D0301852

Musical Works and Performances

A Philosophical Exploration

Stephen Davies

CLARENDON PRESS · OXFORD

2001

OXFORD
UNIVERSITY PRESS

Great Clarendon Street, Oxford OX2 6DP
Oxford University Press is a department of the University of Oxford.
It furthers the University's objective of excellence in research, scholarship,
and education by publishing worldwide in

Oxford New York

Athens Auckland Bangkok Bogotá Buenos Aires Cape Town
Chennai Dar es Salaam Delhi Florence Hong Kong Istanbul Karachi
Kolkata Kuala Lumpur Madrid Melbourne Mexico City Mumbai Nairobi
Paris São Paulo Shanghai Singapore Taipei Tokyo Toronto Warsaw

with associated companies in Berlin Ibadan

Oxford is a registered trade mark of Oxford University Press
in the UK and certain other countries

Published in the United States
by Oxford University Press Inc., New York

British Library Cataloguing in Publication Data

Data available

Library of Congress Cataloging-in-Publication Data
Davies, Stephen, 1950–
Musical works and performances : a philosophical exploration / Stephen Davies
p. cm.
Includes bibliographical references (p.) and index.
1. Music—Performance. 2. Music—Philosophy and aesthetics. I. Title.
ML457 .D38 2001 21—dc.1 [78] 2001016386
ISBN 0-19-924158-9

1 3 5 7 9 10 8 6 4 2

Typeset by Best-set Typesetter Ltd., Hong Kong
Printed in Great Britain by
Biddles Ltd., Guildford & Kings Lynn

Contents

Acknowledgements

The author would like to thank the following for kind permission to reproduce published material: the Medieval Academy of America (Example 2.5), Willem Rodenhuis, Universiteitsbibliotheek Amsterdam (Examples 3.6 and 3.7); Universal Edition (Example 3.9); Editions de Solesmes, Abbaye Saint-Pierre (Example 3.10), Berandol Music Ltd. (Example 3.13); Kluwer Academic Publishers (Example 3.16), Karlheinz Stockhausen (Example 3.17). Example 3.4 © Ernst Eulenburg and Co. GmbH, Mainz. Reproduced by permission of Schott and Co. Ltd, London (MAHLER). Example 3.12 © MOECK MUSIC, D-Celle for all countries with the exception of: © Schott Musik International, D-Mainz for Poland. Example 3.15 © 1929 by Universal Edition London Ltd. © renewed 1956 by Boosey and Hawkes, Inc., New York. Example 3.14 is reproduced by kind permission of Alice Moyle.

PART ONE

Works, their Instances, and Notations

Introduction to Part One

What is a musical work? Are musical works of a single kind? Are free improvisations best regarded as performances of ephemeral works? Can two composers working independently create the same, single piece? Do composers discover or create their compositions? Of what elements are musical works comprised? Is there more to a piece than its sound sequence? How are works specified by notations? Is everything recorded in the score work-identifying and, hence, required in an accurate performance? What conditions must be satisfied if a performance is to be of a particular piece? Can performances that sound different faithfully represent and be of a single work? Can performances that sound the same faithfully represent and be of different pieces? Can a performance simultaneously be of more than one work?

In Part One I answer these and related questions. They concern the ontology of musical works and performances. I focus primarily on pieces that are for performance, though some playing events are free improvisations, not work performances, and some purely electronic pieces are for mechanical playback, not for performance. Moreover, not all works for performance are intended for live rendition; many popular forms of music call for performances relying on the special resources of recording studios. Works for live performance differ considerably in the specificity of their essential details. Pieces consisting of abstract structures of note types are ontologically thinner than those specified at the level of note tokens. Thinner works determine less of the fine detail of their performances than do thicker ones, but performances are always thicker than the works they are of. It is in her manner of going beyond the work's detail to the concrete repleteness of sounded music that the musician reveals her interpretation of the work.

While these ways of categorizing musical works differ from the refined theories of musical ontology usually propounded by philosophers, they are to be preferred because they accord nicely with the considerations in terms of which composers and musicians evaluate and appreciate playings and performances. Because freely improvised music is made up on the spot, it is to be considered for properties not necessarily found in the performance of notationally specified works. Because the studio allows for the electronic sculpting of sound, works created for performance there invite a different mode of appreciation than do live renditions. Because thin works leave more than thick ones to the discretion of the performer, this should be reflected in the audience's evaluation of the composer's and the player's contributions to the resulting performance.

Musical works are usually thought of as sound structures indicated by their composers. It is not straightforward to analyse the relationship between the elements that comprise musical sound structures. Not all pieces share the same lowest or highest levels of musical organization. In general, pieces are arranged multidimensionally with respect to pitch, rhythm, harmony, key, and metre, with these indicated sometimes as specific tokens and sometimes as more general types. These elements are organized into higher structures, such as melodies and movements, some of which supervene non-reductively on their constituent parts.

Philosophers and musicologists disagree among themselves about what, apart from the sonic profile of its instances, contributes to the identity of a musical work. Some regard the use of instruments as indicated by the composer as part of the work, while others see the work as a pure structure that might be realized by any means. Some regard the composer's identity as contributing to the work's, so that no two composers could independently write the same piece, whereas others regard all the circumstances of creation as irrelevant to the work's identity. In my view, such issues are settled by reference to the conventions and practices of the period of the piece's composition. Because those conventions and practices vary from time to time and place to place, so do musical works. Instrumentation might be irrelevant to the identity of a thinly indicated work, whereas it could be crucial to the individuality of a more thickly specified piece. Though I take the work's musico-historical context to contribute to its identity, not all features of that setting are pertinent; in particular, two composers could independently write the same work, but only if they shared the same musico-historical context.

Though I favour a historicized account of musical ontology, and to that extent regard the musical work as a social construction, I reject inferences drawn from these observations by some philosophers and proponents of New Musicology. Regarding the work concept as a recent invention does not provide the most plausible narrative for music's history. My own emphasis on the thinness or thickness of pieces better captures the differences between musical periods and styles while respecting the continuities that unify them. Moreover, I reject views claiming that talk of musical works is at best a useful fiction given the extent to which they are under-specified by composers' notations. A proper appreciation of the gap between the detail of a performance and the work it is of, along with a grip on the distinction between notational indefiniteness and notational ambiguity or incompleteness, should put an end to such radical forms of work scepticism.

Though not all works are specified notationally, many are. Notations with the function of specifying works are scores. These are to be read as instructions addressed to the work's potential performers, and it is by following these instructions that players generate instances of the work. The proper interpretation of a score requires knowledge both of conventions for the notation and of the performance practice shared by the composer with the musicians to whom the score is directed. Not everything recorded in the score has the force of a work-determinative instruction, and some essential elements not registered in the score are implicit in the performance practice. Accordingly, interpretation of the instructions that scores encode is not always easy. To make matters worse, scores may be incomplete or ambiguous. This need not be a deficiency where they serve merely as mnemonics for pieces that are already known. It does create a problem, though, where scores are the work's primary source. In this case, ambiguities or incompleteness in the score can obscure the identity of the piece it specifies.

To be of a work, a performance must satisfy three conditions. There must be a suitable degree of matching between the performance and the work's contents, the performers must intend to follow most of the instructions specifying the work in question (though they need know neither what work that is nor who composed it), and there must be a robust causal chain from the performance to the work's creation, so that the matching achieved is systematically responsive to the composer's work-determinative decisions.

Different performances of any given work are individuated by reference to the spatial and temporal locations they occupy and the identity of the performance group. Players are united as groups on particular occasions of performance in terms of their joint goals and mutual cooperation.

Performances for a public have normativity conditions. For instance, only one work is played at a time, and its performance is more or less continuous, running from the beginning to the end. Standards for the integrity of performances vary, depending on the nature of the work. For example, what counts as 'cheating' in a studio recording depends on whether the piece in question is created for live or studio performance. In the former but not the latter case, the integrity of the performance is undermined if the musicians could not do live and in real time something that sounds the same as what makes its way onto the disc.

1

Musical Works

Augsburg, 24 Oct. [1777] The evening of Wednesday last was one of the most agreeable for the local music-lovers. Herr Chevalier [Wolfgang] Mozart, a son of the famous Salzburg musician, who is a native of Augsburg, gave a concert on the fortepiano in the hall of Count Fugger . . . there was opportunity to include a fine concerto for three claviers. . . Apart from this the Chevalier played a sonata and a fugued fantasy without accompaniment, and a concerto with one, and the opening and closing symphonies were of his composition as well. Everything was extraordinary, tasteful and admirable . . . all the hearers were enraptured. One found here mastery in the thought, mastery in the performance, mastery in the instruments, all at the same time.

(Newspaper report quoted in Deutsch 1966: 167–8)

In this chapter musical works are classified into their basic ontological types. I separate works that are for performance from those that are not, and, within works for performance, those that are for live presentation from those that are not. In addition, I distinguish works rich in properties from those that are not. My account differs from standard ones, which tend to assume musical pieces are of a single type. I sketch the abstract theories of other philosophers at the chapter's close. Mostly, these concern whether musical works are particulars or universals, and whether they are best described as classes, types, or kinds. I claim composers and players conceive of what they are doing more in my terms than in those of such theories. This counts for my analysis, because there is an intimate connection between what we comprehend and enjoy in music and its being purposefully designed to showcase the skills and talents displayed by its creators and performers. I describe distinctions between kinds of music that are crucial to their proper appreciation and I identify as ontologically relevant the sorts of things that make a difference to the way composers, performers, and listeners understand and discharge their socio-musical roles.

Cards on the table

I might as well lay down my hand at the beginning. The following is the schema with which I operate. It is elaborated and defended in this and subsequent chapters. Here is a continuum of cases:

[A] A group of musicians freely improvises in a Baroque style, or a company of actors extemporizes after the manner of Elizabethan theatre.

[B] A group of musicians plays Bach's *Brandenburg Concerto No. 2*, or a company of actors performs Shakespeare's *Romeo and Juliet*.

[C] A group of musicians records Bach's *Brandenburg Concerto No. 2*. Their aim is to simulate the sound of a live performance. Or a company of actors films Shakespeare's *Romeo and Juliet*. Cinematographic techniques are kept to a minimum and the result looks like a record of a stage performance.

[D] A group of musicians records Bach's *Brandenburg Concerto No. 2*. The full range of electronic interventions is used, including multi-tracking and the like. The result sounds like a 'hooked-on-classics' or techno version of the piece. Or a company of actors films Shakespeare's *Romeo and Juliet*. The full panoply of cinematographic techniques is used, including slow motion, superimposition of images, and temporal discontinuities in the ordering of material. The outcome is 'the movie of the play'.

[E] An engineer creates a recording of Bach's *Brandenburg Concerto No. 2*. His raw material includes tape of musicians. They might be playing anything, but perhaps some of them are playing snatches of Bach. Or a film editor creates a movie of Shakespeare's *Romeo and Juliet*. As his source, he uses film of actors, perhaps including out-takes of the film described in [D].

[F] An engineer creates a recording of Bach's *Brandenburg Concerto No. 2*, generating all the sounds electronically. The result sounds like Walter Carlos's *Switched on Bach* (1968), which was created on a Moog synthesizer. Or a film editor creates a cartoon version of Shakespeare's *Romeo and Juliet*.

I divide this continuum as follows: [A] involves neither the composition nor the performance of a work. It is unalloyed playing, unconstrained by the strictures imposed on those who would deliver a work. A piece is performed in [B]. It is of a kind designed for live presentation. [C] simulates a live performance of the same work. [D] describes a different piece. It is intended for performances of a special kind; namely, those that can be done only in studios and with the support of technology. Yet another kind of work is described in [E] and [F]. It is purely electronic and is for playback, not performance. [E] and [F] are pieces conveyed directly, unadulterated by performance. Three kinds of works are identified: ones for live performance, ones for studio performance, and purely electronic ones that are not for performance.

In [B] to [F], I describe various ways a piece by Bach might be handled. It follows from my account that the 'hooked-on-classics' version and the Moog synthesizer work are distinct from Bach's original. And so they are. They transcribe Bach's piece to a new medium and it receives there such a different treatment that the transformation results in a new work (Davies 1988*a*, 1997*b*).[1] The primary piece is the one Bach composed; the other two are derivative, though they provide epistemic access to some of the contents of the original. Though they are autonomous works, their identity is parasitic on Bach's, and they are likely to display this genealogy in their titles. For transcriptions like this, we are interested in, among other things, how they adapt the music for a new medium while retaining a strong connection with the source work.

It is not just classical[2] pieces that are subject to ontological conversions. Popular musicians in blues and rock have moved from acoustic to electric instruments, and from live gigs to the studio. Some popular songs written in the 1950s and 1960s for acoustic instruments began as works for live performance but later were reincarnated or transformed into pieces for studio performance. The early songs of Bob Dylan and Paul Simon, or of 'folksy' groups, fall into this category. Dylan's original of 'All Along the Watchtower' might best be thought of as a work for live performance, but Jimi Hendrix's version treats it as a work for studio performance.

Though I have just described cases in which musical pieces are transcribed for different formats, usually a work is represented only in the type for which it is composed. Béla Bartók's Concerto for Orchestra (1945) is a piece of kind [B], created for live performance. It has been recorded, as in [C], but so far as I know it has been neither transcribed for studio performance nor synthesized in a purely electronic form. Pink Floyd's 'Brain Damage' first appeared on the album *The Dark Side of the Moon* (1972–3) and is a work for studio performance; it is of kind [D]. A different performance is created when the song is re-recorded or 'covered'. Its covers include those by Austin Lounge Lizards (1991), Robert Berry (1995), Bim Skala Bim (1996), and The Batfinks (1998). Karlheinz Stockhausen's

---

[1] In this use, the verb 'to transcribe' refers to the adaptation of a composition to a different set of instrumental resources from that for which it was originally composed. (The term 'arrangement' is also used for this practice.) In another use, it refers to the act of notating a performance or recording. I will refer to these respectively as work transcriptions and notational transcriptions.

[2] I use 'classical', with lower case, much as record stores do, to label Western art music. I use 'Classical' to name the stylistic paradigm that held sway between 1770 and 1810.

Hymnen (1966–7), which takes as its source the national anthems of the world, is a purely electronic piece of type [E], while Milton Babbitt's *Composition for Synthesizer* (1960–1) and the BBC Electronic Workshop's theme for the TV show *Dr Who* are of kind [F].

Why slice the continuum at these points? I do so because they mark places where there is change in the criteria on which we base our understanding and evaluation of what is happening. In order to enjoy music (and works of art in general), one must be able to locate the relevant object and apply to it the appropriate mode of appreciation. In general, we look for certain qualities in works, others in performances, and yet more in improvisations, and, within these categories, we make further distinctions of kind that affect what we listen for. Even if improvisation calls for skills like those displayed by composers who create scored works, there are also important differences depending on the fact that the extemporizer does on the spot what the latter does at leisure. And, even if the person who plays a work must possess skills like those displayed by improvisers, there are also important differences depending on the fact that the former has accepted the task of delivering a composer's work, whereas the latter has not. The intervention of modern technologies can affect the possibilities for a performer's delivery and interpretation, depending on whether they are used to simulate a live rendition or to create a virtual one owing nothing to the constraints of real-time playing. As a result, one looks for distinct features in the two kinds of recording, and their integrity conditions differ. Finally, technology can be used to synthesize a piece that, when finished, requires presentation, not performance, and thereby is more like a novel than a play or a string quartet. It is to be appreciated as a stand-alone work that can be cloned but is not thereby performed or interpreted.

If ontology is to be other than a philosopher's game, it must reflect the 'what's and 'why's informing the esteem that draws us to art works. Musical ontology should be responsive to the ways we engage with and discuss music and its works. The ontological divisions I have limned map usefully on to differences implicit in the modes of description and assessment applied to music of many kinds, I claim. They mirror our ordinary ways of talking about music, at least when it comes to paradigms of the types I distinguish. The argument does not depend solely on this matching, however. If someone insists on calling the business of playing a recording a 'performance'—on the grounds that it has a certain ritual character, say—I would not dispute with him by surveying ordinary usage. Instead, I would argue that following a composer's instructions in order to instance his work is radically more creative than replaying a disc, and thereby different in kind, whether or not we apply the same word to both activities.

Because they fall along a continuum, the boundaries between the kinds I distinguish are fuzzy. Inevitably, there are hard cases. What is the difference between an improvisation that kicks off from some composer's tune and a performance that expands on and decorates the simple melody it is of? Where do we draw the line between recording, electronically enhancing, and electronically transforming a performer's input? In other words, at what stage does the recording medium lose its transparency? And, where we have a single instance of an electronically modified piece, what is the difference between its being a performance of a work for studio performance and its being the embodiment of a purely electronic piece not for performance?

Though paradigms of my musical types should sound different, it is unlikely that pieces adjacent to the borders will be audibly distinct. Does the separation marked by the boundaries correspond to differences in the intentions of the musicians involved? Undoubtedly, but I think intentions are merely mental chatter unless they engage with practices, conventions, or institutions making some difference in the public world. It is the location of a performance event within a tradition or practice, if not the nature of the sounds it contains, that provides the basis for the distinctions I draw. The relevant tradition or practice settles the goals and values of the activity, the peer classes with which the given event should be compared, and so on.

There are times, admittedly, when it is not clear which tradition or practice is being invoked. Jazz musicians and performances usually do not overlap with their classical equivalents, but they can do. Accordingly, it is not always obvious how a particular case should be categorized. Notice, though, that the haziness of the boundaries does not undermine the significance of key differences between more central examples of the various types. Neither does it imply the arbitrariness of boundary drawing within the continuum. That it is not clear whether the line should be precisely here or there does not entail that we could do without establishing a border in the general area. Moreover, it would be foolish to expect things to be neater than this. Works of art are made by people—by their producers, their audiences, and the discourses or language games enveloping them. They are not natural kinds, but humanly constructed ones. As such, their ontologies are contingent and new types can emerge, as occurred when technological changes made it possible to store and rebroadcast sounds.

A person who acknowledges the importance of the distinctions I make might question, nevertheless, whether these are best thought of as distinguishing *kinds of works*. Why not say, for instance, that Bach's *Brandenburg Concerto No. 2* can have different *incarnations* or *realizations*—live, recorded, electronically generated—and the work is what these share in common? After all, I can hum to myself my favourite parts of Babbitt's *Composition for Synthesizer*, and it seems reasonable to say it is his work I am humming, not a transcription I compose as I go along. If we can abstract from its instances in this way, the work is different from the embodiment it receives from its composer.

I reject this option. I maintained above that our appreciation, both of the work and the performance, depends on our awareness of what is supplied by its composer and performer, and why. The view just proposed distorts our perspective on this relation. It distracts us from the source work to an abstraction that does not match it. If the source work is fairly detailed, as is usually the case, what is common to the various realizations it might be given—to all its possible live performances, studio versions, and electronic renditions—is much leaner than the piece as specified by its composer. Bach's work is the one written for live performance, not the lowest common denominator it shares with 'hooked on classics', Moog synthesizer, Swingle singers, and all other transcribed variants. On the other hand, if the source work is *very* thin—for instance, if it instructs the performer to make up most of what she is to play—abstracting what is common to its various realizations may give the impression of a richer piece than is specified by its composer. In either case, thinking of the work as an abstraction is unhelpful. Besides, the majority of pieces are realized only in the medium proposed by the composer. It is unnecessary to imagine they are other than what is offered. And even where the work is treated as Bach's has been, there is usually no trouble in distinguishing the derivative from the original versions. When I hum Babbitt's best tunes, I do not uncover the essence underlying his piece. Instead, I hum snatches of melodies found in his work, and I use synecdoche in speaking of this as whistling his *Composition for Synthesizer*.

Improvisation

This book is mainly about musical works and their performances or instances. There is more to music than its works and their renditions, however. In almost all cultures at all times, one encounters what I call music making *simpliciter*: spontaneous and unregulated musical playings that are not of works. Extended improvisations are of this kind, as are many doodlings and finger exercises. Pure music making always has existed alongside the performance of works and is featured in some highly sophisticated musical categories, such as jazz.[3] Moreover, some have argued that music making *simpliciter* was historically primary, with composed works and their performances coming later. It is appropriate, then, to begin at the beginning.

[3] When modern Western music is discussed, jazz is the type most clearly associated with extemporization. It is worth recalling, though, that attempts have been made to reintroduce large-scale improvisation within classical music—for instance, by Lukas Foss in the Improvisational Chamber Ensemble he founded in Los Angeles in the late 1950s.

Music can be freely improvised. Such playing is not intended to instance a work and is not guided by a composer's instructions, whether notational, verbal, or exemplified in a performance offered as a model. This does not mean the improviser can make any noises she pleases. Not every sound-making action produces music. To qualify as a music-maker, the player must work within the conventions and stylistic constraints for music. These are neither universal nor unchanging. They vary from culture to culture and from period to period. So, what counts as free musical improvisation differs to some extent, both geographically and temporally.

As just indicated, improvising is not random, but conforms to the general social, stylistic, formal, syntactic, and other constraints governing the culture's music. There is another respect in which improvising is structured. The musician usually acquires a repertoire of phrases and figurations. Some of these will be of her own invention and others belong more widely to the performing community. When she improvises, she draws on this stock. The difference between formulaic improvisation and excitingly original improvisation often lies in how the units are combined, contrasted, and developed, not in their novelty.

Nicholas Wolterstorff (1987) argues that the creation of the first musical works presupposed an already established music practice, so music making must be historically prior to the composition of works. He offers three reasons for this conclusion: (*a*) the composer's 'work-specifying rules' assume the wider musical 'grammar' of the culture and period as their background; (*b*) the composer writes for existing instruments and the techniques established for them; and (*c*) the social context of presentation for which the work is intended affects how it is written. Even if they are true, Wolterstorff's observations do not entail that pure music making pre-dates, or is more foundational than, the composition and performance of works. Audiences always have been as much concerned with the appeal of the music made as with the making itself, and have respected the talented few who are able to propose musical ideas worth hearing, singing, or playing. Provided we have a modest notion of 'work', it is possible that works—pieces intended and accepted for repetition on the basis of their initial presentations—have been around as long as music making itself. Be that as it may, two claims Wolterstorff is concerned to accentuate are important. (i) There is much more to music than its works. (ii) Works are embedded in complex social practices, some of which are more narrowly musical and others more widely cultural, from which they cannot easily be abstracted. Also, improvisational skills typically have been valued as highly as the ability to compose in a calculating fashion or to play an instrument to a high level of proficiency. In the Western tradition up to the mid-nineteenth century, leading composers were expected to be able to improvise canons, fugues, variations, fantasias, or impromptus on a theme of their own invention or one given them by another.[4]

It might be thought the distinction drawn between improvising and composing is wrong-headed. Even if an improvisation is not a performance of a pre-specified work, it may result in a piece created spontaneously as it is performed. In this view, an improvisation is itself a musical work. Where it is not remembered, written down, or recorded, which is usually the case, it has only one performance. It is then as ephemeral as its performance, but no less a work for this.

This is the position implied in arguments presented by Philip Alperson (1984) and Peter Kivy (1983). Alperson holds that jazz players are composers and their improvisations are works. (For further discussion, see Valone 1985, Alperson 1991, and Spade 1991; and for the contrary, see Lee B. Brown 2000 and Andy Hamilton 2000.) Kivy makes the same claim with respect to improvisation within classical music. On a famous occasion at Potsdam in 1747, Johann Sebastian Bach improvised on a theme given him by King Frederick II of Prussia. On his return home, Bach wrote out the work known as *The Musical Offering*. According to Kivy, when Bach notated *The Musical Offering* by remembering what he had improvised, he was copying a work that had been composed already.[5] Had C. P. E. Bach later recollected and written down his father's improvising, the work's composer still would be Johann Sebastian, not Carl Philipp Emanuel.

The insistence that all music making amounts to work performance is mistaken in my view. Works intended for performance take part of their point from their multi-instantiability—that is, from the possibility of their receiving more than one performance. In contemplating a musical piece, we consider the different ways it can be interpreted. If someone is interested in a work, she could not be completely satisfied by hearing it performed a single time only. It would be strange for her to say: 'I once heard Mahler's Fourth Symphony, so it is not necessary for me ever to

---

[4] Here are some accounts of Mozart's skills: (1) 'Even in the sixth year of his age . . . one had only to give [Mozart] the first subject which came to mind for a fugue or an invention . . . he would develop it . . . as long as one wished . . . he would improvise fugally on a subject for hours . . . he would extemporise with inexhaustible inspiration . . .' (Placidus Scharl in a memoir of 1808, cited in Deutsch 1966: 512). (2) Writing in 1818, Norbert Ignaz Loehmann recalls a day in June 1787 when Mozart improvised on the organ: 'He now began a four-part fugue theme . . . Mozzart [sic] had soared up so high from G minor . . . that he was able to continue in B minor . . . His 10 fingers skipped around . . . as busily as when ants run about when their ant-hill has been destroyed' (Deutsch 1966: 518). (3) At a concert given on 15 October 1790, the seventh of eight items was 'a Fantasy without music' in which, according to Count Ludwig von Bentheim-Steinfurt, Mozart 'shone, infinitely exhibiting all the power of his talent' (Deutsch 1966: 375).

[5] Most commentators hold that Bach went beyond what he improvised, expanding and developing the theme's contrapuntal possibilities, whereas Kivy suggests Bach did no more than record on paper what he had extemporized for the king.

listen to it again.' A person cannot know and understand a work without having a sense of its offering a range of different prospects for its presentation. By contrast, when people improvise, it is the immediacy and presence displayed in what they do that attracts us (Lee B. Brown 1996, 2000). An improvisation could be taped or written down, and thereby might always be repeated, but that seems incidental to its appeal. (Indeed, some people believe improvisations lose their interest when they are captured on disc, as I discuss in Chapter 7.) Because they can be recorded on tape or paper, free improvisations may be imitated by others, but this potential for repeatability is not sufficient to establish they are works. They are neither intended nor conventionally received as models to be copied.[6] The ethos of music like jazz (which is Alperson's topic) or like the extemporising of performer-composers within the classical tradition (which is Kivy's subject) counts against the idea that improvisations generate musical works, as does the social practice within which improvising is expected and valued. There is, then, no virtue in regarding free extemporizations as works.

What of the case in which J. S. Bach writes down *The Musical Offering*, with the result that we too can perform and hear it? Kivy (1983) considers that Bach merely *copies* a pre-existing piece, one that resides in his head even if he does not get round to notating it. (Others who separate the act of composition from that of specifying performance criteria are Bender 1993 and Robert L. Martin 1993.) Like many others, I am uncomfortable with the Idealist thesis according to which the work exists primarily in the composer's mind.[7] In my view, the work cannot be purely mental; it must be specified in the public domain. Works composed for performance are conveyed via sets of instructions addressed to their potential performers. These might be expressed in a performance, which, by convention, has a socially established status as a model. Or they might be communicated via a score. A piece indicated in this second fashion does not exist until its inscription is completed. A musical idea or gesture does not become part of a work unless and until it is incorporated within a work specification, and work specifications necessarily are public, since they are addressed to performers who may be unknown to the composer (Thom 1990*a*).

---

[6] I do not deny that some recordings of free improvisations have attained the status of works, irrespective of what was intended by the musicians or is standard for the genre in question (see Eisenberg 1988: 115–16). This is not the norm, though. Indeed, it opposes the norm by fixing what was meant to be free. In becoming a work others can perform, the original attains a new ontological standing, one like that of a modern pop recording. This shows only that what starts life as an improvisation can become transmuted into a work, not that, as an improvisation, it is a work.

[7] For criticism of ontological Idealism, see Hoffman (1962), Wollheim (1968), Khatchadourian (1973), Wolterstorff (1980), Ingarden (1986), and Thom (1990*a*). A recent proponent of an Idealist ontology for musical works is Cox (1986). Ingarden (1986) and Pearce (1988*a*) argue that musical pieces are mental constructions, but distinguish their views from Idealism by insisting that musical works have an objective, intersubjective existence.

Bach could have invented some music and heard it play in his mind's ear without writing it down, but I baulk at the idea that musical works exist in this private, mental realm. If he did not write it down, or if he did not execute a performance intended as a model others should emulate, I hold that Bach composed no work. In the case of *The Musical Offering*, much of the labour of composition was done before pen was put to paper. Bach improvised for Frederick; later he wrote *The Musical Offering*. Even if the work corresponds to the improvisation, they are distinct. *The Musical Offering* is the work *as notated* and that writing was not done until after Bach's departure from Potsdam. As I have already observed, it is widely believed that what was notated differs from what was improvised. Perhaps Bach could not recall what he had played, or perhaps he took the opportunity to improve on it. The important point, though, is not the historical one but this: Bach always had the option of departing in the written work from what he had improvised. No one could know how *The Musical Offering* would go until Bach publicly exercised that option one way or another.

How should we describe the situation in which C. P. E. Bach wrote down his father's improvisation? Two possibilities suggest themselves. It could be that he transcribed what his father played, just as ethnomusicologists record in notational form the songs and playings they hear in the cultures they study. As I explain in Chapter 3, notational transcriptions are not work specifications, since they are descriptions, not prescriptions addressed by the composer to potential performers. Alternatively, he could be creating the score of the work by recording work specifications dictated or authorized in some appropriate fashion by his father, not merely copying down what his father happened to play.[8]

Improvisations are not musical works, I say. Does this mean that improvisers are not composers? Here I think one can say what one likes, so long as the issues are clear. It is plain that composition and improvisation involve similar processes—inventing tunes, organizing material, trying to unify the manifold. If 'composer' is like 'swimmer' or 'driver'—if it names the person who engages in a certain kind of activity—improvisers are composers. On the other hand, if 'composer' is more like 'fletcher', or 'wheelwright'—if it names the person who creates a certain kind of product; namely, a musical work—improvisers are not composers, I say. I can accept the first reading, since it allows for the possibility that not all acts of composition give rise to musical works. And the second also may be acceptable so long as one acknowledges, as I do, that improvisers and performers can deserve no less praise for their creativity than composers receive.

[8] Joaquín Rodrigo was blind from the age of 3 and required the help of others in notating his works. Frederick Delius became blind and was aided by Eric Fenby, who offered himself as an amanuensis and notated, among other pieces, *Songs of Farewell* (1930). Both J. S. Bach and G. F. Handel went blind and needed assistance to continue composing.

I have just rejected one challenge to the distinction between free improvisation and work performance, that according to which the player is performing a work she composes as she goes along. One might dismiss the same
distinction in a different way—namely, by arguing that improvisations are
often performances of pre-existing works. I think this alternative is no more
attractive than the one I have already spurned, but I consider it for the further
light it sheds on the relation between works and their performances.

The work-defining features of some pieces are decidedly paltry or 'thin'
when compared to the rich detail of their performances. For instance,
beyond its text, a simple strophic song might be specified merely as a
sixteen-bar melody underpinned by four chords. Minimal though such a
piece is, a performance adhering to the melody and chords is of it. The
performance might elaborate and extend the piece as required by (or as is
consistent with) the performance tradition for the relevant genre. Yet, though
it fleshes out the work's bare skeleton, the playing does not depart from it
and, so, counts as a performance, not as a free improvisation.

Many folk songs and rock songs are of this ilk. A variety of treatments
is available to a singer of 'The Ash Tree', so long as she remains within the
conventions for folk performance. Also, covers of rock pieces count as
performances of the songs, even where there is much that is original along
the way. The crucial point is this: some pieces leave a great deal for the
performer to contribute. What she adds makes her a performer, not an
improviser. Her input is what the work needs to come to life. And, the
argument continues, when a player starts with another's tune and lets it
guide her subsequent playing, she is performing a piece taking its identity
from that tune.

I used to think (Davies 1987, 1991b; see also Gould and Keaton 2000
and Young and Matheson 2000) of renditions of jazz standards in the
way just indicated: as performances of works, even if the work is of interest
only because it provides the occasion for the performers to exercise their
skills. I now reject this view. There is no reason to assume that a playing event
beginning with a particular tune is best viewed as a performance of a work
thinly specified via that tune. The improvisation is inspired by the tune and
is 'after' it, but the whole that is created can be regarded as new and unique.
After all, this is how we regard Bach's efforts. It would be odd to think Bach
was performing a piece of Frederick's and not improvising, just because
Frederick furnished him with the initial tune. Improvisers must begin from
something and often choose another's pre-composed melody, chord sequence,
or whatever, but this does not make their playings into performances of
preconceived works.

What distinguishes a performance of a 'thin' song from an improvisation
based on a song? Here is one line of reply: where improvisations start from
an existing idea, the player uses it as a springboard. This starting melody or

chord sequence is present only to provide a foundation from which the performer pushes off. After its initial statement, the theme might inspire and inform what is played, but does not structure or restrict what is available. The new creation that results is not a rendition of a work; it is an autonomous performance. The proper object of appreciation in improvised music beginning with familiar, pre-composed material is the musical ballet made possible by the gravity-defying departure from that initial foundation. By contrast, a performance of a work should remain faithful to its defining features. Because the performer is always answerable to the piece, she cannot depart from it too far or too long if her playing is to succeed in being of it, whereas we expect a successful extemporization to explore hitherto untried ideas. Also, the risks associated with the performance of works are not like those accompanying improvisation. There is the danger of forgetting what comes next if the score is not before one, and the music may pose a major challenge in its technical demands, but the performer of a piece does not normally face the problem of *deciding* the direction it should take. Even if the work is indeterminate in some respects, the way of continuing it is usually known. Simply, free improvisations are freer than work performances ever can be, because the latter are committed to following the composer's directives, even if these say 'be free'.

Lee B. Brown (1996, 2000) has in mind points like those just raised when he articulates the regulative ideals governing jazz performances that are largely improvised. The player presents music intended to be worth hearing by creating it as she plays and the audience listens. Brown rightly notes that, though improvisers rely on a stock of materials and techniques mastered prior to the given performance, in this respect they are no different from composers, so there is no stronger basis for denying their originality and creativity than there is for doing the same for composers. What is distinctive to improvisation is that the creation takes place before the listeners' ears. The improviser makes, and must be heard as making, on-the-spot decisions. These should sound 'right', but they should also strike us as surprising, as going beyond not only the predictable and clichéd but also the player's zone of comfort.[9] As listeners we should be concerned with the creative immediacy of the performance—that is, we should consider the playing in terms of the opportunities produced and taken by the musicians. As Brown puts it, improvisation has *presence*. A special risk attends improvised performance, because the musicians try to 'put it together' at the very time they make it up—which is to say, before they know how it will continue and end.

---

[9] Kieran (1996) suggests some kinds of music, including free jazz, 'fail to cohere' and some recent theorists have claimed the rejection of formalism as a hallmark of jazz (see Lee B. Brown 1999). Though some performances might be disorganized, I see no basis for taking musical non-coherence to be characteristic of free jazz.

Similar issues are raised by Alperson (1984), who says the criteria by which improvisations should be judged differ from those for performances of pre-existing works. Improvisations thrive on the nervous energy generated by their immediacy and openness. They are to be treated as in-the-moment compositions. If they are at times disorganized and incoherent, this is only to be expected, and, hence, is more tolerable than it would be in other performance contexts. On the other hand, if they are both unified and enterprising, their value is enhanced by the fact that the result is achieved without premeditation. In either event, praise or blame attaches to the performer, not to the composer of the tune from which the musicians began.

I agree with the observations made by Brown and Alperson concerning how improvisation and work performance display and promote contrasting virtues.[10] The regulative ideals they discuss reveal how paradigms of the two kinds of playing differ; they also locate reasons why those differences matter to us. Nevertheless, I doubt that appeal to them will always cleanly capture the distinction between a performance of a 'thin' song and an improvisation based on a song. The fact is, some improvisations are more prosaic and predictable than work performances, and an improvisation can be as rigidly structured around repetitions of a chord sequence as is a Baroque chaconne. Meanwhile, works for performance often leave considerable freedom to the performer. This is apparent in pieces requiring the realization of a continuo part, or melodic decorations, or free cadenzas, as well as in ones instructing the performer to make up what she will play. A work might consist of a sixteen-bar melody and the prescription that the musician continue the piece by improvising on the given theme. A performance of this work could be indistinguishable from a free improvisation that chooses the same melody as its point of departure. If the example just given seems fanciful, one need only recall the great freedom consistent with the performance of songs such as George Gershwin's 'I've Got Rhythm', 'The Girl from Ipanema' by Norman Gimbel and Antonio C. Jobim, or Hoagy Carmichael's 'Stardust' to appreciate that sparsely indicated pieces can sustain extended, complex renditions. Because the songs are thinly specified and the performance con-

---

[10] Carpenter (1967) distinguishes music as process from music as object and approves more of the former, which she associates with non-Western cultures, than the latter, which is exemplified in Western art music. If music is transformed from an activity to an object, as has happened in the West, it 'becomes the total collection of all its pieces, the imaginary museum of musical works' (1967: 68). The theme is recapitulated in Bohlman (1999). An opposite perspective is presented by Lippman (1977). For him, notated music is art, in that it is concerned with pieces presented for attention and contemplation, whereas improvised music usually is too closely enmeshed with the social functions it serves to be appreciated for its own sake. Of course, neither perspective is convincing. There is nothing socially impoverished in the musically and dramatically profound treatment of complex themes in Mozart's *The Marriage of Figaro*, K. 492; and the music made by Miles Davis is no less worthy of contemplation for its own sake than many a classical work. Both kinds of music have their different strengths and values, and fortunately we are not forced to listen solely to one or the other.

ventions tolerate a wide spread of approaches to their realization, renditions of pieces like these can differ considerably. The extended elaboration and variation of material can be no less indicative of work performance than of improvisation, as these examples make clear.

We should sort cases at the borderline by placing playing events within the appropriate social and musical practice, not by inventorying their sounds or the degrees of restraint or freedom those sounds seem to display. It is the performance tradition it taps into and is drawn from that distinguishes free improvisation from work performance. It is the players' and genre's social location and genealogy—the musical practice they assume as their background—that mark the difference. The players' intentions and their notion of what they are doing are also crucial, certainly, but I prefer to emphasize the socio-historical context without which such intentions could have no grip on what is done and what should be understood about what is done.

The socio-musical practices governing improvisation and work performance may overlap and share many equivalent functions, but they differ in obvious respects. The former aims at the presentation of real-time music making constrained only by the grammatical conventions of a style, and the latter is dedicated to the delivery of a faithful instance of a previously composed work, even if it also has other purposes. Once in place, the relevant practices are liable to become self-conscious and to take their own suppositions and conventions as subjects for comment. This is what happens when a contemporary classical work instructs the player to make up her part. What results might sound like a piece of pure improvisation, but it should be judged against the performance and work tradition it invokes, which includes Raymond Leppard playing Bach rather than Charlie Parker improvising on 'Bird Feathers'. Correspondingly, it is the jazz practice of quotation, not the classical performance tradition, that needs to be invoked when a jazz musician quotes a classical piece.

A typology of musical works

Already, in discussing improvisation, I have resorted to the familiar notion of work performance. I now consider the nature of musical works. By way of introduction, I should say my use of 'work' or 'piece' is broad and inclusive. It takes in 'Happy Birthday' and Shania Twain's 'Man! I Feel Like a Woman!' no less readily than Beethoven's Symphony No. 5, Op. 67. Works can be long or short, simple or complex, vocal or purely instrumental, highly detailed in their determinative characteristics or merely skeletal.

There are many ways musical pieces can be categorized besides those just indicated. For instance, record stores class their wares in terms of cultural origin ('Indian', 'Hispanic', 'Celtic'), genre ('opera', 'symphony', 'heavy metal', 'techno', 'film'), period ('Baroque', 'late Romantic', 'golden oldies'), or function ('easy listening', 'disco', 'march'). My way of distinguishing the classes of musical works reflects their ontological variety more directly, I believe. In the first place, I contrast works for performance with those that are not. Later, I make a further division within works for performance, separating those for live performance from those for what I call studio performance.

Musical works for performance

Works for performance can be 'thick' or 'thin' in their constitutive properties. If it is thin, the work's determinative properties are comparatively few in number and most of the qualities of a performance are aspects of the performer's interpretation, not of the work as such. The thinner they are, the freer is the performer to control aspects of the performance. Pieces specified only as a melody and chord sequence are thin. Some tin pan alley songs are of this kind. For them, the player creates the larger structure of the performance by deciding on the number of repeats, variations, elaborations, links, and the like. Moreover, her choices settle many aspects of the performance's micro-detail, including intonation and melodic inflections, timbre and texture, attack and decay, emphasis and phrasing. By contrast, if the work is thick, a great many of the properties heard in a performance are crucial to its identity and must be reproduced in a fully faithful rendition of the work. The thicker the work, the more the composer controls the sonic detail of its accurate instances. Igor Stravinsky's *The Rite of Spring* (1913) is a thick work by comparison with Mozart's Divertimento in D, K. 136. Thicker yet is Edgard Varèse's *Déserts* (1954) for tape, wind, percussion, and piano, because the contribution made by the tape is both essential to the work's identity and extremely specific.

Performances are very rich in acoustic information (as is apparent from the size of sound files stored digitally on computers). Works for performance, however thick they are, are always thinner in properties than any of their accurate renditions (Ingarden 1986). Works for performance leave some options open to their performers. Equally work-faithful performances differ in accordance with the way the players make the choices that are their prerogative. Inevitably, accurate performances display properties that should be ascribed to the musicians' interpretation rather than to the work itself. Performances of thin works are as replete with acoustic information as are those of thick works, but, for performances of thin works, more of this information is referable to the performance than to the work.

Works for performance are conveyed by instructions from the composer addressed to the performer. The prescription is conditional: 'if you want to play my work, do thus and so.' Typically, these instructions are issued in one of three ways: via a score, orally, or by a performance with the status of a model. A work specified via a score might have no instances, because it is never performed. A work indicated by a model performance always has at least one instance. Works of these kinds are *for* performance, however, whether they get none or many.

A score is a written notation but, as I explain in Chapter 3, not all musical notations are scores. Scores are authored by composers, or can be traced to their efforts. Scores have the function of specifying works by instructing performers on how to produce a performance or on what to produce. Interpreting these instructions is not a straightforward matter. Typically, not everything indicated in the notation has the status of a work-determinative instruction, and not everything work determinative is notated. The player can perform the work on the basis of a score only in the light of a clear understanding of the appropriate notational conventions and of the performance practices assumed by its composer.

A model performance is not merely an accurate instance of the work, but one serving as a vehicle for the composer's work-determinative directives. A performance might achieve the status of an exemplar by following the work's score or, alternatively, by being based on some previous performance with the status of a model. If the work has no score, the chain of model performances leads back to the work's first authorized performance. When it comes to basing a subsequent performance on a prescriptive paradigm, the musician's problem is that of extracting the qualities pertaining to the work from the welter of detail inevitably presented by the model (Bowen 1993). In other words, the difficulty lies in separating the 'model' from the 'performance' in the 'model performance'. Though the player can reproduce the work by slavishly following the exemplar, this may be stylistically inappropriate—for instance, where conventions of the musical practice indicate that the work is of a thin kind. The player can treat the work idiomatically on the basis of a model performance only in the light of a clear idea both of the kind of work it is—that is, of its genre and style—and of the performance practice it presupposes. The conventions of rock allow both for slavish reproduction and for contrasting renditions. A song can be covered by emulating the original recording precisely, or by interpreting it in a fashion that is distinctive.

The gamelan *gong kebyar* tradition in Bali is one in which the repertoire is conveyed by example. The composer of a new piece teaches each musician his part. Other groups learn the piece in the same manner, perhaps being taught by someone who was instructed or who learned the parts by observing another group perform. As an example, consider the piece *Teruna Jaya*, which has existed in its modern form for about half a century. It is about 12–20 minutes in length and, like others in the genre, technically difficult and highly complex. One instructor told me it took him about three months to teach the work to a gamelan of already skilled musicians who did not know it. *Teruna Jaya* is played all over Bali and is always easily recognized.

Nevertheless, the Balinese do not approve of mechanical copying. Each group introduces its own modifications and variations and, over the years, continues to alter its account of the work. (There can be debate about how far versions should be varied, or about their style, but not about the appropriateness of introducing innovations going beyond the model.) The Balinese case shows how works can be introduced and preserved over extended periods within an oral tradition, which, nevertheless, is never static or backward looking. A similar but more conservative practice is revealed in the transmission of Roman, Ambrosian, Spanish, Greek, and Coptic chant in centuries prior to the invention of musical notations.

Where works are for performance, the skill of the performer is always likely to be of interest, as regards her general musicianship, her execution of the piece, and her interpretation of it. Indeed, if the work is very thin, the focus usually falls on her. Even where works are thick and much of what the player does is subject to the composer's instructions, the performer makes a significant creative contribution in delivering the work.

As just indicated, very thin works are usually not of much interest in themselves and the prime candidate for appreciation is the performance. As pieces become thicker, they become more worthy of interest. For many kinds of music, both Western and non-Western, the features of works are no less appreciable than are the autonomous aspects of performance. This is not to claim that all musical pieces are created solely to be listened to. Many are tied to functions calling for responses other than the contemplation of the work. Nevertheless, even functional music is usually designed to reward the person who listens to it. The talent for making functionally successful pieces worth listening to is not common, so composers are identified and valued as creators, and the link between a composer and his work is often recognized and noted.[11]

Works for performance are typically intended for singers or for instrumentalists who set resonators in motion by acts of scraping, plucking, blowing, or striking. Some kinds of musical instruments are standardized (violas), others not (rattles); some are complex (organs), others are simple (triangles); some are highly crafted (violins) and others are very plain (wood blocks) or ready-made (conch shells).[12] Sometimes works are written specifically for particular instruments. In other cases, a work's instrumentation is variable, at least within limits set by conventions holding at the time of

---

[11] These generalizations have exceptions. What impresses me, though, is how often and widely they are true. I do not know of any culture lacking musical works for performance—that is, repeatable pieces with titles or identifying descriptions—or that does not acknowledge the special talents of creators of such pieces.

[12] There are difficult cases if one follows standard classifications of musical instruments, such as that proposed in Sachs (1940). For instance, the Mahisu of New Guinea use their mouths as resonators for live sago beetles (Reck 1977).

composition. Works with specific instrumentations are usually thicker than those that can be adapted at will to the available resources. This is because the composer can make timbral and other instrument-dependent features work determinative only when she can require that her piece be played on particular kinds of instruments. Though instrument-specific works are often conceived for orthodox musical instruments played in the standard fashion, this need not be so. The instruments might be unusual. One method used by From Scratch, a New Zealand percussion group, involves tubes of plastic piping that are struck on their ends with rubber footwear. Alternatively, ordinary instruments may be doctored, as happens in John Cage's works for prepared piano, such as *Bacchanale* (1938).

The parts written for performers often call for hands-on music making. Sounds are elicited directly from the instrument, in that they are made by the performer's larynx, say, or by thumping a stretched membrane with a beater. Because one can feel the ground through it, a walking stick is experienced as an extension of one's body. Many musical instruments are similar.[13] This can remain true even when they are electrified. Some of the difficulties associated with playing traditional, acoustic instruments are ameliorated by their electrification, but often not. Sometimes electrification calls for the use of new techniques and the development of different possibilities, as is apparent from a comparison of the acoustic and electric guitars. In yet other cases, electric instruments can be such that playing them is not at all like eliciting sound from a typical acoustic instrument.[14] For example, the performer turns a knob, or interrupts a force field by movements of her body. Instruments such as the Theremin and the Ondes Martenot (for description, see Manning 1993) are of this kind.

As well as employing electronic musical instruments, composers have incorporated the sounds of other electronic devices (such as blenders and vacuum cleaners) in their works. The most philosophically interesting case of appropriation is that in which devices created for the playback or broadcast of music (or sound in general) are assigned the role of musical instruments. In this vein, John Cage created *Imaginary Landscape No. 4* (1951), the score of which directs the performers to manipulate the tuning and volume dials of radios. Along with Lejaren Hiller, Cage also composed *HPSCHD* (1967–9) (see Manning 1993: 244–5), which is issued as an LP coupled with

[13] Michael Bach, the cellist, says: 'It's an extension of yourself, the instrument. It's not an object you are . . . *traktieren*? [German: To treat (as an object), with a connotation of thoughtlessness.] . . . I don't know the English word. It's an object you can use as an extension of your thinking' (quoted in Cage 1996: 272); see also Stubley (1998).

[14] In the rock music world, electronic instruments sometimes are made to *look* as if they operate like acoustic ones. For instance, a pre-programmed drum machine might be activated by being struck with a drumstick, or a synthesizer might be operated via an orthodox keyboard on which each key excites a different pre-programmed loop or sequence.

computer-generated instructions concerning alterations to be made to the hi-fi's dials as the record is playing. (The record jacket claims each LP has a different set of instructions, thus making each properly performed playback a unique performance.) Here, Cage treats the playback device as an instrument that is 'performed' by the user. The piece is not encoded on the record that comes with the instructions. What is found there is better regarded as an electronic, pre-work input. The work itself is instanced by the output resulting from the combination of recording, playback device, and settings-adjuster. The person who obeys Cage's instructions in setting the dials of her stereo is the work's performer.[15] In the world of popular music, composers and performers have been quick to exploit the potential of such 'meta-musical instruments'. For instance, the 'sampling' of material pre-taped by the artists concerned, or taken from others' commercial recordings, is common in performances of hip hop and also in those of many brands of commercial music.

If a work is for performance, it must assign some role to a performer, but this is consistent with the possibility that much of its content is sounded without being performed. Steven Feld (1988) describes how the Kaluli of New Guinea duet with naturally produced sounds, such as those made by waterfalls or cicadas.[16] I am not sure whether they regard such duets as work performances. Whatever the Kaluli's view of the matter, we can easily imagine a composition that combines a soprano with the dawn chorus, perhaps specifying that it is to be given on a fine day in mixed deciduous woodland in Western Europe in May, so as to ensure contributions from Sylvia and Phylloscopus warblers. And we can speculate that, for the sake of more convenient performance times and venues, a different and later version of *Dawn Chorus* will be for soprano and tape (with the tape made at dawn on a fine day, and so on). Works for performance might contain a significant electronic component. One such is Luigi Nono's *La fabbrica illuminata* (1964), which is for soprano and a recording of electronically modified factory sounds and choral singing. Unlike *HPSCHD*, in *Dawn Chorus* and

[15] A person who alters the graphic equalizers on her hi-fi is not a performer when a disc of Beethoven's Symphony No. 5 is on the turntable. Wolterstorff (1980) argues that this is because there is less feedback between what she does and what she hears, and because there is less adjustment in the light of her anticipation of how this will affect the outcome than is the case under performance conditions. If she does qualify as a performer of *HPSCHD*, though, Wolterstorff's argument must be unsound, because her position *vis-à-vis* what is sounded is the same for that work as for the recording of Beethoven's. In my view, what makes her a performer in one case but not in the other is this: whereas she is addressed by and complies with the instructions issued by Cage concerning the correct performance of his work, she is not addressed by Beethoven's instructions and does not comply with them. Moreover, Cage's work is awaiting performance when its disc is on the turntable, whereas the performance of Beethoven's is already over when the disc is released. I elaborate further on related points in Chapter 4.

[16] For examples, hear his CD *Voices of the Rainforest* (Ryko, RCD 10173, 1991), produced by Mickey Hart. Alternatively, listen to any of the numerous New Age 'music for relaxation' discs that impose music on sea sounds, whale songs, burbling streams, and the like.

La fabbrica illuminata, the taped material is part of the work's content rather than raw material on which the performer operates. The tape contributes to the work's contents by being played back as the work is performed. The part in the performance that is *performed* is the soprano's.

Though I mean to take a catholic and non-evaluative approach to the possibilities for music created for performance, some will think I overcommit myself by assuming musical works for performance must involve outputs sounded by or through the actions of their performers. Cage's *4′33″* might be offered as a counter-example to my view, since Cage instructs the piece's performers to be silent. In response, I have argued (Davies 1997*a*) that *4′33″* is a theatrical work about music rather than a musical piece as such. Much avant-garde art has taken music in the direction of multimedia theatre and artists have set out to create works challenging the distinction just invoked. Nevertheless, I hold by it. I am not convinced that Nam June Paik's *Danger Music No. 5* (which has a score instructing the performer to crawl up the vagina of a living whale) or *Performable Music* (1967) (which tells the performer to cut his left forearm with a razor blade) are *musical* works, even if the word appears in their titles and the pieces are discussed in a book entitled *Experimental Music* (Nyman 1981: 72–4). In my view they are theatrical works.

Musical works that are not for performance

Some kinds of works are created for playback, not for performance. The entire piece is stored as code and, when sounded, is retrieved in a mechanical fashion. Pieces of this kind are created for a particular storage medium and for the kind of decoder that can replay the work as sound. For instance, the earliest pieces were stored on a revolving barrel with metal prongs that plucked resonators, or as slots in a revolving metal disc that triggered pneumatic air used to activate pipes. Pieces written for music boxes and calliopes are not for performance in my view. The contemporary American composer Conlon Nancarrow writes for player piano, composing directly onto the roll that, later, controls the pianola. Nowadays, though, the most common storage media are electromagnetic tape or computer disks, and the work is recovered and sounded by tape decks, digital processors, speaker systems, and the like. I call such pieces *purely* electronic.[17] As archetypes, I mention Pierre Schaeffer's *Étude pathétique* (1948), one of the first examples of *musique concrète*, and Herbert Eimert's *Four Pieces* (1952–3), one of the first examples of *Elektronische Musik*.

[17] Electronic pieces can be for live performance. This is the case with *HPSCHD* and with Stockhausen's *Microphonie I* (1964), which is for four performers, two of whom rub microphones against a tam tam or move them around it, while the other pair filter and transform the signals from the microphones before they are passed to loudspeakers. Although the *performance medium* is electronic (as opposed to acoustic) in these cases, the *work* is not 'purely' electronic as I intend that phrase. I use it to distinguish works that exclude the contributions of performers.

The source materials for a composition that is not for performance might be generated electronically, or might be recordings of everyday sounds, or might even be recordings of people singing or playing musical instruments.[18] The work is produced through the electronic manipulation and juxtaposition of these sources—that is, the compositional process takes place in the studio. The piece is finalized when an encoding acquires the status of a 'master', which happens partly as a result of the composer's decisions but also in conjunction with industry and wider social conventions concerning pieces of the relevant kind. Subsequently, the piece is transmitted via copies accurately cloned from the master. An appropriate decoding of the copy, as when a CD is played on a CD player, results in an instance of the work. It is industry and technological norms that determine what counts both as an accurate copy and as an adequate playback.[19] The composer issues a tape or disc, not a standard musical score, because her work is mediated only by a decoding device, not by a performer's efforts.

I like to compare purely electronic musical works with films like *Star Wars* (see also Wolterstorff 1980). A film-maker might work directly on negatives, or might take footage of ordinary events as her raw material, or might get actors to perform before the camera. In any event, the typical Hollywood movie is the information encoded on film stock that is suitably related to a master, and, though acting might have gone into its creation, the movie is for screening, not acting (Carroll 1995). Similarly, musicians who play instruments during the production of a purely electronic work are contributing to its raw materials, not performing it.

As well as being unlike pieces such as Stravinsky's *The Rite of Spring* in not being for performance, purely electronic works differ considerably from it in the extent, depth, and saturation of their work-determinative properties. Previously I described *The Rite of Spring* as thick with work-identifying properties by comparison with pieces composed much earlier, which leave more features of the sounded output to the judgement of the performer. I also observed, though, that works for performance are inevitably thinner than the performances that instance them. The performance is as rich in sonic properties as the ear is capable of discriminating and as the mind is capable of discerning. The electronic work, because it comes via a tape,

---

[18] In the 1940s and 1950s, there was considerable opposition between those who produced *Elektronische Musik* (in which all the sounds were electronically generated) and those who created *musique concrète* (in which tapes of actual sounds were used as the raw material); see Manning (1993). As Nyman (1981) notes, these divisions were rejected as early as 1952 by Cage in *Williams Mix*, which combines the two approaches.

[19] Here I agree with Fisher (1998), who stresses that it is an arbitrary and changeable industry standard, one taking account not only of composers' and musicians' judgements but also of the variability accepted in playback devices and their settings, that determines what counts as an ideal, or merely adequate, or inadequate transmission of a given work.

record, or disc, is at the level of acoustic detail that these media are capable of storing and later conveying. Because an electronic work is sounded directly when it is instanced, the properties defining it are at the same level of detail as those characterizing performances, whereas the work-defining properties of pieces created for performance are not so fine-grained (Lippman 1977).

Works that are not for performance are not quite as thick as the soundings that display them, however. The work would be less articulated than its instance if it is created for a low-fidelity or otherwise unreliable playback device. But even where it is intended for speaker systems responsive across the full pitch and volume range, purely electronic works usually contain slightly less information than the medium can carry, as is apparent from these considerations. (1) Sometimes representations of electronic pieces encode sonic detail that is not part of the work as such and, hence, that should be classed as 'noise'. For instance, unintended tape hiss, which is an accident of the production process, sometimes accompanies a purely electronic work. (2) The method by which copies are cloned from the master usually degrades the quality of the information transferred. If a composer originally operates with two-track tape at 15"/second, yet later accepts that her work survives intact on a commercial cassette, then, plainly, she regards the contours of her piece as less precise than those mapped onto the master. The standard of transmission deemed satisfactory by industry standards falls short of the medium's possibilities under 'perfect' studio conditions. (3) Digital technologies may record features too precise for audition under normal circumstances. In that case, digital representations are more fine-grained than the works they capture, given that the limits of work specificity in music correspond to those of human hearing. In consequence, slightly discrepant digital representations might, despite their differences, denote a single piece.

Interestingly, Linda Ferguson (1983) noted many of the differences between purely electronic works and those for performance. She draws from them a conclusion differing from mine. Having observed that purely electronic works are not for performance and are not composed by writing scores, she decides they are not musical works as such. She assumes, therefore, that *real* music is always for performance and is created in a process culminating in the production of notated instructions issued to the work's projected performers. Because electronic music does not conform to this model, it is 'an artform in search of its metaphysics', according to the title of her paper.[20]

---

[20] Urmson (1976) contrasts music, which is a performing art, with painting, which is not, and accepts that tape compositions fit better with paintings than with music. Unlike Ferguson, he does not mention the warranted conclusion, that purely electronic compositions are not music. Wolterstorff (1980) also notes the existence of works created directly onto magnetic tape. He acknowledges they are not for performance, but does not say how they fit into his general ontology for musical works.

I believe my conclusion is the more appropriate: purely electronic pieces are musical works, though they are ontologically distinct from pieces created for performance. In electronic compositions, the composer works more or less directly with the sounds that concern her, rather than instructing others on how to make them, and this allows to her much more control of their detail, which she is able to incorporate within her work by giving it an electronic representation that can be disseminated and accessed without the assistance or intervention of those traditional intermediaries, musicians.

Ferguson identifies two trends counting against our appreciating the distinctive status of purely electronic music. (1) Recordings are often of works intended for live performance, and our primary access to such pieces is via discs, so we are inclined to think wrongly of *all* recordings that they represent a performance, whereas recordings of purely electronic pieces directly embody the work itself. As she puts it, the person who purchases a recording of a purely electronic work thereby comes to own the genuine article, not merely a 'once upon a time' instance of it. (2) The conjunction of tape with standard instruments in some compositions obscures the contrast between purely electronic pieces and those written exclusively for ordinary instruments.

Ferguson's first point could be developed this way: we are used to encountering pieces intended for performance in the recorded format. A minority of these are 'records' of live performances, but most are made in the studio under conditions unlike those in the concert hall. For instance, multiple takes are made, with the best edited together. Nevertheless, we continue to think of these studio recordings as *performances*. In consequence, we could come to regard all recordings as performances of the pieces on them. This model is inappropriate, though, for purely electronic music.

The second point strikes me as more interesting. As I have already noted, a work might be written for tape *and* performer. Among the earliest examples are Bruno Maderna's *Musica su due dimensioni I* (1952) for flute and tape and *Rhapsodic Variations for Tape Recorder and Orchestra* (1953–4), composed by Otto Luening and Vladimir Ussachevsky. (Stockhausen's *Kontakte* (1958–60) is unusual in being created in versions both for tape alone and for tape and instruments.) It seems reasonable to take such pieces as for performance, even if the live player is given very little to do, for a rendition is incomplete or imperfect if the player's part is left out. So, in some cases, all that distinguishes a purely electronic work from one for performance is the addition to a playing of the tape of a few humanly produced sounds as prescribed by the composer.

I have already acknowledged the implications of this, but two points are worth detailing: works for performance range from those in which the performer plays everything to those in which the performer's part is small, while the bulk of the work is replayed from disc or tape without being performed. The more minimal the input required from the performer, the thicker with constitutive properties does the mixed-media work become. As a result, works for performance range along a continuum, with some very thin and others nearly as thick as the performances that instance them. Works that are for performance in all their parts, that do not contain indeterminacies, and that are conveyed by orthodox musical notations, fall around the continuum's middle. Secondly, though many works for performance are intended for live presentation on acoustic instruments, and works that are not for performance often rely on electronic technology for their creation and dissemination, the ontological distinction between the two kinds of work does not depend on differences in their media. A work for performer plus tape, or an electronic piece like *HPSCHD* that is intended for performance, might incorporate all the features and techniques characteristic of electronic works that are not for performance. The difference does not lie in the fact that one composer uses electronic technology where the other does not, but in the fact that one composer uses the technology precisely in order to exclude the performer where the other uses it to parallel or provide the material for her performance. Whether a piece is for performance depends on how it is issued. Works that are not for performance are issued as discs; these encode the work, rather than a performance of it. Pieces for performance are always presented via instructions addressed to performers.

I have argued that music includes works not for performance. How common are they, though? Nelson Goodman (1968: 190) passingly acknowledged their existence, but his casual comment indicates that he regarded them as rare or exceptional. Perhaps he was right to see purely electronic composition as peripheral to classical music, since in 1968 it was a minority activity and interest within that tradition, but he was wrong to ignore developments within the world of popular music that changed the prospects for electronic non-performance pieces. It is arguable that works not for performance became extremely common from the mid-1960s within the realm of rock music. This was appreciated by Ferguson (1983), who observes that the Beatles' *Sergeant Pepper's Lonely Hearts Club Band* and *Magical Mystery Tour* replaced the dynamism of performance with processes that relied on recording technology. Because the songs on these albums cannot be performed live in real time, the recordings must be considered as tape compositions. In her terms, the recordings are 'produced music' (that is, works not for performance) rather than 'recorded performances'. As she rightly observes, for pieces like these the primary object of interest is the phono-recording, which relegates the concert appearance to an adjunct that admits its subsidiary status by permitting lip-synching.[21]

These themes have been developed by Theodore Gracyk (1996) in his ground-breaking discussion of rock, which he regards as a category covering many types of song with roots in African-American popular music. These songs are united, not in terms of shared auditory profiles, but rather, in their common reliance on recording technology, both for their creation and distribution. In rock, the primary text, the work, is the information stored on a recording or tape. Gracyk characterizes rock pieces in the terms I have used to describe purely electronic works that are not for performance. He denies they are for performance and describes them as ontologically thick with work-identifying properties.

To counter the assumption that recordings transparently copy performances of pre-existing pieces, Gracyk offers many cases in which the final take is cobbled together from the independent efforts of musicians who had no particular result in mind when they laid down what were to become their contributions to the final result. Besides, rock has long exploited and made central aspects of sound for which modern technology is central—for instance, feedback, overdubbing, and mixing. This is not because the musicians lazily fake what they cannot do live, but because they aim to sculpt sound in a fashion distinctive to the electronic medium. Their ideal is not verisimilitude to unelectrified, acoustic conditions, but a soundscape essentially implicating the technology of the studio. Audiences are aware of this. They regard electronically induced timbral details and other subtle aspects of the recorded sound as crucial to the given work, not merely as elements of interpretation. As a result, rock stage acts are measured against their recordings, and not vice versa. Although rock is often promoted as a performing art, this is no more true than is the myth according to which rock artists are social rebels driven not by money but by creative urges and political concerns. Finally, rock has long employed an institutional framework, with new musical works stipulated and disseminated by a process of recording, labelling, and releasing of discs. Hence, rock recordings are electronic works that are not for performance, since plainly they are not 'records' of live performances.

I agree with Gracyk's observations. And if the choice were between classifying rock pieces as either for live performance or purely electronic, I would

---

[21] Griffiths made the point in 1979 and it has often been noted since. For instance, Chanan writes: '[Recording] freezes the work; it reifies the human voice and hand . . . The effect is different in different musical camps. In pop music, this tendency leads to products that depend entirely on recording technique, and which cannot be performed live at all' (1995: 18). Of *Sergeant Pepper's* he observes that it was 'the first of a new kind of studio rock album, composed for recording rather than performance' (1995: 146).

follow him in favouring the latter.[22] There is, however, an intermediate possibility: the object of appreciation in rock music, its 'primary vehicle', is a *recorded performance*, not, as Gracyk maintains, a *purely electronic work that is not for performance*. Pieces for studio performance display all the features to which Gracyk has drawn attention. I accept that, in some cases, the rock song is a purely electronic composition that is not for performance. (The example to which people most often draw attention is the Beatles' 'A Day in the Life'.) More often, though, it is a work for studio performance. The performer's skill is sometimes displayed in the immediacy of the present, as happens with improvised jazz, but it can also be exhibited in a more extended process during which his playing is taped, superimposed, mixed, and modified, until a composite is produced. What happens in the rock studio is a mode of performance, I maintain, and the disc that is produced embodies a performance of a song.

What kind of evidence would help us adjudicate for rock songs between the competing alternatives. In other words, how do we locate the boundary between [D] and [E] type works? Both are issued as discs for playback and rely on electronic manipulation of raw sonic materials. Would reference to the intentions of the artists be revealing? I doubt it. A peek into the mind of the singer-song writer during the recording process would probably leave one little the wiser. (On the admission of some, there would be no more than a puff of herbal smoke to be found.) More helpful is the idea mooted earlier: it is the practices and the traditions perpetuated in rock that reveal how the piece is to be conceived. Two factors lend strong support to my position: the attitude to covers and the criteria for virtuosity.

If rock pieces were purely electronic, we would not expect them to be re-recorded by others. Yet, covers are made of the songs of even those groups, such as Pink Floyd, the Grateful Dead, and Frank Zappa and the Mothers of Invention, that are the most committed to creating an electronic soundscape. Not every rock piece is re-recorded, but there is usually nothing odd at the prospect of this happening.[23] And if rock pieces were purely electronic, new recordings should count as autonomous though derivative works, not as performances and interpretations of the piece found on the original recording. Moreover, covers that depart significantly from their model would be only loosely related to the original. This is not how they are viewed, though. In Joe Cocker's recording of John Lennon

---

[22] Those who come closest to the live performance tradition are blues musicians and piano-playing composers, I think. It seems to me that Muddy Waters and B. B. King, or Elton John and Joni Mitchell, are performers of songs, even when they record.

[23] In fact, for the top groups it is difficult to find uncovered songs. As examples, Gracyk has suggested to me 'Voice of Harold' by R. E. M. and Pink Floyd's 'Several Species of Small Furry Animals Gathered together in a Cave and Grooving with a Pict' from their *Ummagumma* album.

and Paul McCartney's 'With a Little Help from my Friends', the listener is interested in the subtlest nuance of every scream and growling chord,[24] but that is because she concentrates on his performance, not on a tape work different from the Beatles'. Someone who hears Cocker's rendition as only loosely related to the Beatles' (just because it is dissimilar to their *recording* of the song) fails to appreciate it. Cocker departs not from the Beatles' piece but from their recorded performance and interpretation of it. He is appreciated as a consummate performer, not as a composer of a new piece that merely happens to have the same name as one recorded by the Beatles.[25] Also, remixes of earlier recordings, as on 'best hits' compilations, are represented and accepted as versions of the original songs, not as entirely new works.

A further point notes the value placed by rock musicians on the mastery of instrumental technique and the importance they attach to their own apprentice years of mimicry and practice (Edidin 1999).[26] There are groups that rely on anonymous studio musicians to do most of their work for them—Milli Vanilli is a notorious example—but a far greater number pride themselves on their musicianship. The instruments played may be electrified, but virtuosity in their use relies on the kind of labour and talent that has always been necessary for skilled instrumentalists. Overall, the approach to recordings has its roots in, and presupposes many traditions and values of, live performance, though it supplements these with an arsenal of new devices. The facts are these: more groups play rock music than ever are recorded; almost every recorded group began as a garage band that relied on live gigs; almost every famous recording artist is also an accomplished stage performer; although record producers are quite rightly acknowledged for the importance of their contribution, they are not usually identified as members of the band (unless they are so, independently of their producing role).

---

[24] The focus in rock falls more on what is done with timbral qualities and rhythmic subtleties than with harmonic development and complex structures (Baugh 1993, 1995; Gracyk 1996). (As a generalization I am sure this is correct, but as the basis for a distinction between classical and rock music, which is how Baugh intends it, I am more sceptical (see Davies 1999).)

[25] In discussing the collaborative, vague nature of authorship in rock music, Gracyk (1996: 92–3) observes that groups frequently use others' songs without acknowledgement, or even claim song-writing credit when all they have done is arrange a pre-existing tune or change its lyrics. And Frith (1987) emphasizes how copyright has been used in the popular music business to protect the interests more of industrial manufacturers than of creative artists. I accept these claims. My point is this: it is common for an artist to record a song with an established and uncontested identity and to represent his efforts as a performance of the song in question.

[26] To unpublished criticisms along these lines by Kathleen Higgins and Renée Lorraine, Gracyk replies that he should deal with mainstream artists whose works are familiar and successful, just as other philosophers of music and the arts do. This response, even if accepted, does not explain why mastery of musical instruments should be so esteemed by rock musicians if they do not think of themselves (also) as performers.

I have suggested that Gracyk's view, according to which rock songs are purely electronic pieces, makes mysterious our attitude to covers and the frequency with which they are recorded, and it cannot easily be reconciled to the retention within rock of the values, disciplines, and practices that go more with performance than composition. Several replies might be made on his behalf.

Gracyk compares rock pieces with the typical Hollywood film (as does Fisher 1998), which he regards as not for performance. I think he is right about this, but I also think the category of films straddles the border between [D] and [E] type pieces. As I indicated when first I set out the categories, a movie of a Shakespearian play treats it as a work for studio performance. All the film versions of *Hamlet* should be regarded as studio performances, with each offering its own interpretation, not as discrete works. In other words, some films are more like covers than like purely electronic pieces. In particular, this is true of theatre pieces adapted for the screen; they are heir to a performance tradition that allows for multiple renditions and interpretations. We do not think in the same way about typical Hollywood movies because there is not an established practice of remaking such films, though a few, such as *Cape Fear* and *The Thirty-Nine Steps*, have been done more than once. Rock recordings are like films in many respects, but this does not show them to be purely electronic works.

The second defence objects to the exclusivity of the alternatives I have posed. Perhaps a rock recording presents more than one work of art: an electronic piece that is replete with constitutive properties and that is at the same time a realization of a much thinner song. In this vein, Gracyk (1996: 18) writes: 'Recordings are the primary link between the rock artist and the audience, and the primary object of musical attention. These musical works are played on appropriate machines, not performed . . . The relevant work (the recording) frequently manifests another work, usually a song, without being a performance of that song.'

Now, I wonder what it is for a song to be 'manifested' in a recording. The influence of an earlier piece might be heard in a later one—as is so when Carl Orff's *Carmina Burana* (1937) is experienced as awash with effects anticipated in Stravinsky's *Les Noces* (1923)—yet I assume this would not lead Gracyk to say *Carmina Burana* 'manifests' *Les Noces*. He does think Cocker's recording of 'With a Little Help from my Friends' 'manifests' the Beatles' song, however. This suggests that 'manifesting X' amounts to instancing X. But how does Cocker instance the Beatles' song if he is not performing it? The problem for Gracyk is that he cannot say 'on this disc we hear both a purely electronic work that is not for performance and a performance of a song that is for studio performance'. As he is aware, he cannot comfortably allow a performance to sit on a disc occupied in its entirety by a purely electronic work, and this is why he is forced to use the awkward and obscure notion of a manifestation that is not a performance.[27]

At times, Gracyk suggests the rock work is the album, not individual tracks (see 1996: 33). His example is Bruce Springsteen's *Born to Run*; Griffiths (1979) claims the Beatles' *Sergeant Pepper's Lonely Hearts Club Band* and Pink Floyd's *The Dark Side of the Moon* albums ask to be heard as wholes. If Gracyk is correct, as I am sure he is, the thesis that the rock work is purely electronic is strengthened. There is not a normatively sanctioned practice of covering albums, as there is of songs. But even allowing the prominence acquired by the 'concept' album, I think the main rock work remains the song in a majority of cases.

I believe that most people conceive of rock recordings as (studio) performances of songs, not as purely electronic non-performance works (that might also happen to 'manifest' songs). It is necessary to be careful in making sense of these data, I accept. The world of commercial rock music is wrapped about with hype and ideology (Frith 1983; Gracyk 1996), so it is possible that a majority of its practitioners and its audience could be mistaken or confused about its nature. In this case, I doubt this is so. I agree with Gracyk that, in rock, fine details of the recorded sound are of vital interest to an appreciative audience. Unlike him, I take this as showing not that the rock recording encodes a purely electronic work thick with constitutive properties but that more interest is taken in details of the studio performance or interpretation than in the work itself.

Works for live performance and works for studio performance

In developing my disagreement with Gracyk, I have characterized many rock songs as for *studio performance*. Studios create special circumstances for performance. For instance, they permit multiple takes, because tapes of these can be spliced together to create the unity and continuity that marks a performance. In addition, taped sounds can be mixed, overdubbed, multi-tracked, filtered, echoed, and so on. I think works conceived for this setting are sufficiently distinct from those intended for live presentation to deserve their own ontological category.[28]

Many works are conceived specifically for studio, not live, performance. Pieces for studio performance require the electronic manipulation of the

[27] I argue in Chapter 4 that a single performance may be simultaneously of distinct pieces, but these both have to be works for performance.

[28] It has become common for live performers to use electronic amplification, though. Anthony Ritchie's *Guitar Concerto* (1998) relies for a proper balance between the orchestra and the soloist on the latter's being 'miked'. This use of microphones represents a step in the direction of studio performance.

materials finding their way into the performance. Normally, they are not created in real time. Parts are laid down one after the other, and accumulate by addition and juxtaposition. Usually, the result would be impossible to perform in real time—for instance, because a single vocalist or musician records many tracks that later are superimposed. The composite mix is carefully constructed in a complex editing process. The performance is completed when the master tape is finalized.

In my view, works for studio performance are very common indeed. Almost all popular forms of music issued by disc belong to this type. Often the piece is composed collaboratively and in an *ad hoc* fashion during the process in which the performance is created. The works associated with these performances are rather thin as regards their specified content. Hence, a lot of the detail added via the recording process belongs to the performance or interpretation of the song. The composer's disc serves as a model for later ones. Typically, rock pieces are conveyed through exemplars, not by notations. Some musicians read the model as literally as they are able and set out to make sound-alike recordings. Though these might lack originality and interpretative appeal, they are of the same work. Other musicians are interested in the song, rather than in duplicating the composer's interpretation of it. They also take her recording as a source, but they are not concerned with the details of the composer's rendition. Though their performance is faithful to her song, they are not slavishly loyal to the composer's performance. Take the Beatles' original recording of 'With a Little Help from my Friends' as an example. Sound-alike versions of this were made. But the fact that the song's identity survives quite different treatments, as in Cocker's versions, shows that the work is thin, at least by being indefinite with respect to the detail of its contents.

At the same time, works for studio performance are not so lean as their sheet music implies, since the sheet music appears to specify a piece that could be for live performance. In effect, the practice within which popular songs are created assigns a part to the studio engineer and, though details of the treatment and of what should be achieved may be open, requires that the resources of the studio come into play. Just as the notation of a figured bass calls for the middle parts to be filled in, leaving the manner of this to the continuo players, so the conventions of popular songs for studio rendition demand a performance thickened and stiffened by electronic interventions and editing, though the detail of any particular realization is left to its players, technicians, or producers. Rock songs assume the performer and producer have access to the possibilities uniquely provided by studio conditions.

Works for studio performances should be compared with works for live performance. Both kinds satisfy the general description I gave earlier of works for performances. Moreover, works composed for live performance are often recorded in studios, using the special resources available there, and many rock bands play their recordings in live concerts. In what, then, does the difference consist?

A studio performance is one that exploits the special resources of the studio—for instance, in that it involves multiple takes and complex editing. A studio performance of a work originally created for live performance typically differs from a studio performance of a work composed for studio performance. As I explain further in Chapter 4, their integrity conditions are unlike, which is to say that what counts as acceptable musicianly practice in the one case may not do so in the other. If the sound engineer raises the pitch of the singer's voice by a fourth, this may be legitimate in a rock song, where it is not on a recording that is represented as a famous diva's performance of opera arias. The two kinds of studio performance are subject to disparate norms. This is appropriate, because they do not aspire to the same sonic goal. A studio performance of a work intended for live performance aims to provide an aural experience as of a live performance, though no unitary, continuous playing event of the kind the listener seems to hear took place in the studio. Recordings of works conceived for live performance *simulate* live performances. They qualify as performances of works such as Beethoven's Fifth Symphony only because they trade on their relation to continuous real-time presentations that provide the paradigm. By contrast, a recording of a work conceived for studio performance aims to create the sound of a *virtual* performance that is of interest at least in part because of the contribution made to its sound by technological interventions. The recording generates the sound of a performance that not only did not take place live but also could not have done so.

Similar points apply to the appreciation appropriate to the live performance of rock songs intended primarily for studio performance. An industry-conditioned conception of the aural goals and standards at which rock recordings should aim informs the way 'live' performances are approached, both by players and audiences. As much as possible of the technology of the studio is exported to the live venue and the signals passed to loudspeakers are mixed and filtered by technicians and producers. Extensive use is made of synthesizers and of pre-sampled sound sequences. Even then, the attempt to play works for studio performance under real-time circumstances often results in an outcome that is seriously impoverished in sound quality and detail according to the standards of the type. (To avoid this, many recordings represented as of 'live' rock performances are considerably modified in the studio before they are released (Gracyk 1996: 87–90).) The playing is acceptable as a performance of its target piece only because it trades on its relation to the type of rendition that provides the paradigm, which is one relying on the studio's technology.

Philosophers' theories of the ontology of musical works

The major philosophical theories of musical ontology presuppose that musical works are for live performance and most assume that works are transmitted by scores. I have had my say on these issues and will not labour over my differences with these theories in what follows. Instead, I catalogue and describe the more prominent theses and issues. I do so without enthusiasm. The discussions are dry and difficult. (Readers who are not dedicated ontologists might prefer to skip to the next chapter.) Also, the motivations of the protagonists are often neither explicit nor apparent. As R. A. Sharpe (1995, 2000) puts it, ontology is ideology. His point, I think, is that a person's ontology is likely to be shaped by prior commitments—such as the desire to privilege works over performances and composers over performers, or to defend the canon that highlights the works of some composers and marginalizes those of others, or to suppose that music could be valuable only if it has the objectivity and permanence of sculpture—and these prior commitments arise not from philosophical reflection but from attitudes unconsciously shaped by the 'politics' of art and music. (For a discussion of the history of the Western classical musical canon, see Weber 1999.)

Musical works are not concrete particulars, though they are encountered in or through concrete particulars, such as scores and performances. Either they have an abstract existence or they are non-existent. As abstractions, musical works have been described both as universals and as particulars. I begin with these two possibilities before mentioning the third, that they have no existence over and above that of their performances.

Musical works have been identified as universals (Wolterstorff 1975; Kingsley Price 1982; Kivy 1983; Thom 1993). The view is widely rejected (Rudner 1950; Bachrach 1971; Khatchadourian 1973, 1978; Webster 1974; Levinson 1980*a*; Margolis 1980; Ingarden 1986; Bender 1993; Scruton 1994; Sharpe 1995). The main lines of objection point out that musical works can be created and destroyed, whereas universals exist eternally.

Some 'universalists' have responded by arguing that their position is consistent with 'creationism'. Others have denied that musical works are created. Wolterstorff (1975, 1980) belongs to the first camp. It is appropriate, he claims, to consider works as created, even if they are universals, because the composer selects the sound properties required in a correct rendition of the piece. John W. Bender (1993) objects that it is not clear how selection amounts to work creation, since works are not merely sets of properties, and Thom (1993) observes that the composer is better described as directing the work's potential performers than as merely selecting its properties. Some philosophers (James C. Anderson 1985; Cox 1985; Fisher 1998) find a different defence of 'creationism' in Wolterstorff's account, and it is one that could answer the criticisms just made. Wolterstorff views musical works as *norm* kinds, which is to say as allowing both for perfect and imperfect instances (as natural kinds do). Though a *descriptive* kind exists eternally, works are composed through the transformation of a *descriptive* kind into a *normative* kind, which is done by establishing principles regulating the formation and nature of the work's instances. This act of transformation can be seen as one of creation, for the piece comes out of it. On Thom's view also, the composer creates the work and its existence depends on there being a token performance directive issued by the composer. More explicitly than Wolterstorff's defenders, Thom rejects a Platonic account of universals in favour of an Aristotelian one, according to which a universal comes into existence with its first instance and goes out of existence when its last instance disappears. (Khatchadourian 1978 also thinks musical works are more like Aristotelian than Platonic universals, though he rejects both views.)

The alternative response defends 'universalism' by dismissing the intuition that musical works are created. They are discovered instead, or so Kivy argues (1983, 1987). (Walhout 1986 is sympathetic to this position; for a musicologist's affirmation of the view, see Zuckerkandl 1956.) Discoveries can be no less important and valuable than are creations. Also, discoveries can be no less historically relative than are creations, in that a discovery might become possible only after complex social or technological conditions are realized, or a person with particular interests and traits is on the scene. Though such arguments go some distance to defusing this objection to 'universalism', critics of this line (Levinson 1990a; Thom 1990a; Fisher 1991; Sharpe 1995) clearly win the day.

The main alternative to 'universalism' holds that the musical work is an abstract particular or individual. This may seem strange if one thinks of individuals as essentially singular, since musical works can have many instances. In fact, though, some individuals can be described as involving multiplicity. For instance, if a person is a set of time slices, he or she has different realizations at different times. Also, if mental states are characterized functionally, a given state might be manifested differently, either within different brains or within a single brain at different times. More to the point, some classes and types (such as patterns and configurations) are particulars. The design of the Union Jack is one such. As patterns, musical works are both abstract particulars and types (see Scruton 1994).[29] In that case, it will be natural to characterize performances as instances, tokens, or exemplifications of the piece. (These terms are used by those who consider musical works to be classes, types, or kinds. Some philosophers avoid them, because, mistakenly in my view, they do not accept that such entities may be particulars.

---

[29] When Snoeyenbos (1979) considers the idea that a type can be a particular, he interprets it as requiring that the type has one ideal instance. But the number of perfect instances that are allowed has nothing to do with the singularity of the type.

Instead, they describe performances as *realizations* of the works they are of (Webster 1974; Khatchadourian 1978; Bender 1993).)

A standard objection to 'particularism' complains about the reification of the musical work (Rudner 1950; Bachrach 1971; Harrison 1975). The piece is presented as an individual existing in a different but parallel realm to that of its performances, and as sharing properties with them despite their different modes of existence. Moreover, access to this special domain is always mediated by more mundane transactions with the sphere of concrete particulars, such as performances (or recordings and scores). All this suggests that appeal to abstract particulars involves an unfortunate ontological redundancy. This, at least, is the conclusion of those who take the third of the positions previously listed, according to which the musical work is eliminable. It exists neither as a particular nor as a universal. As Robert L. Martin (1993) describes this view: musical works are fictions allowing us to speak more conveniently about performances.

It is important to note the difference between two theses. According to the first, our only epistemic access to musical works comes through particulars such as performances and scores. According to the second, if 'Beethoven's Fifth Symphony' is a referring expression, its referents are past, present, or future performances, or copies of the score. And if it makes sense to say the work is witty or sad, this is because the relevant predicate applies to parts of its performances. Aside from such things, the work is a nothing. The first thesis is an epistemological one; the second is ontological. The first tells us how we learn about musical works; the second says works are nothing more than performances and their parts. A person who subscribes to the second view certainly will agree with the first, but not everyone who adopts the first would accept the second (see e.g. Wolterstorff 1980). I draw attention to this difference because the first thesis is widely held, where the second is not. As a result, one must be careful in interpreting potentially ambiguous claims. For instance, when Kivy (1983: 111) writes 'to make a statement about the work is to make a statement about its instances', he must be interpreted as making an epistemological point given his insistence a few pages before that works are distinct from their performances. Also, we should be wary of arguments that slide from the epistemological viewpoint to the ontological one (as seems true of Harrison 1975).

My interest is in those who unambiguously hold the ontological position according to which the musical piece is nothing over and beyond its performances. That thesis is most forcefully presented by Richard Rudner (1950), who feels aesthetic theory is undermined by the view that works of art are abstract and, hence, cannot be experienced. Other adherents include Monroe C. Beardsley (1958) and Jay Bachrach (1971). Milton H. Snoeyenbos (1979) complains that Rudner's central claim, that 'Beethoven's Fifth Symphony' is non-referring in many of its uses, is no less counter-intuitive than regarding its referent as an abstract entity. And he objects that Bachrach's formulation of the position generates contradictions whenever a particular performance displays a different property from the work (see also Ingarden 1986). Nevertheless, Snoeyenbos is a supporter of the reductionist programme and he is critical only to clear space for his own solution: talk of Beethoven's Fifth Symphony is an elliptical way of referring to *most* (but not all) performances presented as of that piece.

How one feels about the view that the work has no existence over and above its performances is likely to depend on the extent of one's antipathy to the idea of there being abstract particulars. For my part, I think 'the family', 'the US Presidency', 'the Middle Ages' refer to abstract individuals, and I am comfortable in saying the same of 'Beethoven's Fifth Symphony'. Works of art have properties that are not reducible to the properties of all (or even most) of their correct instances. For example, the work can be created in Vienna, be performed simultaneously in Paris and London, and be the last of its composer's juvenilia, with none of these things true of all of its performances. Moreover, works have a role in determining what is to count as their correct performances; without some prior standard, we could not separate faithful from inaccurate instances.[30] Therefore, I do not think the theory is able convincingly to translate all the statements we make about works into ones about their performances.

Most theories of musical ontology concentrate on the relation between the work and the performances that are of it. I did the same earlier, by distinguishing works created for performance from those that are not. In the theories under discussion here, it is assumed that all musical works are for performance and the focus falls on the manner by which that relationship is realized. It is variously characterized as that between a class and its members, a type and its tokens, or a kind and its instances. Much of the debate in recent years has focused on the comparative merits of these outwardly similar proposals.

In line with the nominalist predilections that lead him to shun talk of universals and particulars, Goodman (1968: 210) regards the work as the class of its performances, and counts as performances only those that comply perfectly with the work's specification. On the face of it, the view has unacceptable corollaries. It implies either that all unperformed pieces are not musical works or that all unperformed musical works are the same piece, since the class of performances for all such pieces is null (Webster 1974; Urmson 1976; Wolterstorff 1980; Kingsley Price 1982). For that matter, the view seems to imply that Beethoven's Fifth Symphony is constantly growing larger as it

---

[30] Wolterstorff (1980) offers this further argument: different performances can be of the same, single work; two different things cannot each be identical with the same one thing; so the performances cannot be identical with the work they are of.

receives more performances, yet 'growing larger' is not a predicate we would accept as applying to musical works. This style of objection reads Goodman's equation of the work with a class too literally, however. He might reply: any one performance, taken in conjunction with the appropriate notational system, captures the work and allows for the generation both of a score and of all other possible performances. Alternatively, any score, taken in conjunction with the appropriate notational system, specifies the work and allows for the generation of all its possible performances. We need to talk of the *class* of (possible) performances to acknowledge that perfectly accurate instances of the work can differ, but what matters is that each and every member is a complete and accurate expression of the work. The relevant class, then, is not that of actual performances, but that of the work's possible extension—that is, the class of all performances that would instance the work. There is no reason to think each work is getting bigger, since the class of its potential performances is stable. Neither is there a basis here for identifying unperformed works as the same; their scores determine different putative extensions.[31]

Goodman's general theory of musical works is unconvincing in many respects—for instance, in his account of notations and musical scores, in his requiring perfection for something's satisfying a score and thereby qualifying as a performance, and in his excluding historical and practical matters from the analysis. These and other aspects of his theory are criticized over the course of the next three chapters. But his position is not obviously flawed for regarding the work as the class of its performances, so long as that claim is understood as meaning that the work exists as the possibility of a range of (differing) performances, each of which satisfies it. As this is not equivalent to holding that the work's properties are exhausted by (an appropriate subset of) its performances' properties, his position remains distinct from the one just rejected, according to which 'Beethoven's Fifth' is non-designative in sentences such as 'That was a poor rendition of the Fifth Symphony.'

One common alternative regards musical works as types to which their performances stand as tokens. Richard Wollheim (1968: sects. 35–6) provides the most detailed account.[32] The relation between a type and its tokens is more intimate than that between a universal and its instances or a class and its members, because types share many key properties with their tokens. The

---

[31] Harrison (1975) defends Goodman in such terms. Pearce (1988*a*) characterizes works in much the same way in offering his own intuitionist account.

[32] Other supporters of the position include Margolis (1965), Zemach (1992), Thom (1993), and Scruton (1994). Currie (1988) has developed a theory according to which the work of art is an action type, tokens of which are particular actions performed on particular occasions. Works are distinguished both in terms of their structure and the heuristic path (the history of the artist's creative thought) followed in their creation. For critical discussion of this view, see Wolterstorff (1991) and Levinson (1992).

type–token relation best explains the principles of identity and individuation for works of art, he claims. The theory has had many critics, though.[33] The most substantial objections deny sense to the idea that types transmit properties to their tokens, or to the assumption that works of art share the relevant properties with their token instances.

A rival theory maintains that works of art are kinds. Wolterstorff (1975), the theory's main advocate, distinguishes his account from Wollheim's by noting that he talks of *predicates* shared between the kind and its instances where Wollheim (wrongly) finds properties shared between a type and its tokens. As regards kinds, what makes a predicate true of the kind is that something cannot be a properly formed instance of the kind unless it satisfies the predicate. So, 'growls' is true of the Grizzly, if something cannot be a properly formed grizzly unless it growls. This account is applied to works of art, which are characterized as like natural kinds not only in the way so far mentioned but in another important respect: they can have instances that are well formed and instances that are malformed. This is to say, they are *norm* kinds.[34]

Wolterstorff's account appears to have two advantages over its Platonist rivals (Predelli 1995). It provides a way of explaining how works are created— namely, via those acts that transform a pre-existing descriptive kind into a norm kind. Secondly, by characterizing norm kinds as allowing for malformed instances, it accommodates the familiar understanding that performances that are less than perfect can count, nevertheless, as of the work. In my view, these appearances of advantage are misleading, however. On the one hand, the notion of kinds is no more self-explanatory than is that of types or classes. After all, the ontological coherence of natural kinds is hotly disputed in the philosophy of science. And, on the other hand, I do not see why others cannot co-opt the notion of normativity for their own theories, talking of norm types or norm classes. Although there are differences between, say, Wollheim's and Wolterstorff's analyses, these could be seen as reflecting disagreements about the nature of types just as easily as they can be regarded as concerning differences between types and kinds.[35]

---

[33] These include Rudner (1950), Bachrach (1971), Harrison (1975), Wolterstorff (1975), Snoeyenbos (1979), Kingsley Price (1982), Carrier (1983), Bender (1993), and Predelli (1995). Some, including Kingsley Price (1982) and Predelli (1995), argue that types cannot be created and assume they must be universals. I have already indicated the responses that could be made to this allegation.

[34] For discussion and proposed modification to Wolterstorff's theory, the most detailed version of which appears in his work of 1980, see James C. Anderson (1985), Cox (1985), and Fisher (1998). Levinson favours a revised Wolterstorffian approach to musical works in 1990*a*, having been less accepting in 1980*a*.

[35] Indeed, Wolterstorff may concur, since he writes: 'The concept of a kind, or type, of which I made extensive use in Part One, can be put to use here . . .' (1980: 194). Kivy (1983) characterizes musical works as 'universals/types/kinds'. I think his agnosticism is justified, at least as it comes to choosing between types and kinds.

A final question to be considered asks about the content of the kinds or types that are musical works: they are types or kinds of *what*, exactly? Almost all theorists agree they are sound structures (or sets of sound sequences or sound patterns).[36] They disagree, however, about what the sound structure is comprised of and about what more, if anything, is involved in the work. According to William E. Webster (1974), the essential sound structure of J. S. Bach's Violin Concerto in E major is preserved if the piece is played on the sousaphone and in B major. Obviously he thinks of the sound structure as without key and timbre; for him it is a colourless articulation of intervals. (The work is similarly rarefied, according to Boretz 1970; Kivy 1983, 1988a; Scruton 1994, 1997.) Others insist that the piece's sound structure includes much more than this. It takes in, as well as sounds of the specified musical instruments, also the use of those instruments in producing the required sound (Kendall L. Walton 1988; Bender 1993). A yet richer account argues that different works could share the same sound structure and performance means, from which it concludes that the context in which a work is created affects properties that make a crucial contribution to its identity (Levinson 1980a, 1990a; Currie 1988).

My own approach to such matters can be anticipated from the earlier account of musical works as variously thick or thin in constitutive properties. For all the theories previously listed, there are works for which each is true. Some may be as thin as those that Webster describes and others are as thick as those characterized by Levinson. Equally, no theory is true of all musical works, not even for all musical works created for live performance. I am inclined to think that the thicker view of musical works is true, however, if we confine our attention to classical pieces for live performance composed since 1850. And I also support contextualist ontologies over those that would cut works of art adrift from the social and historical location within which they are generated. These views are developed in the following chapter.

Summary

I have characterized certain ontological divisions as basic to the way we describe musical works and their realizations. In particular, I separate works for performance from ones that are merely for playback, and I distinguish pieces created for live performances from those intended for studio performance. In addition, I have described works, especially those for live performance, as varying considerably in the number and kind of their constitutive properties. The thinner the work, the less it determines details of its accurate

---

[36] Kingsley Price (1982) argues that a musical piece is a collection of *essences* of tones, each of which is characterized by an essence of loudness and of time, and all of which are structured in terms of the order of the notes. It is difficult to understand what could be meant by an ordering of essences, however (Bender 1993).

performances. Meanwhile, even the thickest of works for performance leave considerable interpretative latitude to their performers.

All these distinctions are of significance to the musical composer, practitioner, and listener. They inform at the most practical levels the processes by which music is created, communicated, and received. An appreciation of them is crucial to a proper understanding and evaluation of the contributions made to the outcome of any playing event by composers, performers, and others.

At the close of the chapter, I outlined the esoteric concepts in terms of which the debate about musical ontology is presented by philosophers. Composers and performers typically do not think about what they are producing as universals or abstract particulars, or as classes, types, or kinds. Since they can make music without philosophizing about it, there is no reason why they should. All the same, the fact that my account more closely fits the ways composers and performers conceive of what they are doing does count for it. I emphasize differences between sorts of music that are crucial to their proper appreciation and I identify as ontologically relevant the kinds of things that are significant to the way composers, performers, and listeners understand and discharge their socio-musical roles. For the most part, such things are missing from the monolithic theories advocated by others.

2

Elements of Musical Works

There is only one firm intuition here, and it is that work identity is pre-served just so long as structural integrity is preserved. Indeed, so strong is that intuition that we do not even require *absolute* preservation of structure; that is to say, we only require that structural *relations* be pre-served . . . Performing a Bach fugue with a choir of kazoos may, of itself (although not necessarily), make it a very bad performance; of that there can be no possible doubt. But it cannot, of itself, make the performance a performance of something else.

(Kivy 1988a: 45, 55)

Consisting essentially of nine repetitions of the same sinuous melody and countermelody, varied almost exclusively through changes in instrumen-tation, [Ravel's *Bolero*] would make no sense if rendered on, say, two pianos . . . Nor would it make the sense Ravel gave it if comparable instrumental variety was retained, but not the particular sequence of changes that Ravel prescribed. For example, nothing can substitute for the heightening of sultriness and sassiness Ravel achieves by introducing the tenor, soprano, and sopranino saxes as carriers of his countermelody about halfway through, after all the more reserved and conventional woodwinds have had their say.

(Levinson 1990a: 247)

In this chapter I discuss elements crucial to the identity of musical works. I begin with sound structures, because it is generally agreed that these are central to any piece's singularity. Later, I ask if its instrumentation also contributes essentially to a piece's being the one it is. Finally, I consider issues of ontological contextualism—that is, I enquire whether relations between a piece's raw musical content and the socio-musical setting in which it is created generate features vital to its identity. Before getting down to these tasks, it is important to draw attention to several methodological issues.

When we set out to characterize the nature of limestone, we search for properties displayed by all and only its instances. If not all bits of limestone are found in Scotland, then a Scottish location is not an essential feature of limestone, and if things other than limestone dissolve in nitric acid, then solubility in nitric acid is not an essential feature of limestone. As it turns out, a certain molecular structure is the most plausible candidate for the essence of limestone and other compounds. Following this model, it might be assumed we can discover what is essential to the identity of a musical work by finding what all and only its instances have in common. That supposition is questionable, though, as the following scenario makes clear. Imagine 50,000 performances of a piece with 50,000 notes. The work is specified by a score indicating precisely which notes are to be played. In the first performance, the first note is played wrongly but all the other notes are correct. In the second, the only error occurs on the second note. And so on, to the 50,000th performance and 50,000th note. None of the work's 50,000 notes is common to all the performances, so none is essential to the work's being the one it is. This conclusion is absurd, though. Its note sequence surely is crucial to the identity of such a piece. In each performance, the note executed imperfectly is no less central to the identity of the work than are ones played correctly.[1]

At least two responses are possible. The original supposition—that we can discover what is essential to the identity of a musical work by finding what all and only its instances have in common—can be insulated from the absurd conclusion just drawn by insisting that only note-perfect performances are of the work. None of the 50,000 performances instances the work in question, so their similarities and differences are irrelevant to the identity of that piece. This is the line taken by Nelson Goodman (1968). The alternative accepts that something can qualify as a performance of a given piece despite containing imperfect renditions of features normally regarded as crucial to the work's identity. A less than accurate rendition of Beethoven's Symphony No. 5 may qualify as an instance of the work. A departure from the appropriately specified notes violates the work's integrity, thereby generating an error in the performance, but not all such departures move so far from the piece that the attempt to perform it fails. As I described in the last chapter, this is why Nicholas Wolterstorff (1975, 1980) recommends that musical works be regarded as *norm* kinds. Because wrong notes are imperfections that can properly be disregarded, we are not forced to the conclusion indicated earlier, that none of the piece's notes is relevant to its identity.

The first strategy is very much at odds with ordinary ways of talking about performances. We encounter few note-perfect live performances, and we do

---

[1] Similar claims apply to musical pieces not for performance. For instance, the device used to replay a purely electronic work might be attacked by gremlins in the circuitry, thereby affecting a note or two, yet the device might pass the industry standards qualifying it as suitable for the playback of such works.

not expect to do so. When it comes to identifying the works that performances are of, we are much more tolerant of wrong notes than Goodman's theory suggests we should be. For this reason, and for others to be introduced in later criticisms of Goodman's position, I prefer the second line: not all of a work's identifying features will be present in all its instances, given that performances with mistakes qualify as among its instances. In the light of this, I prefer to refer to *constitutive* properties or features, rather than to *essential* ones, though I can offer no fancy philosophical analysis of the distinction between constitutive and essential work properties and their respective relations to work identity (but see Jackson 1998: ch. 3, where such an analysis is outlined).

Here, though, I am more interested in the fact that neither approach sanctions arguments with this form: *two performances purport to be of the same piece; they differ in their instrumentation; and the work can be recognized in both; therefore, its instrumentation cannot be crucial to the work's identity*.[2] If one holds that performances must be perfect, one must first ascertain whether both renditions qualify as such. Only features unique to perfect performances are relevant to determining a work's identifying essence. Many aspects of the work will be recognizable in renditions that, because of their imperfections, fail to qualify as performances. So, to establish the truth of the conclusion drawn above, one needs more information than is supplied by the premises. Alternatively, if one adopts the preferred second strategy and maintains that a work can be instanced imperfectly, differences in performances are not decisive in assessing the status of a work's identifying properties. It could be that one of the performances is imperfect precisely because it departs from the instrumentation indicated. The moral: we should not expect clean and easy arguments if we cannot count on the presence of all of a work's constitutive features in any attempted performance or instance.

What is a sound structure?

The theories described at the close of Chapter 1 are agreed in regarding a piece's *sound structure* as crucial to its being the work it is, just as word sequence is vital to a play's identity. Some philosophers think its sound structure is only one of several features conferring individuality on a work, whereas others believe nothing more is involved or required, but there is accord on the centrality to a work's identity of its sound structure. Despite its importance, the notion is left largely unanalysed, its nature being regarded as intuitively obvious. A sound structure is a sequence of tones.

As it happens, the concept is slippery and elusive. I drew the analogy between musical works and plays just now, and compared the former's sound

---

[2] It seems to me that Kivy is one who is guilty (especially in 1988*a*) of using the invalid form of argument to which I am drawing attention.

EXAMPLE 2.1. Claude Debussy, *Prélude à l'après midi d'un faune*, opening

structure with the latter's word sequence. A moment's reflection reveals it is not easy to analyse word sequences in a way that casts light on the identity and content of a play. Should a word sequence be thought of as marks on paper, or phonemes, or words, or phrases, or sentences, or propositions? Is it an inscription or a text? Can it be specified without reference to semantic content and, if not, how far should the aura of meaning be extended? Not surprisingly, analogous puzzles arise in describing what a sound structure is. As will become apparent, reference to low-level elements, such as pitched tones, proves inadequate to explain the significance of higher-order structures, such as melodies, expositions, and movements. Two conclusions emerge. The first is that one cannot reduce musical significance to low-level acoustic and 'syntactic' features.[3] Topic neutral descriptions of tones—for instance as frequencies—presuppose a grasp of, and do not explain, their musical significance. Many musically neutral descriptions are made possible by, and in the light of, ones referring to musical meaning or significance, not vice versa. The second conclusion is that there is neither a lowest nor a highest common denominator for musical importance. The lowest level of significance is not always the same in one work as in another. In many it is the pitched tone, but, in others, pitched tones are absent altogether or their pitches are not significant. Similarly, works do not all contain the same higher-order elements. For instance, some possess melodies and an overall structure while others do not.

Suitably forewarned, we can ask: of what are sound structures comprised? Here is a first stab: a sound structure is a rhythmically articulated array of pitched tones (specified by a composer). For instance, the sound structure of the opening of Debussy's *Prélude à l'après midi d'un faune* can be represented as Example 2.1. A different ordering of notes would specify another piece.

Arrays of pitched tones

The current proposal is inadequate, as should be immediately apparent, because there are works in which notes are not specified. Consider a piece with a figured bass or continuo part, as in Example 2.2. The numbers indi-

---

[3] Goodman (1968) seems to assume, wrongly, that this can be done; see Savile (1971). Ingarden (1986) is one who argues to the conclusion I prefer.

EXAMPLE 2.2. Figured bass notation

cate the inner voices of the harmony as degrees of the scale above the notated
bass. *Types* of notes are specified, but the particular *tokens* to be played,
as well as the additional notes needed to fill out the texture, are not. A rather
different illustration is apparent in works that are instrument specific, yet
instances of the instrument differ. The didgeridoo sounds two notes, a
fundamental and a harmonic. The interval between them can vary from
instrument to instrument. If tradition allows the performer to choose his
instrument, the music requires of the didgeridoo accompaniment not
particular notes or intervals but a pattern, the precise realization of which
(as regards pitch) is unspecified. As these cases show, a piece that leaves
its note tokens undetermined cannot be described as an array of pitched
tones.

   Also, there are works in which the specified notes are not pitched tones.
Consider music of the Australian aborigines in which glissandos and portamentos are so prominent that it is misleading to regard the sound structure
as involving discrete notes or intervals. Many works contain untuned musical
sounds—body slaps, hand claps, clap-sticks, rattles, tambourines, castanets,
cymbals, tam tam, drums, unbossed gongs, wind machines, or typewriters. In
the case of the African *mbira*, sympathetic buzzing sounds caused by beads
and bottle caps attached to the instrument are an essential aspect of the
desired sound. Electronically produced sounds sometimes contain many
untuned elements. In brief, music typically contains 'noises' as well as pitched
tones.

   Put aside all such problem cases and also shelve the difficulties that go with
unpacking the notion of 'rhythmic articulation'. Consider a piece in which
all the tones are indicated as precisely pitched notes. Can its sound structure
be characterized as an array of tuned tones? Before this question can be
answered, it is necessary to get a clearer grip on what must be meant here by
'tuned' or 'pitched' tone.

   'The notes' of a piece do not have precise frequencies. The A above
middle C has ranged from 360 to 567 Herz (Apel 1966: 584–5; Ziff 1973).

Relativizing pitches to historical periods does not help because, at any given time, pitches have varied from place to place (A = 440 Herz in the USA as against A = 435 Herz in Europe in recent times) and also from musical type to musical type (J. S. Bach's instrumental music sounded about a semitone lower than today, whereas his organ works, and cantatas involving the participation of the organ, sounded between a semitone and a tone higher than now).

Although the A above middle C lies within a frequency range (say, of 420–460 Herz), this does not mean it can vary at random across this spectrum within a given performance. For a particular occasion of playing, the musicians are provided with a fixed datum from within the pitch band—for instance, everyone tunes to the A of the oboe. But, even in considering the tones of a particular performance, it is not always possible to specify their frequencies with precision. The problem is not that they might be out of tune, though this happens often enough. It is, rather, that micro-tonal deviations from the starting frequencies are often tolerated. In practice, the pitches of tones tend to wander or bend within playings of extended works, especially in vocal and string parts, without thereby sounding out of tune (Cook 1990: 236–7). Also, in string sections, there is a 'choir' effect that comes from microtonal differences in the pitches played by its members. Moreover, the instruments in an ensemble are not always aligned to matching frequencies. Soloists in Western music sometimes tune their instruments very slightly sharp (to 'solo' as against 'concert' pitch), which makes their line stand out more clearly against the orchestra's and adds a certain brightness to the tone. In Balinese orchestras, most of the instruments are in pairs with all the notes for one member of the couple tuned about 6 Herz higher than its mate. When the same notes are played by the duo, about six beats per second can be heard. It is this effect across the whole ensemble that gives to their sound the shimmering brilliance that is so distinctive of Balinese *gamelans*.

Another relevant consideration is this: we experience pitched notes as the 'same' (but higher or lower) at the octave. This (peculiar) experience of affinity is apparent in the way we name notes. Eight different tones, all called 'C', can be found on the modern piano's keyboard. But the likeness we experience between different Cs is not captured by designations of their frequencies. The logarithmic connection between 128, 256, 512, 1024, and 2048 is no more intimate than that between 128, 256, 384, 512, and 640, but this is not how we experience the two sets of frequencies. As a result, not even the notes of an instrument like the pianoforte, which has a fixed (but variable) tuning, can be characterized meaningfully in terms solely of frequencies of vibration.

Descriptions of the way air vibrates are no more successful in separating music from the noise it makes than they are in capturing the meaning of human utterances. Pitched tones should not be conceived in terms of precise frequencies. Indeed, the proposed relation is reversed. We know how to divide the frequency continuum into bands, or how to assign a given frequency to a note, only because we can identify and classify pitched tones independently of an awareness of their frequencies. Accordingly, pitched tones are not reducible to frequencies. How, then, are we to describe them? They are better thought of as tokens of named pitches than as frequencies of vibration—that is, as F, G, A, C, F, rather than as, say, 360, 405, 450, 512, 360 Herz.

This observation inevitably provokes another question, no less easy to answer than the first: on what basis are pitch names assigned and applied? The most plausible answers are these: pitch names refer to (*a*) elements in scales, (*b*) elements in intervallic sequences, or (*c*) a list of tones each of which, as regards pitch, is isolated from its fellows. Before clarifying and comparing these options, it is important to consider their implications for the proposal with which I began, according to which a sound structure is a rhythmically articulated array of pitched tones. Both (*a*) and (*b*) suggest a musical work is more than an ordered array of tones, for both indicate that the relation between notes goes beyond an account merely of their succession. We hear tones not solely according to their order—for example, as F, G, A, C, F—but as sequentially connected—as F–G–A–C–F, either within a tonal or an intervallic matrix. We hear them in terms both of pitches and of scalar relationships. Qualified listeners experience F–G–A–C–F as, say, tonic–supertonic–mediant–dominant–tonic, or as a motive involving two rising whole tones, a minor third, and a falling perfect fifth.[4] The tones of a sound structure are not merely ordered, they are patterned. They are pairs, triples, or whatever, not arrays of otherwise unconnected singletons. I call them strings, as opposed to arrays. They are more like sentences than like words structured only in terms of the order in which they appear in a list. So, now we are considering the proposal that sound structures are rhythmically articulated *strings* of tones with *named* pitches, and our focus is on the three alternatives indicated earlier for explaining the basis on which pitches are named.

The first option maintains that pitches are named, indirectly or directly, with regard to their scalar position. If the notes were F–G–A–C–F and the key were F major, a direct reference to their scalar position would be made both in 'tonic–supertonic–mediant–dominant–tonic' and in 'doh–ray–me–soh–doh', whereas the reference would be indirect in 'F–G–A–C–F in the key of F major'.[5]

---

[4] Yet qualified listeners need not be capable of offering descriptions of their experiences in technical terms, as I explain elsewhere (Davies 1994*a*: ch. 6).

[5] A similar distinction is apparent in the names used for chords: 'F–Dm–C^7–F in the key of F major' is indirect, whereas 'I–vi–V^7–I' is direct.

The direct system that uses doh, ray, me, etc. is known as solfeggio.[6] Solfeggio is employed mainly in training vocalists, not instrumentalists. I think this is because the singer is not aware of, and does not deliberately arrange, the subtle disposition of her tongue, larynx, and tendons in aiming for a particular note and timbre. She takes the note as her direct target, and leaves the mechanics of production to work themselves out. (I do not deny that singers are extensively trained. My point is that they are schooled in singing, not in physiology.) So long as the vocalist performs tonal music, has 'relative' not 'perfect' pitch, and is given the frequency of the relevant tonic before she begins, solfeggio is likely to be more useful to her than indirect tonal indications. Moreover, for vocal pieces that can be performed in any key of the singer's choosing, solfeggio is the more appropriate representation of their notes. The conventions of folk singing might allow the performer to begin a tune on any pitch that suits her tessitura. In that case, the relevant melodies are characterized most conveniently in terms of tonally structured interval sequences, without mention of pitch names.

Instrumentalists are usually addressed by indirect notations. Most instruments allow the player to perform in many keys. Individual notes are produced in particular ways—placing the hands and fingers just here and so, tensing the lips in such and such a fashion—largely regardless of the piece's key. The musician trains his body, so that the appropriate responses are triggered without undue concentration on the mechanics of sound production. Once he has mastered the required techniques, he can concentrate on playing the music, as against getting through the notes. Nevertheless, his work is much more plainly of the hands-on variety than is the singer's. He has to learn where to put his fingers even if, when competent, that process becomes unthinking. And, because the placement of the hands deals with pitches rather than their tonal functions, it is more useful for him to conceive the music through indirect notations naming pitches, rather than through direct ones indicating scalar position.[7]

---

[6] Balinese refer to notes by the terms 'dong', 'deng', 'dung', 'dang', 'ding'. Do these indicate pitch or scalar position? If the same note always were called 'dong', irrespective of the work's mode, the terms would indicate pitch position. In fact, though, the tones are named after their relative location in the mode. For example, in the seven-note *pelog* tuning, 'note 6' is 'dang' in *selisir*, 'deng' in *tembung*, and 'dong' in *sunaren*. (For discussion, see Tenzer 1991: 32.) Therefore, the Balinese pitch terminology for *pelog* is a kind of solfeggio.

[7] Among Western instruments, the guitar and its fretted kin are distinctive in that the neck can be 'capped'. Suppose a guitarist learned chords relevant to E major; for instance, she might be taught that B^7 is thus and so, and also that it is the dominant seventh chord of E major. By this method, she could apply her knowledge to any key, so long as the fingerboard was capped with the lowest unstopped string sounding the tonic. Without learning a new fingering for a D^7 chord, she could play that chord by fingering a dominant seventh when the cap was placed below the fourth fret, making the tonic G. In practice, though, a different approach is taken. Guitar parts in popular music are usually notated in tablature form—a picture of the fingerboard showing where the strings should be stopped—and/or in terms of chords identified by their roots—B^7, Em, $A^{\#6}$, and so on. In other words, popular guitar music is like other instrumental kinds in dealing with notes as pitches, rather than as scalar locations.

Earlier I showed that intervals take precedence over mere note successions, so it is not possible to analyse the former reductively in terms of the latter. It is easy to argue in a similar fashion for the precedence tonality takes over sets of intervals. Many different tunings may be adopted, with all counting as, say, 'major'. In fact, a variety of temperaments have been used in the West (Lindley 1980; Lawrence 1987). As a result, a tonal piece might be played in mean, just, or equally tempered scales, and is instanced in all of them. If all count as performances in the major, say, tonality is not reducible to an ordered array of intervals, since the intervals in the different performances vary microtonally according to the temperaments adopted. The same point can be made with respect to Balinese *gamelan gong kebyar*. By tradition, the fixed-pitch metallophones of such orchestras are tuned to a five-note scale, but the intervals in this scale may vary from orchestra to orchestra (Ornstein 1971: 81–106; Tenzer 1991: ch. 13). Since the same piece can be played by different ensembles, obviously its identifying sound structure depends on its modal realization and not exclusively on an ordering of precise intervals. This means the Balinese five-tone scale, like most Western scales, tolerates a spread of distinguishably different realizations. So, tonal or modal music is not merely a string of intervals, and tonality cannot be analysed reductively in such terms.

I suggested that sound structures are rhythmically articulated *strings* of tones with *named* pitches, and I asked about the basis on which pitches are named. The present discussion indicates they should be understood as representing scalar functions, as against either interval sequences or ordered arrays of tuned notes. Indeed, I do think this is a reasonable claim to make about music that is tonally/modally simple and stable. The problem is that not all music is like this. Some is thoroughly atonal and yet more contains modulations along with other passages that are tonally ambivalent. For such music, or at least for many of its parts, the pitch names refer to sequences of intervals, because the higher level of tonal/modal organization is absent. In a very few kinds of music, it may not be possible to hear strings of intervals in the tone succession, though the tones themselves are of definite pitch. (If successive notes are always more than three octaves apart, for instance, all sense of intervallic progression is destroyed.) For this last kind of music, or at least for many of its parts, the pitch names refer to ordered arrays of tones, because the higher levels of intervallic and of tonal/modal organization are absent.

Previously I observed that, because of variability in their frequencies, the identity of pitched tones depends on their place within sequences of intervals, and that, because of variability within intervals, the identity of intervals depends on their place within tonally structured sequences. This might seem to be inconsistent with the claims just made, which are that some works are organized only at the level of intervals and a few are structured purely in terms of pitch succession. The inconsistency is merely apparent, though. The

dependence referred to has a historical component; we would not individuate pitches as we do had they not been located within sequences of intervals,
and we would not individuate intervals as we do had they not had tonal/
modal functions. But, once we can individuate pitches, we may do so whether
or not they retain an intervallic context, and once we can individuate intervals, we may do so whether or not they retain a tonal/modal setting. Nothing
about the historical record contradicts the claim I make, which is that atonal-
ity was made possibly by the dissolution of tonality, and that music that proceeds without also progressing as a sequence could only have followed after
patterned varieties of music.

Harmony and metre

The points made for sequences of pitched tones apply equally to simultaneously sounded pitched tones. The identity of chords standing in tonally
functional relationships is not reducible to the vertical intervals constituting
them. The significance of a C–E–G chord depends both on the basic tonality and on its local setting. If the key is F, the chord is on the dominant
and leads naturally to an F chord; if the key is B major, the chord is on
the flattened supertonic and might resolve to a B chord. Moreover, not all
dominant chords display the same intervallic structure or notes. In F major,
C–E–G, C–E–B♭, E–B♭–D♭ all function harmonically as V (dominant) chords.
Just as melodic structures are not usually reducible to arrays of pitched tones,
harmonic progressions are more than successions of discrete chords.
Harmonies must be understood in terms of their tonal settings and functional relationships. Not all pieces employ harmonies progressively, however,
or provide a tonal or modal context for vertical combinations.

  Parallel arguments would show that beat, rhythm, and metre form a hierarchy, with the latter not always reducible to a combination of the others.
And again, pieces are not always organized to the highest level. For instance,
metre ceases to be an element within the sound structure when the time signature operates as a notational convenience only, so that bar lines imply no
stresses or pulse patterns. This is the case in the final dance of Stravinsky's
The Rite of Spring, where notated accents destroy a sense of the (irregular)
metre. In the relevant dimension, the highest organizational factor is reduced
to that of beat and rhythm.

Melodies, rhythm, and form

Note sequences structured tonally and metrically are the highest of the
irreducible levels of musical organization so far discussed. Are others higher
yet? For instance, can melodies be analysed reductively as tonally structured

EXAMPLE 2.3. J. S. Bach, *The Art of Fugue*, openings of Fuga 1 and Fuga 9

note strings, or do they exhibit yet more complex levels of organization and count in their own right, therefore, as elements in musical sound structures? The reduction would go through if alterations to a theme's intervals and rhythmic patterns always destroyed its identity. Alternatively, if a theme can withstand such changes in that it remains the same individual, the reduction fails and themes must be treated as autonomous sound structural items.

Compare the melodies in Example 2.3. The second derives from the first, but should we regard it as a *variant* that stands in its own right as a distinct (though related) melody, or should we consider it to be the *same* theme? I think we should prefer the first proposal. I hear the melody of Fuga 9 as different from that of Fuga 1, not as identical to it. There are many cases in which it is intuitively correct to hear melodic relationships as against identity. For instance, in themes and variations, the original melody is often radically transformed in the variations composed on it. These variations achieve musical autonomy, despite bearing the mark of the theme's influence in the family resemblance they share with it.

This demonstrates only that similar, even related, themes can be different. If themes are no more than the elements constituting them, it is necessary to prove their identities never do transcend alterations to those elements, however. But this is an impossible task. Compare the two parts of Example 2.4. Even if we ignore their harmonies and instrumentations, we find differences in their respective interval sequences: the descending run of sixteenth notes in bar 45 involves the intervals of tone–semitone–tone, whereas in bar 228 this becomes tone–tone–semitone; in the first violin part, bars 46–7

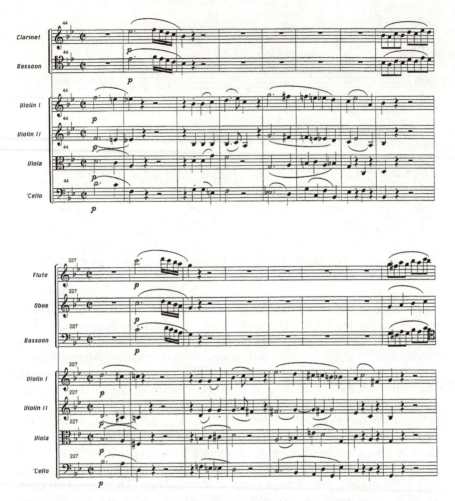

EXAMPLE 2.4. W. A. Mozart, Symphony No. 40, K. 550, opening bars of the second subject in the exposition and recapitulation of the first movement

proceed by tone–tone–semitone–minor third and in bars 229–30 the equivalent intervals are tone–semitone–tone–minor third. A more relevant way of capturing the difference observes that, in the exposition, the melody's tonality is B♭ major and, in the recapitulation, G minor, though incidental chromaticism is a feature of both versions. Of course, the change from the exposition's relative major to the recapitulation's tonic minor is standard for the treatment of second subjects in sonata-form movements in minor keys.

Though their interval sequences differ, it seems to me that one should hear both passages as versions of a single theme—that is, the same theme appears in the exposition and recapitulation. One explanation observes that the alterations are small ones when compared to those leading us to distinguish a theme from an autonomous variant. A second consideration is more compelling. Sonata form takes its structural point from the fact that themes introduced at the outset are later recapitulated. In Mozart's symphonies in major keys, the second subject is clearly the same in the exposition and the recapitulation, despite the change in key. For instance, the recapitulation of the second subject in the first movement of Symphony No. 41, K. 551 (at bar 289) is an almost exact transposition of its statement in the exposition (beginning at bar 101). To understand Mozartean sonata form, one must hear the *same* themes featuring in the exposition and recapitulation. The listener should hear the theme at bar 227 of Mozart's Symphony No. 40, K. 550, as the *same* as the one at bar 44 if she is to follow the work's structure.

The relevant change in the tune might be rhythmic and metric, rather than intervallic. Bill Monroe's bluegrass classic 'Blue Moon of Kentucky' was written and performed for many years as a waltz. Elvis Presley recorded it in common time and Monroe himself then played it that way. These were versions of the same melody.

The relationships between melodies in a given work spread over a continuum. At one end are cases in which a theme is repeated exactly; adjacent to this are ones in which it is accurately transposed to another key. At the other end are ones in which only some of the original elements (key, intervals, rhythm, metre, harmonic progression, instrumentation, dynamics) preserve an audible relationship to the original. Indeed, one of a work's themes might be derived from another yet bear no audible connection to its model. For instance, a tune might be transformed by small steps recorded in the composer's notebook to a point at which, when the finished opus includes only the first and final versions, the connection between them is not discernible. Entirely distinct themes result, though the notebook provides evidence of an ancestral relation. Between the extremes of the continuum is the case in which one theme is a variant on another. It differs enough from its model to qualify as a separate tune, though a similarity between the two is also apparent. Another possibility falls nearer the 'exact repeat' end of the continuum. A single theme, such as the one in Example 2.4, occurs in more than one version.

The points along this spectrum are separated only by degrees. At one end there is a single melody with more than one token; further along, there are related but distinct themes; eventually there are unrelated tunes. There is no obvious place to draw these divisions, yet they are real enough in our experience of music. The twisted and distorted rendition by Jimi Hendrix of 'The Star-Spangled Banner' at Woodstock was a version of the nation's anthem, not a similar but different piece. Indeed, his observation about the United States could not have been understood unless he was heard to play 'The Star-Spangled Banner'.

What I have argued for melodies applies also to complex rhythmic gestalts: they are not reducible to their component bits because the identity of the larger pattern can survive small-scale, local changes. (For analyses of the hierarchical structure of rhythmic patterns, see Cooper and Meyer 1960.)

The same does not apply to structural sections, I think, for these are reducible to the elements of which they are comprised—that is, musical macro-form is generated simply from the order of presentation of lower-level elements that are already accounted for in the work's sound structure. (The same goes for movements that together constitute a work.) Of course, many movement forms (such as rondo) rely on the recognizability of a recurrent motto, and a few musical works display a cyclic structure at the level of movements (with one short passage returning often as a refrain, as occurs with the fanfare in Igor Stravinsky's *Agon* (1957)). If it were crucial in following these works that repeated sections or movements are recognized as the same in their various occurrences, though they display low-level differences, it would be necessary to regard these sections and movements as irreducible aspects of the sound structure. The sound structure would run all the way to the top of the musical hierarchy, as it were. In fact, though, it is sufficient to hear the returning sections or movements as variants on, and as intimately related to, their predecessors, not as the same. In that case, such sections are reducible to the elements from which they are generated.

I have said enough to bring out my main points. Music is organized hierarchically and multidimensionally, with most of the higher structures not being reducible to aggregates or strings of their component elements. Musical identity and significance reach most of the way up the hierarchy. Indeed, the principles of identity and individuation that govern the 'simpler' constituents of musical sound structures usually depend on higher ones. The works composers create need not be organized to the highest possible degree, however. It is an empirical matter, then, to characterize the various elements and levels crucial to a work's identity.

Apart from reinforcing these conclusions, I have other reasons for considering whether a work's tempo and its instrumentation are non-reducible features of its sound structure. The discussion of tempo will serve as an introduction to the views of Nelson Goodman. His theory is outlined and criticized in subsequent chapters. Meanwhile, the discussion of instrumentation interjects several issues I have neglected so far. It leads us to ask if there is more to a work's identity that its sound structure. Moreover, it invokes consideration of the social context in which works are created and performed, a factor conspicuous by its absence from the account so far. It leads us to contemplate the idea that a work's musico-social context can affect what it is possible for the composer to include in her work's sound structure.

Tempo

Does a piece's tempo count as part of its sound structure? Not so, according to Goodman (1968), unless it is indicated by metronome markings under a system universally requiring them and thereby excluding vague, verbal indications.[8] 'The verbal language of tempos is not notational. The tempo words cannot be integral parts of a score in so far as the score serves the function of identifying a work from performance to performance. No departure from the indicated tempo disqualifies a performance as an instance—however wretched—of the work defined by the score' (1968: 185). In Goodman's view, the tempo adopted in playing a work is an interpretational feature of the *performance*, but is not also a property of the *work*. A performance can be entirely satisfactory as a rendering of the piece but, nevertheless, poor as an interpretation if it adopts an inappropriate tempo.

I regard Goodman's position as mistaken. The tempo of a performance could be so slow that it is impossible for the listener to hear other aspects of the sound structure as such. She cannot hear the notes as succeeding each other, or as rhythmically articulated, or as assuming a metric structure, if the tempo of performance is 'crotchet = five years'. That performance strikes me as failing to instance the work, as a non-performance, not as a poor interpretation that otherwise exemplifies the work satisfactorily. A performance in which the work cannot be discerned does not succeed as a performance *of the work*; it does not deliver the work's sound structure to the listener. Unlike Goodman, I place considerable weight on the fact that musical works are revealed in our experience of their performances. One sign that something belongs to a musical sound structure is that a performance is destroyed, both as an instance of the piece and as a sound event that can be experienced as music, if it is ignored. This is the case with tempo. (For further discussion, see Ziff 1971, Coker 1983, Kivy 1984, and Currie 1988.)

If, as I believe, a work's tempo counts as part of its sound structure, then tempo is like pitch in presenting a range of possibilities to the performer. The tempo of a given work might lie within the range of 70–90 crotchets per minute, for instance. Once a *particular* tempo is chosen from within this range for a given performance, that performance should stick close to the tempo until another is indicated (though allowance is made for rubato if this is stylistically appropriate). Even where tempos are specified precisely (say, crotchet = 104), by convention a narrow range around that figure is indicated as legitimate, I think. Notice, by the way, that tempo is work constitutive even where none is indicated in the score by the composer (as is the case with much of J. S. Bach's music). Where this is so, it is the performance practice, aspects

---

[8] Goodman adopts this conclusion because his theory of notations forbids the ambiguity that is ineliminable from verbal indications like *Andante*. I criticize his account of notations in Chapter 3.

of the notation (such as the time signature), and other musical features (such as the melodic shape, the rate of harmonic change, the genre, and so on) that together settle what tempo is called for.

Instrumentation

What of a piece's instrumentation? Is this a crucial aspect of its sound structure and thereby essential to the work's identity?

A few philosophers regard musical works as pure sound structures from which instrumental colour and timbre are entirely absent; call this position 'pure sonicism'. For instance, William E. Webster (1974) holds that J. S. Bach's Violin Concerto in E Major is unblemished if it is performed on the sousaphone. Though Peter Kivy allows that tone colour is crucial to the identity of a few pieces, he claims 'that in the three hundred-year or more history of instrumental music in the West, such cases are rare; that the *tradition* of Western music is one of musical works constituted by musical structure' (1988*a*: 51). Obviously these philosophers regard musical works for performance as ontologically very thin. For them, the choice and use of musical instruments is an interpretative feature of a performance rather than something crucial to the faithful delivery of the composer's work.

The idea that musical works are pure sound structures from which orchestral or instrumental shading and tone are absent seeks support from the following observations: in many pieces, especially early ones, instrumentation is not specified; the historical record often shows that a work's instrumentation was adapted to the contingencies of its various performances; pieces are frequently arranged for instrumental combinations for which they were not originally intended; and most works remain recognizable despite dramatic reorchestrations, so long as their sound structure is preserved in the new versions (Webster 1974; Kivy 1988*a*).

None of these points is decisive, however. Composers take for granted the musical practices they share with the contemporary musicians to whom they direct their instructions. As a result, they say no more than is necessary. In many cases, there was no need to specify the piece's instrumentation, because they were writing for a particular group and a given occasion. And, even if they left the orchestral details open so as to make the work adaptable to a spread of performance circumstances, it does not follow that they regarded its instrumental colour as irrelevant to its character. The most flexible of composers still thought in terms of the resources and instrumental techniques of his period, even if he intended that more than one combination of these would be suitable for the rendition of his work. Moreover, the prevalence of work transcriptions does not support the pure sonicist position. No one should regard a performance of Franz Liszt's transcription for the piano of Beethoven's Fifth Symphony as precisely equivalent to a performance given in the orchestral version Beethoven specified. The work transcription affords a kind of access to the original, but the two are not treated as identical or as intersubstitutable. Rather, work transcriptions are accorded a status as pieces in their own right, though they are also acknowledged as intimately related to their sources (Levinson 1980*a*; Davies 1988*a*; Thom 1993).[9] Finally, it is true that the more obvious aspects of its sound structure are more central to the work's identity than its orchestration (Levinson 1990*a*). This explains why the work usually remains recognizable if its instrumentation is altered. But it does not show that its instrumentation does not contribute to a work's identity.

It is sometimes said that J. S. Bach wrote works that, if not entirely abstract, were intended for instruments in only the most general terms. For instance, 'Klavier' in *The Well-Tempered Klavier* might be translated as 'keyboard' rather than as 'harpsichord' (Rosen 1990). The danger of turning this into a point for pure sonicism soon becomes clear, though. Nowadays, the Klavier-like keyboards of synthesizers may be used to activate pre-taped sound sequences, so that fingering Bach's piece on such a keyboard would not result in a performance of it. And with the aid of an appropriate programme, one could sound Bach's piece by typing this very sentence on a computer keyboard. Neither synthesizers nor computers are among the instruments for which *The Well-Tempered Klavier* was written. Hence, we cannot avoid taking seriously the question regarding which instrument or instruments Bach's piece should be played on by claiming that 'Klavier' is a general term in Bach's title. Inevitably there will have to be discussion about what kinds of mechanisms are activated by a keyboard if it is to count as a Klavier. I accept that nothing I have said so far shows that 'Klavier' must be interpreted as referring only to instruments that Bach might have considered, such as harpsichord, clavichord, spinet, virginal, organ, and the earlier models of the fortepiano. It remains to decide whether the pianoforte and the celesta should be counted as among those for which the piece is written. (I argue that they are not in Chapter 5.) My point is this: even if there is room for considering if Bach's intention for the piece could have been so general that it might have included some keyboard instruments that had yet to be invented, it by no means follows that the work's instrumentation is wide open, even as regards musical instruments triggered via keyboards.

I doubt that Bach's intentions were as vague as I was previously supposing, but if I am wrong, this would make him the exception rather than the rule. There can be little doubt that composers usually conceive their works

---

[9] I am not sure what attitude is adopted in other cultures, but I take the following, which concerns the Venda of South Africa, to support my position: 'a number of different transformations of the national dance, *tshikona* may be performed on Venda musical instruments. They sound different, but they are all called *tshikona* and are conceived as variations on a theme in the "languages" of the different instruments' (Blacking 1973: 41).

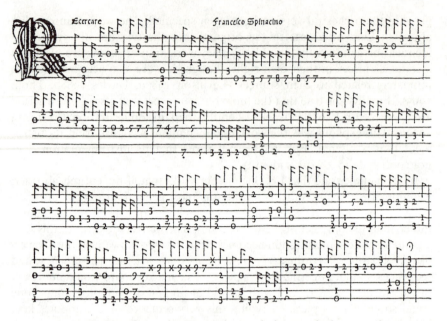

EXAMPLE 2.5. Ottaviano de Petrucci, *Intabolatura de lauto. Libro primo* (Vnice, 1507), 39; after Apel (1953: 63)

for the instruments on which they will be performed, rather than thinking solely in terms of timbreless sound structures. In the first place, this is apparent in the notations by which they communicate their music to its potential performers. Consider Example 2.5, which is an Italian lute tablature. Here, each line represents a string with the lowest at the top; the tuning is that which was standard for lutes at the time. The numbers indicate semitone steps up the fingerboard, and the flags indicate rhythmic values. This notation tells the player where to place his hand on the neck of a lute. It is instrument specific. Rather than thinking of his piece as an abstract sound structure and being indifferent to the manner of realizing it, Ottaviano de Petrucci is addressing himself expressly to a musician who is holding a lute in his hands.

Musical notations became more generic, as I discuss in Chapter 3, but it would be a mistake to overlook the extent to which they employ indications unique to particular instruments or families of instruments. Consider these indications: sul G, pizzicato, martelé, sautillé, jeté, louré, sul ponticello, tremolo, flautando, col legno, ᴠ, ⌐, 𝄴. They could not be other than instructions addressed to string players. It would be a nonsense to direct the clarinetist to play pizzicato, or to request the violinist to use the sustaining pedal, or to mark the pianist's part with breathing places, or to ask the drum player to raise the bell of her instrument. No competent composer would instruct a violinist to play a glissando of chords over three octaves, or to sound the D below middle C, but these can be perfectly appropriate as directives to a harpist.

Here is the point: in the normal run of events, composers rely on musicians for the performance of their works. Even if early notations often look bare, composers' scores are not intended as depictions of abstract sound structures. Instead, they are offered as instructions regarding what is to be played and how it is to be done. This is also how they are interpreted by performers, who expect to be told what to do with the instruments they have mastered. Music has always been thoroughly practical and pragmatic in these respects.

In arguing that a work's instrumentation contributes to its identity, Levinson (1980*a*, 1990*a*,*c*) notes that scores call for the use of particular kinds of instruments and that aesthetic and artistic properties central to the work's identity require their use. He provides illustrations of the following claims: (i) the dialogue between musical parts depends on their being played on different instruments; (ii) expressive properties of the sound rely on the strain placed on the instrument in the making of those sounds; (iii) the virtuosic character of a piece rests on the difficulties of playing it correctly on the specified instruments; (iv) the unusual tonal qualities of the sounds depend on their being atypical of the instrument used; and (v) the work displays the composer's attempt to achieve a balance between the instrumental forces specified.

Kivy has objected (1988*a*) to Levinson's account. Properties like originality and virtuosity belong to the work timelessly, and regardless of how it sounds now. He continues: if they inhere in the work heedless of how it sounds, they are possessed by the work irrespective of the instruments on which it is played. Kivy's second argument concerns expressive properties, such as the cragginess of Beethoven's Piano Sonata No. 29, Op. 106, 'Hammerklavier', or the nobility of the horn tune in the last movement of Johannes Brahms's Symphony No. 1, Op. 68. Here he suggests that the expressiveness depends more on the sound structure than the instrumentation.

Kivy's first argument strikes me as very odd. It appears to be on a par with claiming that, if a work begins with a middle C, it does so timelessly and, therefore, it is a matter of indifference whether we now begin it on that note or some other. In fact, though, to say a work is original or virtuosic is to say something about the properties it has when it is played correctly. Part of Kivy's point is that modern listeners can no longer hear it as displaying the relevant properties, even when it is played 'correctly', so there is little point in trying to be correct. But surely it is false to assume modern listeners are incapable of recognizing the virtuosic character of Nicolai Paganini's music when they see and hear it played on a violin, or to insist they cannot appreciate the originality of Beethoven's late quartets when their listening is informed by an awareness of his own and earlier composers' essays in the genre. And Kivy's second argument fares no better than his first. I doubt that much of the cragginess of Beethoven's work or the nobility of Brahms's theme would survive their rendition on a choir of recorders. Felix Mendelssohn's fairy overture would not lilt so lightly had it been scored for bagpipes.[10]

There is an alternative to pure sonicism that is better placed to deal with many of Levinson's cases. Call the new position 'timbral sonicism'. The timbral sonicist accepts a work's tone colour as part of its sound structure and as crucial to its identity, yet denies that the work's instrumentation is essential to it. On this account, what is important is the sounded outcome, including the full range of timbral qualities, not the means by which this is realized. If an electronic synthesizer could generate the appropriate sound, there would be nothing to choose between its performance and one elicited from the instruments for which the composer wrote. The effect, not its cause, is what is vital. Now, the timbral sonicist can allow to Levinson that the cragginess of Beethoven's 'Hammerklavier' is apparent only when it sounds as if it is elicited from a piano, and that the nobility of Brahms's theme requires the sound as of a French horn. Her claim is that what matters is 'sounds as if made by', not 'sound actually made by'.

Sometimes we characterize noises independently of their causes. For instance, we talk of clicks, ticks, creaks, groans, and bangs all as sounds of the night, without having any idea what makes them and how they are done. But this is not the way we normally listen to music. (Indeed, if we do hear a recording of some foreign music and can form no idea of how the sounds are made, or how many people and instruments make them, it can be very difficult to locate the music in what one hears.) Neither is it how composers and musicians think about their activities. For them, the instrument can no more be divorced from the music made on it than a voice can be separated from the words it speaks. Even if music can be thought of in terms of purely acoustic phenomena that might be electronically analysed and synthesized, in practical reality there is only one way of getting something to sound as if it is played well on a violin, and that is by having a skilled violinist play it.

The point is not simply that habit leads us to associate certain musical instruments with particular sounds; it is not merely that we have trouble imagining the separation of a musical event, qua sonic effect, from the process by which it is educed, qua cause. Rather, it is this: improvisation, the creation of works, the public specification of works, the performance of works, the reception of works—all these assume, involve, and rely on prac-

---

[10] Scruton (1997: 442) sees Kivy as winning the exchange. No doubt this is because his own account regards the identity of sounds as having nothing to do with their causes. (I wonder if he has heard a baby cry, or a fingernail scraped across a blackboard.)

tices and conventions, some of which are predominantly musical and others of which have more to do with wider social structures and purposes. As a result, connections that otherwise might be merely contingent take on a different status because they become normative or regulative within the relevant practice. In music as in figure skating, technical merit counts alongside 'artistic impression.' Within the relevant practices, playing the appropriate instruments is not merely a useful means to the production of the desired result, which supposedly is the creation of an abstract sound structure. Instead, the use of those instruments is part of the end, which is to articulate the specified sound structure on the required instruments (Wolterstorff 1980, 1987; Kendall L. Walton 1988; Bender 1993; Godlovitch 1998). To do otherwise is to 'cheat' and thereby to undermine the playing's status as a performance. I do not deny a modern composer can write works that deliberately specify no instrumentation. Indeed, Percy Grainger did exactly this. I say, though, that Grainger's decision must be understood as rejecting the established practice rather than as the choice of a normal option.

Kivy (1988*a*) asks: would the listener experience the cragginess of Beethoven's 'Hammerklavier' if, unknown to her, it was rendered on a synthesizer that sounded just like a piano? His point is that the music's expressive character must reside in its sound, independently of the means of production, if it is experienced as being present in the synthesized version. (I made a similar claim in 1990; I now think I was wrong.) This is the crunch case for the sonicist, for whom the means by which the sound is produced are irrelevant so long as what is sounded has all the required qualities. Kivy's rhetorical question does not show, though, that expressiveness is independent of the means of production. Instead, it indicates that mistaken beliefs about the means of production can affect what one hears in the sound. The listener should have the appropriate true beliefs if she is to have a proper understanding and appreciation of what she is hearing, however. This necessity is accepted as a convention of musical performance; it is assumed the listener knows or could find out how the sounds are generated. As Levinson (1980*a*, 1990*a,c*), David Carrier (1983), Kendall L. Walton (1988), and Stan Godlovitch (1990*b*) argue, it is precisely because synthesized renditions are not openly substitutable *salva veritate* for ones elicited on the appropriate instruments that sonicism is false. I can make the sounds *as of* a virtuosic performance of Paganini's *Caprices*, Op. 1, by playing a CD of the work on my record player, but I can give a virtuosic performance of those pieces only by playing the violin. A disc jockey is usually not a performer. We accept recordings as substitutes for live performances only because we take them as records of (simulated) performances, as I explain further in Chapters 4 and 7.

So far I have been agreeing with arguments directed against pure and timbral sonicism. I am not an unqualified 'instrumentalist', however. In other words, I do not agree that a work's instrumentation is always essential to its identity. Nor am I convinced by all the reasons advanced in favour of instrumentalism. In particular, one of Levinson's key arguments strikes me as overstated. In considering it, I hope to make clearer how my view differs from his.

Levinson writes: 'Since the expressive value of a passage is partly determined by the musical gestures that are properly heard within it ... expressive content in music is not detachable from the means of performance that are written into musical compositions, and authentic performances of such compositions, seeking to transmit their full expressivity, must observe instrumentation as much as resultant sonics' (1990c: 398–9; see also Laszlo 1967). He then presents a series of examples. To hear a passage as rushed (and hence as exuberant, frenzied, or anticipatory), we must take account of the manner in which it is generated. Strokes on the tympani carry powerful associations with striking, pounding, and battering in the abstract. The searing or caressing character of violin music connects with the manner of bowing.

I accept that the physical action that goes into making the notes sometimes confers dynamic and expressive features to the music that are audible to suitably informed listeners. As I explained in Chapter 1, musical instruments often *feel* like a direct extension of the performer's body. To take a simple example, how hard the tympani is struck translates directly into the percussive impact and volume of its sound. In other cases, however, this correspondence fails. High notes produced by wind players may involve intense strain on the player's diaphragm, but, where the notes should be quiet and tranquil, this tension should not be apparent in the sound produced. Many aspects of sound are apparent to the listener quite independently of her knowledge of the method or mechanism of their production, and, in general, listeners are often unaware (and cannot be expected to know) of register breaks in wind instruments, of shifts in fingering positions on string instruments, of whether a string instrument is fretted, of the internal workings that distinguish clavichords from harpsichords, and so on. The virtuosity of instrumentalists sometimes depends on their ability to disguise from the listener the technical problems presented by shifts in register, say, because the performance relies for its efficacy on the seamlessness of the move from the one to the other.

I have a more general and revealing objection. Levinson aims to show that the manner of eliciting sounds from instruments generates properties constitutive of musical works. From this he concludes that the use of those instruments, played in the appropriate fashion, is required in a fully authentic performance. His examples are well chosen. There are, however, many cases that are relevantly similar, ones in which the composer writes with the distinctive features of instruments in mind, yet musical practice does not regard the use of those instruments as necessary for achieving authentic performance. Nothing in Levinson's account explains how we distinguish the two kinds of cases.

There are innumerable instances in which composers shape their music to accommodate and highlight the timbral, stylistic, tonal, or other proclivities of the particular instruments for which the work was written. Stravinsky conceived the end of 'Evocation of the Ancestors' in *The Rite of Spring* for the tone distinctive to the bassoon players in Russia. Half a century after its composition, when he first conducted the work in Russia in 1962, he is reported as saying: 'The *fagotti* at the end of *Evocation des ancêtres* sounds, for the first time, like the *cinq vieillards* I had imagined' (Stravinsky and Craft 1968: 277). Nevertheless, I do not think we hold that *The Rite of Spring* can be performed authentically only by Russian orchestras, or by ensembles in which the bassoonists are Russian. Béla Bartók wrote violin works for Joseph Szigeti, who played with a metallic, hard-edged tone; Benjamin Britten composed for the tenor Peter Pears, who had a distinctively reedy vocal timbre. Yet we do not regard performances of the relevant pieces as less authentic if they are not played by Szigeti (or by a violinist who plays with a similar tone), or if they are not sung by Peter Pears (or by a tenor who copies the timbre of his voice). Mozart's Constanze was Caterina Cavalieri, his Figaro was Francesco Benucci, his Papageno was Emanuel Schikaneder, and his Queen of the Night was Josepha Hofer. He shaped his music in the most intimate way to suit the ranges, abilities, and colours of the voices of these individuals. Yet it does not count against the authenticity of renditions of the relevant operas that they cast other vocalists in the roles.

The examples just given are ones in which, though the composer wrote for the qualities of a particular instrument or performer, the conventions of the relevant performance practice discount such matters. It is also important to note that, as regards instrumentation, what the composer has been able to determine for his work has varied from time to time. Before the clarinet became established as an orchestral instrument, convention allowed that the oboe or flute (but not, say, the trumpet) could be substituted for it. Though Mozart wrote for the clarinet in his Symphony No. 39, K. 543, of 1788, he could not *require* that it be used.[11] According to Levinson (pers. comm.), because the clarinet has long been standard, *now* its use is required for authenticity; later developments have made Mozart's injunction stronger than it was in 1788. My view is different. I agree that the substitution of oboes for clarinets would be musically undesirable (given that the part was written to feature the distinctive qualities of the latter instrument). I also think the substitution would be perverse, given Mozart's preference and the current

---

[11] There is a version of his Symphony No. 40 in which Mozart dispenses with the clarinets because they were not available.

availability of clarinets. But I do not think the substitution suffers the additional fault of being inauthentic. Whereas Gustav Mahler can make the use of the clarinet mandatory for his music, so that it must be used if the performance is fully faithful, Mozart cannot do the same for his symphony, much as he might like to.[12]

I have presented cases in which the composer takes account of the special qualities of musical instruments or of the performer in writing as she does. In this they are like Levinson's illustrations. He appeals to the fact that composers design their works with an ear to qualities of the instruments to be used in performing them. He takes his examples to demonstrate that a work's instrumentation is essential to it. I agree this is often the case, but I deny that Levinson's method of argument proves this. In my similar examples, the composer writes with the features of certain instruments in mind, but is prevented by the conventions of the relevant musical practice from making them required parts of her work. I conclude that Levinson is not well placed to distinguish a work's constitutive properties from those belonging to its performed interpretations. The reason for this is fairly obvious: he pays little regard to the social conventions of music making and the effect these have in setting limits on what the composer's intentions and instructions can determine. It is these alterable, external conventions, not considerations of expressive detail, that govern which properties constitute musical works and, thereby, indicate what is required in the name of authenticity for performance.

Levinson motivates the idea that instrumental prescriptions generally should be observed by arguing that doing so has direct aesthetic consequences. The use of the relevant instruments typically generates some *other* feature—a dynamic or expressive one—that, because it is both salient and intended by the composer, is relevant to the work's identity. As I made clear earlier, I doubt that employing the required instruments inevitably results in the production of such properties. A work's instrumentation can be among its identifying characteristics even if no additional expressive or gestural feature depends on this. Also, even where the instrumentation desired by the composer generates other properties, it is not always the case that these

---

[12] I take a different view of Mozart's Clarinet Concerto, K. 622, which was written for the basset clarinet, a hybrid between the basset horn and clarinet. The basset clarinet and the clarinet are similar but the former has a deeper range, so Mozart's adaptation of the piece for the latter transposes some passages up an octave. Usually, the clarinet is used in performances of this work. Because it is a virtuosic concerto, a technically challenging work written to highlight the features of a particular kind of instrument, I do not think the substitution can be viewed with indifference. Like Levinson, I regard as absurd Webster's (1974) suggestion that J. S. Bach's Violin Concerto in E major can be played on the sousaphone without loss of authenticity. I also allow, though, that the closeness of the clarinet to the basset clarinet means a performance using the clarinet provides a version of the original, not a work transcription.

are work constitutive. In my view, what faithfulness to the work requires by way of the use of instruments depends, not on the effect of instrumentation on other properties, but straightforwardly on the work's ontological make-up. If the composer determinatively instructs that certain instruments should be used, they must be played if the performance is to be fully authentic. What the composer is able to mandate depends on conventions controlling the musical practice of her time.

In the fourteenth century, convention did not always allow the composer to require a particular instrumentation for his piece, even if he had a clear preference on the subject. Performers could use what was available to them. This is to say, instrumentation was not constitutive of musical works of the period. Various ensembles would be equally legitimate so long as they were consistent with what might have been used at the time. Some combinations would suit a given work better than others, but their adoption could not be required in the name of authenticity, because aesthetic and artistic properties affected by the choice are not work constitutive.

If the period's musical practice does not allow the composer to determine her work's precise instrumentations, are there any restrictions on what the performer may use? He should choose instruments from the range available at the time of the work's composition, I believe. The piece should be played on period instruments or replicas of them. The reason for this should be apparent from the previous discussion. The composer instructs the musicians who would play her work and those prescriptions take for granted the conventions that are the work's background. Inevitably, the composer has the sonorities and possibilities of existing instruments in mind, not those of as yet unthought-of devices, given that she expects her contemporaries to be able to deliver her work.[13] In particular, if the instruments of the composer's day have been replaced by quite different ones, her work cannot be performed in its most authentic version on modern instruments. The rendition of Medieval and Renaissance music calls for instruments such as the rebec, hurdy-gurdy, Krummhorn, rackett, cornett, and sacbut, even if

---

[13] A composer hopes to address future musicians as well as her contemporaries. Moreover, she might intend her music for as yet undeveloped instruments, though I do not think such intentions are common or are accepted by convention as work determinative. But, as I tried to make clear in my previous discussion of the possibility that J. S. Bach's music is intended generally for 'keyboard' instruments, there must be a limit to what will qualify as a keyboard instrument and that limit will take account of what the composer or his contemporaries could recognize on the basis of the keyboard instruments with which they were familiar. In this regard, the case of Beethoven is interesting. The pianos of Graf and Streicher were greatly superior to the earlier ones of Érard, which Beethoven used when he was younger, yet Brendel (1976: 15–16) doubts the authenticity of employing pianos by Graf or Streicher for the later works on the grounds that Beethoven was already deaf before these pianos came into use. (Beethoven owned an English Broadwood and a Graf at his death (see Arnold and Fortune 1971).)

no particular instrumental combinations could be required by the composer. For that matter, members of the viol family are too distant (as regards both playing technique and idiomatic sonorities) from modern violins, violas, and cellos, and the lute is too far from the guitar, for substitutions to be comfortable.

What of the case in which instruments, or families of instruments, existing at the time of composition have remained in use, albeit with modifications? Most of the strings, woodwind, and brass found in today's symphony orchestra attained their modern form 200 or more years ago. The basic design was established then, even if key systems, valves, different bows, metal strings, and many other 'improvements' were added subsequently. In playing Western classical music of the past 200 years, is it necessary to use (replicas of) period instruments or is it sufficient to use their modern cousins? For the so-called 'authentic performance movement' and its opponents, this is the $64,000 question.

I address the query just posed and related issues in Chapter 5. Here is my answer in brief: very subtle shades of treatment can be of vital importance in performances of works of the past 200 years and this is because those works are made to be thick and complex by their composers, who lavish considerable care on many aspects of fine detail and on practical considerations that affect the realization of such details. From the time they could make instrumentation work determinative, composers devoted careful attention to the contribution made by the instruments they specified. Because even small changes in those instruments can compromise effects on which composers relied, the highest degree of authenticity can often be attained by using only the best instruments that might have been available in the composer's day. There is another side to this coin, though. Where the instrument used is a modernized version of one for which the composer wrote, the departure from ideal authenticity is comparatively modest. Certainly it falls far short of destroying the identity and interest of the relevant performance. There are worse crimes, even in the world of music, than playing J. S. Bach's suites for unaccompanied cello on an instrument that, in comparison with the one Bach knew, has a rest peg, metal strings, a rounded bridge, a bass bar, and a modern bow. As I see it, performing Bach's keyboard music on a grand piano, though it is inauthentic, should be faulted more for tastelessness, given the way the instrument muddies textures that should be clearer and cleaner.

Here is an analogy. In literature, the work cannot be replaced by a paraphrase in modern-speak because the story told is not separable from the manner of its narration. One can paraphrase Jonathan Swift, say, but one loses his work of art in doing so. What goes for literature applies yet more clearly to music. Because music does not have semantic content, its message resides entirely in its accent and inflection. As regards the 'story' of an older instrumental work, there is simply nothing that could be paraphrased in a more up-to-date musical idiom. Musical works are not meaningless, as the sound of the wind is. Composers have something to 'say', but, because what they say has no independently specifiable semantic content, it can be successfully communicated only in their own accents and idiolects, even if these are local to a particular time and place. It is the sounds of the instruments they knew and for which they wrote, as much as the syntax of their musical expression, that capture the tonal nuances of their utterances. To hear their voices at their clearest, we must listen to performances on period instruments.

Levinson's definition

Already I have mentioned Levinson's views on the centrality of its instrumentation to a piece's identity. That is only one element in the detailed account of musical works he developed, taking as his paradigm pieces such as Beethoven's Quintet for Piano and Winds, Op. 16. Because my own views come nearer to Levinson's than to any other's, in the remainder of this chapter I concentrate on his theory.

Levinson's definition (1980*a*) was: a musical work is a sound/performing means structure as indicated by a composer at a given time. Although he later defended his general approach (1990*a*), Levinson modified his definition. He replaced 'sound/performance means structure' with 'performed sound structure', on the grounds that the former wrongly implies both that two antecedently specified things are brought into conjunction and that the performance means structure has the same reality and importance as the sound structure.

Following criticism that the notion of 'indication' is vague (James C. Anderson 1985; Thom 1990*a*, 1993; Bender 1993), Levinson accepted a suggestion made by James C. Anderson: 'indication' can be elucidated by reference to the idea (derived from Wolterstorff 1975) that, in creating a piece, the composer makes it normative that 'note N is to be played here and so'. By introducing the idea that composers' specifications are normative and not merely descriptive, Anderson's suggestion improves the definition, I think. Nevertheless, talk of 'makes normative' is only marginally less vague than Levinson's original 'indicates'. The problem is that one can imagine many ways in which a composer might 'indicate' something 'prescriptively' to the work's performers, with only some of these connected to the business of specifying a work. For instance, as the conductor of a performance of her work, the composer might make normative very precise details of phrasing and attack that are not indicated in her score. In this case, her 'indicating' or 'making normative' affects, not the work's identity, but that of the interpretation she proposes through her rendition.

Levinson's account has no resources for distinguishing acts of indication belonging to the process of work creation from those made by the same individual in her capacity as performer. To fill out what is missing, it would be necessary to distinguish musico-social roles (composer, conductor, performer) that might be occupied at different times by a single individual. Or, alternatively, one could explain what it is that brings to completion an act of composition, so that 'indicatings' coming later have a different prescriptive force from those defining a work's contents and boundaries.

Contextualism

Sometimes a thing's properties depend not solely on its internal structure or character, but on some relation between it and its wider environment. Being tall, or being an aunt, are properties of this relational kind. Now, the characteristics identified as aesthetic were described in traditional theories of the eighteenth century as intrinsic and non-relational. In the latter part of the twentieth century, some people argued that many (perhaps most) of the features crucial to a work of art's nature depend on its relation to its setting, especially to its art-historical location.[14] This last position, which I endorse, is sometimes called *contextualism*. Contextualism can be applied to the ontologies of works of art, as well as to their artistic properties. According to contextualist ontologies, the properties making a given work the piece it is include ones depending on its relation to circumstances, events, or facts lying beyond its immediate boundaries. (For examples of contextualist ontologies of art, see Margolis 1980, 1999; Carroll 1988; Currie 1988.)

Contextualists can and do differ about which external features affect the properties of works of art, which features are affected, and whether they are crucial to their works' content or identity. For instance, whether a work of art is famous or influential might depend on relations between it and contexts arising after the time of its creation, and it might be held that such properties are irrelevant to the work's identity and even to its artistic meaning or content. In the following discussion, I focus on versions of ontological contextualism maintaining that a musical work's identity is fixed at the time of its creation and that this identity is shaped in crucial ways by the piece's relation to its natal setting.

---

[14] Danto (1981) is the strongest exponent of this view. This is evident in his philosophical method. He starts from cases that are perceptually indistinguishable yet crucially different and considers what it is about their relational, non-intrinsic properties that accounts for the difference. For instance, he asks what separates Marcel Duchamp's *Fountain* from other urinals, such that Duchamp's piece is a work of art whereas look-alike urinals are not. For discussion, see Fisher (1995).

Levinson is an ontological contextualist of the variety I have just identified.[15] This may have been apparent from the earlier discussion of his views on instrumentation. If a musical work is instanced only by playing the appropriate instruments, so that an electronically synthesized version of the sound structure does not qualify even when it is aurally indistinguishable from a performance on the specified instruments, then a relation between the sounded outcome and the means of its production is crucial to the performance's being of the work. Which is to say, it is vital for the work's identity that its performances are produced in the specified fashion, independently of whether this is the only means available for generating the required sound structure.

As well as by regarding a work's instrumentation as central to its identity, Levinson's contextualism is apparent in the references made in his definition both to the time of composition and to the composer's identity.[16] For Levinson, these two aspects of the context are crucial to the work's identity. The general musico-historical setting encompasses cultural, social, and political history at and up to the given time, along with the musical activities of the composer's contemporaries and musical developments, styles, and influences that were then widespread. The composer's identity makes relevant his style and influences on this, as well as his repertoire and œuvre. Levinson provides examples of aesthetically significant properties affected both by the general musico-historical setting and by the composer's individual situation. Arnold Schoenberg's *Pierrot Lunaire* (1912) would have been yet more anguished if it had been composed by Richard Strauss; whereas Mendelssohn's style was original, someone writing in the same style in 1900 would not be; a work could be Liszt-influenced only if written after the relevant compositions of Liszt; Johann Stamitz's 'Mannheim rockets' were exciting in the mid-eighteenth century but would be quaint and funny in works of more recent times; Bartók could not have been satirizing Dmitri Shostakovitch's Symphony No. 7 (1941) in his Concerto for Orchestra (1945) if it had been written in 1939; a composer's work is properly heard in relation to his other compositions and would differ if his œuvre did. Levinson argues for the aesthetic significance of contextually relative properties for the works in which they are generated. He does not explicitly add that these properties are crucial to the identity of the pieces in which they occur. Presumably, their aesthetic

---

[15] Kendall L. Walton (1988), Pearce (1988*a*), and Margolis (1993) regard music in similar terms.

[16] James C. Anderson (1982) thinks Levinson is wrong not to treat the composer's identity as a variable within his definition. Unlike Levinson, who maintains that *only* Beethoven could have written the *Eroica*, Anderson allows there are possible worlds in which the *Eroica* was written by someone else and, hence, he regards the composer's identity as contingently connected to the work's identity. Nevertheless, he insists for any given world that only one person can compose the *Eroica*. He agrees with Levinson that two composers, working independently, could not produce a single work.

significance is supposed to speak for their centrality to work identity. His conclusion is that the indication of otherwise identical sound structures results in the creation of *non-identical* musical works if these acts of prescription occur in contrasting musico-historical contexts and/or are made by different individuals.

Like Levinson, I think (Davies 1994*a,b*) a piece's identity depends on properties some of which are contextually relative and, in consequence, that it can be identified and appreciated as the work it is only by those with the relevant knowledge. I agree that the musico-historical setting within which the work is created contributes to its identity. I disagree, however, with Levinson's further claim, that the work's identity depends on the composer's. I turn to our differences later, but I begin with a discussion of the ground we share in common.

If two composers independently indicate the same performed sound structure in different musico-historical contexts, they write different works. Where these composers belong to different times or cultures, then their musico-historical situations differ. If a mid-twentieth century composer 'indicated' a work that sounded when performed accurately just like one of J. S. Bach's *Brandenburg Concertos*, it would not be the same piece as Bach's because many of its artistic properties would differ from those of Bach's concertos. The modern work would be conservative and mannered in its use of an outdated style and in its reliance on ancient instruments, such as the harpsichord. It would be replete with quotations of and reference to Baroque mannerisms and idioms. It would be expressively understated. It would be significant for all the possibilities and techniques—for instance, dodecaphonism, electronic synthesis, metric irregularities, melodic fragmentation—that it deliberately excludes. Bach's *Brandenburgs* have no such properties, of course. (Neither does the Postmodern 'Brandenburg' of an early twenty-first-century artist, which is self-conscious and witty in its appropriation of a past style.) This is relevant to the identities of the works in question; characteristics of these sorts contribute significantly to a piece's being the one it is.

A given sound structure takes some of its properties from the musico-historical setting within which it is proposed. If that same sound structure were indicated in another musico-historical situation, it would take on characteristics sufficiently different to make it another piece. Two composers living centuries apart, or in very different cultures with little musical contact, operate in dissimilar musico-historical locations. If they indicate the same performed sound structure, they produce different works—not because they are different people but because of their contrasting musico-historical contexts. The composers would create different works by indicating identical performed sound structures if one were a fifteenth-century Chinese whereas his contemporary was born, raised, and lived in Paris, or if one heard only jazz and the other heard only punk, or if their works were separated by 100 years though both participated in the Western classical tradition.

Any definition must tolerate a degree of uncertainty in specifying the temporal or cultural parameters that fix the work's musico-historical locale. Imagine a world closely related to the actual one. In this possible world, Bach pauses for a cup of tea and moves his manuscript from the desk to a chair before writing the last note, whereas, in the actual one, he completes the work without hesitation where he is. I wish to say he writes the same work in both worlds (and I assume Levinson would agree with this). Perhaps this is what James C. Anderson (1982) has in mind when he holds that the *time* of a work's composition is contingent to its identity. If he means to insist that the *Brandenburg Concertos* would have been the same works were the set to have been finished a few minutes, hours, weeks, or even months after the actual moment on which Bach completed it, I agree. But if he means that, had Bach never written the *Brandenburg Concertos*, I could compose them now, at the dawn of the twenty-first century, were I to indicate in the counterfactual world a performed sound structure just like that specified in the actual world by Bach, I think he is wrong. The work specified by my instructions would differ significantly from Bach's, as I have just described. I distinguish the cases, though both involve differences in time, because a few days or months would not have altered the musico-historical context of Bach's compositional efforts, whereas a shift to the twenty-first century brings us into a quite different musical era. The *time* of a work's composition is irrelevant to its identity only if differences in time do not correspond to significant differences in musico-historical contexts.

How should we identify 'significant differences in musico-historical contexts'?[17] There is no algorithm for doing so, but apparently it is possible when temporal distance allows us to pick out styles, periods, and trends, since musical historians make judgements of this kind all the time. Musico-historical periods are not of a consistent duration, though. Eras of relative stasis and consolidation alternate with ones of rapid, revolutionary development. Sometimes the musical world can be turned on its head in a short time; for instance, for the West in the period it took Léonin to create the first polyphonic pieces, or Claudio Monteverdi to pen his *Orfeo*, or Beethoven to write his Symphony No. 9, Op. 125, or Stravinsky to compose *The Rite of Spring*. Other epochs are comparatively stable, as was the case in Western classical music from 1700 to 1740. As a result, pieces written in a given place a few years apart might or might not differ in their musico-historical backgrounds.

---

[17] Dipert (1993) objects that contextualists simply have not done enough to explain how musico-historical settings are individuated and identified.

Can a musical work have more than one composer?

Like Levinson, I believe a work's identity depends on its musico-historical situation (and thereby on the place and time of its composition). If two composers independently specify acoustically identical performed sound structures, their indications determine distinct works provided their musico-historical locations differ sufficiently. Levinson's contextualism extends further, though. He argues that a musical work is specific to its composer. If two composers independently indicate the same performed sound structure *at the same time and place*, they compose different works. I disagree, and in this section address the arguments with which Levinson supports his conclusion. (For additional criticisms, see Currie 1988, and for Levinson's response, see his 1992.)

There are many apparent counter-examples to Levinson's claim, none of which he considers. Many works include the efforts of more than one composer. For instance, countless pieces quote the opening notes of the Dies Irae sequence dating from the Middle Ages, and many others include the BACH motive Johann Sebastian employed as his musical signature. Peter Tchaikovsky's *1812 Overture* contains 'La Marseillaise', which was not written by him. In reply, it might be said these are cases of quotation or inclusion. We do not regard the composer of the source material as co-author of the piece into which it is incorporated. The *1812 Overture* has only one composer, Tchaikovsky, though he took parts of it from pieces by other composers.

This response is not adequate to a different set of cases—namely, ones in which works are cooperatively produced. Many popular songs are created in the studio by a group effort, with no individual identifiable as the composer (Frith 1983, 1986; Gracyk 1996). In China, the *Butterfly Lovers' Concerto* was composed by a committee. And many of the Beatles' songs were written jointly by John Lennon and Paul McCartney.[18] Here I suppose Levinson would allow that the work belongs to a team, not to an individual, while denying this counts against the intention of his thesis. He aims to rule out the possibility in which different composers *working independently* create a single work.

What is to be said about the case in which Walzer von A. Diabelli invited several composers each to write a set of variations on his theme? I assume they did not work together as each fulfilled his individual commission. Perhaps, though, the coordinating role played by Diabelli in gathering together the contributors' efforts makes it the case that they did not work

---

[18] I realize that, even from their early days, they did not cooperate on the composition of all the songs listing them as joint authors. (Indeed, I have a point to make about this later.) For the time being, I am concerned only with the songs that resulted from their combined inputs.

independently. This suggestion will not cover a piece such as Mozart's *Requiem*, K. 626, which, because it was completed after his death, cannot easily be viewed as arising from cooperation.[19] Instead of joint authorship, here we have a rather special composite: Mozart's *Requiem* in a performing *version* produced by Joseph Eybler *et al.* (It was in such terms that Deryck Cooke's treatment of Mahler's Symphony No. 10 was advertised.) Or, if the original is too fragmentary, we might describe the later piece not as a performing version of the first composer's work, but as 'after' it.

As I have interpreted it, Levinson's claim is not that there can be no more than a single composer for any work but that composers whose efforts are not coordinated or otherwise interdependent must write different pieces, even if they indicate otherwise identical performed sound structures. To support the conclusion, he offers this general argument:

Composers who produce identical scores in the same notational system with the same conventions of interpretation will determine the same sound structure. But the musical works they thereby compose will generally not be the same. The reason for this is that certain attributes of musical works are dependent on more than the sound structures contained. In particular, the aesthetic and artistic attributes of a piece of music are partly a function of, and must be gauged with reference to, the total musico-historical context in which the composer is situated while composing his piece. Since the musico-historical contexts of composing individuals are invariably different, then even if their works are identical in sound structure, they will differ widely in aesthetic and artistic attributes. But then, by Leibniz's law, the musical works themselves must be non-identical; if W_1 has any attribute W_2 lacks, or *vice versa*, $W_1 \neq W_2$. (Levinson 1980a: 10)

Had the work been composed by a different composer, it would fall within a different œuvre, and this would alter expressive and other properties arising from its relation to surrounding works. Had Richard Strauss written in 1897 something the same as Schoenberg's *Pierrot Lunaire* (1912), Strauss's piece would have been even more anguished and eerie than Schoenberg's is. And if a composer had duplicated Schoenberg's output with the exception of *Verklärte Nacht* (1899), her *Pierrot Lunaire* would differ from his, which resonates with the Expressionist sighs of *Verklärte Nacht*. Composers are mentioned in Levinson's definition as a way of locking onto fine-grained aspects of the creative context not covered by the more general notions of time and place.

Kivy (1987) has objected to Levinson's argument. He points out (as does Carrier 1982) that Leibniz's law does not distinguish between a thing's essential and its accidental properties. Appeal to it does not settle whether a piece's musico-historical setting is essential to its identity or, instead, affects only its

---

[19] Three composers were involved: Joseph Eybler and F. J. Freystädtler realized the orchestrated version of Mozart's 99 sheet *particella*, whereas Franz Süssmayr was the main copyist because his handwriting was most like Mozart's (Robbins Landon 1989).

accidental properties. Kivy's intuitions fail him when confronted with some of Levinson's fictional illustrations; for instance, that in which Richard Strauss produces in 1897 a score identical to Schoenberg's *Pierrot Lunaire*. He declares the example to be 'impossible'. His intuitions are clearer about an actual case he offers as an antidote to Levinson's position: a fugue once attributed to J. S. Bach is now known to be by his older cousin, Johann Christian Bach (1642–1703). Kivy allows that the piece has 'gained' some properties and 'lost' others, but denies it has changed its identity. His feeling is that the work is the same, whether composed by J. S. or J. C. Bach and, hence, that changes we hear in it when we learn of its true authorship are alterations in its accidental, not essential, properties. To this, Levinson (1990*a*) responds by arguing that his examples are logically possible ones. He admits that Leibniz's law does not distinguish between essential and accidental properties and, hence, a thing might remain self-identical although it differs (in its accidental properties) across possible worlds. But, within a particular world at a given time, differences in properties signify differences in things, he emphasizes.

It may be that Levinson takes this to be sufficient to show no two composers could independently compose the same work, for the results of their efforts would coexist in a single world at a given time, and must be different because they do not share all the same relational properties. That seems to be the gist of the following: 'it makes no difference whether the distinguishing property is essential or accidental, relational or non-relational, important or unimportant: if one piece has got it and the other not, then they ain't the same piece!' (1990*a*: 226). If that is his line, I think it is mistaken (see Davies 1992). Where Leibniz's law entails that things are not identical, it remains to determine just *what* things are different. Levinson's wording presupposes it is the musical works that differ—'if *one* piece has got it and the *other* not, then they ain't the same piece!' (emphasis added)—but this is only one possibility. My copy of Leo Tolstoy's *Anna Karenina* is distinct from yours, but this does not mean both cannot instance the same, single work of art. Similarly, my composition might differ from yours in some of its contextual properties, but this does not mean we have composed different works. *W*-as-composed-by-*A* might be a juvenile work that is soon forgotten, whereas *W*-as-composed-by-*B* might be an influential, mature piece, yet '*W*' might be a single composition. This is apparent, I think, if we consider a different sort of case. Sometimes people have independently invented the same thing. This happened with television, the creation of which is now attributed both to John Logie Baird and Vladimir Zworykin. As it happens, the result of Baird's efforts was taken up and became famous, whereas Vladimir Zworykin's work at first slipped into obscurity. Such differences in relational properties do not entail that two things were invented, though they do require a difference between *some* things somewhere. In this kind of case, we distinguish as necessary between the television-as-invented-by-Baird and the television-as-invented-by-Zworykin.[20] The appeal to Leibniz's law settles nothing, then.

I concur with Levinson that two composers working independently and specifying conspecific performed sound structures compose different works if they operate at a cultural or historical remove from each other. Unlike Levinson, I believe two composers can independently create the same work if they share the same musico-historical location. In this last claim I agree with Kivy, but we differ in our reasons. I am a mild contextualist who thinks Levinson has taken matters too far in regarding the composer's identity as affecting the work's, whereas Kivy rejects contextualism in general and equates a work with its pure sound structure. For him, coincidences in sound structures always mean that only one work is on show. To test these various intuitions, consider further Levinson's arguments.

Levinson (1980a) touts as an advantage of his account that it provides the composer with a logical insurance that his works are his very own and he asks rhetorically why a composer should have more fears on this count than a painter who uses oils. It seems to me that what the composer should be guaranteed depends on the nature of his product. It is an abstract individual, not a concrete one like an oil painting or a hewn statue. To be *sure* it will be acknowledged as his, he should get his work into the public domain, or obtain copyrights or patents. (In this respect he is no worse off than designers, inventors, legislators, and many other artists, such as architects, novelists, poets, choreographers, playwrights, and cinematographers.) If he does so, then he can be certain it counts as his, though he cannot also be certain it will not be rightly identified also as a work of one of his contemporaries. Even if he does not get a *logical* assurance that the work is exclusively his, he can get a pragmatic one that is good enough in practice. Musical works are usually of a complexity making independent duplication very unlikely. If a heavenly requiem is performed in the chapel of Count Franz Walsegg zu Stuppach's castle and he claims it as his own, yet it is identical to one penned by the dying Mozart, who will be impressed by Franz's claim that it is logically possible for him to write the same piece independently? Because plagiarism is much more likely, the onus of proof will fall on him.

Levinson's next point is that, if two composers independently determine the same performed sound structures, these structures will diverge in their properties over time, even if they seem to be very similar when they begin

---

[20] The same point can be made for discoveries. The structure of DNA was discovered independently by the teams of Francis Crick and James Watson, and of Oswald Avery. The discoveries differed in terms of properties that depended on the scientists' identities, on their circumstances, and on their subsequent histories—for instance, the one discovery earned the Nobel prize whereas the other did not—but this does not mean that what was discovered by Crick and Watson thereby differed from what was discovered by Avery.

life. 'W_1 will eventually be seen properly against A's total development, and W_2 against B's total development. W_1 may turn out to be *a seminal work*, whereas W_2 turns out to be *a false start*' (1980*a*: 24–5).

Levinson does not presuppose that the future changes the past. In fact, he is a realist about historically conditioned aesthetic qualities (1994) and believes that properties like originality are present from the outset (1988). What changes is not the meaning or content of the work, but our access to this and the significance we accord to what we find there (see also Ingarden 1986: 155–6). Nevertheless, there is one case according to Levinson (1996) in which the past is altered by the future—namely, that in which an artist's early work takes on a new meaning in the light of later developments in her œuvre. This is possible because it is reasonable sometimes to see an artist's output as an extended but unified 'utterance'. Just as the meaning of the early parts of a narrative can be affected by the later unfolding of the story, so the content of one work can be altered by the nature of later pieces with which it is continuous and united via a complexly articulated but singular act of artistic creation.

Now, one might propose that some of the properties Levinson seems to have in mind, such as expressive ones, might better be seen as relative to artistic genres, schools, and the times than to the œuvre of the individual artist. To return to an earlier case, Richard Strauss's (fictional) *Pierrot Lunaire* would be more anguished and eerie than Schoenberg's actual one, not because of differences in the expressive vocabularies of the two composers, but because (in the example Levinson imagines) Strauss's piece is written in 1897, whereas Schoenberg's is from 1912. Those fifteen years saw a major and final shift in the treatment of harmony and tonality. The fluid chromaticism of Wagner and Mahler gave way to the isolation of brutal discords and a more aggressive atonalism. *Pierrot Lunaire* is more expressively extreme if it is located against the works prior to 1897 (such as Strauss's *Thus Spake Zarathustra* of 1896) than those immediately prior to 1912 (such as Schoenberg's *Erwartung* of 1909 and Stravinsky's *Petrushka* of 1911). It is possible to account for much of the character of the 1897 *Pierrot Lunaire* in terms of its relation to its specific historical context, without reference to the stylistic predilections and idiosyncrasies of its composer.

Suppose I am mistaken. For the sake of the discussion, concede to Levinson the truth of the claims he makes about the dependence of some of a work's properties on its relation to features of other works belonging to the composer's œuvre. Even then, one can deny the conclusion he draws. There is often a deep, close connection between one piece and later ones by the same composer, but this does not show that a work can have only one composer. What follows, instead, is that it is reasonable to expect an intimate connection between a given piece and later ones produced by its creator *or creators*. It may be true that the futures of different composers affect relational properties of the products of their earlier creative efforts, but it does not follow that they could not independently have created the same work in the past. That W-as-composed-by-A comes to differ from W-as-composed-by-B as the careers of A and B take divergent paths does not show that 'W' cannot refer to a single work. Individuals who go on to have contrasting lives might independently invent, say, the typewriter, or discover, say, the structure of carbon.

Here it is worth recalling the case of Lennon and McCartney. They went on to compose independently. The cooperatively produced songs of their earlier period can be properly seen against the total musical development of Lennon, but also, and with no less propriety, against the very different total development of McCartney. Indeed, because they were created as much by the one as the other, the fullest appreciation of the co-authored songs requires that they be considered in the light of the later careers of both their writers. If this real-world case is unproblematic, it is hard to accept Levinson's argument. Though Lennon and McCartney cooperated at the outset, whereas Levinson's hypothetical composers do not do so in indicating the same performed sound structure, that is irrelevant, because the argument appeals to what happens *after* the initial act of composition. In the real world, Lennon and McCartney took separate paths as composers. This does not show they could not jointly author some of their early songs, since they did so in fact. By analogy, the contrast in the careers of Levinson's A and B does not demonstrate that they could not have authored the same work.

Levinson's final claim (1980a) is that, for a performance to qualify as of a given work, it must be connected to, and guided by, the composer's act of work specification. I share this view, but I deny the entailment detected by Levinson: musical works must be specific to a single composer. Accept that a performance is of a given work only if there is an intimate connection between what is done and what is indicated to its performers by the work's composer. (I argue for this view in Chapter 4.) Also suppose (contrary to Levinson's view) that a work might be composed independently by more than one person. Though Levinson's approach suggests it should be impossible to marry these two hypotheses, this is not the case. If the work has more than one composer, it is performed only if what is played depends either on the one composer's work indications or on the other's. So far as I can judge, this formulation meets Levinson's requirement that there be a tie between what the performer achieves and what the composer specifies.

On several previous occasions I have invoked Lennon and McCartney against Levinson's position. Here is another reason for doing so: Levinson writes of creation as a natural process—for instance, by describing it as autonomous and individual rather than as essentially social. And, in a move that is reminiscent of John Locke's theory that labour mixing is a natural process by which property, and rights to it, are generated, he suggests that the composer's creative intervention in the world leads to her possessing the works she writes. In other words, he slides effortlessly from arguments about the creative role of the composer in bringing a work into existence to further claims about that individual's exclusive ownership of what she has created. Yet, the fact that not all the songs identified as by Lennon and McCartney were written jointly by them should lead one to pause over the equation of creative responsibility with authorship. Some of the songs attributed to the duo were created by only one of the pair. Nevertheless, it is not obviously mistaken or silly to regard them as co-authors of these songs: they cooperated as composers over a decade and viewed themselves as members of a song-writing team. As I see it, this indicates that there is a social aspect— which is to say an arbitrarily conventional, socially relative element—to the notion of 'composer' or 'composer's work', just as there is a communal dimension to the notion of 'owner' or 'property' going beyond anyone's 'natural' engagement with the relevant material. Even if the creation of musical works usually results from the autonomous actions of individuals, it does not follow that one cannot become a work's composer in other ways. A person might compose a work by writing it at much the same time as another of its composers does, or she might acquire responsibility for a piece simply by belonging to a team identifying her as the co-author of everything that is written, whichever member of the team did the work.

To my mind, the sandbar that forces one to right or left is Kivy's real-world example of the fugue by J. C. Bach that was wrongly assigned to his cousin, J. S. Bach. A relevantly similar case occurs when a composer's symphonies are not numbered in chronological order of composition, as was the case for Antonín Dvořák, whose symphonies of 1880, 1885, and 1875 were first published as numbers one, two, and three. The symphony of 1875 was his fifth and now bears that number.

Levinson (1990a) suggests that, when we learn the facts of the case, what has changed is not the work's identity but the audience's epistemic access to its properties. If it seems to be different now, this is because we are in a better position to discern qualities depending on the context of its generation, which was previously misidentified.[21] This response is fine as far as it goes, but it does miss the intended point, which is that the audience is no less well positioned to identify the work in question prior to the revelation of the composer's identity than afterwards. As Kivy allows, some features of the piece are experienced differently when it is correctly attributed, but (he claims) we are more inclined to think the *same* work is slightly altered than to believe it is not at all the work we formerly supposed.

---

[21] I assume Levinson would deal in a similar way with pieces from a known location and period that have anonymous composers. Rather than insisting that we cannot identify such works, he could argue that we can discern enough of their outlines to make a qualified identification, though we cannot appreciate their fine-grained features because we are ignorant of the more subtle aspects of their genealogy.

For a case like this, I agree with Kivy. Imagine that, working independently, the young Mozart penned a piece note-for-note identical with one written at the same time by his contemporary, the 'London' Johann Christian Bach, son of Johann Sebastian, a composer he then admired and emulated. It is not obvious to me that the differences between what each produces—the one being a juvenile piece and the other the work of a mature composer; the one at best a hint of the heights to which its creator would aspire and the other the composer's best possible effort—suggest there are two works here rather than two specifications of a single work. As concerns the properties relevant to the appreciation and understanding of the work as a musical piece, they may be identical. The work-as-composed-by-Mozart differs from the work-as-composed-by-J. C. Bach, since the one fits into a corpus of compositions distinct from that of the other. But such contrasts result in different works only if one accepts that the identity of the work is indexed to the identity of its composer, which is the assumption I am inclined to reject.

I do not undervalue the achievements of actual composers, or treat the authorship of works as of only passing interest. The reverse. The line I take is no friend of the 'death of the author' view that treats authorship as of little relevance to the manner in which we enjoy and understand actual works. As will become apparent in subsequent chapters, I place considerable store in the fact that, for many if not all kinds of music, we appreciate works as of their authors. In explaining why this is so, it is not necessary to provide a logical guarantee of individual ownership, as Levinson tries to do. It is sufficient to realize how complex extended musical works are.

So far I have been agreeing with Kivy against Levinson: a given work might have had a different composer, and two composers might independently create a single work. In general, though, I am more sympathetic to Levinson's characterization of musical works. It is time to criticize the grounds on which Kivy rejects contextualism.

When it comes to assessing the significance of historically relative artistic properties to the identity of musical works, Kivy (1987) is not sure what to think. Where the cases are clear, they point to the sound structure as the only viable principle of work identity, he believes. It is apparent, however, that his scepticism is fuelled by two assumptions, each of which is rightly questioned by Levinson. The first is that the contextually relative properties of a work change through time, as its context alters. What was virtuosic, original, or exciting in a piece at the time of its composition ceases to be so later, when instrumental technique improves and the audience becomes habituated to newer, more exaggerated, idioms (Kivy 1987, 1988a). If these properties do not endure, though the work's identity does, then they cannot be essential to its identity. Levinson responds (1990a): artistic properties do not alter through time. The work takes on the relevant property as a result of standing in a particular relation to its musico-historical surroundings, but having acquired that property—and thereby having established an identity shaped by that property among others—it retains it so long as it remains the work it was. If the work is original at its inception, it continues to be so thereafter. Kivy (1988a) seemingly anticipates this reply. He allows that a piece might continue to possess a property that can no longer be exhibited in any performance of it. Not surprisingly perhaps, he is unconcerned in making the concession. If his opponent's account of work identity makes much of characteristics that inevitably become inaccessible to the work's audience, so much the worse for the theory. This is not what Levinson intends, however. Properties relative to the work's musico-historical situation might not be apparent to a person who takes the work to belong to a time and context later than that in which it was created. But that person *mishears* the work (Levinson 1990a). A person who listens in terms of the appropriate expectations and knowledge, which are those possessed by a suitably informed audience of the composer's time, will hear in an adequate performance the artistic properties belonging to the work.[22]

The second of Kivy's questionable assumptions is apparent in his suggestion that a work's artistic properties could not be essential to it, since a listener might be aware of its identity even if she cannot (or could never) experience its artistic qualities. Kivy's strategy is the one to which I made objection earlier. He argues, if a work can be recognized as such in a performance lacking a given property, that property is not essential to the work's identity. As I have already explained, this approach mistakenly conflates a thing's identity conditions with the criteria for its individuation. Kivy's argument fails to take account of the fact that a musical work can remain discernible in a seriously deficient performance, such as one peppered with wrong and missing notes, chords, or even themes and sections. As crucial parts of its sound structure, such things are essential to the work's identity on most accounts, including Kivy's own. If the work can be identified, albeit in a crippled version, when not all its constitutive features are manifest, then Kivy cannot show that a work's artistic properties are merely contingent by noting that auditors who are unaware of such features in a performance can, nevertheless, discern which work is being instanced.

Until now I have been discussing Levinson's definition without acknowledging an important restriction he places on its scope. He writes: 'I am confining my inquiry to that paradigm of a musical work, the fully notated "classical" composition of Western culture, for example, Beethoven's Quintet for piano and winds in E-flat, Opus 16' (1980a: 6). Immediately, this excuses

---

[22] In Chapter 5 I consider in more detail whether the listener of the present day can hear old music as its original audience did. I suggest she cannot do so in all respects, and that she can be in a better position to understand and appreciate the piece for this very reason, but I also indicate that conceptual adjustments making possible an experience of the artistic features of old works are possible.

Levinson from addressing counter-examples coming from other eras or from non-Western cultures. Kivy (especially in 1988*a*) invokes works from earlier periods in developing objections to Levinson's position, and Levinson (1990*a*) defends himself by drawing attention to the injustice of this, though he does not confine his response to that complaint.

What is one to make of all this? Is Levinson's frame ridiculously narrow or is Kivy taking unfair advantage in ranging against him pieces from the sixteenth century? How one answers is likely to depend on the status of works such as Beethoven's. If they are typical of a wide corpus and if they are paradigm examples of a tradition that continues to inform current compositional practice, we might applaud Levinson's efforts. He is justified in confining his perspective (for the sake of achieving focus and clarity), because his analysis can be generalized across an extensive range of musical types, so long as this is done with care. Alternatively, if Beethoven's works represent only one point along an unfolding continuum, with no better a claim to privileged status than countless other pieces of very different kinds, we might doubt the value of Levinson's account even if it is correct for Beethoven. Was Beethoven a watershed, both summarizing what preceded him and setting the agenda for what was to follow, however much both of those differed in incidental respects from what he achieved? Or was Beethoven no more important than his Western predecessors and successors? Were his efforts, for all their merit, more uniquely representative of *musical* works than the different ones of composers in Medieval times, in non-Western cultures, in ragtime, blues, rock, and pop, in electronic music and the avant-garde? Levinson titles his article 'What a Musical Work Is', so it is not unreasonable to object to his account if it is not insightful when applied more broadly.

In my opinion, Levinson's concentration is too narrow, and this undermines its wider relevance and credibility. Beethoven's pieces are specified in some detail, as regards both sound structure (at the level of note sequences, phrasing, dynamics, attack, decay, and the like) and instrumentation. In my terms, they are thick with properties as works for performance go. Later, classical composers could assume more by way of uniform skill in professional players and standardization in instrumental ensembles, so they were able (permitted) to specify works that were yet more detailed than Beethoven's, but this should be seen as an extension of, rather than a departure from, the early nineteenth-century classical practice. In many respects, though, pieces of this thickness are untypical within music, viewed broadly across history and cultures. Frequently, works are much thinner than Beethoven's. This applies to the orally transmitted musics of non-Western cultures and in eras prior to Beethoven's, as well as to the present in the West, so long as one includes within music's ambit the folk and popular traditions that have always been vital to our culture's musical life. Within them, the *song* has been treated very freely, not only as regards instrumentation but also with respect to key, overall structure (repetition and order), melodic elaboration, accompaniment, and lyrics. For instance, consider how many covers there are of some songs written by Lennon and McCartney and how much these differ from each other though qualifying unmistakably as instances of the song in question. In my view, Beethoven's works are atypical in being much thicker—which is to say, much more specifically detailed in many of their musical dimensions— than the wider spread of musical pieces. As a result, Levinson's analysis of musical ontology is difficult to generalize.

The musical work as social construct

Another philosopher, Lydia Goehr, contrasts her perspective with Levinson's. The focal point for her theory is a proposal 'regarding the time of the emergence of the work-concept, which places that time at the end of the eighteenth century' (Goehr 1992: 4). Moreover, it is not the case that prior composers operated with an implicit, inchoate notion that emerged more fully in 1800. 'Central to the historical thesis is the claim that Bach did not intend to compose musical works. Only by adopting a modern perspective— a perspective foreign to Bach—would we say that he had ... musical practice before 1800 precluded the regulative function of the work-concept' (1992: 8).

What is in question is whether musicians before 1800 (or at any time), though conditions forbade overt expression, none the less were thinking about musical production in terms of works. There are historical reasons for rejecting this conclusion ... Prior to its explicit emergence, there is no evidence to suggest that persons were *really* (whatever that means) thinking about something in conceptual terms distinct from those indicated by their expressed thought and behaviour.   (1992: 114)

We can still say that J. S. Bach produced works; the point is that, in doing so, we project our later concept onto the past. 'Given that we have an explicit concept of a work, Bach composed works ... since about 1800, it has been the rule to speak of early music anachronistically; to retroactively impose upon this music concepts developed at a later point in the history of music' (1992: 114–15). Even if it is true now that works were composed prior to 1800, it was not true prior to 1800 that this was the case.[23]

---

[23] Lippman adopts a similar methodology and criteria, but arrives at a different date for the emergence of the work concept: 'The basic conceptions that define the musical work of art and the expression of these conceptions in practice belong to the 16th century. It was then that the fixity of notation and the artfully composed work were explicitly contrasted with improvisational practice, that individual genius and personal style became conspicuous as musical values, that the musical work of art was regarded as a self-contained and perfected entity, and that music was thought of, like the other arts, as a creative, or "poetic", endeavour based on science, with products that merited preservation and imitation' (1977: 204).

In arguing for her conclusion, Goehr adopts a very thick view of musical works. She takes the work concept to be one in which musical pieces are specific and determinate at the level of notes; scores are un-ambiguous and sacrosanct, with every mark indicating an essential feature of the work. In other words, she builds into the 'work concept' all (or more, even) that it came to mean to the Romantic sensibilities that took root early in the nineteenth century. Not surprisingly, she finds different attitudes ruling in prior times. As she rightly observes, earlier composers were more relaxed than later ones when it came to settling details of sound structure and instrumentation, to achieving similarity between performances, and to reusing their own material or appropriating others'. And it was not until Beethoven's time that purely instrumental music became fully respectable, and music generally was presented as worth hearing solely 'for its own sake.' She concludes there were no musical works prior to the dawn of the nineteenth century.

One could appeal to the historical record in challenging Goehr's con-clusion. Though composers in the West have often been treated by their em-ployers as anonymous servants, the interest in authorship is a long-standing one. Composers were often recognized, respected, and valued as such from well before the end of the eighteenth century. Their names were known to their contemporaries and some have been passed down. For instance, we are familiar with the names of composers of many polyphonic pieces created in the twelfth and thirteenth centuries. Not much is known about the life of Léonin, but his music has survived. His greatest work was *Magnus Liber Organi* and he was known as 'optimus organista' (the greatest composer of organa), whereas his famous student, Pérotin, was known as 'optimus discantor' (the greatest composer of discanti or clasulae). Even if, in the fourteenth century, the various sections of masses were usually cobbled together from individual movements written by different composers, still we know the author of one of the first complete settings of the Ordinary: Guillaume de Machaut and his *Messe de Nostre Dame*. And it is interesting to observe that music publishing began very shortly after the invention of the printing press. Petrucci's *Harmenice musices odhecaton A*, a collection of ninety-six songs by various composers, is from Venice in 1501 and was followed by two further volumes. The musical practice of making a perma-nent, public record of notation as a signature of compositional finality appar-ently coexisted with the same practice for literature, philosophy, drama, and science.[24]

---

[24] R. A. Sharpe poses similar objections to Goehr's thesis with reference to music by Josquin de Prez, Thomas Tallis, William Byrd, and Franz Joseph Haydn. He writes: 'in many ways musi-cians prior to 1800 behaved much as they do now with respect to their creations. They behaved as if they had the concept of a work and it regulated their practice though they did not refer to the "work" as we do' (1993: 294). For further criticisms, see Scruton (1994) and White (1997).

Here is a later example from Robert Dowland's preface to the *Varietie of Lvte Lessons*, an anthology of lute pieces published in London in 1610:[25] 'To the Reader whosoever. Gentlemen: I am bold to present you with the first fruits of my Skill . . . Touching this I have done, they are Collections gathered together with much labour out of the most excellent Authors, as well of those beyond the Seas, as out of the workes of our owne Countrimen.' It is clear that 'worke' here does not solely mean 'thing made by labour or travail' but also quite pointedly identifies pieces as the product of an author.

Take a very different case and musical context: although Balinese music is primarily oral and the tradition values innovation and alteration in established works, the composers of many pieces are known, remembered, and honoured. One of the most renowned, Bapak Wayan Lotring, was born in 1898. Jacques Brunet writes of him: 'in Bali, pronounce the name Lotring to an urbanite, a peasant, or an adolescent, and before you a face lights up, seeming to dream of the stars, which says: "He was a great musician!" and the humming of music immediately floods his ears. Lotring, a name that is still practically magic in Bali'.[26] Even in cultures (such as Australian Aboriginal and Amerindian ones) that believe songs are dreamed, and thereby are gifts given by the gods, distinctions are drawn between those who dream good songs and those who do not.

Goehr has a reply to objections accusing her of distorting the historical record. She accepts that many concepts and terms associated with the work concept operated prior to its emergence. Among the related notions that she mentions are composition, performance, autonomy, repeatability, permanence, and perfect compliance; the terms used prior to 1800 that are nearly synonymous with 'work' are 'piece', 'composition', and 'opus'. Her claim is that the work concept became regulative only when all these elements coalesced and functioned together, which did not happen until about 1800 (Goehr 1992: 119).

Goehr can always locate some difference between the practice or attitudes of post-1800 and earlier times; her opponent denies that the difference proves there were no works before 1800; Goehr demurs. The appeal to historical facts is inconclusive precisely because it is their weighting and interpretation that are at issue. How should this debate be continued and adjudicated, then?

---

[25] As well as works by Robert's famous father, John, the *Varietie* includes items by Alfonso Ferrabosco, Anthony Holborne, Thomas Morley, Landgrave of Hessen, Daniel Batchelar, and others. My source, Stan Godlovitch, notes: one story about the *Varietie* was that John Dowland's work was being pirated in unauthorized publications (for example, William Barley's), and he was so appalled at the poor quality of the pirated versions, he wanted to get his own work on the record.

[26] Record notes to [1], 22. (Numbers in square brackets refer to recordings listed in the Discography.)

The choice is between two perspectives on the trajectory of music history. The first locates and emphasizes a radical discontinuity in the historical record—a quake after which musical things could no longer be the same. In 1800, an entirely foreign beast, the musical work, came into existence and immediately went on to eclipse all earlier approaches to the organization and presentation of musical materials. The musical piece was determined in all its detail by its score. Because it has a datable origin, the concept of the musical work is a historical construct. The second, offered by Goehr's opponent, draws attention to the manifest continuities common to many centuries of music making, and views change and development against that unifying backdrop. It observes that the works of earlier periods tend to be thinner than those of later ones; thin works are often indefinite, or deal in note types, without indicating all the note tokens that might be played in an accurate rendition. In 1800 and subsequently, composers continued a long-standing process—one that began with the invention of notations, with the dissemination of the printing press, with the standardization of instruments and ensembles, with a move to public or repeated performances that would not always be under the control of the composer—as a result of which their pieces became thicker, even to the point where scores specified each and every note to be played. In this view, the work concept has been around for a long time and has an important role in explaining the development and perpetuation of musical practices over many centuries. The concept is not historically recent. It is the conditions for satisfying it that altered and evolved, and these changes spread over many hundreds of years.

The best way of choosing between these perspectives is by considering which offers the most coherent narrative of the history of musical change. Can we make more sense of the music on either side of 1800 by emphasizing the discontinuities or the continuities? The first approach has a degree of plausibility. Often, the more narrowly we focus on a given moment, the more we are struck by its uniqueness and disassociation from its local surroundings. (Perhaps this is why the present always seems so different from the immediate past.) Those who operate very closely with the minutiae of restricted musical periods can become overly impressed by the differences between their topic epoch and others that are very similar. Also, when we compare historically distant ages, the contrasts are more striking than the similarities. But in this case, it is a span of eight centuries of change in Western (art) music that is being described. On that wide stage, the more plausible story is the one that finds continuities, rather than the alternative that emphasizes radical interruption. The notion of a musical piece altered and developed slowly, with works becoming thicker in essential properties as time went on. To appreciate this, what is required is not the dramatic identification of this or that moment as the one at which the work concept emerged, but rather, a sense both of the historicity of the work concept and of the narrative unity that underpins its unfolding.

Goehr's account loses its grip on the history of Western music by denying significance to the manifest continuities linking musical creations across the centuries, I claim. History is not a matter of succession but of self-conscious reflexion. The present develops, reacts against, transforms, reinvigorates, or repudiates its past. It does not simply ignore what happened, inventing a replacement from thin air. It is better to acknowledge that musical works and composers have long been with us, which also means accepting the flexibility and the social relativity of the relevant concepts, than to lose sight of the continuity that underlies eight centuries or more of Western music. We should approach the history of works within Western music as a unified process that evolves over many centuries.

In fact, Goehr is guilty of doing what she criticizes in others, Levinson included. She privileges the works of Beethoven. Although she attempts a deconstruction of the work concept and rejects the enterprise in which Levinson is engaged, that of work definition, Goehr no less than Levinson affirms Beethoven's compositions as paradigms. She over-contextualizes the musical work by taking features local to a particular musico-historical setting as essential to the work concept, thereby allowing the musical creations of other times and places to qualify as works only as a result of the imposition of a concept that is alien to them.

The form of her argument betrays her commitment to aspects of the work concept, even as she debunks other of its features. She claims: if the work concept is correct, there were no works before 1800. Only two conclusions can be derived validly (by *modus ponens* and *modus tollens*) from a premiss with this conditional structure: there were no works before 1800, or the work concept is not correct. The second of these conclusions follows when one rejects the truth of the conditional's consequent by asserting there were works prior to 1800. This is the line I would take. The nineteenth century work concept, according to which musical works are always thoroughly determinate at the level of note tokens, is too narrow to accommodate the full range of cases, even if it does apply to some works after 1800. The work concept is mistaken in assuming works have to attain this level of definiteness and specificity to qualify as such. Goehr plainly opts for the first, not the second, conclusion, however. There were no musical works before 1800. To arrive validly at this conclusion from the conditional premiss with which she begins, she must affirm its antecedent; that is, she must assert that the nineteenth century work concept is correct.

Goehr's project is primarily negative. She means to attack a mistaken ideology of the musical work that has held musicologists captive. What she opposes is evident from the way her discussion continues. She combines the conclusion of the previous argument—there were no works before 1800—

with a new conditional—if the work concept is ahistorical, stable, and immutable, then musical works are made and exist throughout musical history. From these premisses she validly derives the conclusion that the concept of the musical work is a historical construction. Musical works cannot be defined in terms of some eternal, unchanging essence.

Some musicologists have applauded Goehr's fashionable scepticism with regard to ahistorical musical essentialism. They are similarly doubtful that musical scores could play the role theory has so often assumed them to perform, that of specifying as definite particulars all the individual notes and features that would be heard in a faithful account of the work. Indeed, in that spirit they have pushed the date of the emergence of the work concept to a later time than Goehr nominates (see e.g. Treitler 1993 and Kallberg 1996). Moreover, in consequence of rejecting the authority and definiteness of scores, they have come to doubt the objectivity of judgements concerning the faithfulness of performances.

I consider the concern about scores in the next chapter, and the question of authenticity in performance is taken up in Chapter 5. Here, my aim is to draw attention to the way Goehr's analysis has her endorsing some key aspects of the prevailing ideology regarding musical works. Indeed, doing so is a precondition of the argument by which she reject other parts of this ideology. The form of her argument commits her to the view that musical works require the definiteness and specificity of nineteenth-century works. Without endorsing the correctness of the nineteenth-century work concept, she cannot logically derive her final conclusion, that the work concept is a historical construction. That is why I maintain she accords to the works of Beethoven an undue and unexpected importance. Indeed, she goes much further than Levinson in this regard; by her account, Beethoven could have said: *après moi, les œuvres.*

The New Musicology

At the close of the previous chapter I complained that ontological theories of analytic philosophers are too abstract to map conveniently onto works and performances as these are understood by musical practitioners. Now it is the musicologists' turn to face the music. According to their prevailing ideology, musical works are vague to the point of not being identifiable. This view surely is not much closer to the ordinary musician's or listener's understanding than are the technicalities of the philosopher.

In the 1970s and 1980s, a new musicology emerged. Among its tenets are the claims that musical works are historically conditioned social constructions and that scores do not fully specify the works they are of. (Other of the assumptions and methods of the New Musicology are contested by its proponents (Tomlinson 1993*a,b*; Kramer 1993; Treitler 1999)). The New

Musicology defines itself by contrast with the Old Musicology that is also the target of Goehr's critique. It is not surprising, then, that her musicologist critics are few (White 1997) and her work is cited with approval (e.g. by Treitler 1993, Samson 1994, and Erauw 1998). Indeed, Nicholas Cook (1999) goes so far as to claim that Goehr has answered definitively the puzzles of musical ontology; no philosophical problems remain to be solved. Nevertheless, the New Musicologists should think Goehr is in error about the date of the emergence of the work concept, since they argue this had not occurred even at the time of Chopin's works, as I discuss below. More significantly, some of their claims—for instance, that scores can never accurately specify the works they are of (Boorman 1999) or that the concept of the musical work is a myth, albeit a useful and potent one (Samson 1994)—are at odds with hers. These musicologists apparently do not appreciate how Goehr's argument weds her to some aspects of the Old Musicological view, even as she challenges other of its elements. As I explained above, in denying that the *Werktreue* notion truly characterizes music prior to 1800, Goehr must maintain that the concept accurately represents some works when it emerged in later times.

The New Musicology has generated exciting, innovative results through musicological analysis. I am unconvinced by the veneer of philosophical speculation that often is laid over these. In my view, the New Musicology is no less extreme, dogmatic, and silly than the predecessor it rightly rejects. Explaining why this is will not only recall some arguments already presented but anticipate important ideas to be developed in later chapters.

Works of New Musicology frequently begin with a detailed, technical discussion of a composer's music or notations. Conclusions are drawn from these about the nature of the pieces in question and, in some cases, these conclusions are extrapolated into universal claims about the nature of musical works. Take the treatment of Chopin's music, which is a favourite topic. Impressive scholarship has shown not only that published versions of Chopin's pieces differ from printer to printer or edition to edition, but also that pre- and post-publication autographs and copies differ in yet other respects (Treitler 1993; Kallberg 1996: ch. 7). Cone (1995: 244) observes:

The performer's first obligation, then, is to the score—but to what score? The autograph or the first printed edition? The composer's hasty manuscript or the presumably more careful copy by a trusted amanuensis? The composer's initial version or his later emendation? The first German edition or the first French edition? An original edition or one supposedly incorporating the composer's instructions to his pupils? Those involved in the attempt to establish a canonic text of Chopin's works face all these decisions.

Kallberg (1996) concludes that Chopin's pieces have no clear completion. The argument continues: there is a continuum of cases falling between the works of Chopin and, say, Brahms. So, what goes for Chopin's music can also be said of other composers' works (see Cone 1995).

I have two initial comments. The seamlessness of continua is a two-edged sword, because the argument runs equally smoothly in either direction. If properties can be transmitted one way along a continuum, there is no reason why they might not also go in the reverse direction. So it is moot whether Brahms's works are as vague and ambiguous as Chopin's or, instead, if Chopin's are as solid and secure as Brahms's. But anyway, and this is the second point, properties need not be transitive across continua. The colour spectrum is continuous, but this does not mean that blueness is a property of yellow or vice versa. In fact, there may be very good reasons for drawing impermeable boundaries within continua, even if these borders are arbitrary and have hazy edges. Red and orange are different colours, though the frontier between them is a vague one. Accordingly, the possibility that Brahms's and Chopin's pieces could be connected by intermediates along a continuum ranging from ambiguously to clearly specified works does not show that distinctions of kind cannot or should not be drawn.

Another version of the continuum argument extrapolates from the freedom of jazz to the nature of the classical piece (see Bowen 1993). This approach faces the problems already mentioned; for instance, even if there is a continuum between thin and thick works, it does not follow that the mode of performance and appreciation appropriate to the one goes also for the other. Very thin works are merely pegs for performances, whereas thick ones are usually of as much interest as the performances that are of them. Moreover, there is a difference between taking a tune as the starting point for an improvisation and performing a thin work, as I argued in Chapter 1. To the extent that jazz renditions are free improvisations rather than work performances, the analogy between jazz playings and performances of classical works is on shaky ground.

A different position offered in support of the New Musicology appears to have a basis that is more philosophical than historical. Boorman (1999), whose conclusion is described as a 'critical orthodoxy' among musicologists (Cook 1999: 209), claims that the search for authoritative sources fully representing composer's intentions is a search for something that cannot exist. The irremediable incompleteness of notation means there is no way composers can specify all the detail of what they want. Moreover, not everything recorded in the score is work constitutive and there is no way anybody can tell what is essential and what is contingent, except through the process of educated guesswork known as interpretation. Boorman (1999: 422) concludes: 'The text, as it appears in sources, is not . . . a simple definer of the work.'

This argument displays a crucial confusion between indefiniteness and incompleteness in scores. An incomplete or ambiguous score under-specifies features that are work identifying, and therefore underdetermines the work it was intended to specify. If we found the violin and viola parts for a previously unknown Haydn string quartet, for example, the composite would be incomplete because the cello part was missing. It is not the case, however, that the silence of the score regarding details of performances is always a sign of its incompleteness. In the case of a figured bass, only note types, not the various tokens that could satisfy them, are indicated. In fact, a degree of indefiniteness is present in all scores; there are many more subtle shades of dynamics, attack, and phrasing than are covered in readable musical notations. This does not mean notations are incomplete if the indefiniteness of the score accurately reflects an indefiniteness in the work itself. As I have already explained, works for performance are thinner than the performances that accurately instance them, and the performer's resolution of these indefinite or unspecified elements goes beyond the work in constituting her interpretation of it.

Either Boorman makes the absurd assumption that musical pieces must be as ontologically thick as their performances, so that the notation's underdetermination of the performance's full detail is a sign of its incompleteness and, hence, of the impossibility of its unambiguously determining the work's identity. Or, more likely, he (along with Cook 1996) carelessly elides the distinction between an indefiniteness in the notation (which completely and accurately indicates an indefiniteness in the work) and an incompleteness in the notation (which thereby fails fully to determine the identity of the work it is of). The confusion is not entirely surprising, given that what would be an appropriate indefiniteness in one musical era or genre might, in another, amount to a failure of notational completeness. But musicologists, above all, should be sensitive to these historical relativities in notational and performance practices. And it is precisely in terms of these that performers and editors do discriminate quite properly between work-determinative instructions and merely recommendatory advice within scores.

Is it not true, though, that the musical work is a social construction? Since the creative acts in which they have their genesis can be understood only in terms of the social practices and conventions they presuppose, it is reasonable to describe musical works as socially constructed. The concept is historicized, which is to say, what could be made a musical work depends on when and where it was done. Musical works are created against the background of musical practices that constrain what may or may not be work determinative, and these practices evolve and alter through time so that what is musically possible in one era might not be in another.

The New Musicologists are inclined to interpret the social constructedness of musical works in more radical, and I think implausible, ways. As I noted above, some follow Goehr in taking the historicized nature of musical works to entail that there is a recently datable moment, such as 1800 in Europe, when the concept came into play. Against this, I have suggested that a better way of constructing a coherent narrative for Western music's history is by distinguishing between thick and thin works and by recognizing the historically conditioned limits on the degrees of work density available to composers at different times. The view I have supported does not show the work concept to be unstable or arbitrary, if this entails that just anything at any time might have merited the name 'music'. As I will argue in later chapters, the notion of works as the creations of their composers may be central to our conception of music as such, even if it is true that not all music is composed and that not all composed music interests us in terms of its authorship.

Other New Musicologists (such as Cox 1986; Bowen 1993, 1999) maintain that the identity of the work is altered by new performances. In other words, its performances contribute to the piece's identity, which constantly expands through time; that is, an ongoing process of social construction controls the work's evolving identity.[27] In its most radical formulation, the thesis is that there are no old musical works as such, only reconstructions shaped in the present (Howard Mayer Brown 1988; Morgan 1988; Tomlinson 1988). Unlike the views previously considered, which acknowledge the existence of historical facts even if they dispute the way these are often interpreted, the current theory rejects the idea that there are facts about the past that are independent of present construals. History, as an academic discipline, really is bunk.

The first version fails for the reason that the work's identity does not derive from the set of its performances. We do not classify performances as of the same work merely in terms of their similarity. Instead, it is because various performances are regulated by reference to its score that they qualify as of the given piece. The shared class membership of the performances is apparent only when they are identified in terms of the work they are of. Moreover, it is not clear that changes in the work's performances or reception do affect its identity in the way claimed (Davies 1996). As for the radical version, it would take us too far astray to explore in detail the incoherence of the suggestion that the past is no more than an aspect of how the present seems to us. But perhaps that journey is unnecessary anyway. I readily concede that events after the work's creation affect its properties and the way it is currently received. Whether it is influential and significant, for example, depends on the history of its relationship to subsequent pieces and the trajectory taken by music history. It is also true that our epistemic access to the work can be inhibited by its treatment through time. If it becomes fashionable to shroud all performances in a patina of Romanticism, our contact with Baroque and earlier works may be significantly compromised. These concessions, which

---

[27] Notice that this argument is not easily reconciled to the earlier one appealing to the alleged indeterminacy and incompleteness of Chopin's pieces. The case of Chopin creates leverage against the Old Musicology only if his notations are indefinite about details that, for works of the period, should be work determinative. If the identity of such pieces constantly alters, there is no reason why Chopin's works should be more relevant than Brahms's to the rejection of the Old Musicology.

often seem to be all that the musicologists in question are after, do not entail that the identity of musical works constantly alters, however.

What, though, should we say about the case of Chopin? To begin, not all the alternatives that Cone poses are on a par. Where the composer's annotations deal with details of his performance interpretation, it is a mistake to treat them as work determinative. Where the notation concerns matters the practice treats as non-determinative of works, they should be read as recommendations that might be ignored. Where the differences between scores result from manifest notational errors, they can be corrected. When all this is done, a residue of difficult cases remains. If the scores are incomplete or ambiguous with respect to matters that should be work identifying for a piece of the given kind, as is so in these cases, is its identity not unstable and vague? I think not. Such ambiguities and difficulties can usually be resolved by identifying a given performance as of the version of 1845, or of the Paris edition, and so on. This approach is not a pragmatic way of ducking intractable ontological questions; instead, it accurately reflects a sustainable malleability in the work concept. (The New Musicology remains in thrall to the Old Musicology to the extent that it does not see how the work concept can survive the rejection of the Old Musicology's obsession with authorial univocity.) Earlier I argued that melodies are not reducible to rhythmically articulated intervallic sequences because, sometimes, a single melody can be instanced in non-identical intervallic sequences. A similar move can be made in this case; we can talk of versions of a single work. What distinguishes a piece with versions from a distinct but similar piece is settled by reference to the composer's intentions and the causal nexus of creation. From his treatment, we can know both that Chopin conceived of himself not as creating a new composition but as fiddling with an old one, and that his fiddling is causally continuous with many earlier processes involved in the complex, unified act of composing the given piece.[28]

The completion of a work usually has two aspects: the intention to bring it to a close and its public validation and presentation as such. The case of Chopin reminds us that these two aspects can be pulled apart, at least to some extent. In the same way, continuity of memories and of personality, not to mention bodies, contributes to personal identity, but these elements sometimes rub against each other, as in cases of amnesia, or of apparent memories of events at which the person's body was not present, or of personality shifts. Such tensions do not show that the contributions to personal identity made by continuity of memory and personality are ultimately independent

---

[28] Some musicologists (Bowen 1993, 1999; Kallberg 1996; Cook 1999) invoke Ludwig Wittgenstein's notion of family resemblance as explaining how differing versions could be united. This positive use of the idea is well known to be problematic (see Davies 1991a: ch. 1) and goes beyond the negative application Wittgenstein intended, which was that of showing there are not always perceptible properties common to the instances of a concept.

or separable. An equivalent point applies for musical identity in cases such as Chopin's. The public confirmation of his works as finished may sometimes have been out of synchrony with his intentions regarding their completion,[29] but this does not show that these factors, and indeed their mutual interaction, can never establish completed, stable identities for musical compositions.

What is a musical work?

I have not set myself the goal of defining what a musical work is. Still, it is interesting to consider how Levinson's definitional framework should be modified to reflect the variety of contextualism for which I have argued. Here is a first suggestion: replace Levinson's 'a musical work is a performed sound structure as made normative by a composer at a given time' with 'a musical work is a performed sound structure as made normative in a musico-historical setting'. (Also, let the musico-historical setting encompass the social and institutional conventions and practices defining the relevant roles—such as composer or conductor—and the process of production—such as that by which a work is brought to completion and issued, as opposed to its being circulated in a draft version. I indicated at the beginning of my discussion of Levinson's definition that such matters would have to fall within its scope.)

In Levinson's definition, 'as made normative by a composer at a given time' is not separate and additional to the work's musico-semantic content, but identifies the relational components that combine with the performed sound structure to generate the work's semantic signature. In mine, 'as made normative in a musico-historical setting' has a similar function. It makes explicit that a musical work is a musico-semantic structure generated through the appropriate contextualization of a performed sound structure. Both definitions avoid implying that the work's musico-semantic structure is insulated from, or independent of, whatever essential features are added by the musico-historical context. They differ over whether the composer's identity, in addition to the wider musical setting, makes a crucial contribution to the work-defining environment (and I have explained already why I reject Levinson's account).

Why not prefer the simpler and more elegant 'a musical work is a prescribed, performed sound structure'? If the listener's beliefs affect how the work *sounds* to her, then the compression may be acceptable, though it does subsume, and thereby hide, the relational nature of musical content. But if one wants to consider the work's sound structure as an abstract particular

---

[29] An alternative description is available, though. It could be that Chopin was psychologically incapable of leaving his finished works alone. As someone who is inclined to modify and rewrite papers even after they are published, I have no trouble with the plausibility of this hypothesis.

existing independently of the manner in which it is or should be experienced—as some kinds of formal musical analysis may do, for instance—the reduction is unappealing.

Summary

I began by considering what a sound structure is, since all theories of the nature of musical works make a piece's sound structure central to its identity. The notion turned out to be far from straightforward. Not all works are organized to the same hierarchical level; for instance, some lack tonality and themes. Yet, many aspects of higher musical structure resist reduction to lower levels. Indeed, the path of explanation often seems to lead in the reverse direction, in that the basic categories are sometimes identifiable only in terms of higher ones in which they are elements.

The identity of musical works typically goes beyond their purely sonic profile. For instance, a work's instrumentation may be essential to its identity, and not solely in cases where its instrumentation produces sonic or expressive effects that could not be duplicated by other means. It is the socio-musical conventions obtaining at the time of the work's composition that settle whether a particular instrumentation is mandated, or recommended only. Within the Western classical tradition, instrumentation became work constitutive from the time orchestras became standardized.

In the latter part of the chapter I have argued for a contextualist ontology of musical works. Some of a piece's identifying features depend on the musico-historical setting in which it is created, so that composers at a historical or cultural remove from each other specify different works even if they prescribe otherwise identical sound structures. Some ontological contextualists go too far, however. Levinson over-contextualizes the work in making its identity depend on that of its composer. Against his view, I argued that two composers working independently could create the same, single work if they operate within a shared musico-historical setting and specify equivalent performed sound structures. Goehr attacks the idea that musical works can be defined in terms of an unchanging essence, but she over-contextualizes the work by linking its identity to a concept applying mainly to nineteenth-century Western classical pieces. Though there has been change in the detail at which works could be indicated, and different audience regards for works in recognition of this, there is a tradition of work creation, and respect for work authorship, that extends to much earlier periods of Western classical music. Both Levinson and Goehr are too parochial in concentrating on works such as Beethoven's, which are thick in constitutive properties by comparison with many pieces outside the Western classical tradition.

3

Notations

A twentieth-century composer uses notation in accordance with the conventions of his own time, and there is therefore little chance that a twentieth-century performer will misunderstand him. A composer of the eighteenth or the sixteenth or the fourteenth century also used notation in accordance with the conventions of his own time, but there is therefore every chance in the world that a twentieth-century performer will entirely misrepresent his music through an inadequate knowledge of these conventions, for the most part long obsolete and forgotten. In a word, when a modern performer looks at a piece of early music he must not take for granted the significance of any of the symbols he sees.

(Dart 1967: 13)

As I explained in previous chapters, some musical works are not for performance and others, which are for performance, are transmitted via instances that function as models, rather than via notations. Nevertheless, a majority of musical pieces are for performance and many of these are transmitted via musical notations. In this chapter I consider the nature of musical notations, distinguishing various types in terms of their primary functions. Following the common practice, I call notations with the main purpose of prescribing works 'scores'. Not all musical notations are scores, however. For instance, some describe musical works, performances, or styles and are notational transcriptions, while others serve as mnemonics. At the level of inscription, there may be nothing to distinguish a score from a mnemonic or a notational transcription. The primary function of a notation is not always apparent on its face, and a notation with one function might sometimes be employed for another. For example, a score might be used for analysis rather than performance. As well as elaborating the distinctions just introduced, I examine the theory of notations developed by Nelson Goodman.

Scores

In my sense of the term, a score is a musical notation the main purpose of which is to serve as a work prescription. It records a set of instructions, addressed to performers, the faithful execution of which generates an instance of the piece it specifies.[1] The instructions transmitted via a score must be sufficient to characterize a work of the kind in question.[2]

Scores have taken many forms. Polyphonic music prior to 1225 was notated using the method of vertical alignment. With the rise of the motet, there was a move to the use of choir-books, with the parts for each voice appearing on opposite pages of an open book, so they can be read by singers standing around it. From the mid-sixteenth century, performers worked from separate part-books. With the rise of instrumental music from about 1600, the modern score—with uniform barlines, a stave for each instrument or group of instruments, and a vertical arrangement of voices—was adopted. Parts used by individual players were then copied from the composite score. As I use the term, 'score' covers all of these. So long as it is recalled that part-books are not separable from the set to which they belong, since the full instructions are encoded only in the relevant aggregate, they count as scores in my view.

How are scores read? Consider Example 3.1, which is meant to be typical. Some of its elements might readily be seen as instructions (pizzicato, con sord, arco, the downbows indicated in bar 4 of the violin part). These deal with the method of inducing sounds from the instruments. A majority of its components (pitches, durations, phrasings, crescendo, staccato markings) are suggestive not of what is done but, rather, of the result achieved. Other elements (tempo and dynamics) seem to be ambiguous between these two possibilities.

To the extent that Example 3.1 is more concerned with the result to be realized than with the techniques involved in achieving it, with musical ends rather than practitioners' means, we might doubt that it is a set of instructions. This conclusion would be hasty, however. Because the composer can assume the musician's competence in the use of her instrument, his instruc-

---

[1] Among those who regard scores as instructions directed to performers are Cone (1967), Silliman (1969), Wolterstorff (1975, 1980, 1987), Urmson (1976), Khatchadourian (1978), Kingsley Price (1982), Coker (1983), Ingarden (1986), Dipert (1988), Thom (1990a, 1993), Levinson (1990a), Robert L. Martin (1993), Porter (1996), and Cochrane (2000). Sparshott (1987) and Grossman (1987) deny that the score is prescriptive on the grounds that it always allows a degree of interpretative freedom to the performer. The two claims are not exclusive, though. The composer can instruct some things while leaving others to the musician, as I explain later. Scores can be produced where it is known they will not be performed—for instance, by students in a course on composition. Cases of this kind are derivative; they are parasitic on the primary one.

[2] Notations with the purpose of jogging the musician's recollections can be adequate to the transmission and preservation of pieces that have already been committed to memory. These would not be scores, however, unless a suitably schooled and prepared musician who did not already know the piece in question could perform it on the basis of her following the notation.

EXAMPLE 3.1. Anon., Trio

EXAMPLE 3.2. Guitar tablature

tions relate more often to the work played than to the mechanics of playing it. They are of the variety 'achieve this' rather than of the kind that says 'put tab *A* into slot *B*'. They take for granted the means by which the result is brought to fruition. If 'instruct' is read as 'teach', the composer teaches the musician that in which the work consists, not how to play her chosen instrument, except in so far as the method of playing is distinctive to the work at hand.[3]

The notation of Example 3.1 is generic; the parts for the different instruments use much the same notational system. This was not always the case. In the previous chapter I used an Italian lute tablature of the early sixteenth century to illustrate a notation that is specific to a particular instrument (see Example 2.5). These remain in use, as in the guitar tablatures of jazz and popular music (see Example 3.2).

Instrument-specific notations are relatively impractical for works involving a mix of instruments. If the playing method of each instrument must be shown in the notation, the score of such a piece requires as many notational systems as there are kinds of instruments used in it. Moreover, such notations tend to presuppose that the composer is a skilled practitioner on each instrument for which she writes. And the specificity of the notation counts against the adaptation of the piece for other ensembles. It is not difficult

---

[3] Seeger (1958) labels as 'prescriptive' notations dealing with the method of sound production and as 'descriptive' those that record the outcome. I claim the elements Seeger would call 'descriptive' have a prescriptive function when they appear in scores.

to see, then, why generalized musical notations became dominant. The composer did not then become indifferent to the manner in which her music was generated from the instruments for which she wrote. In fact, generic notations were harnessed by composers to issue increasingly complex and detailed instructions about the results they wanted, and these outcomes typically depended on the use of the specified instruments.[4]

As is apparent in Example 3.2, notations often have an iconic character. In this case, the fingers' disposition on the neck of the instrument is depicted. Iconic elements are apparent also in generic notations, but for these it is the music's sound structure that is mirrored. Typically, scores are less like verbal orders than like prescriptions delivered by means of pictures.

Some theorists have criticized a 'Platonic' view that equates works with their scores (Jacobs 1990; Higgins 1991: 40–6, 1997; Goehr 1992; Porter 1996). It is not entirely clear who holds the view attacked, though it is sometimes attributed to Goodman. In fact, he explicitly denies that a work of music is its score, regarding the work as the class of compliant performances (1968: 210, 1972: 140). Wilson Coker is one who comes close to making the equation when he writes: 'a score oddly is both a particular instance or token of an imagined work and also a schematic symbolization of the universal, the type(s) of sound structures and their ordering' (1983: 156). But then he observes: 'The score alone is not the music itself. The score is just a complex of written symbols for the music' (1983: 157). This last claim is developed by Ingarden (1986: ch. 3), who identifies many ways scores and musical works are irreducibly different: scores have properties (such as a mass and a distribution of ink on paper) not shared by the work, and the work has characteristics (such as having instances with loudness and duration) not also shared by the score. In fact, the score employs a system of signs to designate musical works. It is worth noting, though, that scores provide a different and sometimes clearer route to the work for the purposes of analysis than do performances (Silliman 1969). And this observation by Edward A. Lippman (1977: 200) is astute: 'Musical notation not only provides the permanence and textual authenticity that artistic composition deserves, but . . . it changes the process of composition itself so as to foster the very properties of unified diversity and qualitative interest that it permits us to preserve.'

Whether or not it is strictly accurate, the complaint that theorists mistake scores for works is prompted by a justifiable unease about the extent to which works, and the scores through which they are accessed, can become an exclusive focus of attention. All too often, musical works are treated as separable from the social context in which they are created and performed. An unper-

---

[4] Dorian (1942) observes that scores became increasingly detailed as composers were distanced from the presentation of their works. As their direct participation in performance was reduced, composers attempted to retain control over the performer by means of the notation. See also Goehr (1992: 224–5) and Bujic (1993).

formed piece is accorded the same status as one that has been performed. It is assumed that scores record the sum total of the musical work and of all music making. The sound structure of the work is indicated as the proper object of attention, whereas dynamics, colour, and expressiveness, as well as the creative input of the performer, are disregarded. The writing of scores is treated as of a higher interest and value than other musical practices, such as improvisation.

When we [musicologists] discuss works, we usually only discuss the score. We rarely look at performance practice, much less the performance culture which surrounded the creation of a new bit of musical sound. We usually consider performance practice a separate subject from the discussion of the work and thus our very methodology tends to undercut the position we want performers to take, namely that performance practice matters. (Bowen 1996: 25)

A regrettable consequence of these faults is the glorification of composers over performers and listeners, as well as the valorization of Western classical music, with a consequent disdain for the music of other cultures and subcultures, especially those with oral traditions.

These objections have substance, I agree. The point I would emphasize is this: any tendency to talk of scores as if they can be substituted for works undoubtedly arises from the way scores present their instructions. It would be a rare foolishness that led a person to take the instruction 'Shut the door!' for the action exhibited in fulfilling the injunction. The verbal order and its execution are too dissimilar to be confused. Unlike spoken commands, however, musical scores resemble the works they designate. I doubt that they are often genuinely mistaken for pieces, but I do think that they are often discussed as proxies for works. In the same way, I doubt that realistic paintings are often taken for the persons they depict, but, because they provide epistemic access to the appearances of their sitters, it is understandable that viewers talk of them as if they are in the presence of the persons represented. This manner of talking of scores, as if they are the works they indicate, need not be misleading, though it is possible that it sometimes has led to the faults listed earlier.

The conventions for interpreting scores

Even where they appear to display the work's sound structure, scores are by no means always transparent to the work. What is written is often not what should be sounded and much of what is to be played is not recorded in the notation. In order to interpret correctly the instructions in the score, the performer needs to know the notational conventions used in it and the performance practices that are assumed without being explicitly indicated. The naive performer who considers only the score and who takes it 'literally' would misunderstand its instructions.

EXAMPLE 3.3. A more 'literal' version of the clarinet part in Example 3.1

In developing these points, I return to Example 3.1. The second F in bar 3 of the clarinet part is not indicated as sharpened but convention dictates that the accidental at the start of the bar applies to it (but not to the Fs in the next bar). The sharp in bar 5 of the cello part does not pertain to the F an octave higher; only notes at the exact pitch of an accidental are modified within a bar. Had the sharp been indicated in a key signature, it would apply to all Fs at any octave unless countermanded within a given measure. Meanwhile, the dots indicating staccato under the notes in bars three and four of the clarinet part mean those notes are sounded for less than the duration shown. A more noteworthy departure from the literal notation arises from the fact that the clarinet (here tuned to B♭) is a transposing instrument. The notes written in the score are one whole tone higher than the ones sounded.[5] A more literal notational rendition of the clarinet part might be that indicated in Example 3.3. Had 'scordatura' been specified for the string instruments, a similar consideration would apply to them, for the notation would show the notes to be fingered were the tuning of the strings standard, not the (different) pitches that then would be obtained. (See Example 3.4, from Mahler's Fourth Symphony, in which the solo violin has each string tuned up one tone; the part is written a tone lower than it sounds.) Even where the notation is iconic, it is not indifferent to the means by which the musician is to realize the result, so that, where transposing instruments or non-standard tunings are employed, the notation indicates what is fingered rather than the sonic outcome that should result. Though it is iconic in character, the notation in these cases does not map literally onto the pitches that are sounded.

The notation must be read in terms of the musical practice it assumes. Chopin's semiquavers should not all be given the same length, and this rhythmic flexibility should also be extended to the treatment of tempo. In dance band music, the notated metre may be squarely 4/4, but many of the instruments should play around the beat, so that the music swings.[6] In the

---

[5] Among the transposing instruments in the standard symphony orchestra are alto flute, cor anglais, clarinet, French horn, and trumpet. Even in the full score, the parts written for these usually depict the pitches to be fingered as against what will be sounded. The parts for some other instruments, such as the piccolo, contrabassoon, and string bass, are notated an octave from the pitch that is sounded.

[6] Lee B. Brown (1996) suggests jazz cannot be notationally transcribed because the notation loses the 'swing' that is an essential part of the music. Baugh (1993, 1995) makes the same claim for rock music. These objections wrongly assume notations must be literal and transparent.

II.

In gemächlicher Bewegung. Ohne Hast

*AB Der 1. Sologeiger hat sich mit 2 Instrumenten zu versehen, von denen das eine um einen Ganzton hö-
her, das andere normal gestimmt ist.*

EXAMPLE 3.4. Gustav Mahler, Symphony No. 4, Second Movement
(London: Ernst Eulenburg, Ltd), No. 575, p. 73

Viennese waltz, the second beat should sound a little earlier than the notation suggests. In Baroque music, appoggiaturas were variously treated,
depending on their context, according to rules so well understood that they
were formulated in textbooks.

The absence of notational signs can also be significant. Pizzicatos can be played in at least three ways. The G in bar 4 of the cello part of Example 3.1 could be played on the open string with the fingering, rather than the bowing, hand. If this were required, the note would be marked with + as well as with pizz. Also, a pizzicato might be so violent as to cause the string to snap against the wood of the fingerboard. If this is what the composer wanted, the note would have been marked with ⊘. The absence of these supplementary signs makes clear it is the orthodox pizzicato that is required.

It should also be noted that not everything explicitly notated in the score is thereby mandated. Composers sometimes mark fingerings, for instance. Usually these are recommendatory only. In the eighteenth century, when first they were introduced, marked dynamics and phrasings would probably have been treated merely as suggestions. The same probably applies to pedallings notated in the nineteenth century. In twentieth-century works, of course, these same indications must be followed in a faithful performance (Davies 1987; Kendall L. Walton 1988).

So far my examples have drawn attention to conventions governing the interpretation of the notation. Others, ones no less vital to the work's correct performance, may not be covered by notations at all. These are resident to the performance practice assumed by the composer. For instance, there is no notational indication as to whether the string players in Example 3.1 should use bows or wooden spoons on the strings, but this does not mean the latter is a genuine possibility. The relevant performance tradition and the place of notations within this together make the use of bows required.[7] In the case of a piece composed in the early eighteenth century, the melody line should be decorated in repeats, vibrato should be used sparingly, and rhythms marked as 'dotted' in the score should be played as if they are double-dotted. If the piece is a Sarabande, the stress normally falls on the second beat of the bar, not the first. In a late-nineteenth-century classical piece, some string vibrato is required. The established conventions of the style or genre determine the 'default' condition, so no sign of what is expected is needed in the score. If the composer aims to instruct something not standard within the practice or its notational resources, this must be indicated explicitly. So it is that Gioacchino Rossini stipulates in the score of the overture to *Il Signor Bruschino* that the string players tap their music stands with their bows.

---

[7] '[The composer] tells us, say, that the composition is for violin. He does not go on to tell us how those instruments called "violins" are to be constructed, nor does he tell us how he wants them played. He *presupposes* the existence of musical instruments of the species: Violin, and of a practice tradition for playing instruments of that species; and he *takes for granted* that some of his readers will know which instruments those are and what the practice tradition is' (Wolterstorff 1980: 70).

I have been arguing that scores, even when they contain iconic elements, are not transparent to the works they specify. In being depictive, the score is sometimes inaccurate to the work, just because what is shown connects to the method of production rather than to the result achieved (scordatura tunings). Not every element indicated in the score specifies a definitive feature of the work (recommendations rather than injunctions). Not all the definitive features of the work are indicated in its score (the use of bows rather than wooden spoons). The instructions issued by scores are interpreted with respect to both the performance practices against which they are written and the notational conventions of the composer's day. Where these are not known, as is sometimes true of works written in periods chronologically distant from our own, the score's interpretation presents difficulties. This is reflected, for example, in the current debate about *musica ficta* in music from the tenth to the sixteenth centuries. Fortunately, we do know enough about the *Aufführungpraxis* and notational conventions of the last few centuries of Western music to be able to decipher composers' instructions and, hence, to perform their works.

This claim is hotly disputed, of course. Philip (1992) demonstrates by reference to early recordings that some performance practices, such as a universal string vibrato, are much more recent than is often supposed, and that others, such as portamento, which are not now regarded as tasteful, were common in earlier times (see also Bowen 1996, 1999). Philip (1992: 240) concludes: 'However carefully we choose the instruments and read the documents, we have really very little idea what a performance of the 1740s [of Handel's *Messiah*] would have sounded like. To judge by the way things have changed over only the last hundred years, it might have been almost incomprehensible to us.'

I do not deny the problems. When it comes to subtle aspects of past performance practice, we are forced to rely on performance treatises, descriptions of what was done and how it sounded, paintings, and other frustratingly indirect sources. Yet there can be no gainsaying the progress that has been made both in scholarship and in the mastery of early performance instruments and techniques. Performers and their audiences should be aware of what they do not know and should acknowledge the extent to which they exercise judgements of taste that may be biased to their own times when they resolve these epistemic uncertainties by playing one way rather than another. Equally though, we do know a great deal about the music of prior ages and about the interpretations valued at those times. It surely is an over-exaggeration to maintain that Mozart would not recognize his own works in contemporary 'authentic' performances, or that he would find those renditions incomprehensible.

Performability and readability

I take the requirement that a score be usable to entail that, in principle, it is humanly performable at the rate of one second of playing per second of music, on the instruments for which it is written. If a piece specified for solo violin can be rendered at the required speed only by the combined efforts of 1,001 violinists, its notation would not qualify as a score in the fullest sense. I do not deny, of course, that scores can *become* unperformable. This might happen where the instruments for which they are written are lost, or where the performance techniques needed to play those instruments are forgotten, or where the conventions for reading the notation are no longer known. Nor do I deny that parts of scores might be unplayable—for instance, as a result of a blunder (such as specifying that a normally tuned violin play an F below middle C) or by exceeding the limits of instrumental technique (as Charles Ives's *Concord Sonata* (1910–15) may do).[8] But where such things occur, it is usually the case that only a small part of the score cannot be performed as written. My claim is that a notation fails to qualify as a score if most of it is unplayable (by acknowledged experts) on the instruments for which, purportedly, it is created.[9]

The requirement that a score of a piece for live performance be performable in real time does not entail that it be readable in real time. The full score of a work written for large orchestra usually could not be followed by the conductor in all its detail at the appropriate speed at a first reading. And a written instruction in a score might take longer to read than it takes to execute— 'play an out of tune middle C at the tip of the bow for the shortest time interval that will be audible'. The conventions of performance normally allow for practice and I know of no works that forbid rehearsal. Indeed, convention recommends that instrumental soloists memorize their music. In a few cases, such as that of the clarinet part of Karlheinz Stockhausen's *Harlekin* (1975), this is instructed. This is appropriate where the nature of the performance would make sight-reading impractical—for example, where singers must also dance. On the other hand, orchestral musicians standardly play from their parts during public performance and, given the extent of the repertoire they might be expected to master, those parts mostly should be readable in real time.

---

[8] In Iannis Xenakis's *Evryali* (1973) for piano, the composer acknowledges that the piece may not be accurately playable; it is the energy of the attempt he is after. It would be appropriate to regard this score as a sophistication on the usual one, in that the implied injunction is 'try to do this for the sake of the effect produced, even if accuracy is not attainable', not the standard 'do this'.

[9] I allow that a score might consist of a single note, middle C, and specify this for an instrument that cannot play it, such as a piccolo. The result is a conceptual work. It is not a musical work, though it takes musical works as its reference. Thom (1990*a*) discusses a similar case and arrives at a similar conclusion.

Some peculiar cases

Around 1917 Igor Stravinsky experimented with pianolas, intending to include them in *Les Noces*. He notated their parts in the fashion standard for pianos. Because of difficulties in coordinating the pianolas, he abandoned them in favour of four pianos. Suppose he had retained them. The resulting notation would have been a score, because it addresses human vocalists and percussionists. A work for performance can include parts that are for playback, not performance as such. For example, it could be written for an instrumentalist who combines her part with taped sounds, as is the case with Mario Davidovsky's *Synchronisms No. 1* of 1962, for flute and tape. In Ottorino Respighi's *Pines of Rome* (1924), a taped nightingale sings along with the orchestra.

What, though, of the case in which the notation is of a piece entirely for mechanical playback? I have in mind works such as those written by Mozart for mechanical organ (K. 594, 608, and 616). These were indicated in the orthodox fashion, but they are not for human performance in the ordinary way. As instructions, they address the craftsman who creates the barrel or metal disc that controls the operation of the mechanical organ.[10] Mozart's notation is like an orthodox score in having a prescriptive function, but this is not directed to a performer, who is the target of an orthodox score's instructions. Is it a score? I think one can say what one likes, so long as the differences are kept in mind.

Another odd case is one in which the composer supplies instructions apparently more to do with how to compose a new piece than about how to perform one that already exists. For instance, she might indicate that a note sequence should be generated through the use of a randomizing procedure, such as the rolling of dice. How this example should be described depends on how the prescription is to be understood. If it has the force of 'compose a musical work by this method', it charges its executor with the creation of a score of a new work.[11] In that event, it is not itself a score, because it does not specify a musical work. If there is a work of art here, it is better thought of as a performance piece about music than as a musical work as such. On the other hand, if the directives issued by the work's creator have the force of 'select the notes to be played by this method and then play them', it is a score that, instead of indicating particular note tokens, is like a figured bass in specifying its contents by reference to note types (namely, to the type that can be instanced by applying the method specified).

---

[10] They are treated as if they are scores, however, when organists play from them. The same applies when Joanna McGregor plays Conlon Nancarrow's pieces on an ordinary piano.

[11] Mozart's *Musikalisches Würfel Spiel*, first published after his death, was a kit for composing minuets. For the opening sixteen-bar theme, two options were supplied for each of bars 8 and 16; eleven alternatives were written for each of the remaining bars. For the Trio, six choices were offered for each of the sixteen bars. Dice were rolled to make the selections.

Scores and interpretations of works

Scores, I have said, are vehicles by which composers issue instructions to performers for the instantiation of their works. One performs the given work by following the instructions determinative of it. The discovery of those instructions requires an appropriate interpretation of the score. But when this is achieved, many details of the given performance remain unspecified (Ingarden 1986; Davies 1987; Cochrane 2000; Gould and Keaton 2000). The performer must decide what to do about them. This requires a further act of interpretation (Coker 1983; Thom 1993; Edlund 1997; compare with Howat 1995, who suggests that the music's interpretation is just the interpretation of its score). Whereas the first concerns the interpretation—that is, the reading—of the score, the second focuses on the interpretation—that is, the rendition—of the work.

Earlier I suggested that the melodies of many works composed in the early eighteenth-century should be elaborated, especially when they are repeated. In my view, these works (not just performances of them) contain decorations, since the performance practice makes elaborations mandatory. Moreover, there are limits to what is tolerable by way of decoration within the given style. But, provided she stays within those limits, the performer is free to decorate as she pleases.[12] Similarly, I think works composed in the late nineteenth century include vibrato unless this is explicitly counter-indicated, but, within the boundaries of what is idiomatic, the performer is free to choose the degree and manner of vibrato she will use. The relevant works require melodic decoration or vibrato, for such characteristics are among their identity conditions, but, so long as the selected tokens of decoration or vibrato are of the required types, their particularity contributes to the performance interpretation rather than to the work's identity.

There are many respects in which musical works underdetermine the concrete details of performance. The faithful execution of the composer's work instructions leave open a multitude of choices that a performer must make in giving a performance. Typically, the use of many subtle nuances of attack, decay, balance, and phrasing are consistent with scrupulous allegiance to the composer's work indications. As a result, performances differing in these respects can all be equally and ideally faithful to the composer's piece. The interpretative element added to the performance by the musician depends on

---

[12] A position like mine is defended in Cook (1999)—though I do not agree with the ontology he proposes to derive from it. Cook rightly argues that not all differences between its accurate performances are irrelevant to a work's identity. The piece might be more than bare notes, its being essential that this foundation be decorated in an appropriate but unspecified manner. Also see Boorman (1999). For discussion of the stylistic constraints, see Neumann (1993). Not all the possible options will be apt or tasteful for the work in hand, but faults revealed in the performer's choices apply to her interpretation, not to the accuracy of her performance, so long as those choices are consistent with the work's genre and style.

decisions she makes concerning matters on which the composer's instructions and the relevant performance practices are mute. The performer's choices do not affect the work's properties but do affect properties of the performance and, thereby, properties of the interpretation provided by that performance. In this sense, performance interpretation goes beyond the work (Lippman 1977; Callen 1982; Davies 1987; Levinson 1993).[13]

The two kinds of interpretation made by the performer are crucially different. The first concerns the discovery of the composer's instructions, so that an accurate performance of his work can be achieved. Works for performance are always ontologically thinner than their performances, however, and the second sort of interpretation involves the performer's choices about how this ontological gap is filled. At this level, the performer is free within broad limits set by the style and genre of the piece.

Because the two kinds of interpretation differ, though each is involved in performance, it is important not to confuse them. One who does so is Michael Krausz (1993*a*,*b*). He holds that a work's score underdetermines its interpretations and illustrates the claim with the following: in the first movement of Beethoven's Symphony No. 1, Op. 21, the upbeat run preceding the 'Allegro con brio' that follows the introductory 'Adagio' might be played in accordance with either tempo. He writes (1993*a*: 79):

Most conductors hold the view expressed by Riccardo Mutti that it is a 'mistake' to perform the work as written [that is, Adagio]. Good reasons can be given for performing the passage either way, that is, according to the principle of faithfulness to the score [Adagio], or according to the principle of aesthetic consistency [Allegro]. Despite the fact that the overwhelming tendency is to favour the principle of aesthetic consistency, neither is conclusively right.

In the same vein, he comments elsewhere (1993*b*: 20): 'certain indications that a score mandates may arguably be overridden for good reasons.'

My first objection here is to the literalism with which Krausz reads Beethoven's score. I doubt that 'faithfulness to the score' requires an adagio tempo, just as I would deny that faithfulness to the score requires the clarinet player in Example 3.1 to play notes sounding at the pitch indicated in her part. (Would Krausz maintain, I wonder, that those who play transposing instruments deviate from the composer's mandated instructions in sounding pitches other than those recorded in the notation?) The case to be made for

---

[13] Perhaps it was this idea that led Langer (1953: 138) to suggest that the performer *completes* the work, a view rightly criticized by Wacker (1960), among others. There is an echo of Langer's claim in Porter (1996) and Hall (1999). I agree with them that the work goes beyond its score, in that it presupposes a performance practice, but I also think that performers go beyond the work in interpreting it and, accordingly, that some of the features appreciable in a performance belong to the particular interpretation, rather than to the work as such. In giving credit to the performer's creativity, it is neither necessary nor usual to regard her as a co-author of the work, as opposed to its interpreter.

an allegro account of the upbeat is plain enough. Both the performance tradition in its treatment of upbeats and later appearances of the run in the
movement suggest the faster tempo is required. In my view, Krausz conflates
the interpretation (reading) of the score with the interpretative side of performance, thereby obscuring the distinction between features of the work and
properties of particular interpretations. Though he recognizes that *performance* is a social practice, he does not acknowledge the extent to which the
correct manner of reading musical notations is similarly contextual and conventional. As a result, he treats the naked notation as expressing the directives determined by the composer and regards departures from these as
overriding such instructions. I hold, by contrast, that the score reveals what
is instructed only when it is taken in conjunction with the social practices
brought to its comprehension by musicians. Contrary to his perception,
Krausz's arguments concern the discovery, not the disregard, of the instructions expressed within the score.

In consequence, I do not accept that, as regards rightness, there is nothing
to choose between the adagio and the allegro tempo for Beethoven's upbeat.
Moreover, it is oxymoronic to claim one is interpreting a composer's work
in systematically disregarding the instructions that are determinative of
that piece. (I allow, though, that questions can often be raised about the
accuracy of a given notation.) One can interpret a work only in the act of
delivering it, and one can deliver it only by accepting a commitment to following the composer's work-determinative instructions, as I explain further
in Chapter 5.

Krausz's account of performance interpretation is doubly mistaken. It con-
fuses the interpretation of the composer's work-determinative instructions
with the interpretative freedom brought by the performer in going beyond
those instructions to the creation of a performance. And it states plainly
that the performer is free to disregard the composer's mandates (though it
misidentifies these), thereby failing to acknowledge the differences described
previously between the two kinds of interpretation in which the performer
engages. Though I am unconvinced by his examples, I agree with Krausz
that the work and its score underdetermine the performed interpretation. I
do not mean to downplay the creative freedom brought by the musician to
her account of the piece. My point is that the distinction between constitutive properties of the work and interpretative properties of the performance
needs a more careful treatment than is given in Krausz's account.

A non-Western example

When one reads a familiar musical notation, the conventions to which one
resorts are so well known that their operation is likely to be unintrusive. It
is useful, therefore, to illustrate the points made previously by considering

Ladrang Asmarandana   (*Slendro manyura*)

Buka   . 3 . 2   . 3 . 2   3 1 3 2   . 1 2 6̱

                            2 1 2 6̣   2 1 2 3̂

                            5 3 2 1̣   3 2 3 1̂

                            6 3 2 1̣   3 2 1 6̣

                            5 3 2 1̣   3 2 1 6̱

EXAMPLE 3.5. Kepatihan notation of a central Javanese piece for gamelan

GENḌING *GUNUNGSARI*; KENḌANGAN KETAWANG KENḌANG 2 ¹); PAṬET MANYURA ²)

EXAMPLE 3.6. Ladder notation of a central Javanese piece; after Kunst (1973: 493)

symbolisms unknown to most readers, those for central Javanese gamelan. Example 3.5 is of modern cipher notation (*kepatihan*). In this, which is read from left to right, the numbers signify the pitches of the main melody and other symbols indicate kinds of gongs. Example 3.6 illustrates late-nineteenth-century 'ladder' notation (*titlaras andha*). Each ladder is read from top to bottom and ends with the large gong. Each beat is marked by a horizontal line; the notes of the main melody are marked as dots; kinds and

EXAMPLE 3.7. A transcription of central Javanese gamelan music attributed
to M. Ng. Lebdapradongga and M. P. Jatiswara and dating from 1923;
adapted from Kunst (1973: 484–5)

combinations of gongs are shown on the left and drum strokes on the right.
The ladders suceed each other from left to right. (For a discussion of the
history of Javanese musical notation and of its impact on the musical practices of the island, see Becker 1980: ch. 2.) The simplicity and economy of
these scripts are striking when one considers the duration and textural complexity of performances. A rendition of the work designated by Example 3.5
might take ten minutes or more and, if a fragment of this were transcribed
into Western notation, it would look like Example 3.7.

In Example 3.7, it can be seen that the lower *sarons* (*barung, demung, slentem*) carry a cantus firmus around which the highest *saron* (*peking*), *bonangs*, *gambang*, and *genders* weave improvisations.[14] The woman vocalist (*pesinden*), flute (*suling*), and solo string instrument (*rebab*) provide freer melodies, with the whole underpinned by the gong section (*kempyang*, *ketuk*, *kenong*, *kempul*, *gong agung*) and by drums (*kendang*). In Example 3.5, the numbers refer to degrees of the scale and their series indicates what I called the cantus firmus. Supplementary symbols indicate the gong pattern. More interesting, though, is what is not notated. The variations made on the cantus firmus by instruments such as the *bonangs* and *genders* are not shown; also missing is the drum part; and neither the melody nor the words sung by the vocalist are recorded.

Example 3.5 can function as a score, however, because there are conventions governing how the musicians might derive their parts from the notated melody. Take the line sung by the *pesinden*.[15] Usually she sings melodic formulas, or *cengkok*, which are common to many different works. These vary to some extent from mode (*patet*) to mode. Allowing for octave equivalence, the pitch of the last note of the *cengkok* is the same as that of the last note of each four-beat grouping (*gatra*) played by the *sarons*, though the singer often arrives at this note well after the *sarons* have sounded theirs. Each of the other elaborating instruments has its own, idiomatic repertoire of *cengkoks* and derives its part in similar fashion. Because the *cengkoks* offer the musician a range of choices, there is constant variety in the treatment of ideas.[16] Moreover, new formulas can be added to the *cengkoks*. As for the words sung by the *pesinden*, these are chosen from a variety of poetic texts, with the structure and length of the piece determining the choice of poetic genre. At specific points in the structure, non-obligatory, semi-nonsense words (*isen-isen*) may also be sung. Finally, the pattern of pitched gongs and the number of beats between each sounding of the deepest gong are indicative of the work's micro-structure and, thereby, its type. In practice, the unfolding of the work's extended form is controlled by the drummer or the *rebab* player, who decides the repeats and tempo changes to be followed.

[14] Apart from *gambang*, which is a wooden xylophone, all these instruments are metallophones. Many orchestras would also contain a string zither, *celempung*, which is not present in Example 3.7. For a description of these and the other instruments in the ensemble, see Kunst (1973) and Becker (1980).

[15] In the following discussion I am indebted to Susan Pratt Walton. Note that she quotes experts as insisting that all the polyphonic lines, *including the notated tune*, are based on an underlying melody that is never stated literally or fully sounded, one that exists in complete form only in the minds of the musicians (1987: 6–7).

[16] Hood (1959: 208) writes of Javanese gamelan: 'One might wonder how "set" an "improvised" part becomes. This varies somewhat with the type of instrument and with the individual player. On some instruments and with some players once a part has been "worked out" it remains more or less the same for repeated performances. More skilled players, however, manage a flexible and expert improvisation under the guidance of the *rebab* player.'

Despite its apparent simplicity, Example 3.5 contains sufficient information for the generation of instances of the work it specifies, this being one indefinite in much of its detail and, hence, allowing considerable latitude (within limits governed by conventions depending on the work's form, style, and genre) to the performer. As a notation, it addresses 'insiders' who are already steeped in the performance tradition presupposed in its interpretation and realization. In this respect it does not differ from Western scores. If Example 3.5 does not look to Westerners like a score, this is because they are unaware both of the conventions in terms of which it should be read and of the practices and skills required for its realization.

Kepatihan notation is adequate to the complexities of the works it specifies. Formerly it was not widely employed, because the central Javanese tradition was mainly oral. Most gamelan musicians learned particular pieces by example. Now though, *kepatihan* is regularly used by Westerners learning to play Javanese music and, increasingly, by indigenous students in Javanese music conservatoriums. Given that *kepatihan* notation has no function other than to specify works and that it is used as such by some, if not all, gamelan musicians, Example 3.5 qualifies as a score.

One final point: where the notation comes out of a performance tradition other than that from which the work arises, as is the case with Example 3.7, it is very unlikely to be playable for, as an instruction to performers, it could address only those who are at home with the appropriate instruments and performance practice as well as with the alien style of notation, and who also possess the imaginative ability to apply the latter to the former. Even then it would not be adequate to the given work because what it notates is too specific. Whereas the work is indefinite as to the particular *cengkok*s to be used, Example 3.7 shows those that have been actually chosen and presents them in a notational style that wrongly implies that those particular realizations are mandated. Example 3.7 is a notational transcription of a performance, not (part of) a score for the work being performed. I return to this point later, when I discuss the difference between notational transcriptions and scores.

Indeterminacy in works and scores

Can scores designate works if they underdetermine what the performer must do? I have already suggested that scores leave many decisions to the performer—for example, as regards the detail of decoration. Read in conjunction with the appropriate conventions, decoration is mandated for some works, but the precise form of decoration is not indicated (though conventions of the style set limits on what would be acceptable). This does not mean the work is under-specified; rather, the work contains stylistically appropriate decorations, but no particular set of these. In settling on which decorations to employ, the performer makes a decision affecting the interpretation projected by the performance. All decisions consistent with the performance practice appropriate to such pieces are faithful to the given work.

In some cases, the performance practice reveals a liberal and flexible attitude to the treatment of works that is not apparent, perhaps, from their scores. 'We know more or less what [a seventeenth-century opera director] would have done [in producing a new performance of John Blow's *Venus and Adonis*], since baroque revivals of opera were frequent, and scarcely ever without substantial alterations either to suit altered circumstances, or to take advantage of available singers, or merely for the pleasure of having something new' (Donington 1989: 65). A more modest example of the same liberality is in the use of decorations in early eighteenth-century music. The indeterminacy is not explicit in the notation itself, which occupies all the beats of the bar with notes, but becomes apparent when the score is read in terms of the performance practice it assumes. In other examples, the relevant indeterminacy is apparent in the notation itself, as in the tempo indication 'Andante', which is vague. The same point applies, though: scores with explicitly specified indeterminacies are sufficient to characterize their works if the work itself is indeterminate in the indicated respects.

For illustration, consider the thorough-bass notation that was common in music of the eighteenth century (see Example 2.2). As is observed in the *Harvard Dictionary of Music*: 'A good thorough-bass accompaniment is considerably more than a mere translation of the figures into musical notes. At the proper places, the musical material used in the solo parts (voice, violin) should be incorporated into the accompaniment, in free imitation, or in doubling thirds, or in contrapuntal contrast' (Apel 1966: 745–6). The limits of what is acceptable in realizing a figured bass are set by the appropriate performance practice but, within these, the performer uses her own discretion. (For detailed discussion, see Lester 1992.)

Such a notation does not violate my earlier insistence that the score specifies the piece in its entirety, for the score indicates an indeterminacy that is constitutive of the work. The notation is read in conjunction with the appropriate performance practice, which dictates a filling-in of the middle parts; that is, works of this kind contain middle parts and a harmonic structure as indicated by the numbering. But the detail of that realization is undetermined; a particular rendition characterizes properties of the given performance that are not thereby properties of the work as such. Where pieces are indeterminate, the score, taken together with the performance practice, must indicate the limits of indeterminacy. The score is not less accurate as a designation of the work for the fact that it does not constrain those details of performance that go beyond the piece in embodying it in sound.

EXAMPLE 3.8. Two Australian folk tunes in waltz time and C major

Some musical works contain high levels of indeterminacy in their sound structures.[17] The sound structure indicated in the score is far less detailed than that realized in a performance, but this is because the work has no fixed sound structure at the concrete level of pitches, rhythms, and timbres, as is clear from its score. Suppose a work had a score specifying that two flutes play any two Australian folk tunes in waltz time and C major. In that case, Example 3.8 might count as an accurate notational transcription of a performance of the given work but would not thereby provide an accurate instance of the work's score. (For discussion of notational transcriptions of works containing indeterminacy, see Behrman 1976.) The performance (necessarily) achieves a specificity the work lacks, and that specificity carries over to the notational transcription of the performance. Given the conventions, the notational transcription, were it mistaken for a score, would be read as mandating the simultaneous playing of particular note sequences and would thereby misrepresent the work, which, though it contains note sequences, construed broadly as types, need not contain these particular tokens.

There is no difficulty in regarding Example 3.9, a notation consisting of purely verbal instructions, as (part of) a score. These injunctions tell the player what to do (pizzicatos, spoken utterances), but many particulars of the sound structure are not specified. This is because the piece in question lacks them, not because the notation is inadequate as an indication of the work's determinative properties. The more indeterminacy (as regards details of sound structure and the like) a work contains, the further its score is likely to differ from an iconic depiction if it uses orthodox musical notations (since these usually are iconic in their manner of indicating a specific sound structure).

---

[17] One who denies this is Cone (1967: 104): 'There is something intuitively wrong in saying, of several pieces [that is, performances] of music that sound completely different from one another, that they are all valid realisations of one and the same composition because they were all obtained by faithfully following the directions of the same score.' Cone appeals to this intuition in order to ground the conclusion that Stockhausen's *Piano Piece XI* (1956) is not a musical work since different, accurate renditions of Stockhausen's score can sound very unlike. I think Cone is mistaken here.

SONANT (1960/....)

für Gitarre, Harfe, Kontrabass und Fellinstrumente

FIN II / Invitation au jeu, voix

Kontrabaß (Stimmen-Partitur)

Mauricio Kagel

T / P		
00" / 10"		Sie können beginnen, der Herr Gitarrist hat Ihnen ein Zeichen gegeben. Spielen Sie bitte zwei pizzicati - molto vibrato - auf der V. Saite im Abstand einer kleinen None
	p	(BEGINNEN WIR MIT DER ABSCHAFFUNG EINIGER ELEMENTARER EINWÄNDE); klingen lassen.
10" / 18"	mf	(SIE SPIELEN HIER PROGRAMMUSIK : WERKTREUE KANN NUR ILLUSION SEIN.) Noch ein pizzicato. Um ein Schnarren hervorzubringen, heben Sie kurz nach dem Zupfen den Finger der linken Hand langsam von der Saite; währenddessen trommeln Sie mit der rechten Hand auf den Korpus (in der Nähe des Steges). Setzen sie den Dämpfer auf.
	pp	("BEI BEETHOVEN SIND SOZUSAGEN DIE EFFEKTE SCHON IM VORAUS VERTEILT".)
28" / 11"	f	Führen Sie auf zwei Saiten gleichzeitig COL LEGNO BATTUTO sechs oder sieben GETTATO-Striche ( ) in verschiedenen Geschwindigkeiten aus. Dabei sollen Sie die linke Hand zwischen der 2. und 5. Position bewegen; die Intensität
	mp	des Bogenanschlages von PIANO bis FORTE heftig verändern.
39" / 24"		(In den 'Heures Séculaires' schreibt Satie :
	mf rall.	"ICH VERBIETE JEDEM, WÄHREND DER AUFFÜHRUNG LAUT DEN TEXT ZU LESEN.
	f	JEDER VERSTOSS GEGEN DIESE ANORDNUNG WIRD MEINE GERECHTFERTIGTE UNGEHALTENHEIT GEGEN DEN
	p	DREISTEN NACH SICH ZIEHEN. AUSNAHMEN AUF GRUND PERSÖNLICHER BEVORZUGUNG SIND AUSGESCHLOSSEN" Dagegen bitte ich Sie, Herr Kontrabassist, diese Aufforderung laut zu verlesen, während Sie spielen.)
'03" / 13"		Ein pizzicato auf der I.Saite in der 8.Position; noch eines, und spielen Sie nun, immer schneller, eine große Anzahl von pizzicati über alle Saiten wandernd; begleiten Sie diese Passage mit Glottisschlägen (die dem Klang der pizzicati ähneln)
	f	und Akzenten auf Korpus und Zarge. Entwickeln Sie zum Schluß GROSSE AKTIVITÄT AUF DER IV. und V.Saite, durch
	mp	PIZZICATI, COL LEGNO BATTUTO, Schnarren, schnellsten Aufstrich und ABSTRICH, übertriebenen Druck des Bogens mit
	mf	halbem col legno tratto. DANKE.
'16" / 20"	p	BEREITEN SIE SICH BITTE AUF DIE PETITE PIECE DE RESISTANCE VOR. Während die linke Hand die Stellung der Finger und ihre Lage dauernd ändert, führen Sie arpeggierte Akkorde auf den

EXAMPLE 3.9. Mauricio Kagel, *Sonant (1960/...)*, bass part, after Karkoschka (1972: 107)

Incompleteness and ambiguity in scores

Earlier I maintained that scores, when approached in terms of the relevant conventions, must contain sufficient information to characterize the works they designate. Obviously, problems arise for the identification of a work where its score is incomplete or the instructions it conveys are inconsistent or ambiguous concerning matters that should be work determinative.

Incomplete pieces include J. S. Bach's *The Art of Fugue*, Mozart's *Requiem*, K. 626, Franz Schubert's Symphony No. 8, D. 759, Modest Mussorgsky's *Khovantchina*, and Gustav Mahler's Symphony No. 10. Where the work stops short of its end, but is fully detailed up to that point, it can be performed as an incomplete piece. This is how Schubert's symphony is usually played. When large parts of the work are incomplete because they exist only in short score, as is so with Mahler's Tenth, a performance is possible only if someone expands upon the composer's effort. A score can be 'short' of any of the elements constitutive of works of the relevant kinds, not just notes. For instance, a piano score of an orchestral work might leave most of the instrumentation undecided. Where the incompleteness is more radical, with no hints or guides left by the original author, a later composer might undertake the task of finishing what was written. Many have completed Bach's mighty final fugue; Mozart's students concluded his *Requiem*; and Nicolai Rimsky-Korsakov reworked and added to Mussorgsky's opera.

I see no problems with such cases, so long as the performance is advertised as incomplete because the work is, or as completed in a performing version by someone else. If the case of Mozart's *Requiem* is controversial, this is because it was originally offered as entirely his own, and the contributions of the student composers were not easy to sort out. And if Rimsky-Korsakov's zeal is sometimes criticized, it is for his tendency to try to rewrite harmonies and orchestrations that were already complete.

A score is ambiguous if it issues conflicting instructions or in some other way fails to clarify matters that are work constitutive in pieces of the kind at issue. The inconsistency may be explicit in the score or can arise from a conflict between what is written and the relevant performance practice or prevailing musical grammar. An example of the first kind of ambiguity is in Frédéric Chopin's *Mazurka*, Op. 7, No. 5, where there is a 'repeat to the sign' marker at the end of the score, but no 'sign' earlier (Treitler 1993). Schubert instructs pedalling over staccato or detached chords. Often, different editions of the score indicate different notes at equivalent points in the piece. Paul Ziff (1973: 715) writes:

In adapting and editing for viola [Bach's] first violoncello suite Lifschey notes with respect to the twenty-sixth measure that[,] while there is no accidental before the second B of the measure either in the Anna Magdalena manuscript or in that supplied by Kellner[,] B♭ appears in all the early editions . . . The Bach-Gesellschaft edition makes the flat optional. Neither choice poses any harmonic problems. Melodically the augmented second supplied by B♭ was not implausible for Bach. Which is correct? Evidently either will do but what Bach wrote is not known.

The second kind of inconsistency has a score at odds with the musical practices it presupposes. For instance, the musical syntax might suggest a given note should be 'natural', while the score shows that note as subject to a sharp that was applied earlier in the bar and was not cancelled. Sometimes Beethoven's tempo specifications seem inappropriate; he apparently relied on a faulty metronome.

Ambiguities may occur within the composer's autograph manuscript as a result of his slips of the pen (Keller 1956–7; Wolterstorff 1980: 68–9). Alternatively, the copying or printing process can be the source of errors. This is apparent when copies and printed editions are compared with each other and with autographs (Brendel 1976: 21–2; Howat 1995). Typically, notational mistakes of the type just described occur by accident, though some may be deliberate. It is possible that on rare occasions composers have intentionally recorded conflicting instructions, perhaps in order to indicate some desired effect for which the notation seemed inadequate (Epstein 1995), or to provoke the performer to think more carefully than usual about how to proceed.

When an error is uncovered, it should be corrected. Where we cannot tell which of the conflicting alternatives was intended, the ambiguity should be noted by the edition's publisher. (For a discussion of music editing, see Caldwell 1985, Taruskin 1985–6, Brett 1988, and Grier 1996.) Although small-scale, local ambiguity is annoying for those who would prefer things to be tidy, the identity of works is not threatened by a few ambiguities. If necessary, the performer can footnote in the programme notes which edition is followed, or how the ambiguity is treated.

Not all ambiguities are tiny, though. One of the most common kinds is also one of the largest, that in which there are significantly different versions of the score with none established as authoritative. The following examples are typical: the compositions of Chopin exist in many notational variants, many of which were made by him. For instance, his *Nocturne in B♭*, Op. 62, No. 1, differs in its published forms (Treitler 1993; for many other examples, see Kallberg 1996: ch. 7). Franz Liszt was apparently not committed to the idea of a single, authoritative version of his works, either. Mussorgsky wrote several variants of parts of his opera *Boris Godunov*. Nineteenth-century non-French operas were usually modified to incorporate a ballet for their Paris productions. Edward Elgar sanctioned a trumpet part different from the score for a performance of one of his symphonies. Many composers have altered their scores in the light of rehearsals or official performances of their music. When *Don Giovanni* was given in Vienna, Mozart cut some numbers from the Prague production and added new ones. Anton Bruckner continued to revise many of his symphonies after they had been published. Stravinsky revised his early works for later publication. Beethoven suggested in 1819 that the 'Hammerklavier' could be published in London without the Largo, or without the fugue but with the Scherzo as finale, or even that the first movement and Scherzo might form the entire sonata. (Kinderman 1995: 304 suggests he did so to obtain additional profit from a work that was being properly printed in Vienna.)

If one thinks works can be indicated definitively by scores only where a complete and unambiguous *Ur-text* can be located, these and countless similar examples might lead one to speculate that the 'work concept' was established, if at all, well after 1800 (cf. Goehr 1992). My conclusion is different. Even if the cited examples show that scores are often ambiguous, the identity of musical works is clearly flexible enough to survive the haziness created by such cases. The number of variants is usually comparatively small and there is no doubt that they were conceived as versions of a single work. Their common genesis, along with the huge overlaps they share in common, are sufficient to unite them. The ambiguity remains, of course, but can be dealt with easily enough by specifying 'Prague version of 1843' or 'one of several undated versions composed between 1870 and 1879' or 'from the Artaria edition of 1777'. A degree of ambiguity need not undermine a work's identity, though it requires acknowledgement that the piece exists in several versions. Also, ambiguity does not present an insuperable barrier to performance, though it must be addressed and resolved if a piece is to be played, and should be described in programme notes.

As I explained earlier, a score can be indefinite without being incomplete or ambiguous. It is not incomplete or ambiguous if it is indefinite about matters or elements with respect to which the work it specifies is also indefinite. If a score calls for a trill without indicating precisely how fast the trill must be, it is indefinite but not incomplete or ambiguous, provided the work it specifies necessarily contains a trill that may be realized at any speed within the range accepted by the performance practice relevant to pieces of that genre, place, and period. (Discussion of the manner of playing trills takes nearly 100 pages in Neumann 1993.) By contrast, an incomplete or ambiguous score is indefinite about something that should be definite, because that something typically is work constitutive for pieces of the relevant kind.

In practice, the distinction can be difficult to make. More detail in the decorations is recorded in the scores of some of Mozart's piano concertos than in others, with the works intended for performance by others more heavily notated. Does this mean the less detailed scores are incomplete? Or instead, are they indefinite because the works are? The answers to these questions depend on the practice and understanding of the times. For instance, if the written-out decorations have the status of mere recommendations—even if Mozart's students would have felt obliged to follow them— then the lighter scores are better considered complete, though indefinite. Here is another case: in some of Schubert's piano sonatas, dynamics and phrasing are marked more frequently in their earlier sections. Are the scores incomplete, then? That depends on whether the practice of the time expected detailed and frequent indications throughout and treated these as determinative. In cases where the composer is addressing himself, it can be particularly difficult to know if lightly notated passages leave out essential detail (that he counts on remembering), or if heavy annotations go beyond the work to record details of an intended interpretation. It is the conventions applicable to music of the relevant kind, not the detail of the composer's realization in performance, that determines what should be counted as essential in his work. Sometimes the practice and conventions might be interpreted either way, but often the distinction is clear enough.

Although there may be practical difficulties in distinguishing incomplete scores from indefinite ones that accurately specify a work-constitutive indefiniteness, it is important to be sensitive to this contrast if one is teasing out the ontological implications of the role of scores in performance practices. As mentioned in the previous chapter, New Musicologists do not always display the necessary subtlety. Neither do Goehr (1992: 187–9), Krausz (1993*a,b*), and Hall (1999). Goehr characterizes scores produced before 1800 as imprecise and incomplete, because composers did not write out the embellishments performers were expected to add according to the established performance practice. She describes as incomplete any score that does not establish a rigid distinction between extemporization and work performance. This way of talking supports the conclusion she would draw: the work concept was not established prior to 1800. But her examples seem rather to be ones of indefiniteness, not incompleteness, and indefiniteness in scores is perfectly consistent with the conscious creation of ontologically spare musical works, as I have already argued.

Mnemonic notations

A special class of incomplete notations deserves mention—namely, those with the function of reminding a performer of a work the detail of which she has already committed to memory. The notation is incomplete, not merely indefinite, because the piece is constituted at a higher level of complexity than is captured by the notation. Example 3.10 is of neumatic notation from the eleventh century. It is of the kind called chironomic, staffless, non-diastematic, oratorical, or *in campo aperto* (in the open field). This notation indicates the general contour of musical motion, as against the exact pitches and intervals constituting the melody. It serves primarily as a mnemonic for singers (or a choir director) already familiar with the indicated melody. In this case, the notation underdetermines the melody in that it contains a kind of indeterminacy not present in the melody itself. Because Example 3.10 is inadequate to characterize fully all that is constitutive of the piece in question, it is not a score (in my sense of the term).[18] This does not mean the notation is inadequate to its purpose, which is to support a strong oral tradition of works. Indeed, it is precisely the kind of notational system that could be predicted to arise from a context in which, in the absence of notations, centuries already had been spent communicating and preserving a large body of musical material.

Earlier I said central Javanese music is mostly transmitted orally, but I also suggested Example 3.5 could serve as a score. What distinguishes Example

[18] In discussing medieval notations, Treitler (1992) notes that some indicate precise intervals though others do not. He suggests that, where systems of both kinds were in simultaneous use, the former was for a less familiar repertoire than the latter. In other words, the latter were mnemonics. Also, Morrow (1978) believes traditional notations of the songs of troubadours, trouvères, and Minnesingers are inadequate to the pieces they specify, and that this is a general feature of monophonic, folk-based traditions. If he is correct, such notations would be mnemonic, in my terms.

EXAMPLE 3.10. Staffless notation from Hartker, Antiphonary (Saint-Gall 390) of around 1000 (*Paléographie Musicale*, series 2, vol. 1, p. 215)

3.10 from Example 3.5? The difference is this: the performance practice in Javanese music provides 'rules' allowing the musician to derive his part systematically from *kepatihan* notation. There are quite definite conventions (though these may be relativized to occasions of performance, regions, genres, styles, and instrument types) governing the derivation of individual parts from the basic melody. Such rules do not determine all the interpretative choices made, but they take all the parts up to the level of complexity that is work constitutive. By contrast, there are no conventions (or so I believe) allowing the performer of Example 3.10 to move with exactitude from the notation to the pitches and intervals in terms of which chants are individuated as particular works. In this case, it is memories, not established performance conventions, that bridge the gap between the notation and the melody constituting the given work.

In a suitable context, a notation identical to Example 3.10 might be a score. As such, it would specify a monophonic, melodically indeterminate piece. One cannot recognize a score from an otherwise identical notation merely by looking. As I have emphasized, notations can be interpreted correctly only against the background of the musical practice and notational conventions they presuppose, so that they are not meaningfully separable from those contexts. What makes Example 3.10 a mnemonic rather than a score is its role within a performance tradition having pieces that are more specific than what can be recovered from the notation alone. These scripts serve to refresh the memory, not to specify the details constitutive of the kind of melodic piece that is in question.

How should we regard sheet music sold in the popular market? Usually it is for keyboard and indicates only the melody, the basic harmonic structure, and the words. 'Bess, You is my Woman Now' receives its definitive treatment in George Gershwin's *Porgy and Bess* (1937). In that setting it has a detailed instrumentation. The sheet-music version of the song ignores its orchestration, and there are no conventions allowing recovery of the orchestration from what is written there. Printed versions of pop songs are similar. Even if such pieces are not purely electronic, their definitive first versions contain much more than is recorded in the sheet music issued subsequently. Though these publications are obviously intended for performers, they under-specify a great many of the details constitutive of the pieces they represent.

There are two ways of describing the status of the sheet music: as a mnemonic for the more detailed, definitive version, or as the score of a work transcription that transforms the original into a simple song for piano and vocalists. The use to which the performer puts the sheet music settles which of the two descriptions is the more appropriate.

Non-standard notations

Western composers have explored the use of many non-standard notational systems in recent decades. (For examples, see Cage 1969.) Provided these are issued as instructions to players, can be interpreted, and establish public standards allowing one to distinguish acceptable from inaccurate readings, I do not see them as posing a problem for my view. For instance, Example 3.11

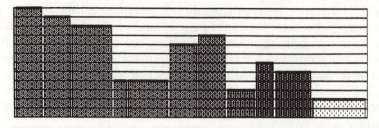

EXAMPLE 3.11. Graphic representation of violin part from Example 3.1

might be offered as a graphical representation of the violin part of Example 3.1. The horizontal axis indicates the duration of notes, the vertical axis notates pitches, and the patterns of the columns indicate the volume of sound (the darker the louder). Admittedly, Example 3.11 contains less information than does Example 3.1; phrasing, tempo, bowing, and metric indications are absent. If further symbols dealing with such matters were added to Example 3.11, along with a similar representation of the other instrumental parts, it would be functionally equivalent to Example 3.1 and could serve as a score of the same work. If no further markings were added to Example 3.11, it might be a score nevertheless. Then it would specify a different, though similar, work to that indicated by Example 3.1. This new work would be less determinate in some of its features (such as phrasing and metre) than is the work designated in Example 3.1. Only if Example 3.11 were offered, unmodified, as representing the violin part in the work indicated by Example 3.1 would it fail to be a score in the fullest sense, for then it would underdetermine some of the properties essential to the identity of the given work.

Where the notation is non-standard, there are unlikely to be established, commonly understood conventions for its interpretation. If such a notation is to specify a work, thereby qualifying as a score, it should supply the rules according to which its indications are read. Unless there is the possibility of a distinction between correct and incorrect interpretations, the notation requires nothing from the performer and, hence, fails as a score. (Even the freest work—one with a score instructing the performer to play whatever she likes for as long as she wants however she chooses—establishes a standard for compliance, albeit one very easily satisfied.) It is not surprising, then, that some scores come complete with a key to the intended meanings of the unorthodox symbols they employ. Example 3.12 reproduces a page of Penderecki's *Fluorescences for Orchestra*, as well as some of the rules for its interpretation. In this example the notation underdetermines the sound structure of any given performance. It is apparent, though, that the notation specifies the work's indeterminacy, not that it fails to characterize details constitutive of it, so there is no difficulty in regarding Example 3.12 as a score.

Example 3.13, the first two pages of Schafer's *Epitaph for Moonlight* for

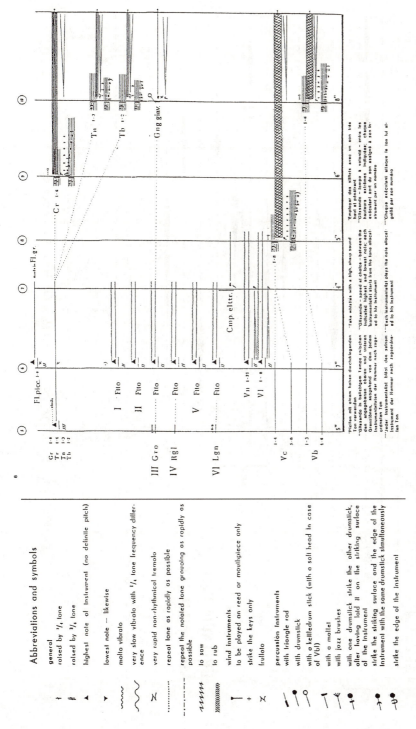

EXAMPLE 3.12. Krzysztof Penderecki, *Fluorescences for Orchestra* (Celle: Moeck Verlag, 1962), extracts from introductory instructions and p. 8

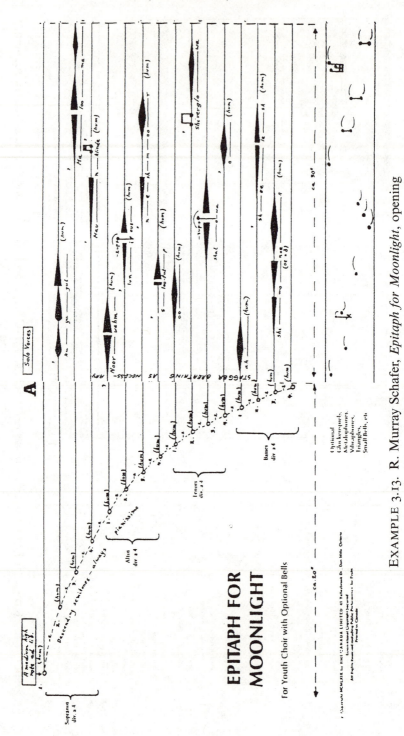

EXAMPLE 3.13. R. Murray Schafer, *Epitaph for Moonlight*, opening

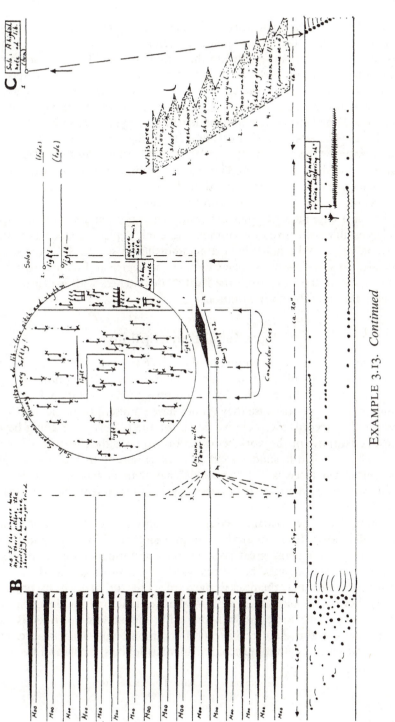

EXAMPLE 3.13. *Continued*

youth choir with optional bells,[19] might seem problematic from the perspective of my theory, because no guide to the interpretation of the notation is provided by the composer. But in this case it is not difficult to see how it should be read and one can appreciate the character of the work it specifies. As in Example 3.11, the horizontal axis indicates the temporal order, as is so with orthodox musical notation. The various parts are indicated on the vertical axis. Sound structure and volume within the parts are shown by pictorial shapes. The interpretation of these allows the performers some freedom but, obviously, the work itself is indeterminate in the relevant respects. One can easily see how accurate and inaccurate renditions could be distinguished by someone possessing the score, though very different performances could be accurate in being consistent with the score.

This last case indicates that the composer can often appeal implicitly to widely established conventions for reading iconic depictions (such as pictures, cartoon strips, and graphs) in creating unorthodox scores. Since the score is intended to specify a work, one can infer the degree and nature of indeterminacy within the work from the level of definiteness with which it is possible to interpret the given notation.

Notational transcriptions

I have so far mentioned two notational transcriptions (Examples 3.7 and 3.8). Transcriptions of this kind, which provide notational descriptions of works or performances, differ from scores and mnemonics. Notational transcriptions are not scores because they do not have a prescriptive function. Moreover, if they record interpretative details of the performance going beyond those constitutive of the work being performed (as is the case with Examples 3.7 and 3.8), when misunderstood as work prescriptions they would imply the performed piece is ontologically richer than in fact it is. This is no fault, of course, where the transcriber intends to represent the performance, not the piece.

Though any performance could be transcribed into notation, it is those that arise from an oral or improvising tradition that most often are. The solos of many great jazz and rock performers have been notated. These transcriptions may be for analysis, but also they are used by young performers who treat them as if they are scores, or, at least, as providing a way they can emulate their idols—John Coltrane or Jimi Hendrix, say— and thereby come to terms with the skills and idioms involved. Because many non-Western cultures have oral traditions, notational transcription is a central tool in ethnomusicology. In what follows, I concentrate on the

---

[19] The entire piece is published in Schafer (1970).

special issues raised by transcriptions in which the music of one culture is recorded via the notational system of another. The object work or performance could be a Western one. For instance, a transcription by Tsun Yuen Lui of 'Greensleeves' for the Chinese pipa is shown in Hood (1971: 77), along with other examples.[20] But I focus on the case where the notational system is Western and the object work or performance is non-Western. Example 3.14 is of this kind.

The ethnomusicologist faces many problems in transcribing the music of a non-Western culture. There is the obvious one of using a notation evolved to record one kind of music in describing another that might involve, say, subtleties of pitch, rhythm, and timbre that are foreign to classical Western music (for discussion, see Seeger 1958 and Kunst 1959: 38–41). In Example 3.14, portamentos in the vocal part are indicated by an unbroken line (see bar 2) and tonal interference in the *didgeridoo* part, caused by vocal sounds made into the instrument by the player, is indicated by a special symbol, 'V' (see the second note of bar 1). Though much is made of the difficulties of using Western notation in recording non-Western music, it should be recalled that this system includes many symbolic resources. For instance, portamento is a feature of Example 3.15 and Iannis Xenakis's *Metastasis* (1955) is a seven-minute work built on string glissandos. Also, the Western system allows for supplementation by diacritical signs. Béla Bartók's notational transcriptions of Serbo-Croatian folk songs are replete with such markings (see Example 3.16). Finally, in the ideal situation, the one ethnomusicologists most desire, the transcription accompanies a recording and is read alongside the actual performance.

A more significant issue is faced in deciding the kind and degree of detail to transcribe. The problem is that of knowing what is significant in the musical culture being studied. To put the point crudely, if the smallest unit of pitch significance is the tone, with finer intervals always classified as instances of the nearest whole tone, then it would be misleading to notate finer pitch differences, even if the transcriber hears these played. Alternatively, if micro-tonal deviations from the primary pitches of the scale are important, for instance as decorative devices, then it is appropriate to indicate them. Some ethnomusicologists (e.g. Hood 1971: 55–61) distinguish 'phonetic' from 'phonemic' transcription, with the former as detailed as possible and the latter concerned with more general features of shape. To regard these as equally acceptable styles of notational transcription would be to fudge crucial questions (see Nettl 1964: 105, 1983: 69; Bowen 1996): what is the transcription of, and what is it used for? Among the considerations relevant to fixing the level of detail appropriate to a notational

---

[20] For discussion of this and similar notations, see Kaufmann (1967).

EXAMPLE 3.14. Transcription of an Australian aboriginal song by Alice
Moyle; after Moyle (1967: 86)

transcription is a determination of the object of transcription—the piece
(should the culture have them) or the performance. A transcription of the
work should aim to capture properties of which it is comprised, leaving aside
those nuances and shades that are features of the performance, whereas a
transcription of a particular performance or performance style will include

EXAMPLE 3.15. Béla Bartók, String Quartet No. 4 (London: Boosey & Hawkes, 1939), no. 9043, p. 10

such subtleties.[21] And if the concern is to capture the personal idiom of a particular performer, yet finer details would have to be noted. It is my impression that ethnomusicologists' notational transcriptions are usually at the level of performance, though this is not always made clear.

How is the transcriber to know, for all the aural discriminations that might be made, which are musically significant within the culture, style, work, and performance? (For that matter, how is the ethnomusicologist to know important discriminations that are not audible, so that someone is rated a good singer as much in terms of how he dresses as how accurate his pitches are?) Progress can be made by the use of standard techniques of musical analysis and tests of statistical significance, but, as ethnomusicologists have always appreciated, there is no substitute for an intimate knowledge of the musical culture and tradition. It is desirable to talk to competent performers in their native language, to hear much music and to consider the social context in which it arises, to see instruments made and played, and so on. The notation must be no less responsive

---

[21] Treitler (1992) discusses the notations of tropes in the Duchy of Aquitania between the tenth and twelfth centuries. He suggests that these specify a level of detail going beyond the tropes themselves; in my terminology, they are best viewed as notational transcriptions of performances, not work scores.

EXAMPLE 3.16. Transcription by Béla Bartók; after Bartók (1967: 285)

to the performance practice in this case than in the Western classical tradition.

Non-musical notations of performances and works

There are many ways of representing performances or works that do not qualify as *musical* notations because they are not of a kind that can be read as indicating what should be played.

Performances can be recorded as holes punched in rolls of paper or in metal discs, as grooves in vinyl, as electromagnetic patterns on tape, or as extended sequences of 1s and 0s. Usually these are sourced from the actions of musicians. Such grooves and patterns are not musical *notations*, however, because they are not readable by, or addressed to, musicians. They represent performances and the works the performances are of, but not as musical notations do. (Moreover, they include details belonging to the performance interpretation rather than to the work as such.)

Some musical works are not for performance, as I explained in Chapter 1. A few purely electronic compositions are accompanied by a pictorial representation of the piece's soundscape. One such is the picture graph of Stockhausen's *Studie II* (1954) (see Example 3.17). This records pitch, density, volume, and note mixture overlays. Notations of this kind resemble some of the non-standard ones mentioned earlier, and they invoke similar conventions: the higher a mark is on the vertical axis, the higher its pitch; temporal sequence reads from left to right. Nevertheless, they are not scores because they are not directed to performers, since such works have none. They also fail as non-standard musical notations. There are no conventions allowing the listener to extrapolate from such pictures to the level of detail constitutive in works of this kind. The notation of Example 3.13, Schafer's *Epitaph for Moonlight*, is adequate to the work it specifies, since that piece is no more precise in its detail than is the notation itself. By contrast, an electronic work, such as Paul Lansky's *Table's Clear* (1990–1), has an extremely complex and specific content. If it were accurately depicted in a 'picture', the graphic representation would have to be no less intricate and articulated than is the work itself. If musical notations must be adequate to capture the works they prescribe or describe, these fail as musical notations.[22]

Is a more accurate notation available for electronic pieces? There is. Depending on the work's medium, it is the analogue or digital specification of the composer's master. An electronic work composed on a computer is saved as a file and this file can be represented in turn as a series of 1s and 0s. Even if such notations are accurate, they count neither as scores nor as musical notations for reasons already rehearsed. They are not scores because they are not issued as instructions to performers and they are not *musical* notations because they cannot be read as such by musicians. Besides, they are not always accurate work depictions. As I noted in Chapter 1, analogue or digital specifications often contain information that is extrinsic to the work itself, such as tape hiss, acoustic detail that is subsequently lost in the dubbing process, or data that are too fine for most humans to register.

Nelson Goodman on musical notations

In this final section, I consider the account of musical notations and scores offered by Goodman (1968), because he devoted more attention to this topic

---

[22] If these pictures are merely gestural in that they under-specify the works in question, why were they produced? There are several answers to this question, but one is both unexpected and interesting. In the early days of electronic composition, there was no way for the composer to copyright his work, so it was the 'score' that was copyrighted (see Chew 1980 and Ferguson 1983).

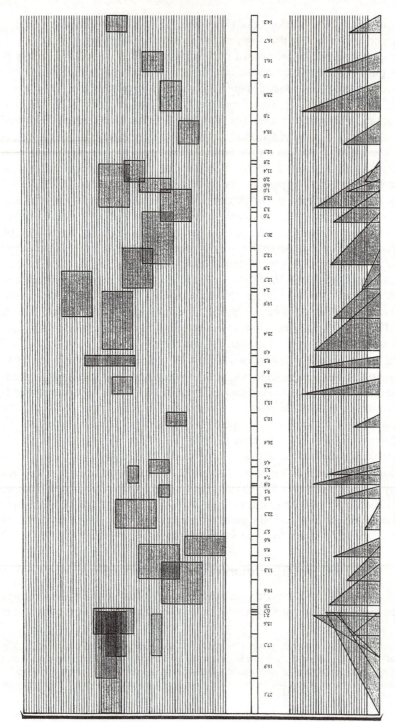

EXAMPLE 3.17. Karlheinz Stockhausen, *Studie II* (London: Universal Edition, 1956), 13

than other philosophers. His conclusions differ from mine. In criticizing them, I hope to reinforce some of the key points made in the previous discussion.

According to Goodman, a score is a character in a notational system (1968: 177). Where works are complex and articulated, 'character' refers to a string of syntactically connected 'atomic' notational elements. The main function of a score is to identify a work. Since, for Goodman, a work is a class of performances (1968: 210) or is the semantic structure they share in common (1968: 184), a notation identifies a work by accurately encoding its distinctive semantic signature. In describing the work it denotes, the notation must uniquely identify each and every performance that is of the given work and, in its turn, it must be uniquely identified by any performance taken in conjunction with the relevant notational system.

A score, whether or not ever used as a guide for a performance, has as a primary function the authoritative identification of a work from performance to performance ... [E]very score, as a score, has the logically prior office of identifying a work ... First, a score must define a work, marking off the performances that belong to the work from those that do not ... Not only must a score uniquely determine the class of performances belonging to the work, but the score (as a class of copies or inscriptions that so define the work) must be uniquely determined, given a performance and the notational system. (1968: 128–30)

Goodman proceeds by considering what conditions must be met by any notational system if it is to fulfil this primary function. He identifies two syntactic requirements (1968: 130–47)—disjointness and finite differentiation—and three semantic ones (1968: 148–52)—unambiguity, disjointness, and finite differentiation. Both syntactic conditions are met when no mark belongs to more than one character (with the result that marks correctly judged to be joint members of a character will always be true copies of one another) and it is theoretically possible to determine of a mark that it does not belong to at least one of any two characters. The semantic conditions on notational systems require them to be unambiguous (so that the compliance relationship is invariant), their compliance classes to be disjoint, and it to be theoretically possible to determine of an object that it does not comply with (fall within the extension of) at least one of any two non-synonymous characters.

In sum, the properties required of a notational system are unambiguity and syntactic and semantic disjointness and differentiation ... [These features] derive from the primary purpose a score must serve; and all are categorically required for any even theoretically workable notational system. A system is notational, then, if and only if all objects complying with inscriptions of a given character belong to the same compliant class and we can, theoretically, determine that each mark belongs to, and each object complies with inscriptions of, at most one particular character. (1968: 156)

Though redundancy is a fault in a notational system, it is tolerable if it does not lead to semantic ambiguity.[23] In music written for even-tempered instruments, notations of G♭ and F♯ involve different characters. Since these determine co-extensional compliants within a notational system for even-tempered instruments—that is to say, since all and only that which is denoted by one character is denoted by the other—the redundancy is harmless, because it leads to semantic synonymy (1968: 151, 181–2).

Having outlined the general features of ideal notational systems, Goodman goes on to consider the characteristics of actual musical scores. Though most musical notations appear to meet his syntactic requirements, it is doubtful they satisfy the semantic ones. He deals with difficult cases in various ways.

In some instances, the problem is merely apparent. For example, an atomic character might seem to be ambiguous until it is linked to others with which it forms a compound character. In a work for piano and violin, there is no semantic distinction between G♭ and F♯ within a given octave as regards the former instrument, whereas there is one as regards the latter. Nevertheless, the condition of semantic disjointness is not violated. 'Each of the two characters can be considered a vacant atomic character that combines with different specifications of instrument to form different prime characters' (1968: 182). A simpler illustration of the same point is the following: a note on the top line of the stave denotes one pitch at some times and others at others; the relevant compound character is determined not solely by stave position, but in conjunction with the clef, key signature, and accidentals, so there is no ambiguity (1968: 141).

Just as atomic characters need to be situated within the compounds of which they are part, scores need to be considered in relation to the notational systems under which they are created. Take compositions written with a figured bass. 'Now so long as such scores determine comparatively broad but still mutually disjoint classes of performances, they cause no trouble; what counts is not specificity but separateness' (1968: 183). There would be a difficulty, though, if a score with a thorough bass were matched with another that spelled out a realization of the continuo part. These two scores, 'even though they have some common compliant performance, will not thereby be semantically equivalent; and two performances complying with the former may severally comply with two specific scores that have no compliant in common. The comprehensive language of musical scores, insofar as it offers free choice between figured-bass and specific notation, is thus not truly notational' (1968: 184). This consequence is avoided by regarding figured bass and note-specific notations as belonging to different subsystems within the wider language of musical nota-

---

[23] Notice that what is acceptable is redundancy in the notation. Redundancy in a performance—as would occur if the performer repeats each note before moving on to the next—is not tolerable for Goodman. It would result in a semantic content different from the given work's and, thereby, would fail to be a performance of it.

tions, with the work relativized to only one of these. The same applies in the case of cadenzas. 'Unless there is a way of determining in every case whether a solo passage is to be fully specified or indicated as a free cadenza, we must again recognize that the language of musical scores is not purely notational but divides into notational subsystems' (1968: 184).

In effect, Goodman adopts a similar approach in dealing with works allowing considerable freedom to the performer. 'Such latitude is not incompatible with notationality; even a system with only two characters, one having as compliants all piano performances beginning with a middle C, and the other having as compliants all other performances, would be notational—though for this system there could be only two different works' (1968: 190).[24] Here again, if the notation succeeds in identifying a work, it does so only in relation to a distinct notational system.

Not all elements in musical scores can be accommodated by Goodman's theory of notations, though. He responds by excluding these from the notation and, hence, from the score. Now, the limits on notations correspond to limits on the kinds of properties that can be work constitutive, since, for Goodman, the work is the class of performances compliant with the score. As a result, when he demotes some mark from the musical score, he also excludes it from the piece denoted by that score. Goodman can and does use his account of notations to determine the properties that identify works. This is apparent in his banishing verbal tempo specifications, such as 'allegro', from the score because they are ambiguous and are not finitely differentiated.

Where the failures are yet more radical, so that none of the marks used falls within a notational system, no score is produced and no work is identified. According to Goodman, this is the case with John Cage's graphic indications for *Concert for Piano and Orchestra, Solo for Piano* (1960); the system is not notational and, therefore, no work is specified. 'There are only copies *after* and performances *after* that unique object as there are only drawings and paintings after a sketch' (1968: 190). The inscription can inspire and inform a performance, but that performance cannot instance a work indicated by the notation, since none is.

If a notation fails, it could be that no work is indicated, as in the example just described, or it could be that a work exists independently of that particular notation. Medieval chironomic inscriptions (such as Example 3.10) served as mnemonics to those already familiar with the melody by indicating its general contour.[25] They are inadequate as scores in Goodman's sense, because they do not unambiguously indicate pitch details essential to the identity of the tunes they represent. Such pieces are 'scorable' in Goodman's

---

[24] One who fails to appreciate that Goodman's theory can allow for pitch indeterminacy is Porter (1996).

[25] Goodman's example—BN, Paris, Lat. 7211, fo. 127ᵛ—is unfortunate. It does specify definite pitches, despite the absence of stave lines.

terms, and this is why they count as works, though the actual notations that assisted performers do not qualify as scores.

Notations are also inadequate for purely electronic music, because purely electronic pieces are more like oil paintings than like the kinds of works indicated via scores. Electronic music is semantically dense; that is, many of the semantically significant properties (which is to say, work-constitutive features) of such pieces cannot be assigned unambiguously to finitely differentiated notational characters. Accordingly, purely electronic works cannot be specified notationally. They are of a non-notational type. In Goodman's terms, they are 'autographic', whereas works transmitted via notations are 'allographic' (1968: 191). 'Autographic' works can be multiply instanced by being cloned from a master, but any independently produced replica is a forgery distinct from the original. By contrast, any accurate replica of an 'allographic' work provides yet another copy of that work.[26]

Criticisms of Goodman's account of musical notations

Though Goodman sometimes writes that scores prescribe works, he does not regard them as *instructions* issued to performers; rather, he sees them as identifying *descriptions* of works. Performance is a matter not of *following* a score but of *matching* its semantic content by any means whatever. His account is dictated entirely by his goal of analysing what it is about notations that allows them to perform their primary function of specifying works uniquely and unequivocally. He explicitly ignores such matters as

ease of writing or reading . . . or of ready duplicability or performability [because] none of this has anything to do with the basic theoretical function of notational systems. Throughout, I have been stressing the nominative or predicative aspects of symbols, not their assertive or imperative or interrogative force, and have taken characters more as predicates or labels than as sentences. This is natural in the present context; for in notational systems the grammatical mood of a character seldom matters much . . . The point is that . . . mood is irrelevant [to logical languages] insofar as they are notational.   (1968: 154–5)

Even if Goodman accepts that the composer issues a conditional imperative via her score, he regards this as irrelevant to his theoretical enterprise.

Goodman is wrong to disregard the variety of functions served by musical notations and the historically mutable conventions on which their proper interpretation depends. Not all musical notations have as their prime function the specification of works. Ethnomusicologists' transcriptions, for example,

---

[26] See Goodman (1968: 113–23) for a discussion of the distinction between autographic and allographic art. At first (1968, 1972), Goodman regarded all works of art as covered by the distinction. Later (1984: 139), he allowed that Cage's non-notational works may have to be counted as exceptions to the rule. For criticism and discussion of difficulties in applying the distinction to music, see Webster (1971), Levinson (1980*b*), Currie (1988), Jacobs (1990), Margolis (1993), and Lee B. Brown (1996).

are descriptive. They are to be read, not followed by players, and they are as likely to document performances as works. And even when the prime function of a notation is to specify a work, it does so not by 'describing' it but by instructing performers about what is to be achieved and how this is to be done. In my view, scores contain, as well as work-determinative instructions, recommendations, and the like. Not everything recorded in the score has the same force or status. What makes the difference is neither the manner nor the system of notation. It is, rather, conventions governing the interpretation of scores of the kind in question. The correct reading of musical notations requires that they be approached in terms of the appropriate conventions and against the background of the performance practice they assume.

My account comfortably handles cases presenting Goodman with problems. In the eighteenth century, cadenzas were often improvised, but composers sometimes wrote them out in full, either for their own use or to instruct pupils. A performer, when faced with a score containing a written-out version of the cadenza, may choose to play it. Equally though, she retains the option of improvising one of her own design. In terms of the kinds of works they determine, scores from this period with notated cadenzas are not different from those that simply mark the place where the cadenza is to occur, because in either case the performer is free to improvise her own. By contrast, Goodman is forced by his view of notations to regard the two scores as crucially different. He must say that exclusive notational systems are in use, with each specifying a different work. In regarding scores as descriptions of works that can be separated from the performance practices that are their background, Goodman is bound to take all that is expressly notated as work identifying. He can acknowledge the semantic synonymy of scores containing different notes only by supposing those scores to involve different notational systems.

As I see it, Goodman's indifference to the manner in which scores are interpreted and used, rather than permitting a clearer account of notational theory, distorts the proper view both of notations and of works. Consider his discussion of enharmonic equivalents in piano music: they involve (benign) notational redundancy, since they do not mark a semantic difference relevant to the work's identity. Is this really the case? One reason to be wary of his conclusion is the systematic care with which composers distinguish (even in music for the piano) between the possibilities of, say F♯ and G♭. In tonal music, they hardly ever treat these as interchangeable.[27] And

---

[27] If Goodman's claim ever holds true, it does so in non-tonal, non-harmonic music. Twelve-tone compositions are often just that—that is, they are not seventeen-tone compositions acknowledging semantic distinctions between G♭ and F♯, A♭ and G♯, and so on. If the notation for such a work employs enharmonically equivalent characters, it involves notational redundancy. But notice that this depends on the kind of work and not the temperament of the instruments for which it is written. The redundancy remains, even if the work is for a string quartet.

EXAMPLE 3.18. Different resolutions of enharmonically equivalent chords

the reason for this is readily apparent. Particular harmonic and voice-leading tendencies are implied in the choices made.

Example 3.18 shows various resolutions of a diminished chord and the different notations that go with them. For Goodman, the semantic character of the diminished chord is indifferent to its notation, but he surely is wrong if the notation plainly reflects harmonically functional relationships that differ according to their context (Webster 1971; Edlund 1996). The four diminished chords in Example 3.18 might all be analysed as different (flattened ninth) major chords, each of which resolves to the major chord a fifth lower. As such, each diminished chord has a different (unsounded) root. Now, if chord progressions are semantically significant, as surely they are, and if different enharmonic notations indicate different chords, even in piano music, then Goodman is mistaken in treating the use of enharmonic notations in piano music merely as involving notational redundancy.[28] The point just made—namely, Goodman is mistaken in regarding individual notes as the basic semantic units to which higher-level musical structures can be reduced, is one to which I return in the next chapter.

The cases mentioned previously are ones where Goodman's account of notations suffers from his assumption that the fundamental elements of musical works are individual, pitched tones. Elsewhere, though, it is Goodman's theory of notations that influences his ontology of musical works, as when he dismisses as irrelevant to work identity features, such as tempo, that are often semantically significant within musical pieces. Indeed, some of Goodman's most controversial claims are forced on him by his theory of notations. For example, he must regard a symbol such as *tr* as non-notational, because it fails to meet his requirement of semantic differentiation (since there is indefiniteness about how many notes any trill should contain). He has to treat the trill, not as part of the work, but as an inter-

---

[28] A similar objection is raised by Webster (1971): in tonal music, it is scalar functions rather than pure pitches that are semantically significant; the significance of a tone does not lie solely in its pitch.

pretative aspect of performance. This makes a nonsense of one of the more significant semantic features of a work such as Guiseppe Tartini's *Devil's Trill Sonata* (Ziff 1971). Moreover (as Jennifer Judkins has reminded me), this approach ignores crucial discrepancies in the significance of *tr* when it is directed to different instruments. It calls for a rapid alternation between notes of adjacent pitch from a violin, but, when the instrument has a fixed pitch or is untuned, it calls for a roll.

I regard trills, vibrato, tempo, cadenzas, figured basses, and the like as part of the work. Where the detail of realization is left to the performance practice, the relevant instruction applies not to particular tokens but to sound types or playing types. For instance, vibrato is mandated in late-nineteenth-century string music unless contra-indicated, but the performer is free within bounds set by the performance practice to style her vibrato as she chooses. Or a cadenza is required at a given point in an eighteenth-century concerto, and so counts as part of the work, but the detail of what is presented is left to the performer. By contrast, Goodman regards the relevant inscriptions as non-notational and, therefore, treats trills and the like as not part of the given work. His goal is to explain how notations can capture and preserve work identity, but he does so in a way that ignores semantically significant musical contents.

Goodman assumes notations can specify works uniquely and definitively only if they include all that is constitutive of the given work.[29] In consequence, he thinks that notations can perform the job of specifying works only if everything relevant to the work's identity is captured in the notation. (No doubt he takes social context to be irrelevant to the work and its notation because his account assumes notational systems are self-contained.) I think a digital print-out of a purely electronic work comes nearer to being a score in Goodman's sense than do actual musical notations (although, for him, purely electronic works are autographic, not allographic). The print-out, taken as a string, is a character in a notational system that maps onto the work with the exactitude Goodman admires and requires. Such a rendition is unreadable by musicians, it could not be followed, and it post-dates the work's creation, but none of these points would bother Goodman. His approach is subject to this objection, which is

---

[29] Actually, his requirement is stricter than this. He asks what notations must be like if they can definitively identify a work 'fully freed from the history of production' (Goodman 1968: 122). Wolterstorff (1980; see also Sparshott 1987) rejects this question as without consequence, since, on Goodman's own admission, musical works survive and are transmitted in the absence of notations, and actual notational systems convey works although they do not satisfy all of Goodman's conditions for notations. Subscribers to the kind of contextualist ontologies described in Chapter 2, such as myself, see no virtue in Goodman's self-imposed enterprise. They deny that theories dedicated to slewing off the history of the piece's production are suited to revealing its nature.

adapted from Ludwig Wittgenstein: no notation, however detailed and highly structured, can determine its own application; all notations must be interpreted. To the extent that he ignores this, Goodman misconceives the nature of notations. The socially established conventions of music making within which scores play a functional role inevitably return to haunt his theory, despite the pains he takes to exclude them.

As he is aware, Goodman's account requires not that a score is followed by performers, but that one be recoverable from any performance instancing the work.[30] He writes (1968: 178):

A class is uniquely determined by the score . . . but a score . . . is also uniquely determined by each member of that class. Given the notational system and a performance of a score, the score is recoverable. Identity of work and of score is retained in any series of steps, each of them either from compliant performance to score-inscription, or from score-inscription to compliant performance, or from score-inscription to true copy . . . [I]n a chain of the sort described, the score-inscriptions may not all be true copies of one another; yet all will be semantically equivalent— all performances will be of the same work. Work-preservation but not score-preservation is ensured; and insofar as work-preservation is paramount, and score-preservation incidental, redundancy is tolerable.

Is the score always recoverable from a note-perfect performance? On the face of it, the answer must be 'no' (Tormey 1974). Take some hypothetical examples. The twentieth-century sound-appropriator Ribaldi creates a work that is like Antonio Vivaldi's *Four Seasons*, except his specifies that the twelve movements can be played in any order. One possible performance of this piece is indistinguishable from a performance of Vivaldi's.[31] Or consider Symphony No. 5 of the Martian composer Marthoven (see Kendall L. Walton 1973, 1988). In Martian music, the focus falls on

---

[30] Only note-perfect performances instance their works, according to Goodman. (I consider and criticize his reasons for this claim in the next chapter.) It is beside the point, then, when Carrier (1983) observes that we could not recover Frédéric Chopin's scores if we worked from Vladimir de Pachman's recordings, since these contain wrong notes. For further discussion of difficulties attending the recovery of a score from a performance, see Davies (1991*b*) and Edlund (1996).

[31] Savile (1971) described a case in which Stockhausen composes a work which, to someone unaware of its origin, sounds exactly like one composed by Johann Stamitz 200 years earlier. The example I discuss is after one described in Ziff (1973). (Unlike me, Ziff tends to treat any works that closely resemble each other merely as variants of a single piece. For criticism, see Kendall L. Walton 1973.) The composer, Christopher Hobbs, uses traditional works (of Joseph Lanner, Johann Strauss, John Bull, Alexander Scriabin, Peter Tchaikovsky, etc.) as sources for his own (Nyman 1981: 140–2). In *The Remorseless Lamb* (1970), a two-piano version of J. S. Bach's 'Sheep May Safely Graze' was cut up. The right- and left-hand parts of each bar were separated and then randomly reorganized. Suppose the random ordering happened to correspond exactly to Bach's . . .

subtle aspects of timbre, attack, decay, and the like, whereas the order of notes is of no special importance. One possible performance of Marthoven's work is aurally indistinguishable from a performance of Beethoven's Fifth Symphony. Or compare a work like that described by Goodman, one having as compliants any harpsichord performance beginning on middle C, with the first of Bach's *Two Part Inventions*, which begins on that note. In all these examples, pairs of different works, each specified by a different score, appear to have possible instances in common. Where a performance falls within the intersection, nothing about it determines which score should be recovered.

I mention these outlandish cases just because Goodman emphasizes that his interest lies with what is theoretically possible, not with practicalities. But it is worth noting that ethnomusicologists' transcriptions of a given piece of music often differ markedly, even where they share the same 'object', be it work or performance.

Now, the theoretical cases I have offered do not directly trouble Goodman's theory. He has an obvious resource for dealing with them. The score is recoverable *only where the notational system is given*, he insists. The works I have described are created under different notational systems. Provided we know which these are, sound-alike performances will give rise to scores that differ appropriately. Though they lead to *sound-alike performances*, these works do not have any *compliants* in common, since compliants capture work-defining contents and the works, as described, are different just because they are semantically distinct. Given the notational system, all this should be reflected in the scores that are recovered.

This reply deals with the problem in hand, but it also draws attention to a weakness that undermines Goodman's general account. Notice how much work is being done here by the notion of a notational system. I doubt it can sustain the burden Goodman places on it.

Suppose I set out to recover the score of the first of Bach's *Two Part Inventions*. I work in terms of the appropriate notational system, but, whereas Bach's score is in common time, mine is in 4/8, with all the rhythmic values halved (see Example 3.19). Goodman has two ways of describing my score. He could say I am mistaken about Bach's notational system and thereby have misrepresented Bach's piece. That line strikes me as unconvincing. The two notations are semantically equivalent, with mine as good as Bach's in recording his work. Alternatively, Goodman could accept that my score is semantically equivalent to Bach's. In that case, he would have to explain the differences between the two scores as non-semantic and hence as *purely* notational. For his theory, this means arguing that the differences are the product of benign notational redundancies. If it were appropriate to assume the piece is for a well-tempered instrument, my score might have differed from Bach's in beginning with

EXAMPLE 3.19. The opening of J. S. Bach, *Two Part Invention in C*, as compared to a transcription in 4/8 time

B♯, not C, but, for Goodman, these two notations would capture the same semantic content and, hence, could be interchanged.[32] But, although Goodman can allow that 'true' scores might differ where the notational system allows for redundancy, it is not obvious that this strategy can deal convincingly with my example. My score contains notational symbols, such as semi-quavers, that also appear in Bach's, but mine do not belong to the same pitches as his. Those semi-quavers are neither notationally nor semantically equivalent in the notational system my score shares with Bach's, so the difference between our scores is not covered by the notion of redundancy.

The strategy of explaining away the notational differences in terms of redundancy is the appropriate one in my view, but the relevant argument is not available to Goodman. The redundancy becomes apparent only when the connection between tempo and rhythmic values is accepted. My score should be taken at approximately half the tempo of Bach's and this is appropriate for the 4/8 metre, given the rate of harmonic change, and so on. Goodman cannot appeal to such matters, though, since he does not count tempo as part of a work. Moreover, because Bach gives no tempo indication, Goodman is doubly barred from attaching significance to it. I can take account of conventions in the performance practice regarding tempo and its relation to metre; he cannot, because he regards

---

[32] I have already objected to Goodman's treatment of enharmonic equivalents. No one who understands the work's tonality could begin it with a B♯. That point is irrelevant to the present *ad hominem* argument, however.

such matters as non-notational. As a result, Goodman cannot satisfactorily explain the status of the score I have recovered from a note-perfect performance of Bach's work. It is counter-intuitive to dismiss it as employing a different notational system, but neither can Goodman explain how it is semantically equivalent to (and therefore different only in matters of notational redundancy from) Bach's.

Here is another example that presents a problem for Goodman's view. Imagine a score containing the instruction that the work be played once only. In this case, I would argue that the composer's exhortation has the status of a wish and is not work determinative. Not everything recorded by a composer in her score must be taken as required, even if she would like the musicians to follow her every indication. The musical tradition within which scores are produced and works are played does not recognize the legitimacy of instructions of the kind mentioned, I think. Such an indication should be regarded as recommendatory, rather than compulsory, given the appropriate conventions for reading scores. The recommendation might be respected and enacted but, or so I maintain, a failure to do so would not otherwise render a performance of the work less authentic or accurate.[33] In that case, a notation accurately transcribed from the work's one and only performance is not demoted from its status as a score solely for its failure to capture and record the composer's unsuccessful attempt to forbid subsequent performances.

Goodman does not allow for the possibility that a composer's indications might range between the mandated and the merely recommended. He takes inscriptions either as work definitive or as non-notational. A composer's written instructions are work defining just in case they meet his notational conditions. In terms of those conditions, he should regard the specification that a work be played only once as part of the score so long as it is recorded on it; that is, he should treat this as a work-identifying feature. Now, one could retrieve much of the score of this work from (a recording of) its single performance, but nothing about that performance would allow one to discover the restriction on the number of performances. In this case, one could know what notational system was employed, and, hence, recover the work's score, only if one had access to the composer's original or a copy of it.

Goodman is obliged to treat some other examples similarly. Suppose a score indicates that the piece begin and end on C if it is played on a Monday, on D if the performance is on Tuesday, and so on. Apart from this, any notes

---

[33] Alban Berg requested that the seventy songs he composed between 1901 and 1908 should not be given public performance. Had he indicated this on the manuscripts themselves, his desire would not thereby have become mandatory, I claim. Many recordings of these songs have since been issued. These are not any less genuine as instances of his works for ignoring his expressed preference.

may be played. Again, it appears that one could fully understand the notational system used by the composer only if one could view his score, and one could not recover the full score from any single performance of the work.

In this last case, I accept that a copy of the score could not be derived from a single performance of the work, even if one knew it was of a kind permitting the performer a great deal of freedom. Indeed, I think it would be very difficult to retrieve the score of this work even were one to analyse many of its performances.[34] But no taint attaches to my own account in conceding that performances can sometimes be judged to be accurate only in the light of awareness of the score that is followed.

This discussion leads to two observations, neither of which is congenial to Goodman. Either it is performance practices and conventions, rather than a set of abstract rules characterizing a notational system, that must be taken into account in deriving a score from a performance. Or prior knowledge of (at least some) details of the score followed by the musicians is necessary if a copy of that score is to be derived from an accurate performance. These claims can be generalized. The first point is an epistemological one: often we could not know on the basis of a note-perfect performance what notational system is given for a particular work. The second goes deeper: appeal to notational systems (taken in conjunction with a performance) will not suffice to specify works unless that appeal admits by the back door the social aspects of performance that are excluded from Goodman's account.

What could be meant by 'notational system'? For Goodman, presumably the terms refer to a set of syntactic and semantic rules governing the use of a notation the primary purpose of which is to specify works. Now, if there are comparatively few notational systems, and if they correspond neatly to historical periods and distinctive styles of music, it does not seem to be troublesome to assume we could take them into account. On the other hand, if they are only marginally less varied than are works themselves, little territory will be gained in claiming that pieces are specified under notational systems.

As I see it, Goodman should regard notational systems (or subsystems) as many and diverse. Each kind of temperament implies a different notational system; to the extent that notational elements are specific to particular instruments, each orchestral combination demands its own notational system; different methods for introducing indeterminacy in pitch sequence (or in any other element deemed semantically significant by Goodman) call for their own notational systems. Across the spread of musical works, many of the

---

[34] I have argued (Davies 1991*b*) that scores should be recoverable from performances, provided one has a sufficient number of them and an idea of the work's period, genre, and style. I now think this claim is mistaken, at least as it regards pieces that organize indeterminacy according to arbitrary principles.

items mentioned are variable. As a result, a great many Goodmanian notational systems are in use. But this is conceptually profligate. When notational
systems come close to being unique to each particular work—as they do
under Goodman's theory—they become incapable of contributing usefully to
the analysis either of works or of notations.

The importance of the role Goodman assigns to notational systems stems
from his desire to capture all that is essential to the work's identity in the
notation for it. It is the rules governing the notation that allow an inscription
to function as a score. His approach is misconceived, however. Goodman's
notational systems must become as elaborate and individual as the scores
specified under them. A better alternative recognizes far fewer notational
systems and acknowledges that their application in particular cases may
be both subtle and flexible. This approach does not undermine the integrity
of musical works specified by scores, because it allows that their interpretation is controlled by public conventions and practices the composer assumes
and shares with the musicians he addresses. These take up the slack, as it
were, between the work and its notational expression within a rather general
notational system. This approach also entails that, often, the musicians can
deliver the composer's work only by following his score, and, hence, that
sometimes we can test the accuracy of a performance only by comparing
it with the composer's score. In this respect (but this respect only),
scores take precedence over performances. None of this need cause difficulty,
however, provided we accept that it is not incidental to the nature of
scores as work specifications that they play a functional role in established
musical practices. In particular, they guide performances and, to do so, must
pre-date them. It is not a matter of theoretical indifference within musical
traditions relying on notations for the transmission of works that the score
comes before the performance.

Summary

Whether or not something is a musical score depends not on its form but on
its primary function. Scores designate works and are instructions addressed
to performers. They must be read in terms of the relevant conventions
and presuppose familiarity with the performance practices they invoke.
Some Western scores contain iconic elements depicting (parts of) the sound
structure of the work they specify, but this is not necessary for something's
functioning as a score. Moreover, iconic elements in scores sometimes
depict not the structure to be sounded but another—for instance, where
the composer writes for transposing instruments. Scores may be indeterminate if the works they designate are the same, but incompleteness and
ambiguity in scores are undesirable. Nevertheless, scores with these defects
can be adequate in practice to the specification of works and as guides to

performance. Incomplete notations may serve as mnemonics for musicians already familiar with the piece at issue. Notations offered as descriptions of works or performances, rather than as prescriptions, are notational transcriptions. And, finally, scores are distinct from the works they designate.

As for Goodman, I have argued that he requires too much of notations in expecting them to specify works while divorcing them from the historical context in which they are produced, from the demands of using and following them, and from the conventions and practices they assume.

4

Performances

The setting: a prestigious international piano competition presided over by a panel of judges drawn from the most accomplished, respected, and astute virtuosi, pedagogues, and critics currently active. The session rules have been altered. Under the pretext of minimizing predictable nationalistic and doctrinal prejudice, not only the players' identities but the players themselves have been concealed from the judges. The judges are blindfolded before entering the hall. Each player is labelled by number. The judges are also unaware that not a single person will participate in the competition. The prize will go to a program which drives a conventional piano. No human player participates.

The contest proceeds. Although the level of talent is impressive, the accolades converge in the end on one player whose future developments will be anticipated eagerly, so the judges inform the musical world. The call goes out for the winner to appear. Player #8 appears in a clear acrylic jacket and is respectfully laid on a disk stand specially fashioned for the occasion. As from one voice, a great gasp echoes through the hall.

Something seems to have gone wrong . . . Are we witness to a musical performance here?

(Godlovitch 1998: 125)

In this chapter I discuss musical performances. I have allowed that musical performances need not be of works, in that they can be freely improvised, and I have noted that some works are not for performance. Most pieces are for performance, though. Of these, not all are intended for *live* performance; some are for what I have called studio performance. Nevertheless, many works for performance are intended for live performances, and I concentrate on these.

My focus is on the relation between live performances of works and the works they are of. I begin with this question: what makes a performance of Beethoven's Symphony No. 5 a performance of Beethoven's Symphony No. 5? Other queries quickly follow. If two performances sound the same, are they always of the same work? If two performances sound different, can they be of the same work? Is it possible for a performance simultaneously to be of more than one work? How do we individuate performances of a given work? How do we individuate performance groups?

Necessary conditions for performance

Matching

Works for performance are communicated via instructions addressed to their potential executants. (The relevant directives might be conveyed via model performances but I mainly consider those specified notationally.) The given instructions are mostly work determinative, but may also include recommendations concerning aspects of the work's interpretation. If the performer is to deliver the composer's work, he must satisfy those of the composer's instructions that are work identifying. As was seen in Chapter 1, philosophers vary in their views about what is determinative of musical works. Some regard the work as a timbre-less sound structure (Webster 1974; Kivy 1983), others as a performed sound structure (Levinson 1980a), and yet others as a semantic content generated under a notational system (Goodman 1968). Though they differ in their accounts, all agree that a fully faithful performance must capture whatever is work constitutive. For instance, if a given work is a performed sound structure, an ideally accurate rendition will employ the appropriate instruments to generate the sound structure made normative by its composer. It seems reasonable to propose as a necessary condition for something's being a performance of a given work that it matches what is prescribed as work determinative by the piece's composer (Currie 1988: 123; Hermerén 1993), though it remains to analyse what 'matching' entails.

Not all matching performances of a given work will sound the same. Works are ontologically thinner than the performances instancing them—that is, a performance must, and always does, go beyond the work in embodying it in sound. The composer's instructions, even when taken in conjunction with the appropriate notational conventions and performance practices, leave unsettled many details of the performance. It is for the player to make the relevant decisions. Necessarily, the work is interpreted in being performed, which is why we regard performance as an 'art' in its own right. It follows, then, that two performances of a given work can sound unlike because they involve different interpretations, even though both are completely faithful to the composer's work-determinative instructions. Each performance complies exactly with the composer's specification of the work, though they diverge in their respective interpretations.

There is a second way performances can differ: one might contain mistakes the other does not. A performance might fail to satisfy some of the composer's work-defining directives. For instance, the horn player might fluff his entry. In complex works, a great many things are instructed by the composer and these are frequently extremely difficult to carry through, so it is rare under conditions of live performance to achieve perfection. What is the status of putative performances containing errors?

Performance is a success notion. One can aim to perform a piece and bring it off, but one can also aim to perform a piece and fail in the attempt. If I tried to play Beethoven's Piano Sonata No. 23, Op. 57, 'Appassionata', I would not succeed. My efforts would be so dismal that no one could count them as a rendition of Beethoven's work, not even as a poor one. How, though, are we to regard the efforts of a pianist who comes much closer than me to meeting Beethoven's requirements, but without satisfying all of them? Is success an all-or-nothing affair when it comes to performing musical works, or does it admit of degrees? For some activities, success is hit or miss. I succeeded in turning off the gas before I left home *only* if I extinguished the flame. In other contexts, I can be more or less successful. I succeeded in the exam by passing, but my success was not unqualified because I did less well than I hoped or expected. In some cases we measure success on a scale. If one falls below a minimum standard, one fails in one's aim, but if one meets or surpasses it, one is successful to a degree that depends on the margin by which the threshold is exceeded. The question, then, is this: for a performance to be of a given work, must it meet every one of the composer's instructions, or, instead, do we accept as performances attempts falling short of the ideal? And, if the latter is the case, where and how do we draw the line between performances that are imperfect and those that fail to instance the given work?

Ordinary usage suggests that, as regards performances' instancing works, success is a threshold notion allowing of degrees. We distinguish between good and bad performances, and do so with reference to the accuracy with which the composer's work indications are met, as well as to the interpretation offered. In general, even if a performance contains some errors of which we are aware, we do not hesitate to identify it as of the given work.[1] Indeed, some interpretations, such as Arthur Schnabel's of Beethoven, are highly esteemed despite being peppered with inaccuracies.

Nelson Goodman rejects ordinary language as inadequate to the characterization of musical works. Philosophical theory should not be measured against common discourse, which often muddles crucial distinctions, he thinks. Goodman argues that only a rendition perfectly matching the work's content counts as a performance of it. A performance's success in instancing a work is an all-or-nothing matter.

---

[1] Among the philosophers who hold that errors need not be fatal to performances are Beardsley (1958), Webster (1974), Wolterstorff (1975, 1980, 1987), Kivy (1984), Dipert (1988), Kendall L. Walton (1988), Hernadi (1991), Thom (1993), Hermerén (1993), Predelli (1995), and Edlund (1997).

According to Goodman, a performance of a work is one compliant with its score. Recall that his notion of a score is not the standard one: a score is a character in a notational system. To qualify as such, it must meet certain syntactic and semantic requirements. Not all the elements used in actual musical notations satisfy these conditions, and these elements do not count as part of the score. In particular, the verbal language of tempos ('allegro', etc.) is not notational (Goodman 1968: 185). To comply with a score, the performance must (re)produce those elements denoting the work's semantic content. Conspicuous among these are sequences of pitched notes. Not all compliant performances need to contain exactly the same tones. The score might not prescribe all the notes to be played in a performance. Provided the relevant notational system does not allow for more specific indications, this would be the case for works with a figured bass, or for ones requiring an improvised cadenza (see Goodman 1968: 183–4; 1970: 569; 1972: 98). Performances complying with these notational systems will probably differ (at the level of note sequences) in their realizations of the notated indeterminacies.

So far I have been clarifying what is involved in Goodman's notion of score compliance or work compliance. Now I look more closely at one of his more central and controversial claims: nothing less than perfection is required if a rendition is to qualify as a performance of a work. Why does Goodman think so stringent a condition is called for? He does so because he believes a weaker one would lose its footing on a slope made slippery by the transitivity of identity. It is worth quoting the relevant passage in full, for it contains much that needs discussion.

Since complete compliance with the score is the only requirement for a genuine instance of a work, the most miserable performance without actual mistakes does count as such an instance, while the most brilliant performance with a single wrong note does not. Could we not bring our theoretical vocabulary into better agreement with common practice and common sense by allowing some limited degree of deviation in performances admitted as instances of the work? . . . But this is only one of those cases where ordinary usage gets us quickly into trouble. The innocent-seeming principle that performances differing by just one note are instances of the same work risks the consequence—in view of the transitivity of identity—that all performances whatsoever are of the same work. If we allow the least deviation, all assurance of work-preservation and score-preservation is lost; for by a series of one-note errors of omission or addition, and modifications, we can go all the way from Beethoven's *Fifth Symphony* to *Three Blind Mice*. Thus while a score may leave unspecified many features of a performance, and allow for considerable variation in others within prescribed limits, full compliance with the specifications given is categorically required. This is not to say that the exigencies that dictate our technical discourse need govern our everyday speech. I am no more recommending that in ordinary discourse we refuse to say that a pianist who misses a note has performed a Chopin Polonaise than that we refuse to call a whale a fish, the earth spherical, or a grayish-pink human white. (Goodman 1968: 186–7)

Here is a gloss of Goodman's argument. From a performance of Beethoven's Fifth with one wrong note, derive a score. Perform that score with one wrong note and extract another score from the latest performance. And so on. If the first of the derived scores specifies the same work as the original, then so do the subsequent ones, even if their realizations would sound more like 'Three Blind Mice' than Beethoven's Fifth. Unless one accepts the sameness of Beethoven's piece and the nursery tune, one must deny that the work's identity survives the first note change in its score.

Before tackling Goodman's argument, it is worth considering his examples of slackness in ordinary discourse. He says we call whales fishes. Well, I do not think there is much excuse normally for confusing these and would correct those who do so if this could be done politely, especially if something hangs on the distinction. (Suppose it was said that, because they are fishes, it must be that whales do not care for their offspring.) Pink-and-grey white people? But surely 'white' is often used in this connection to indicate ethnicity or cultural heritage, not colour. Describing the globe as spherical? I am inclined to do that, I suppose. But why think my usage is confused or crude just because a more precise specification is available? When it comes to determining the winner of the 100 metres in the Olympic Games, differences of 0.01 seconds can be extremely significant. The standard of temporal sameness appropriate to other contexts is more relaxed, though. We arrive at the restaurant at the same time so long as we get there within a minute or two of each other. The criteria for sameness, synonymy, and identity do not always cleave to the most precise level of discrimination that is possible. I am not convinced that Goodman succeeds in making his case against ordinary language by noting that a level of precision beyond what is usually sought can be achieved by the canny philosopher.

Do these last comments point to a fault in the slippery slope argument? Does Goodman set an increment of change—one note per version—that is too precise? If it were always the case that one wrong note is harmless whereas five destroy a performance, Goodman's position could be criticized, because changes or errors in a few notes could be acceptable where large-scale alterations would not be. In that case, accepting as legitimate a performance of Beethoven's Fifth Symphony containing one wrong note would not commit one to regarding Beethoven's piece as ultimately indistinguishable from 'Three Blind Mice'. This objection fails, though. At the level of notes, there is no magic number or percentage that must be right if a performance is to qualify as such.

The problem with Goodman's argument is not that it sets a unit of change that is too precise, but that it relies on an inappropriate one. So long as the notational system of the musical work accords significance to tones of determinate pitch, as is true for the majority of pieces he considers, Goodman regards the fundamental units of the work as its notes. He treats the (performed) sound structure of such pieces as successions of tones, all of which are equal in significance. Of course he is wrong to think this way. In the political economy of music, not all notes are equal (Boretz 1970; Webster 1971; Edlund 1996). In tonal or modal music, the tonic is crucial. In chords, the root is basic (even if it is implied rather than sounded), whereas sixths add seasoning. In melodies, the notes constituting the structural skeleton are more significant than embellishments, passing tones, grace notes, and appoggiaturas. In brief, we experience some notes as more important than others. We hear hierarchically connected gestalts—chords, rhythmic and melodic motives, phrases, themes, expositions, codas, and the like—not solely a procession of pitched tones.

In Chapter 2 I observed that, in sonata form movements in the minor key, the second subject theme typically appears in the relative major in the exposition and in the tonic minor in the recapitulation. Usually it differs in these versions by at least one note. Now, by the slippery slope argument, we should deny that the *same* theme appears in both places, because to accept its identity in these occurrences should commit us to regarding it as equivalent to all others. Of course this is a nonsense. We should identify the theme as the same in its recapitulation and we cannot comprehend the music's structure unless we do so. Insisting on the non-identity of the respective themes would engender, not clarity and precision, but confusion and misunderstanding.

A musical pattern can survive the reorganization of some (sometimes many) of its elements, and can also be destroyed by the slightest alteration in others. If the melody, exposition, and movement survive changes to their notes, then the work can, because melodies, expositions, movements, and the like are the units constituting its identity. And if a different alteration renders the melody irrecoverable, the attempt at performance collapses. There can be every reason for discriminating between wrong notes, accepting one yet being flummoxed by another. In consequence, Goodman's slippery slope argument fails, and does so because it wrongly assumes all notes recorded by the notation to be on the same footing. Had the argument appealed to gestalts, like melodies, it could be endorsed. If none of the themes of Beethoven's Fifth Symphony can be heard in a playing episode, is that event a performance of Beethoven's symphony? Of course not!

Tones are basic elements in semantically significant musical structures (such as chords, motives, and themes), and it is at the level of notes (usually) that composers write scores. To change the specified tones is to ignore the score and, thereby, is to make an error. Musical works are heard, however, not as a succession of unrelated tones, but as patterned sound (Scruton 1974, 1997; Harrison 1978; Ingarden 1986; Kendall L. Walton 1988; Davies 1991*b*). Goodman has nothing to say about the way we *experience* sounded music (Ackerman 1981; Raffman 1993*a,b*). (As I have already indicated, this is apparent in his characterizing tempo as an interpretative feature of performances, not a work property, which entails that a performance can instance the work perfectly although it cannot be *heard* as music, so slow is it.) Accordingly, he treats any wrong note as fatal to work performance. In fact, our recognition of themes, sections, and the like—that is, the kind of experience involved in judgements of musical sameness, of identity—operates at a higher and more sophisticated level than Goodman supposes. His account of the relation between musical works and their performances does not achieve a perspicuity fuzzied over by ordinary discourse. The reverse. It generates false and irrelevant distinctions as a result of misidentifying the elements crucial to the identity of works.

Another challenge to Goodman's slippery slope argument also stresses his indifference to the manner in which music is experienced. Wrong notes could easily mislead the listener if she were incapable of detecting them. Very often, though, she can recognize performance errors as such and knows what tone should have been sounded instead, even on hearing a work for the first time (Ziff 1973; Davies 1991*b*; Edlund 1996). Detected wrong notes do not undermine the identity of the work to the same extent as unrecognized mistakes. The context established by the earlier parts of the work sometimes assists the listener in locating mistakes in its performance; at other times, her knowledge of the work's general style and genre makes this possible. Goodman ignores the relevance to the listener's experience of her prior familiarity with the work in hand, with similar pieces, and with musical styles and genres. He treats all performances as if they are encountered in a cultural vacuum, whereas, in fact, the relevant background knowledge is required in the accomplished listener.

A further feature of the performance context is ignored by Goodman: the performers' intentions and the audience's awareness of these. In performance, most departures from the work are the result of unintended slips. Goodman is indifferent to the way inaccuracies occur; from his point of view, it does not matter if they are accidental or deliberate. There is an important difference between these possibilities, though. Deliberate departures should be considered for their significance and effects, whereas unintended errors are to be disregarded. Slips do not count in the performance as the correct notes do. The listener knows the musicians usually aim at perfection, which is difficult to achieve, so she treats wrong notes as at odds with the goal of performance (Predelli 1999). She might regard blunders as detracting from performances— in that sense they count—but, where the identity of a performance is in question, she puts them aside.

In trying to achieve precision in his analysis, Goodman offers an account of the work and its performance that abstracts and decontextualizes them.[2] He regards the score as a specification or description, rather than as instructions issued by the composer to the performer. In this way, he cuts the work loose from its creator and the context of composition. His notion of performance requires merely that the score be *matched*, not *followed*. Yet, if scores are instructions, then performance must be intentional, because following an instruction—doing what is required because it is instructed—must be a deliberate action. In treating scores merely as notational descriptions of works, Goodman's account leaves aside the intentional and normative aspects of performance. Also, it reduces the piece to the level of tone succession and thereby divorces it from many of the features normally regarded as giving musical pieces their identity. Higher semantic units, such as themes and their development, seem to drop out of the picture, along with their expressive or referential qualities (Ackerman 1981; Clark 1982; Pearce 1988b). Finally, he removes the work from the listener's experience of sound, and the recognizability of a performance no longer counts as a criterion of its success in instancing the given work.

Goodman's approach is neither appropriate nor successful. For all the pains he takes in abstracting musical works from their social setting and the human element involved in their creation, performance, and reception, his emphasis on scores, to the extent that what he says seems plausible, is bound to smuggle in such factors, though he allows no legitimate place for them within his theory (Ziff 1971). As I emphasized in the previous chapter, musical notations can be understood only in terms of the conventions and performance practices assumed as their background. The appropriate interpretation of a musical notation requires that it be contextualized. Admittedly, Goodman calls for scorability, not scores that dictate work performances. So, he might accept that a work could be promulgated via a model performance. But this would not save his theory. Since the semantic content identifying the given work falls short of the model's full detail, it must be by reference to conventions and practices that we sort properties of the work from local performance features. Because these are historically and socially relative, the implicit appeal to contextual features cannot be avoided (Levinson 1980b; Lee B. Brown 1996).

I have written enough here and earlier to make clear my disagreements with Goodman. I think a performance can be of a work although it contains wrong notes. Such a performance instances the work imperfectly, but instances it nonetheless. It is a virtue of my view that it accords with ordi-

---

[2] Pearce (1988b) characterizes Goodman's account as *extensional*, because it takes no account of intentions or other propositional attitudes and it ignores the social settings in which works are produced and performed. See also Margolis (1993).

nary parlance in this respect, for such ways of talking are neither confused nor unsatisfactorily approximate, as Goodman maintains. Also, I believe the features crucial to the identity of musical works are generated at the level of motives, chords, melodies, harmonic progressions, and so on, not at the lower level of note successions. I regard tempo, expressiveness, and appropriate embellishment as constitutive properties of musical works, not merely as aspects of performance interpretations. I accept, though, that the performer is often free within limits set by the composer to vary such factors. And I take the listener's experience and awareness of such features as central to the way performances, and the works they instantiate, are identified and described. Furthermore, I regard scores as prescriptive and, thereby, as distinguishable from other (descriptive) varieties of musical notations. As a corollary, I think performance is an intentional activity. Scores implicate the historical and social contexts in which they are generated, for the instructions they encode can be understood only by the person aware of the conventions by which they are to be read. Many qualities integral to a work's identity depend on performance practices that, because they are taken for granted, are ignored in the work's notation. In consequence, a musical work cannot be equated with a score's semantic content unless it is also accepted that this content depends as much on cultural practices and contexts that are its background as on the syntactic character of the system of notation that is used. In brief, I reject Goodman's extensional account of musical works and their performance in favour of an intensional one.

Jerrold Levinson's theory is intensional in that it regards musico-historical relations, including the identity of the composer herself, as among the factors determining a work's identity. How does he handle the issue of wrong notes? In the first place, he makes a terminological distinction (1980*a*: 26; also 1987). A *performance* of a musical work is a sound event intended to instantiate the work—that is, it is an attempt to exemplify the work's performed sound structure in accordance with the composer's indication of it—and that succeeds to a reasonable degree. An *instance* of the work is a performance that conforms *exactly* to the work's performed sound structure. Because most performances fail to some extent in their goal of exemplifying the work's performed sound structure, not all performances of the work are instances of it. Incorrect performances *are* performances, but they are not instances.

I find this terminology cumbersome. The distinction between performances and instances can be indicated well enough by distinguishing, among performances that instance the work, those that are accurate from those that are less so. The performances of a work can be more or less well formed—that is, musical works are *norm kinds* (as recommended by Wolterstorff 1975).

The terminological issue is not of much importance, though. The crux concerns the boundary between failed and imperfect performances. It is because Goodman doubts there is a principled way of making this distinction that he

avoids facing it by insisting that any departure from the specified sound structure results in failure. How does Levinson draw the relevant distinction? To
qualify as such, a performance must 'succeed to a reasonable degree' in exemplifying the given work's performed sound structure. 'What constitutes a
"reasonable degree", and thus what differentiates poor or marginal performance from nonperformance, is for many compositions perhaps marked by
the ability of an informed and sensitive listener to grasp, at least roughly,
what [performed sound] structure is struggling to be presented' (1980*a*: 26
n. 33; for Levinson's account of the informed and sensitive listener, see
1990*d*). Elsewhere Levinson (1987: 76) adds this:

> The line between *somewhat incorrect performances* and *nonperformances* is not a
> sharp one. I am inclined to think of a questionable performance of a work as still a
> performance (albeit incorrect) if its shortcomings are largely a matter of *execution*,
> while inclined on the other hand to discount it as a performance at all when its
> shortcomings are largely a matter of substantial *modification or flouting* of defining
> features.

Levinson is right to be wary of being specific. As I wrote earlier, there is
no measure at the level of notes such that a performance fails if the total of
errors exceeds that amount. This is because not all musically significant
elements—themes and the like—can be reduced simply to tone sequences.
Levinson is also wise to emphasize that the listener's experience of the putative performance is relevant to our assessment of its success or failure as an
instance of the work. If one cannot tell what work the musicians are trying
to play, the performance is a failure. On the other hand, if one can hear the
work in a performance, distorted as that experience may be by mistakes, the
performance qualifies as of the work (provided the other necessary conditions for work performance are satisfied). It is worth recalling how resilient
pieces can be. The school orchestra can deliver what is unmistakably the
march from Bizet's *Carmen*, although the performance is riddled with wrong
and out-of-tune notes.

What a listener recovers of the work from her experience of its intended
performance obviously depends not just on the players' efforts but also on
the listener's knowledge and experience of the work's style and period, of the
composer's output, of other renditions of that same work, and of the score
(if there is one). Inevitably, this introduces a degree of relativity into the
account. But it does not entail that the notion of performance is entirely
subjective. As noted previously, musical works are written for sophisticated
audiences. If they are to be understood, the listener must bring with her a
considerable familiarity with musical and performance conventions and practices. (This is not to suppose that she requires formal training; the appropriate knowledge might be acquired through attention and exposure to
performances of many works (see Davies 1994*a*: ch. 7; 1994*b*).) Finally,

Levinson is correct to stress the relevance of the audience's grasp of what the performers are trying to do. As I have explained, one important reason why wrong notes need not prove fatal to the attempt at performance is that they can be identified as errors by the listener. This is made possible not only by the listener's prior acquaintance with the work, its score, or its style, but also by her assurance that the performers are doing their utmost to present the advertised work. Performers do sometimes ignore or flout the composer's instructions, but, in general, must intend to follow these where their aim is to deliver his work. If we know the performer has no intention of sticking to the majority of a composer's instructions, we are liable to regard her playing as 'after' the work it resembles, but not as *of* that work.

So far I have examined the claim that it is a necessary condition of something's being a performance that it matches or reproduces the work's contents. Though some, such as Goodman, insist that 'matching' requires perfection, I have recommended a more relaxed view. An ideally correct performance requires exact matching, but a performance can qualify as such although it adds a few notes or note types not specified by the composer, or omits others that are determinatively indicated, provided that the higher semantic structures remain sufficiently intact that they can be recognized by appropriate listeners, these being ones possessed of the kind of background knowledge that places them to identify works of the relevant kind. What is necessary for performance is a degree of matching; enough, that is, to allow the listener to make out the work, however dimly. Obviously the listener will be seriously handicapped in appreciating and understanding the work if, because of performance mistakes, she can be confident of little more than its identifying outline. But this is what one would expect. If we desire to understand and appreciate works, inaccuracies usually detract from their performances. Even if errors do not defeat the minimal success of a performance's attempt to instance the given work, they are undesirable, given that the usual aim of performance is to make the work comprehensible and appreciable, not merely to make it identifiable.

At the outset I mentioned that, as a condition for performance, it is the work's contents that must be matched, though I tried to be neutral about what these are in light of the many theories on this topic. In the discussion, I tended to concentrate on matching at the level of sound structures and tone sequences. This was natural for several reasons. The most obvious performance blunders arise at this level. And all theories count these basic elements as central to work identity, whatever else they might add to the list of a work's ingredients. Now, though, it is important to register again the point that most theories of musical ontology regard pieces as more than indicated sound sequences. In consequence, they can hold of two sonically indistinguishable performances, each of which is note perfect, that they might instance different works.

Levinson makes the point explicitly (1980a: 25–6): two composers, working independently at the same time and place, create different works even if they produce identical scores. Performances of these two works could sound exactly the same, though one was of the first and the other of the second. (As I discuss later, he rules out the possibility that each performance is of both works.) More surprising, perhaps, is the fact that Goodman could make the same point, though his examples would have to be different. In the previous chapter (pp. 144–5) I described the works of Marthoven and Ribaldi. An ideally accurate performance of the Martian's Fifth Symphony could sound just the same as a perfect rendition of Beethoven's Fifth Symphony; similarly, the sound appropriator's piece might sound in performance just like Antonio Vivaldi's *Four Seasons*. For Goodman, a performance is one compliant with the work's score. These various works are written under different notational systems that, taken in conjunction with the sound sequence displayed in the performances, give rise to differing musico-semantic structures. If we know the notational system applying to the performance of Marthoven's work, we find exemplified in the Martian performance a semantic content (and, hence, a work) different from that generated by the sound-alike performance of Beethoven's Fifth. The same applies to the performances of Ribaldi's and Vivaldi's pieces. These all instance different works because they express or represent different musico-semantic contents, as is apparent when the raw sound sequences are located within the various notational systems in which they operate as characters. Even if matching at the level of raw sound sequences is necessary for Good-manian compliance, it becomes sufficient only when taken in conjunction with a notational system through which it expresses the relevant (that is, work-identifying) semantic content.

David Pearce (1988b) claims it is implausible to hold that the total of all perceivable qualities of a performance as a sound event do not suffice to determine which of two different musical works is being played.[3] He proposes this as an objection to Levinson's view and implies Goodman's theory avoids the difficulty. Levinson (1990a) responds: what Pearce finds implausible is, nevertheless, manifestly true. I agree, but I draw attention to the exchange to make another point. Goodman's theory of compliance does not entail the conclusion Pearce finds desirable. Only theorists who analyse musical works as pure sound structures *simpliciter*, and who regard matching both as neces-sary and as sufficient for performance, would agree with his conclusion.[4]

---

[3] A related view is presented by Cone, who writes: 'a score can be said to embody a compo-sition only if its directions, correctly followed, lead to results that can be aurally recognised as performances of the same piece of music' (1967: 104). Cone adopts this stance because he wishes to deny to indeterministic avant-garde pieces by Stockhausen and Cage the status of musical works.

[4] Several critics (Savile 1971; Levinson 1980b; Carrier 1982; Wilsmore 1987) have suggested

Performance intentions

Even if it is necessary that a performance matches or reproduces to a reasonable extent the identifying features of a work, is this all that is required for its being a performance of the given work? Is matching also a sufficient condition for work performance? There is good reason to think not. Suppose I improvise on my harpsichord something that happens to correspond to J. S. Bach's *Two Part Invention in C major*, though I know nothing of it—unconscious memories and the like are ruled out. Do I perform Bach's piece? Goodman would maintain I do, perhaps, but here is another case where his theory runs counter to widely held intuitions. I deny that my improvising counts as a performance of Bach's *Invention*, though it sounds like Bach's work and a listener might incidentally learn from my playing how Bach's piece sounds.[5] To be a performance of Bach's *Invention*, more than an accidental correspondence is needed between my output and what Bach specified. The further condition most frequently identified as necessary for performance requires that the player *intends* to achieve what the composer specified as constituting her work (Tormey 1974; Wolterstorff 1975, 1980; Dipert 1993). In this account, with which I concur, performance necessarily is intentional. Works are promulgated via instructions issued by their composers and they are performed only when it is by following these instructions that matching is achieved.

There is an obvious difficulty with the notion that performance necessarily is intentional—often musicians intend to play one work and succeed in realizing an entirely different one. In the past, players aimed to perform a trumpet voluntary by Henry Purcell but ended up playing one by Jeremiah Clarke, or they intended to play Franz Joseph Haydn's String Quartet, Op. 3 No. 5, but delivered a serenade by Pater Romanus Hofstetter instead, or they performed a mass by Noel Bauldeweyn though they intended to give Josquin de Prez's *Missa Da Pacem*. The work the musicians intended to execute did not exist. It was attributed to one composer when, in fact, it was written by another. If they performed Clarke's, Hofstetter's, and

that Goodman's theory cannot cope with non-identical but perceptually indistinguishable works, because he ignores the contextual factors that make the difference between them. My claim is that, by relativizing works to the notational systems under which they are specified, Goodman imports enough contextual factors to avoid this objection's first thrust. It is true, though, that he denies the relevance of the work's setting and seems not to appreciate the ontological implication of his appeal to differences in notational systems.

[5] Among the philosophers who do not think this kind of improvisation results in a performance of Bach's music are Wolterstorff (1980), Levinson (1980*b*), Mark (1981), Carrier (1983), Kendall L. Walton (1988), Thom (1993), and Predelli (1999*b*). Dipert (1993) and Godlovitch (1998) stress the special kind of agency—an agency that is missing from my example—involved in musical performance.

Bauldeweyn's works, which seems reasonable to me, then this suggests there was no connection between what they intended and what they achieved. They intended to play pieces by Purcell, Haydn, and Josquin, but instanced ones by Clarke, Hofstetter, and Bauldeweyn, composers who might have been completely unknown to them. Though they intended to perform a composer's work, it looks as if that intention was irrelevant to what they did, and, hence, irrelevant to performance, since they succeeded in performing works other than the ones they took themselves to be playing.

I do not believe these examples force one to abandon the claim that performance must be intentional, but they do invite a careful consideration of the intentions a performer might have. These can be separated into three levels. Typically the performer intends:

(a) to follow the determinative instructions issued via the score or model performance (irrespective of who first specified them),
(b) to play X's work (where 'X' is the name of a composer), and
(c) to satisfy (b) as a result of achieving (a).

In the standard case, (a) and (b) correspond. I aim to perform Beethoven's 'Appassionata', I intend to follow the instructions encoded in the score in front of me, and let us suppose that the score in front of me truly represents Beethoven's 'Appassionata'. Naturally enough, I do not distinguish between the relevant intentions, since I take them to be transparent to each other.

Cases of the misattribution of authorship reveal that the (a)-level intention does the work, whether or not the performer distinguishes this from the higher-level (b) or (c)-type intentions he has. The same conclusion is implied by other familiar cases. Players can present pieces whose composers are unknown. I am not debarred from performing a work whose composer is indicated as *anon*. Moreover, many pieces, such as 'Happy Birthday' and 'Auld Lang Syne', are played by people who have no idea who composed them. These examples suggest that, even if performance necessarily is intentional, it does not require knowledge of the composer's identity. All that is needed is an appropriate (a)-level intention.

Although (a)-level intentions are indifferent to the composer's identity, they cannot also be unconcerned with the musico-historical context in which the score was penned. In order to satisfy the (a)-level intention—that is, to follow the determinative instructions issued via the score—the performer must be able to recognize those instructions and, as I argued in the previous chapter, this means he must be aware of the notational and performance conventions and practices presumed by the work's composer. Because the relevant conventions and practices vary from time to time and place to place, it follows that, if he is to perform the given work faithfully, the player must be able to locate the work's score in the appropriate cultural and historical setting, even if he cannot identify (or if he misidentifies) its author.

Levinson (1980*a*) insists that that performance must be intentional. Pearce (1988*a*) objects on the grounds that this rules out the possibility of an *accidental* performance of a musical work. Levinson (1990*a*) agrees but wonders why this is proposed as an objection to his view. If a performer creates a performed sound structure that happens to correspond to the work's, he does not perform it if there is no connection between what he does and the composer's writing a work by issuing instructions to its potential performers. It is plain, though, that Levinson has in mind a certain kind of case and he is right to want to exclude it. It is one where there is a coincidental resemblance between what the performer does and a given work. It would be wrong, I think, to allow that I accidentally perform Bach's *Inventions*, or that the Berlin Philarmonic could be playing Marthoven's Fifth when they take themselves to be giving Beethoven's Fifth. There is another possibility Levinson overlooks, however, and it may be the one Pearce has in mind. One can play Hofstetter's serenade by accident. This occurs when one sets out to play a piece by Haydn that happens to be by Hofstetter. A performance results, and it might reasonably be described as serendipitous in that it was never in the performers' minds to play any work by Hofstetter, a composer of whom they might never have heard. As I see it, Pearce is right to think a performance can be accidental and wrong to believe this is prohibited by the claim that performance must be intentional. Meanwhile, Levinson is right to deny that unintended similarities are sufficient for performance, but wrong to think the intentionality of performance rules out all possibilities of accidental renditions. In other words, neither Pearce nor Levinson distinguish carefully enough between the low-level intention that is crucial for performance and the higher-level intentions that are not.

So far I have been stressing that, though performance necessarily is intentional, the required intention is rather weak. It is not directly aimed at a particular composer or work. It focuses on the score in hand and, apart from identifying the musico-historical context relevant to interpreting the notation, it leaves connections between the score and its composer to take care of themselves. Alternatively, it latches onto a model performance and, apart from distinguishing work-determinative features from performance details in the light of a historically informed view of what kind of piece the model instances, it leaves connections between the model performance and the work's composer to take care of themselves.

Weak though it may be, it might be thought that my specification of the necessary intention is yet too strong. Performers sometimes deliberately ignore composers' work-identifying instructions, but succeed, nevertheless, in performing their works. Suppose for the sake of this argument that its performance means is among the work-defining features of Bach's *Inventions* and also that the modern piano is excluded from the list of possible performance means. Knowing this, I might still choose to play the *Inventions* on my piano, and it seems reasonable to conclude I might succeed. Therefore, it is not necessary for a performance's being of a work that the player intends to follow all the determinative instructions issued via its score.

To the extent that it fails to instantiate an identifying feature of Bach's piece, my piano performance is less than perfect. I noted earlier, though, that a performance need not be ideal to qualify as such, so long as the work can be perceived by a suitably qualified listener in the flawed rendition. A work often remains recognizable when its instrumentation is altered, provided its sound structure is preserved. This does not show that its performance means is never part of a work—I argued in Chapter 2 against that view. It does indicate, however, that deliberately introduced changes in instrumentation are usually less disfiguring of performances than are alterations undermining high-level sound structures. Errors in execution need not lead to the failure of an attempt at work performance. I allow here that the same applies when departures from the composer's instructions are deliberately introduced. It is appropriate to ameliorate the requirement that performances be intentional. If he is to succeed in performing the composer's work, the performer must intend to follow at least as many work-determinative instructions as will make the performance recognizably of the work in question. In practice, this means intending to follow most of them, though some—instrumentation, dynamics, marked repeats—are more dispensable than others.

The causal connection

At this stage two conditions have been identified as necessary for something's counting as a performance of a given work: the playing should match the work (more or less) and the performer should follow the composer's work-determinative instructions (more or less). Are these two jointly sufficient, or is a further necessary condition needed? I believe one is. It is possible the performers intend to follow the instructions in the score in front of them and their playing matches some work, but the work matched is not the one specified in the score. (Perhaps an evil demon controls the musicians' actions.) If the first two conditions can be pulled apart in this way, we need a third that can be guaranteed to keep them together.[6] If any performance is achieved, I think it must be of the work specified in the score the musicians are trying to follow. The matching that is the goal of performance should not arise by a fluke. It should depend on an unbroken chain of connections that leads

---

[6] Predelli (1995) maintains that a *reasonable* intention to perform a work is sufficient to ensure its performance, but he builds much more into the notion of 'reasonableness' than is usually associated with intentions.

from the sounds made to the performer's actions and intentions, from those to the notation in front of her, and from that via accurate copying processes to the score written by the composer.[7] This new condition requires a robust causal chain linking the work specified by the composer to the sound event produced by the performer, so the match between the two depends on their systematic and intimate connection.[8]

This addition provides a new perspective on the earlier discussion of imperfect performances. In considering why we would be prepared to accept performances as of the target work despite their containing mistakes, I have suggested this is because they are intended as such, with the errors resulting from accidents, and because we can often tell what would have been correct. To this it can now be added that the errors, as much as the right notes, connect to the composer's act of work creation if the performer who made them was trying to follow a score that is causally related to the one made by the composer. Despite its malformedness, a performance with errors instances the work at least because it possesses the same causal pedigree as correct performances.

Furthermore, the causal condition helpfully provides a new way of describing the second requirement concerning the performer's intentions. The low-level intention I have identified as necessary for performance—the intention to follow the score (whoever wrote it)—always tracks the causal chain leading back to the work's composer. Because the intention is referentially opaque, the performer cannot be sure to whom it leads, but he can be certain it hits its target. From his point of view, if he does not know or care who wrote the piece, the intention begins and stops with the notation he plays from. Nevertheless, since the intention assumes there are instructions and, hence, someone who issued them, it seeks out that person. Now, higher-level intentions, such as intending to play Beethoven's Fifth Symphony, will also track the causal chain, if Beethoven wrote a fifth symphony and the music before the players represents a true copy of his score. The situation is different when the performers intend to play Purcell's *Trumpet Voluntary*. Their higher intention goes astray. It connects with Purcell but it bypasses Jeremiah Clarke, the composer of the performed work. Because low-level intentions must cleave to the causal chain that runs to the work's composer, they are the

---

[7] As Fisher observes (1998), a different causal line traces the connection between a purely electronic work and the disks that encode it—namely, the disk must be produced by causal processes emanating in the right way from the original master.

[8] There is a parallel here with the theory of perception. For genuine perception, not only should the subject's sense impressions match the way the world is, but also this should depend on a direct causal relation that generates the resemblance. Without that mechanism, there may be no distinction between one's seeing the scene before one and one's imaging that scene in one's mind's eye while being oblivious to what actually is there. (Hermerén 1993 draws a similar parallel with the causal theory of reference. I prefer my analogy, if only to avoid considering some of the objections faced by the causal theory of reference (see Kroon 1987 and Jackson 1997).)

ones necessary for performance. Because high-level intentions might always take their own route, one heading away from the composer of the work played, they are not necessary for performance.

Levinson considers as significant the causal link between the performance and the composer's act of creation. He writes (1980*a*: 26): 'an instance of [a work] *W* is typically produced, either directly or indirectly, from a score that can be causally traced and is intentionally related by the performer, to the act of creation of *W* by [the composer] *A*.' Elsewhere he is more explicit about the path connecting the composer's work indications with the performance. 'If Haydn pens a piano trio in 1789 and the Artaria publishing house sets up galleys based on Haydn's autographed manuscript in 1790 and some Viennese amateurs correctly produce an instance of the involved [sound/performance means] structure by reading from one of those Artaria editions in 1791, a genuine instance of Haydn's trio . . . has been sounded' (Levinson 1980*b*: 374). Moreover, he allows, as I would also, that performances treated as models preserve an appropriate causal tie to the composer's creation of the given work. 'If Schwartz listens to Milstein play the chaconne from Bach's Violin Partita in D Minor and subsequently (*mirabilu dictu*!) plays perfectly what he has just heard, Schwartz probably produces an instance of it, even if he does not know what a chaconne is or who Bach is' (Levinson 1980*b*: 374).

Levinson also mentions the causal bond between the composer's work-indications and the players' performance in the following passage:

It seems that, in order for a performance to be a performance *of* [work] *W*, not only must it fit and be intended to fit the [sound/performance means] structure of [the composer] *A*'s work *W*; there must be some *connection*, more or less direct, between the sound event produced and *A*'s creative activity. Whether this is primarily an intentional or causal connection is a difficult question, but, unless it is present, I think we are loath to say that *A*'s work has been performed. Consider two composers, Sterngrab and Grotesteen, who compose quartets with identical [sound/performance means] structures, suppose even that they share the same musico-historical context. Now imagine that the Aloysius Ensemble, who are great friends of Sterngrab, give the ill-attended premiere of Sterngrab's Quartet op. 21. Clearly, the Aloysius have performed Sterngrab's Quartet op. 21—but have they also performed Grotesteen's Quartet op. 21? I think not. Why? For several reasons: they don't know Grotesteen; they weren't using Grotesteen's scores; they didn't believe themselves to be presenting Grotesteen's work—in short, there was no connection between their performance and Grotesteen the creator. Grotesteen's creating his op. 21 Quartet had nothing whatever to do with the sound event produced by the Aloysius Ensemble on the afore-mentioned occasion. (Levinson 1980*a*: 25–6)

Recall from Chapter 2 that Levinson believes musical works are specific to their composers and that composers independently producing otherwise indistinguishable work indications at the same time and place write different pieces. I disagree. In my view, only a single work is composed if two composers from the same musico-historical situation independently produce semantically equivalent scores. Accordingly, I would give a different account of the scenario described earlier. Any performance traceable to the compositional acts of either Sterngrab or Grotesteen instances the same piece. If the causal chain terminates with Sterngrab, he is the source of the work that is given, but that work is the same as Grotesteen's. This difference between Levinson and myself is not directly relevant to the point at issue, though, so let us assume that Sterngrab and Grotesteen operate in different musico-historical circumstances, so that in my view as well as Levinson's they compose different works. For example, imagine Sterngrab worked in late-nineteenth-century Europe, whereas Grotesteen is a deliberately retrogressive composer living in mid-twentieth-century America. (Also assume the notational conventions and performance practices have remained much the same and that the scores are identical.)

Levinson gives three reasons why the Aloysius quartet performs Sterngrab's, not Grotesteen's, work. One of these—that the musicians do not know Grotesteen—is entirely without merit. One need not *know* a composer, or even know *of* her, before one can perform her piece.[9] How many of those who have sung 'Joy to the World' know it was written by Handel? Another of Levinson's reasons—that the musicians do not believe themselves to be presenting Grotesteen's work—is equally inadequate. As observed previously, one might end up performing a piece by Jeremiah Clarke, although one does not believe oneself to be playing a work by him. If Levinson is correct in thinking Sterngrab's piece is performed, as I believe, it is for the other reason he offers: the musicians were using Sterngrab's score, not Grotesteen's. This is to say, via the scores they use, the performers' efforts are causally connected to Sterngrab's compositional efforts rather than to Grotesteen's.

Though Levinson endorses the importance of the causal connection under standard circumstances, he is reluctant to accept it as a necessary condition for performance. This is because he can imagine cases where one work is performed, yet the causal chain appears to lead, not to the act of creation in which the performed work had its genesis, but, instead, to a different compositional event. Here is his reasoning:

Suppose I intend to play a famous waltz by Y I have not heard and have never seen the score of. Someone devilishly gives me a score of the Dadaistic composer Z's recent waltz, which strangely enough has the same [sound/performance means] structure as Y's waltz. I would think that the sound event I produce is a performance of Y's waltz,

---

[9] Not even Levinson can take himself seriously. As I have just recorded, he writes that Schwartz plays Bach's chaconne by copying Nathan Milstein's performance, 'even if he does not know . . . who Bach is' (Levinson 1980b: 374).

not of *Z*'s waltz. Yet there is no continuous causal chain running from *Y*'s creative act of indication to my performance of *Y*'s waltz. (There is only my *intentionally* relating what I am doing to *Y*'s creative activity.) This suggests that at least in some cases it is what you think you are reproducing or performing, not what copies or scores you are actually using, that determines what work the result belongs to—assuming the appropriate pure structure gets instantiated. I am inclined to think that in any case in which intentional and causal criteria are in conflict, the former will determine the identity of the performance.   (Levinson 1980*b*: 382 n. 25)[10]

If we assume the prankster knew of the identity of *Y*'s and *Z*'s scores, I share Levinson's intuition that *Y*'s work is the one performed. I do not agree, however, with the moral he draws, that high-level intentions sometimes trump causal connections in settling which work a performance is of. Before getting to that, it will help in clarifying the issues to consider some similar examples. In all these fantasies I believe the outcome is that Sterngrab's piece, not Grotesteen's, is played.

Levinson's tale includes devilish deception. This may be crucial in assessing if works and performances can be forged (Janaway 1999) but is not relevant to the present discussion, as the following scenarios show. All copies of Sterngrab's score are mislaid prior to a projected performance of his work. Knowing that Grotesteen's score is identical, the Aloysius Quartet substitutes it and goes ahead with the concert. Here is another plot. When Sterngrab's score comes to the publisher, it is seen to be the same as Grotesteen's, which was published earlier. A new title page is created, but the plates prepared for printing Grotesteen's piece are used in running off editions of Sterngrab's. In aiming to play Sterngrab's piece, the Aloysius Quartet uses one of these editions.

So far the substitution is always made by someone who knows the scores are the same. It is not necessary, however, for the person who makes the substitution to be the one aware of the correspondence. For example, I might make public my intention to play Sterngrab's piece (with which I am not familiar). I accidentally grab Grotesteen's score from the shelf. An observer notices my oversight but does not intervene, believing that, since the scores are identical, I can play Sterngrab's piece by reading Grotesteen's score.

In the cases already described, someone is aware the scores are the same, but here are two others in which no one knows of the change. I intend to play Sterngrab's piece, but grab Grotesteen's score, and do not recognize my error precisely because, being familiar with Sterngrab's piece, nothing about the music alerts me to my mistake. Alternatively, at the publishing house, the printer enters Sterngrab's piece into a computer. Neither he nor anyone

---

[10] Notice that, in a later reprint of this paper, Levinson weakens his claim slightly (see 1990*b*: 99–100 n. 23).

else knows it is the same as Grotesteen's, which was published earlier. As it is designed to do, the computer tidies up its hard disk by automatically running a utility that erases redundant data. The electronic representation of Sterngrab's score is expunged. After this process, two separate header files 'point' to the block of data that was created when Grotesteen's piece was entered into the computer. Again, scores are printed and the Aloysius Quartet intends to play Sterngrab's work from one that identifies Sterngrab as the work's composer.

Now, I assume all these examples would be accepted by Levinson as equivalent to his earlier one. For that, he says Sterngrab's work is played, though there is no continuous causal chain running from Sterngrab's act of work indication to the Aloysius Quartet's performance of Sterngrab's piece. Because he thinks the causal chain leads to Grotesteen, though Sterngrab's work is indeed given, Levinson looks for some other connection between the performance and Sterngrab's act of composition. He believes it is the performers' high-level intentions that do the job of identifying which work is performed.

I have suggested that the intention to perform X's work, where 'X' is a name, is not essential to performance. And I would go further: even where this high-level intention is present, it does not take precedence over causal chains from which it deviates. Where there is no principled way of showing what distinguishes the two sorts of cases, I think it is implausible to hold that the causal link sometimes trumps higher-order intentions in determining which work is performed (as is so when the musicians intend to play Haydn but succeed in performing Hofstetter) while the higher intentions are dominant at others (as is allegedly so in the puzzle cases just described). To defend my view that a performance of a given work is necessarily connected by a causal thread to the composer's creation of it, I need to argue that the puzzle cases are ones in which, contrary to Levinson's perception, there is a robust causal chain between the performance and Sterngrab's act of composition, since it is his work, not Grotesteen's, that is played.

When we trace the causes of a present situation back to the past, many paths open before us. Where the current event arose from a confluence of factors, we might first isolate one and look for its determinants, then another, and so on. This process reveals a reticulated web of causal lines, some of which will be more significant than others in explaining the eventual outcome. What settles which these are? One way of discovering this would be by changing the past and then observing the ramifications in the present. We would tweak prior elements of a given causal chain to see if bells ring in the sector of the present that interests us. Of course, we cannot really tickle the past to see who laughs now, so the experiment must be counterfactual. We can test the causal possibilities for robustness by considering if there is a counterfactual dependency between present and historically prior events. If the relevant part of the present would have been other than it is had a given bit of the past been different, there is a robust causal connection between the two. But if the relevant part of the present would not have been affected by a change in a given bit of the past, the connection between the two is fragile or non-existent.[11]

The counterfactual dependency apparent in my puzzle cases reveals a more robust connection between the present performance and Sterngrab's compositional acts than between the present performance and Grotesteen's. Had Grotesteen's score been different from Sterngrab's, the performers would still be playing the same notes (that is, Sterngrab's). Simply, the substitutions would not have been made because they would have been known to be ineffective in carrying through the goal of playing Sterngrab's piece. Or the overlooker would have pointed out that I had grabbed the wrong score. Or I would have realized this for myself. Or the computer would not have erased the file representing Sterngrab's piece. By contrast, had Sterngrab composed his score differently, this would have been reflected by differences in what the performers play. The substitutions would not have occurred, the overlooker would have intervened, I would have recognized my error, or the computer would have preserved the file representing Sterngrab's musical notations. In brief, if Sterngrab had written something other, the present performance would have differed correspondingly, whereas it would not have been affected by alterations in Grotesteen's composition. The present performance depends not on Grotesteen's creative acts, but on Sterngrab's. The intuition that Sterngrab's piece is played is not at odds, then, with the requirement that a performance of a given work be causally tied to the composer's creation of that work. Even if one causal strand links the performance with Grotesteen's efforts, another that is stronger (in that it affects the contents of the given performance) connects the performance to Sterngrab's. Causal continuities, not the performer's higher-level intentions, are crucial in these cases, as in ordinary ones, in determining what piece gets performed.[12]

Contrast this with the following scene. Unbeknown to them, performers intending to play Sterngrab's quartet have Eissberg's score before them. They know neither work. Eissberg's is very different from Sterngrab's. The musicians follow the instructions in the score. Naturally enough, they end

---

[11] In analysing what makes something a correct instance of a work that can be multiply instanced, Currie (1988) applies a similar test to art in general.

[12] What if the belief that the scores are the same were mistaken? Then the performance would have been of Grotesteen's work. This is not solely because the matching would be nearer his work than Sterngrab's but also because the details of the performance would be affected by his creative decisions, not Sterngrab's. The counterfactual dependency of the performance would be altered, so that the robust causal chain led to Grotesteen. Only if the scores were so similar that a perfect performance of Grotesteen's might be consistent with an inaccurate, but still discernible, rendering of Sterngrab's would there be scope for uncertainty about which is the stronger causal connection.

up performing Eissberg's, not Sterngrab's, piece. Had Eissberg composed her work differently, this would have carried through to the performance, whereas nothing Sterngrab did to his piece would have affected what they played.

Now consider the same scenario, except with Grotesteen replacing Eissberg. The scores are identical, but no one knows this and neither is it the case that their synonymy has been established by a machine, such as a computer, or by someone's mistaking the one score for the other simply because they are the same. My intuition here is that, despite the performers' high-level intention to give Sterngrab's work, Grotesteen's is played. In considering Levinson's example in which the score of the Dadaist *Z* replaces that of *Y*'s waltz, I said I was assuming the trickster knew these scores to be identical when I agreed that *Y*'s piece is performed. The significance of that assumption should now be evident. Unless the substitution depends on a person's knowing the scores are the same, or on some other process that checks directly or indirectly for synonymy, it would be *Z*'s piece that was played.

One objection to my view might begin with this observation: if the audience believes itself to be hearing Sterngrab's piece, the musicians take themselves to be playing Sterngrab's quartet, and Sterngrab's score is just like Grotesteen's—yet, by my account, the performance is of Grotesteen's quartet because his score is used and it has never been tested or checked for its similarity to Sterngrab's—then everyone has the same access to the sound of Sterngrab's work in this performance as in one that is of his work. Is that not sufficient to show Sterngrab's piece is played?

I agree that this performance provides the auditor with epistemic access to Sterngrab's work. In this respect, it might be as useful to him as a performance of Sterngrab's quartet. But this does not settle which composition is performed. Consider this actual case: Charles Gounod's 'Ave Maria' incorporates the C major *Prelude* from J. S. Bach's *Well-Tempered Klavier*, which is treated as the accompaniment for a vocal melody added by Gounod. With a bit of selective attention, one can learn a great deal of Bach's piece by listening to Gounod's, but this does not mean Bach's work is performed when Gounod's 'Ave Maria' is.[13] (Simply, an accurate rendition of Gounod's work contains too much that is redundant for it to qualify also as a performance of Bach's. Bach's *Prelude* has no singer, no words, and no sumptuous melody.) And, to return to the fictional, where the performance is intended to be of Grotesteen's quartet and uncontroversially is of that piece, it still is true that the listener who knows of its similarity to Sterngrab's quartet can learn how

[13] There is an analogy in the realm of paintings. One might learn from Rembrandt van Ryn's *Bathsheba*, or from Édouard Manet's *Olympia*, a great deal about the appearance of Hendrickje Stoffels or Victorine Meurent, because Hendrickje and Victorine sat for the artists and the paintings bear their likenesses. Nevertheless, the paintings' titles determine that they represent Bathsheba and Olympia, not Stoffels and Meurent.

Sterngrab's piece would sound. The objection fails, then. It falls to the observation that we can sometimes learn about one work by listening to the performance of another.

Another projected criticism makes this point: the performance interpretation will be affected by the performers' beliefs about the identity of the work they are performing. They will conceive their account of the piece in terms of its connection to others in the composer's œuvre and this will lead them to play it one way rather than another. If they believe the work to be by X rather than by Y, the performers will contextualize the work differently and, as a result, will make salient in their playing some features rather than others. If they take themselves to be rendering Sterngrab's work, they will play it as his. Is that not sufficient to show Sterngrab's piece is played?

I accept that performers' beliefs about the composer's identity are likely to affect their interpretation, but I deny that the manner of interpretation settles whose work the performance is of. No doubt those who tried to play Haydn's Op. 3 No. 5 highlighted its Haydnesque qualities, but their performance was of Hofstetter's piece, whether or not their playing was best suited to his style. It is a commonplace that many orchestras play Beethoven's music as if it were by Brahms and Brahms's as if it were by Mahler. The identity of the works presented in these performances is not affected by the style of interpretation. (Pearce 1988a holds that only if performances project hearably different interpretations is there any ground to ascribe them to different works. Levinson 1990a denies this, and rightly so in my view.)

Levinson is reluctant to consider as necessary for performance a causal connection between the performance and the work's composition. This is because he thinks the causal chain sometimes does not latch onto the piece that is performed. In those cases, the connection is made by the performer's higher-order intentions, he maintains. I have tried to show Levinson is wrong to think relevantly robust causal connections do not go through in these cases. My aim has been to defend the necessity of the causal condition for performance. Moreover, I have suggested that higher-order intentions, because they can always miss their mark, are not up to the job.

It is possible, however, to imagine examples where there is matching coupled with an appropriate higher-order intention, but in which low-level intentions and causal connections are absent. For instance, someone who has heard of Beethoven, but who knows nothing of his music and has never seen his scores, might announce her intention to play a piece by Beethoven and, miracle of miracles, she provides a note-perfect rendition of the 'Appassionata'. Would we not say she has performed Beethoven's work? And does this not show, after all, that Levinson is right to think higher-order intentions can secure a performance in the absence of the usual causal links?

My first inclination, I confess, is to suppose this prodigy has performed the 'Appassionata'. But that is because I would suspect a causal chain lurks somewhere in the background. Perhaps, as a very young baby, the pianist heard Beethoven's music and her playing is guided by unconscious memories. Or perhaps there is a spirit world that interacts with this one, and Beethoven's shade guides the pianist's fingers. By hypothesis, all such explanations are ruled out. The case we are to imagine posits a causal void between Beethoven's creative acts and the player's efforts. With that point taken firmly on board, what is my second inclination? To be frank, I do not know I have one. My intuitions give out. It is not that I am sure the work is performed, but am uncertain how this could be. Rather, I am no longer confident the playing counts as a performance. In any event, I do not feel tempted to revise my previous account in the light of the hypothetical possibility just described.

Simultaneous performances of two works

A quick way to deal with the problems posed by the similarity between Sterngrab's and Grotesteen's scores would have been to suppose the Aloysius Quartet simultaneously performs both works. Previously I rejected the view that matching is sufficient for a performance's being of a work. It is counterintuitive to accept that a performance of Beethoven's Fifth Symphony is also one of Marthoven's Fifth, that Ribaldi's work is performed whenever Vivaldi's *Four Seasons* is, and that my improvised Baroque ditty happens to be at the same time a performance of Bach's C major *Two Part Invention*. But suppose we endorse, as well as matching, the necessity of an appropriately low-level performance intention. In that case, performances of Beethoven will not also be performances of Marthoven, since the scores of the works differ, and my improvisations will not also be a performance of Bach's *Invention*, because I have no intention of following Bach's score. Now, if we reject my third condition, which requires a robust causal link between the performer's output and the composer's act of first specifying her work, we could allow that any performance of Sterngrab's piece is also a performance of Grotesteen's different work, since their scores are the same and the intention to follow the score (whoever wrote it) does not discriminate between their respective work indications.

My objections to the idea that the performance of a work involves only matching and low-level intention should be plain from arguments made in the previous section. The low-level intention tracks the causal chain leading to the work's creator. If that aspect of the intention is ignored, the intention is idle. The position sketched in the previous paragraph counts the low-level intention as necessary but, then, gives it no work to do. The intention reaches the score, but goes no further. Or perhaps it does not go even that far if an evil demon intervenes to control the performer's actions so that, though he intends to follow the score, he plays something that matches another piece instead. My intuition is that the low-level intention is relevant mainly because it retraces the connection between the part-music from which the performer plays and the composer's writing of the work's score. As I have claimed, for a performance to be of a given work, there must be, as well as matching and an appropriate low-level intention, a causal connection guaranteeing that the matching is not a fluke or accident. Indeed, acknowledging the importance of a robust connection between the performance of a piece and the composer's creation of that same work may be crucial in justifying the earlier claim that imperfect matching is otherwise sufficient for a performance's instancing a given work. At the very least, our inclination to count an inexact performance as of a given work is more understandable if there is a strong causal tie between the performance and the creation of that work, whereas no equivalent connections hold between the performance and acts of composition that gave rise to similar, but different, pieces.[14]

In consequence, I am bound to reject the suggestion that any performance of Sterngrab's piece is simultaneously a presentation of Grotesteen's, assuming they have composed different pieces. Which work is performed depends on who is at the termination of a robust causal chain running from the performance to the act of work creation, where the strength of that chain is tested by reference to the relation of counterfactual dependence between its two ends, not simply by considering whose scores are used.

Levinson, who requires for performance a connection that is either straightforwardly causal or secured by higher-level intentions, draws a similar conclusion. In response to Pearce's claim (1988*b*) that he is committed to believing no two works could have any performances in common, Levinson (1990*a*) agrees and suggests we do take for granted that there is a unique answer to 'What is this a performance of?' where there is any answer at all. It seems to me Levinson's reply is hasty on two counts. First, it is always possible that the performing musicians have the high-level intention to perform the works of both X and Y in one hit. Having realized that Sterngrab's and Grotesteen's quartets have congruent scores, the members of the Aloysius Quartet might intend to perform the two pieces together, combined in a single rendition. I do not see how Levinson can deal easily with this possibility, given his view that high-level performance intentions trump ordinary causal connections under equivalent conditions. Here again, I believe the significance attached by Levinson to higher-level intentions trips him up. The second point is more general: even if Levinson thinks no performance of

---

[14] Fisher (1998) criticizes Wolterstorff (1975) and James C. Anderson (1985) for not discussing this condition on our accepting as instances of natural kinds malformed individuals. A male lion that cannot roar is a lion because it came from a lion zygote. Like me, Fisher thinks instances of musical works, especially malformed ones, must stand in an appropriate causal relation to the composer's creation of the work (though his focus is on music conveyed only via recordings).

Sterngrab's quartet is, at the same time, a performance of Grotesteen's, it remains to be seen if the necessary conditions for performance enunciated previously rule out the eventuality that a single performance instances more than one work. I explore the issue in some detail, both because of its intrinsic interest and its relevance to the question before us, which is 'what makes a performance of a given work?'

Suppose that, as a result of a misunderstanding, the orchestra has the parts of Peter Tchaikovsky's Piano Concerto No. 1 on their music stands, but the soloist believes himself to be playing Edvard Grieg's Piano Concerto in A Minor. They begin, with neither side prepared to give way. (Offered as an example of musical humour, this is what happened at one of the concerts arranged by Gerald Hoffnung.) In my view, the débâcle that results is not best regarded as a single performance that is simultaneously of two works. Rather, two performances, each of a different work, take place at the same place and time. These performances are imperfect, since neither uses the full complement of musicians. The same applies when, prior to a performance by the Aloysius Quartet, someone drops the scores of Sterngrab's and Grotesteen's pieces. In the panic that follows, Sterngrab's violin parts are mixed with Grotesteen's viola and cello parts. Provided the equivalence of the two scores has not been established, I think two incomplete performances take place. It is possible the error is not detected, of course, and that everyone is satisfied with the epistemic access they gain to the work of their choice, but such are happy accidents rather than evidence of a successful, single performance.

Here is a second case that need not detain us long. Suppose some performances are works of art in their own right.[15] In that case, when one hears Alfred Brendel play a sonata by Franz Schubert one is presented with two works of art. Still, it is not the case that a single performance is *of* two works. There is a performance of one work, Schubert's, and that performance qualifies as a work of art, but the performance is not also *of* itself.

We come closer to what we are after if we regard the interpretation as a work of art. A performance might be *of* a single interpretation, as well as *of* a single composition. If interpretations are works of art, such a performance will be of two: the interpretation and the piece played. There is, however, an intimate dependence of the one work of art, the interpretation, on the other,

---

[15] Among those who hold this view are Mark (1981), Kivy (1995: 125–8, 261), and Edidin (1997). By contrast, Thom (1993: 3) denies performances are works of art. It seems to me it need not matter much what we say, so long as we acknowledge all that the performer brings to the performance and that, often, we are more interested in this than in what the composer provides. The performer makes a crucial aesthetic contribution and we can and do evaluate this independently of evaluating the work itself. Of course, where pre-composed works are minimal or absent—that is, where music mainly is improvised—it is common to regard good improvised performances as works of art (Alperson 1984; Lee B. Brown 1996).

the composition. The interpretation could not exist independently of the composition.

In retrospect, it can be seen that the original question was directed towards a different possibility: can a single performance simultaneously instance two works with an independent existence?

In many pieces, one gets all or part of another for free. Sometimes reference is secured by explicit quotation. Beethoven quotes Diabelli's theme at the beginning of his variations on it; Tchaikovsky's *1812 Overture* contains 'La Marseillaise',[16] and military songs and rags are included in the movement 'General Putnam's Camp' from Charles Ives's *Three Places in New England* (1914–23, revised 1929). In other cases, material from one work is simply incorporated into another, with no reference intended. For instance, bits of Handel's *Arresto il passo* and *Apollo e Dafne* were often reused by him in his later works. Is it the case that, whenever the *1812 Overture* is played, one gets as a bonus a performance of 'La Marseillaise'? Perhaps so. Yet, still, this is not a *single* performance that is of two independent works. *This* performance of the *1812 Overture*, the one we are interested in, begins *here* and, twenty minutes later, ends *there*. The performance of 'La Marseillaise', if there is one, is not co-extensive with the performance of the *1812 Overture*. Rather, the performance of 'La Marseillaise' is contained within that of the *1812 Overture*. The playing of the former is a part of the performance of the latter, but is not identical with the totality of the latter's rendition.

Matters are not improved if we consider a work comprised entirely of others. Igor Stravinsky's *Pulcinella* (1919) is made up of pieces by Giovanni Pergolesi, and the music for the ballet *Les Sylphides* joins together works by Frédéric Chopin. Even if we ignore changes introduced to Pergolesi's originals, a performance of *Pulcinella* contains renditions of many pieces and none of these corresponds to the performance that is of the whole of *Pulcinella*. In other words, though independent compositions make up all of Stravinsky's piece, their proximity is characteristic of his work rather than of their independent existence. If all the *parts* of a performance of *Pulcinella* are performances of independent works, it does not follow that there is some other piece the playing of which is co-extensive with the performance of *Pulcinella*.

The examples just discussed make yet clearer what is at issue. If a single performance is of two independent works, both must run through the entire performance. Now, some cases display the temporal correspondence that

---

[16] The words are omitted. The same occurs in Schubert's String Quintet, D. 667, 'The Trout', one movement of which is based on his song of that name. In other examples, the original words are replaced by others, as happens to the songs included in John Gay's *The Beggar's Opera*, or to the arias from the previous opera season that find their way into Mozart's *Don Giovanni*. Changes of these sorts, along with others in orchestration and harmony, complicate matters in a way I deliberately ignore.

has just been required, but fail, nonetheless, to count as simultaneous performances of two works. In a rendition of Gounod's 'Ave Maria', the notes of Bach's *Prelude in C* run without pause from its beginning to its end. But I would deny that Bach's *Prelude* is played when Gounod's 'Ave Maria' is. As I wrote earlier, Gounod's piece is a different one from Bach's in that it contains material that Bach's does not. That material is present in a performance of Gounod's piece. In being faithful to Gounod's score, the singer is systematically unfaithful to Bach's. By checking Gounod's score against the performance, we can know the departure from Bach's work indication is deliberate and is controlled by Gounod. So we should not regard the performance of Gounod's piece as simultaneously of Bach's.

Here is another, very common kind of example that is similar. Many works are transcribed for instruments other than those for which the original was written. This almost always requires some adaptation of the original's sound structure. Indeed, the success or otherwise of a work transcription depends on how these changes are managed, the goal being to preserve the impression of the original despite filtering its contents through another medium. As a result, work transcriptions are best viewed as pieces in their own right (Levinson 1980a; Davies 1988a). When a work transcription is played, one does not get a performance that is simultaneously of the transcription and of its topic work, however. Because the performance is faithful to the transcription's score, which differs from that of the topic work, it is not also a playing of the original. When one plays Brahms's piano transcription of the Chaconne from Bach's *Partita in D Minor for Violin*, one does not also perform Bach's Chaconne. Of course, it is perfectly natural to say one hears Bach's Chaconne in Brahms's work transcription. Besides being natural, this is correct. The transcription would be a failure if it did not provide the auditor with epistemic access to (much of) Bach's work. But, as I have argued, a performance offering indirect acquaintance with one work need not be *of* that work.

Earlier I suggested a performance is of a work only if there is a robust causal connection between the performance and that work's creation. Typically, the relevant causal chain does not stop just there and then. It passes on into the past, seeking out the influences leading to the composition of the work under consideration. Mozart's *Haydn Quartets* (K. 387, 421, 428, 458, 464, 465) were written under the influence of Haydn's Op. 20, *Sun Quartets*. The causal path leading from a performance of one of Mozart's quartets continues to Haydn's, and on from Haydn's to other pieces that shaped his development, and so on. Similarly, there is a continuous regress of causal links from a performance of Brahms's work transcription to Bach's *Partita*. As it recedes into the past, the causal chain usually becomes less robust. Had Haydn's *Sun Quartets* been different, Mozart's *Haydn Quartets* may have been, though it is difficult to be sure in what respects. Had Bach's *Partita* taken a different course, Brahms's transcription would have done likewise, but, again, it is difficult to predict exactly how Brahms's piece would have mirrored Bach's.

When we are trying to determine what work a performance is of, how do we know when to stop retracing the relevant causal path? If causal chains gradually lose robustness, when are they too flabby to help us any longer in our quest for the work being performed? The answer to these questions is apparent from the previous discussion. If the contents of the performance match one work but not its predecessors, that is the piece played. Even if the performance displays a residual counterfactual dependence on earlier pieces, if it also contains redundancies or omissions with respect to their work-identifying contents, the earlier works are not performed.

At last it is possible to spell out all that is implied by the query 'can a single performance simultaneously be of two works?' The works in question must have an independent existence but be historically related, both works must be present throughout the entire performance, and the performance should be no less accurate in instancing one than it is in instancing the other. Are there any works whose histories and contents are so related that a single performance could be of both? I can think of some examples.

Some songs are ontologically thin, consisting of a melody and chord sequence but allowing considerable freedom to the performer as regards details and structural development. In the mid-twentieth century, many songs were performed in band arrangements. For instance, Benny Goodman's band featured George Gershwin's 'Fascinating Rhythm' and Glenn Miller's band played 'In the Mood' by Garland Razaf. These arrangements achieved the status of works in their own right. They were printed with due acknowledgement. Other bands played them. As a work, the band arrangement is much more detailed than the song, but it contains no material redundant to the song's identity. Everything added to the band arrangement is consistent with the song's faithful interpretation. When the band arrangement is played, the song is performed, as well as the more intensely specified piece, the arrangement, based on the song but with an independent existence. The musicians intend to perform both the song and the arrangement, and the song is no less directly present in the performance than is the band arrangement (whereas, by contrast, a performance of Brahms's work transcription is not, at the same time, a faithful performance of Bach's *Partita*). The band version of the song is not a work transcription of it, but is a fully faithful instance of the song as well as being a work with an independent existence. A performance by Benny Goodman's group of 'Fascinating Rhythm' or by Glenn

Miller's of 'In the Mood' is of two works—of the song and of the band arrangement.[17]

These cases rely on the dependence of the more complex piece on the simpler one. Where the relationship goes in the other direction, the performance is not simultaneously of both works. A piece for studio performance might be issued on sheet music as if it were a simple song. Because the thin song is the derivative piece, when the original studio performance is played back there is no reason to think the simple song is also instanced. (And a rendition of the thin song is not also a performance of the piece conceived for the studio, of course.) Also, the possibility of co-extensive work instances is defeated when the more complex piece is not for performance. Playing back a purely electronic transcription of a piece conceived originally for performance, like the Moog version of Bach, does not result in the sounding of any performance, since no performance is present on the recording. And Bach's piece is not simultaneously instanced when the transcription is, as I argued above.

My next example of a performance simultaneously of two pieces is that of the conceptual artist whose work is specified by the instruction 'Play any piano sonata by Beethoven while wearing a party hat'. (In this vein, the composer La Monte Young has created a work specified as 'Prepare any piece and play it'.) Again, a faithful performance of the conceptual work must also be a faithful performance of one of Beethoven's piano sonatas. This second case differs from the first, which is one where both of the pieces performed are musical ones. The conceptual piece, in contrast, is best viewed as a work of performance art about music, rather than as a musical work as such.[18] A single performance is of two works, but one of these is musical and the other is theatrical.

The requirement that there be a robust causal link between a performance and the work it is of usually guarantees a performance can be of only one work, but this is not inevitable. Where one work derives from another, and a performance of this second piece is also faithful as a performance of its predecessor, a single performance might be of both. In other words, when the causal route passes through one piece and goes on to another without any diminution in its robustness, a performance could instance both pieces.

[17] I am grateful to Jonathan McKeown for drawing my attention to the implications of this type of example. I find it difficult to think of plausible classical cases. The best candidates, perhaps, are adaptations of folk songs; for instance, Ralph Vaughan Williams's *Fantasia on Greensleeves* (1934) (arranged by R. Greaves from *Sir John in Love*). As a folk song, 'Greensleeves' allows for a liberal treatment in its performances, so a rendition of Vaughan Williams's fantasia might also qualify as a simultaneous performance of 'Greensleeves' qua folk song.

[18] Cone (1967) conceives of a piece with the score 'Play any phonograph record in your collection'. He denies both that this work is music and that it is a work of art. I agree on the first count, but not necessarily on the second.

Are any other conditions necessary for performance?

I have argued that three conditions must be met if a performance is of a given work: (1) there must be (a suitable degree of) matching between the performance and the work; (2) the performers must intend to follow (most of) the instructions specifying the work in question (though they need know neither what work that is nor who composed it); (3) there must be a robust causal chain from the performance to the work's creation, so that the matching achieved is systematically responsive to the composer's work-determinative decisions. Is the satisfaction of these conditions sufficient for a performance's being of a given work, or are further ones necessary? I believe they are jointly sufficient. One who disagrees is Thomas Carson Mark. As I am about to argue, he mistakes a feature that may be a good thing in performance for one that is necessary.

Mark (1981) analyses performance on the model of linguistic quotation. Quotation must be intentional. One does not quote another merely by saying what she did independently of her saying it. Moreover, though Mark does not make the point, it is also low-level intentions that are necessary for quotation. I need not know who said what I am quoting, only that the utterance was made by someone to whom I refer (opaquely) in repeating her words. In these respects, quotation is an apt model for musical performance. But Mark overdraws the analogy with language (Carrier 1983; Kivy 1995: 119–22) and, in doing so, introduces a condition for musical performance that goes beyond those considered so far. He denies that performance is achieved when a professor plays a few bars in class or a musician rehearses. In these cases, the act of quotation is 'inert'. For performance, the composer's utterance must not only be quoted, it must also be 'asserted'. Performance is assertion effected through quotation, as when I say 'to thine own self be true' and *mean* it. If the performer is to assert what he is quoting, he must feel himself in possession of the work's meaning; he cannot assert via quotation except under some interpretation of what the 'utterance' means. Mechanical playing drains away the assertoric force of the player's rendition and, therefore, does not qualify as performance.

Mark admits the analogy with language is partial at best (1981: 317). What does it mean to say the performer must *use* ('assert'), not merely *mention* ('quote'), the composer's ideas? Mark means to insist, obviously, that the performer must be in possession of the work's musical sense before he can perform it. Part of the point, I guess, is that a player without a grasp of where a theme begins or ends is unlikely to present it clearly. But Mark must mean much more than this, since he dismisses mechanical playing as nonperformance. A rendition that has become mechanical through repeated practice might slavishly reproduce an interpretation worked out earlier, or one made by some other performer, and in either case retains the work's musical sense. So, Mark's condition is a strong one: performance involves not just the preservation of the music's sense and structure, it also requires the player somehow to engage personally and on the spot with all that, so his performance counts truly as a personal statement of his, made at the time of playing.

I have suggested it is necessary for a performance to be of a given work that the performer aims to follow (most of) the composer's work-determinative instructions and succeeds in doing so for the most part, so that the piece can be recognized in the noise he ends up making. Because the correct reading of scores presupposes a knowledge of notational conventions, familiarity with the performance styles presupposed, and competence with the relevant instruments, some of what Mark desires in performances is already covered by my analysis. Only a musician who can recognize and phrase themes, feel the tonality, and so on is likely to be able to satisfy these requirements.

Beyond what has just been allowed, I do not see the need to accept Mark's 'assertion' condition for performance. This condition identifies a feature that makes for good performances—or, at least, one that is present in many great performances, as well as some that are patently bad—but it is inappropriately restrictive in characterizing what makes a performance of a given work. Simply, I think mechanical or mindless renditions should be counted as performances. Indeed, such a performance could be ideal as a work instance—for instance, where the piece expresses the mind-numbing dreariness of repetitive labour. If such a manner of playing is unsatisfactory, it is likely to be so at the level of performance interpretation, rather than of work delivery. So I do not endorse Mark's 'assertion' condition for performance.

Another who sets an inappropriate standard for performance is R. A. Sharpe (1979). He holds that a performance is a token, not of a work, but of an interpretation. His reasoning is as follows. Part of one token can be substituted for the equivalent part of another. Part of one musician's performance of a musical work cannot be substituted for the corresponding bit of another person's rendition of the same work without destroying both performances. The performances having inter-substitutable parts are those that are tokens of a particular musician's interpretation of a given work. (Interpretations are types that, as such, can be multiply instanced.) So, the type to which the performance stands as a token is an interpretation, not the work.

Two points dispense with Sharpe's argument. A token might instance more than one type. Moreover, one of the types instanced might depend on the other, which subsumes it in the way that the work subsumes the interpretations that are of it. In being a token of the type 'Mazda 323', my vehicle also is a token of the type 'car', because the type 'Mazda 323' is itself a token of the type 'car'. So, even if musical performances are tokens of interpretations, this does not mean they are not also tokens of the works they are of (Dipert 1980*a*; Davies 1991*b*); in fact, the reverse. The second point simply denies the truth of one of Sharpe's premisses. It is not the case that an interpretationally inconsistent presentation fails to count as a performance (Kivy 1983; Davies 1991*b*; Godlovitch 1993). A performance might be defective to the extent that it does not project a unified interpretation, but, in any event, it qualifies as a rendition of the given work if it follows the composer's work-identifying instructions. In fact, it is not uncommon to encounter faithful performances that present internally incoherent interpretations.

The individuation of performances

If the band at the head of a procession is playing the march from Georges Bizet's *Carmen* and the band at the tail is doing the same, do we have two performances or only one? In this section I consider how performances are individuated or counted.

I observed earlier that, if the orchestra plays Tchaikovsky's music while the soloist embarks on Grieg's, the result is not a single performance but two incomplete ones. This suggests performances are individuated in terms of the works they are of. Usually, there are at least as many distinct performances as there are works being performed. That cannot be all there is to performance individuation, however. This is not solely because a single performance might be of two works, as I explained previously, but also because it does not answer the question just posed: do the bands give a single performance of the march from *Carmen*, or two that are simultaneous? What other conditions are involved in the individuation of performances?

Performance typically requires the spatial contiguity of the performance group and the temporal synchronization of their playing. If one group plays in Paris and the other in London, distinct performances result, even if they are of the same work. If the orchestra plays on Wednesday and the soloist sings on Thursday, the outcome is not a single performance.

These generalizations need to be treated carefully. What counts as spatial contiguity depends on the work in question and on performance conventions relevant to it. Giovanni Gabrieli wrote pieces that exploit the spatial separation of the musicians around galleries in Venice's St Mark's. Many works call for contributions from offstage. Béla Bartók's *Music for Strings, Percussion and Celesta* (1937) plays one string group off against another. Karlheinz Stockhausen's *Gruppen für drei Orchester* (1955–7) is written for three orchestras, each with its own conductor. The spatial separation of the performers might be much greater than it is in the examples mentioned so far. One can imagine an avant-garde composition requiring the performers to be out of earshot of each other (with their efforts coordinated by a conductor shown to each on closed-circuit television). Finally, a band might march across the countryside as it plays a piece.

Similar reservations apply to the suggestion that a performance is marked by the synchronization of the efforts of the performance group. In most extended works, different instruments are used at different times, so the players do not always begin and stop together. Also, recall Yehudi Menuhin's tale of a performance of Felix Mendelssohn's Violin Concerto with a conductor who had only one tempo. In the finale Menuhin went his own way. Half the orchestra followed him, the rest staying with the conductor. This suggests strict temporal coincidence is not always required, if Menuhin did play the work with the orchestra. And one can imagine an avant-garde piece specifying that year-long gaps should separate the playing of each of its several movements. Though the musicians might begin and end together as they play each movement, temporal continuity is not preserved in the usual fashion across the entire performance.

Even if we could come up with a workable account of the space–time conditions that govern performance identity, we would still face problems in disambiguating performances. When forty string musicians play Mozart's *Eine Kleine Nachtmusik*, K. 525, at the same time and venue, it could be that two performances are heard, each given by an orchestra of twenty members. As this example makes clear, the individuation of performances depends on the identification of performance groups or orchestras. What unifies a bunch of players as an orchestra or group?

Many performance groups have an established identity. The orchestra has a name and the musicians are contracted to an organization. When one such group performs a given work—when a Beethoven symphony is given by the Academy of St Martin-in-the-Fields, for instance—there is not much doubt about how to identify the orchestra. Still, this formal characterization of the players cannot explain what unites them. This is apparent from several cases. Some works involve the combined efforts of several such groups. A performance of Gustav Mahler's Eighth Symphony might bring together several otherwise distinct organizations—the Vienna Philharmonic, the Vienna Opera Chorus, and the Vienna Boys' Choir. Also, pieces can be played by 'scratch' orchestras, by an ensemble that comes together only for a specific concert. Finally, when the Vienna Philharmonic plays Beethoven's Symphony No. 2, Op. 36, the trombonists are not included among the players, though they are no less members of the Vienna Philharmonic than those who take part.

It is better, then, to identify the performance group on a particular occasion in terms of their cooperative enterprise. What links them is their working together with the goal of playing the given piece (Stubley 1998). It is the musicians' intentions as regards their activity that unite them as performers of the work at hand. The relevant intentions are mutual and reciprocal;

they intend to pool their joint efforts. It is not simply that each intends to play his specified part, but also that they aim to do so together and acknowledge each other as members of a team.

One does not qualify as a member of the performance group merely by making music at the concert. Percy Grainger's setting of the Lincolnshire song 'Brigg Fair' was adapted for orchestra by Frederick Delius in 1907. Joseph Taylor, the singer from whom Grainger had made a notational transcription of the melody, was present at the first London performance of Delius's music. 'Legend has it that on hearing "his" tune, Joseph Taylor immediately stood up and began to sing along with the orchestra' (Bird 1976: 111). Taylor could not qualify as one of the performers because no role is provided for him as a member of the performance team. The same applies to a member of the audience who whistles along with the first violins. Delius wrote no parts for singers or for whistlers in his work.[19] Neither does one qualify as a performer merely by following Delius's work instructions. A member of the audience who pulls out a fiddle and joins with the second violins in playing the music written for them is not a performer if the other players view him as an interloper (Davies 1997*b*).

Performances are individuated by reference to the works they are of, the spatial and temporal locations they occupy, and the identity of the performance group. Players are united as groups on particular occasions of performance in terms of their joint goals and mutual cooperation.

General conditions for performance

I have concentrated to date on the relation between performances and the works they are of, and on the individuation of different performances of a given work. Now I discuss more general constraints governing the live performances of works. I base my remarks on an analysis offered by Stan Godlovitch (1993, 1998). He aims to identify the criteria underlying our expectations regarding coherence, unity, and completeness in performance. The account is normative. It sets out a regulative ideal, not necessary and sufficient conditions, for performance. Also, the focus is restricted to the classical tradition in which works are played for audiences whose principal interest is in listening to them. Godlovitch's criteria are as follows: only one work is performed at a time; its proper sequence is respected, as is the indicated rate of delivery; the performance is continuous, without unjustified breaks; performers comply with the appropriate roles (and do not, for example, swap parts midway through). Also,

[19] Delius wrote no part in the score for a conductor, yet he is a member of the performance group. This is a case where the relevant role is implicit in the performance practice assumed by the composer. For discussion of the conductor's role, see Ross and Judkins (1996), and, for a political perspective, Goehr (1992).

the audience is in a position to receive the entire performance in its detail.

I begin with two clarifications. Instrumentalists sometimes 'double' parts. The third clarinettist might also play the alto saxophone and the bass clarinet, and take up these instruments as required by the score. A percussionist might play the xylophone, triangle, bells, and tam tam within a single work. When Godlovitch insists that the players do not swap parts, by 'part' he means not 'instrument' but performer's role. How do we define that? To rely on the easiest case, the role is the one indicated in the score. The score might call on a given musician to play different instruments at different times. Here is the second point: some works leave the sequence in which things are played to be settled by the performer or by chance procedures. For instance, Stockhausen's *Piano Piece XI* (1956) has seventeen sections, the order of which is determined by the performer. In many other cases (figured bass, cadenzas, parts requiring improvisation or embellishment), no particular *note* progression is specified by the composer. When Godlovitch requires that 'the proper sequence be respected', he means a specified sequence *type* should be followed—for instance, one determined by the performance practice governing the realization of a figured bass, or the embellishment of a melody, or, in a contemporary piece, the throw of dice, say.

Godlovitch's standards are not always satisfied in public concerts. I attended one where, because of a power failure, Schubert's Symphony No. 8, D. 759, really was unfinished. I have seen performances halted by spectacular errors or as a result of a player's becoming lost. On another occasion, the soloist's violin part in the Agnus Dei of Beethoven's *Missa Solemnis*, Op. 123, was taken over in mid-movement by the second player on the first desk when the leader could not continue, owing to a major structural failure in his instrument. As I have already observed, in a concert arranged by Gerald Hoffnung, the orchestra and soloist embarked on different pieces.

Godlovitch is well aware of cases of these kinds and supplies examples of his own. Also, he allows that, in rehearsals (which he plainly regards as distinct from performances), it is common for his playing conditions to be violated. In particular, passages are often repeated and played out of sequence. His central point, which surely is correct, is that these events or practices do not offer acceptable routine options for public performance.

Godlovitch is also aware that his audience condition is often not met. The musician might play alone at home for her own amusement. It may be that no one is in a position to hear all of Handel's *Water Music* as the musicians play on a barge that floats by. Still, he insists, the point of performance is to deliver a complete work to the audience (see also Thom 1993: ch. 7 and Putman 1990). There is no inconsistency in maintaining that the goal of performance, in general, is the public transmission of composers' works, while accepting that many particular performances are not intended for a public. The criterion identifies a central feature of our concept of performance, one without which it would not be as it is, but not one every particular performance must be directed towards fulfilling.

If I have a reservation about this conclusion, it concerns its exclusivity. Many kinds of work performance do not have as their primary aim the presentation of a composer's piece for the listener's contemplation. The bugler plays Reveille to waken sleeping troops. The piano player who accompanies a silent film changes what he plays to suit the action, whether or not he has finished the piece. Priests in monasteries intone liturgical music that is associated by tradition with their devotions. In Balinese temple festivals, the music is directed to the gods rather than to the humans who are present. Bands spaced through a parade provide entertainment for onlookers, none of whom can hear all that is played. Many kinds of works provide background or attendant music for other activities, for dining, dancing, shopping, or whatever. In short, much music is functional. It is not clear that playing this kind of music has as its main purpose the delivery of the work to the audience. The music is part of a wider social ritual or context in which it is subsidiary.

Godlovitch insulates his analysis from such counter-examples by explicitly focusing on works of a particular kind—ones specifying performance roles, a sound structure, a rate of delivery, and that are intended for listening. Inevitably, this carries with it assumptions about the circumstances under which works should be presented and about the motivations bringing people together in such sites. Works of that sort are common enough, and not solely in the classical Western tradition. Nevertheless, in protecting his position, Godlovitch guarantees the result he wants. He goes too far, perhaps, in characterizing performance as primarily concerned with conveying musical pieces to listeners. All the same, he may be correct to regard this purpose as foundational—not because all music making is dedicated to it, but because a concern with music as such very frequently supposes an awareness that playings are of works.

Godlovitch goes on to consider the conditions underwriting expectations regarding the honesty and accountability of performers. Here he anticipates his conclusion:

I try to show that performance integrity requires that a performer be fully in a position to take credit for the performance, and that, to do so, it is not sufficient that the appropriate sounds be causally related to the performer's musical activities. Rather, a special sort of causal relation is expected, one characterized in part in terms of what we take the work to be performed to exact fittingly from the player. And the fittingness of such demands is, in turn, a function of certain traditions of music-making. (1993: 579)

In developing his view, Godlovitch considers the way supplementary electronic paraphernalia might make it possible for the player to output technically difficult works by inputting something much less demanding. In that event, the player is not appropriately responsible for what is played. For that, the performer must use the specified instrument in the way determined as normative by the heritage and profession, and he must play the work in real time. The use of the relevant instruments and the technical demands they make on the players are essential elements in performance. Performance is not solely a matter of making the right noises, but of generating an instance of the work in real time from appropriate instruments under the technical constraints those instruments impose on the task.

The theme of performance integrity, considered from the performer's viewpoint, is tested through a series of papers (Godlovitch 1988, 1990*a,b*, 1992, 1997) that are brought together and developed in Godlovitch (1998). He explains how improvements and changes in musical instruments are acceptable, whereas technological developments that threaten to dispense with the musician are not. Musical instruments are used not merely as means to the production of sounds, he argues. They cannot be dropped in favour of superior technologies, such as synthesizers, allowing for simpler methods for generating the same sounds (also see Levinson 1990*c*). The use of the musical instrument, as well as a mastery of its difficulties through hard-earned skill, is a core aspect of the musician's role. Violinists are violinists only if they play violins, not synthesizers that sound like violins. Accordingly, musicians are trained to achieve proficiency on their instruments, and also to preserve and revere the traditions of the performance community, which functions like a Guild into which they are inducted (see also Wolterstorff 1987 and James Ross 1993). This community operates to conserve a hierarchy of talents, with only a minority of practitioners achieving virtuoso status. It is in terms of this Guild tradition, not merely of efficiency in making appropriate sounds, that innovations to instruments are considered. Only innovations that do not threaten the Guild's structure can be accommodated. Instruments can be improved, but only so long as the change keeps intact the difference in skill separating the virtuoso from the person who is merely competent. Other improvements, ones challenging the existence of the Guild by making everything so easy that the hierarchy of skill is obliterated, are rejected.

Godlovitch is scrupulous in refraining from moralizing about his observations. Should we reject the values of the Guild as a fusty hangover from an outdated past? He does not say. I claim we should not if we are interested in musical works created in a social context that assumes the existence of a community of skilled performers. Godlovitch's is a sociological analysis, but it is not thereby concerned with something peripheral to work performance. Works that are for live instrumental performance not only rely on but are dedicated to fostering the performance Guild. Not all pieces are virtuosic, but all make demands intimately connected to the use of the instruments for which they are written. The performance heritage is not solely an aspect of the historical context in which the work first appeared, but remains relevant to its present performance. The moral is this: if we value such works and wish to hear them played live, we must also respect and preserve the traditions and musico-social structures that nurtured them and make possible their presentation.

Contemporary musicians can and do use the resources of the new technology, both in composition and in the instruments for which they write. When they do not dispense altogether with the labours of musicians, it is interesting to see many values associated with performing earlier music kept intact. For instance, rock music retains a place for virtuosity.[20] Fans can still be offended on learning that pop stars are incapable of playing the music issued on recordings as their own work, as witnessed by the response when it became known that Milli Vanilli did not play or sing the songs attributed to them.[21]

Studio performances

Earlier I recognized as one ontological type musical works for studio performance. In these, the technology of the recording process makes an essential contribution to the work's properties, so it cannot usually be played live.[22] Performances of works of this kind depart from the conditions normative for live renditions. To mark the difference, I refer to them as 'studio performances'. In the studio, the performance need not be continuous, the players can swap roles (or one performer might take several of the roles finding their way onto the disc or tape, as when Steve Winwood plays all the instruments on the album *Arc of a Diver* (1980)), and it may be that no audience is present. Moreover, temporal and spatial contiguity is not required. Players can tape their parts at different

---

[20] Baugh (1993, 1995) argues that virtuosity in rock music is of a distinctive, 'visceral' type. I think he is mistaken. Jimi Hendrix and Eric Clapton exploit the special qualities of electric guitars, but in many respects their skills are admired for the kind of technical mastery that has always been valued as the hallmark of fine musicianship.

[21] Frith (1986) notes that, in 1981, a band sponsored by the Musicians' Union was not allowed to perform because it used a drum machine. In this case, the ban reflected union policy opposed to replacing musicians with machines. Even now, when most groups rely on synthesizers that play programmed or pre-sampled tracks, their members are expected to contribute something to the recording.

[22] Studios are becoming more portable. Where the electronic equipment on which the performance depends can be taken from place to place, performance of such works might be possible at concerts. There is even a device allowing the vocalist to double or harmonize with himself.

sites and at various times.[23] In consequence, the individuation of studio performances is not like that of live performances. They may be identified partly in terms of the performance groups they involve, but the notion of 'group' here is weakened. For instance, 'session' musicians are used on many recordings and these players do not always work together or even know each other. Studio performances are also frequently identified in terms of the works they are of. Sometimes, though, the piece evolves through the recording process and some of the musicians involved in the recording have no clear idea of the outcome to be achieved and their place in it. The crucial factor in individuating studio performances is the product issued, the disc or tape. The performance is what ends up on the master tape, and the performance is over when those with the authority determine the master tape has reached its definitive version (Davies 1997*b*).[24]

Because a studio performance relies on technology for its realization, those who control the recording equipment play a crucial role in the creative process.[25] In some cases, it is appropriate to regard them as co-performers.[26] The names of some producers of recordings of popular music—Sam Phillips, Phil Specter, Berry Gordy, George Martin—are as well known to aficionados as are those of the musicians they worked with (Elvis Presley, the Beatles) and the distinctive sound environments they created (such as the Detroit sound of Tamla-Motown). Nowadays, many pop musicians produce their own recordings, so important to the final result is the contribution made by the manner of managing studio techniques.

---

[23] One or more of the performers might be dead at the time the others record their parts. Natalie Cole has duetted with her deceased father and the surviving Beatles have recorded a song with John Lennon. If these examples are not convincing, because Nat King Cole and John Lennon did not conceive of the tracks they recorded as for this later use, consider the case in which two musicians intend to play together and one of them dies before the other's part has been taped.

[24] Just as the musical work is not a score, so the recorded performance is not a master tape, and for similar reasons, which is why I say 'what ends up on'. An attempt to be more explicit about the nature of this 'what' is found in Fisher (1998).

[25] A fascinating and inspiring account of the techniques involved in creating the Beatles' *Sergeant Pepper's Lonely Hearts Club Band* LP and other of their songs is offered by George Martin (1994). Frith (1987) notes that, in the 1920s, it was accepted that copyright should go to composers, since record companies merely reproduced their works, but, by 1980, sound engineers were classified as songwriters. For discussion of the role of the record producer in popular music, see Frith (1983: 110–14), Eisenberg (1988), Gracyk (1996), and Porcello (1998).

[26] In 1925, Leopold Stokowski became the first conductor to record electronically. 'In 1929 he began broadcasting, and at the first rehearsal was shocked when he noticed the mixer and learned his function: "Then you're paying the wrong man. He's the conductor and I'm not. I don't want this to be broadcast under my name if I'm not controlling the *pianissimo*, the *mezzo forte*, and the *fortissimo*." After several attempts to work the dials himself while conducting, he settled on making the engineer a member of the orchestra, to be cued as he would cue the first bassoon' (Eisenberg 1988: 124).

In these cases, record producers deserve the listing they receive on record labels (Frith 1986; Chanan 1995; Gracyk 1996; Fisher 1998).

Meanwhile, the demands made in the studio on the musicians differ from those applying to live performance. The possibility of retakes nullifies, at least to some extent, the risk of mistakes.[27] Difficult passages can be recorded at a lower speed or in fragments. This is not to say things are always easier for the studio performer. The medium generates new demands, as well as new opportunities. While a certain rawness can contribute to the simulation of the kind of spontaneity that goes with live performance, crude blunders that survive the recording process are less forgivable than infelicities made under live conditions. In any case, the traditions and standards of the performance community as described by Godlovitch do not apply as stringently to those who specialize in playing works for studio performance.

The vast majority of the musical pieces conceived for studio performance are of the popular variety, but the interaction of musicians with recording technology has repercussions reaching far beyond that arena. Works intended for live performance are often recorded, and are known more widely through recordings than live performances. As he is aware, this has implications for Godlovitch's conditions for performance integrity. I explore them here, though I return to them also in Chapter 7.

I noted that studio performances depart from the normative conditions applying to live performances. This remains true in the case of studio performances of works created for live performance. Most involve multiple takes that later are edited together; they do not always observe the work's sequence or play it through without breaks; the performers may be separated in space and time when they lay down their tracks. As studio performances, these renditions are individuated in terms of the technological process from which they result. A performance is finished when it is 'in the can', ready for issuing.

Godlovitch maintains the performer should be causally responsible for her performance, not just in the sense that her actions lead to an appropriate output, but because she produces it from the required instruments in the manner prescribed by the performance tradition. To be blunt, recording technology provides the possibility of 'cheating'. As Denis Dutton (1979) puts it, if we learned that a classical pianist had recorded a difficult passage at half

---

[27] It is not the case, as yet, that wrong notes or poor intonations can be corrected digitally. If a passage is to be 'patched in', it must come from another take. 'If you are recording a single performance, there's not much you can do to improve the final result other than adjust the mix of signals from a multitrack device . . . [As John Eargle, a Grammy-nominated engineer, says:] You can't go in and fix a single instrumental note, so you have to hope that you have another version of that section with a better note and no other problems. If you don't, you may be in deep trouble' (Wilkinson 1997: 72).

speed, the performance represented on the recording would be regarded as a forgery. This is not to say we think such cheating occurs often.[28] The issue, rather, is this: because the recording is not transparent to the process by which it is created, a performance on disc cannot *display* integrity, even if it has it. At least, it cannot display integrity as does a live performance, where one can see the relation between what the musician does and the sounds he produces.[29] So, it declares its sincerity in another way—by outlining the conditions of performance in the liner notes.[30]

Though some practices would undermine the integrity of a studio performance of a work created for live performance, others do not. The musicians do not cheat when they record the piece over several days and make many takes. Why not? Because we recognize studio performances as just that; because we appreciate they are not transparent *records* of live performances. What is involved here is not merely acceptance that things are different. Clearly we apply distinct standards to the two kinds of performances and evaluate them accordingly. To anticipate an argument to be made in Chapter 7, note perfection is more important in a recording (of classical music) than in a live performance, so it is appropriate the musicians are given the latitude to redress errors that occur. Despite the acknowledged differences between live and studio renditions, Godlovitch's integrity conditions are by no means irrelevant to studio performances, though they enter the equation in a slightly different place. Where they play pieces created for live performance, we expect the musicians who make a studio recording to be capable of playing the piece to a professional standard were they to give it live.[31] A condition for

[28] A much discussed case is that in which the young Elizabeth Schwarzkopf dubbed some of the high notes for Kirsten Flagstad in EMI's 1953 recording of Richard Wagner's *Tristan und Isolde* (Eisenberg 1988: 94). Only a few notes were substituted and the recordings made available one of the era's most famous interpretations of the role.

[29] I allow, though, that live performance can involve dissimulation. Many an aria has been transposed down a semitone or two to allow a fading diva to create the impression she can still hit the high notes. Bernard Holland in the *New York Times* (27 Oct. 1992, B1 and B4) discusses a live concert in which Luciano Pavarotti lip-synched to one of his recordings (see Lee B. Brown 1996). Some people might think it is sanctimonious to complain about this, since the practice is tolerated from rock musicians. The basis for protest should be apparent, however, when the difference between works for live performance and works for studio performance is given its due. Pavarotti is a member of the tenors' Guild, after all, whereas rock musicians belong to a different performance community.

[30] Many recordings advertise themselves as employing authentic instruments or replicas, and as being guided by research into the performance practice of the relevant period. Sometimes all the instruments (makers and dates) are listed. In addition, details of the recording venue and circumstances are usually provided. For an example, see Jaap Schröder's and Christopher Hogwood's recording of Mozart's Symphony No. 41 (L'Oiseau-Lyre, Florilegium Series 411 658-2, 1984).

[31] Things are more complicated in the case of pop groups. They are not expected to include in their live concerts all the session musicians who may have been involved in their recordings. Queen's 'Bohemian Rhapsody' has a section for choir, a tape of which was played when the group performed on stage.

194   *Works, their Instances, and Notations*

the integrity of recorded performances of most classical works is that the players could perform the work in real time according to the usual norms (Godlovitch 1998: 27).

Multimedia playings

Some recordings are designed to elicit the participation of the user. I have in mind 'music-minus-one' recordings and karaoke multimedia disks. (Karaoke is not much discussed by musicologists or ethnomusicologists, an exception being Keil 1994.) How should we describe the interaction between the recorded performers and the person who responds by playing or singing along with the disc?[32]

Since the case involves a studio performance, the spatial and temporal separation of the recorded musicians from the disc's user does not prevent their uniting as a group. Nevertheless, the disc's user cannot become a co-performer, for the simple reason that the studio performance to which he joins his efforts is over and done. The result of playing the recording is not a *new* performance, but instead is the playback of the studio performance finished before the record was issued. Even if the studio rendition is incomplete as regards the number of musical roles it contains, it is not unfinished as a performance. The person who provides the missing instrumental part as the music-minus-one record is played parallels the recorded performance, but he cannot fuse with it or become a co-performer. He plays in tandem with the studio performance, but the two cannot meet as one. Karaoke is similar if the relevant pieces are ones intended for performance. Singing along with a karaoke disc fosters the illusion that one is a co-performer, without making it the case that one is.

The same point applies to the idea (should one be disposed to entertain it) that the person who adjusts her hi-fi as she listens to a recording thereby becomes one of the work's performers. Her efforts might drastically affect the sound of the record's playing. She could make Johannes Brahms sound like Richard Strauss. Or she could set the volume to zero throughout. She can affect the playback of the recording, but she cannot touch or join in the performance, which was completed before she takes to the dials of her player (Godlovitch 1992). Besides, if the work is by Brahms, its score does not instruct the actions she executes, and she does not comply with those that are prescribed. And, if the recording is of an electronic work that is not for performance, she does not alter its ontological character by fiddling with the settings during the playback

---

[32] In the following I rely on arguments published in Davies (1997*b*). Similar conclusions are reached by Saltz (1997) in considering 'interactive' computer disks.

process. This last observation remains true even in the case in which the work's score contains roles for knob-twiddlers. John Cage's *Imaginary Landscape No. 4* (1951) is written for performers who manipulate the volume and tuning knobs of twelve radios. Even if it is a recording of this piece that is on the listener's turntable as she jiggles the graphic equalizers on her stereo, she can no more join in the performance than can the violinist who plays along with a music-minus-one recording on which the solo violinist's part is omitted.

A provocative exception is provided by Cage's *HPSCHD*, which was described in Chapter 1. In this piece, the playback device becomes an instrument performed by the user. Another case in which the recording becomes a *medium* for performance is hip hop as it was originally performed, live. The rap artist samples and 'scratches' the recordings of others—that is, they are treated as the raw source for his production, rather than being for playback. As well as imposing a structure on these materials, the rapper adds his own commentary. The result is a performance in its own right (Shusterman 1992: ch. 8; for a less romantic view, with more detail on the techniques involved, see Chanan 1995: 150–66).

The key point is that, where works for live or studio performance are recorded, the performance is finished when the recording is issued, even if it is incomplete as regards the number of parts or is otherwise faulty. Subsequent changes to the record's output—for instance, caused by its becoming scratched or warped, or by alterations to the settings of the playback device—do not alter the identity or properties of the recorded performance. Neither do supplementary sounds created as the disc is played (as when the user sings along) affect the identity or properties of the recorded performance. If one is a performer, one's efforts have to be such that they can affect the identity and properties of the given performance.

It might be suggested that the music-minus-one version is a recording of a work transcription. As such it would be distinct from the original. Whereas the original is a piece for live performance, the work transcription would be a multimedia piece for disc and instrumentalist or singer. In playing or singing with the disc, one would be performing the work transcription, joining in the performance that was begun in the studio and bringing it to completion in one's home.

I am inclined to resist this suggestion, because I doubt the appropriateness of viewing the music-minus-one disc as part of a multimedia piece. Recordings of works intended for live performance are not normally regarded as work transcriptions. There are, certainly, important differences between live and studio performances of such pieces, but we would not usually maintain that, in purchasing a CD of the Vienna Philharmonic playing Beethoven's Fifth Symphony, one has come to possess (merely) a transcription of Beethoven's work. The recorded version is classed alongside the orchestra's live performance, not with acknowledged work transcriptions, such as Franz Liszt's for the piano.[33]

Though I do not class music-minus-one discs as parts of multimedia pieces, there are recordings that certainly belong in this category. They are conceived for live performer, tape or record, and playback device. An example is *Philomel* (1964) by Milton Babbitt, which is for voice, taped voice, and taped sounds. In the case of a multimedia piece in which the tape features edited recordings of musicians, how should we describe the relation between the live player and the recorded musicians? Though the live performer's efforts should be spatially and temporally contiguous with the tape's playing, obviously they do not stand in that relation to the efforts of those who contributed to the tape's contents. Those who make the tape might be regarded as performing in that they elicit music from their instruments, but it would be inappropriate to see this as a performing *of the work*. Rather, they lay down the part of the work that is for playback, *not* performance. The tape does not 'record' a performance of the piece. In works of this kind, only those who play their parts live, in conjunction with the tape, count as performers.

The same point applies to those who supply material for purely electronic works. They contribute to the work's creation and their input comes to a close before the piece is finished. If they follow a composer's instructions, her directives concern the work's composition, not its performance. What these musicians do is very like what is done by the makers of a recording of a piece for studio performance, because in both cases the input is subject to electronic manipulation and the output is for playback, not performance. The difference lies in the way the product is offered and received, and in the traditions it invokes. A recording of a piece for studio performance conveys one interpretation of a work that can have others. As such, it embodies a performance. By contrast, the recording of a purely electronic piece directly encodes the work, which is also present on clones of that master.

Summary

Three conditions are necessary for a performance of a work and together are sufficient: (1) the performance matches the work's content, more or less; (2) the performers intend to follow most of the instructions specifying the work, whoever wrote them; and (3) a robust causal chain runs from

[33] It may be plausible to suggest that karaoke involves work transcription if we think of the originals as electronic works that are not for performance (as Gracyk 1996 has recommended for rock music), or even as works intended purely for studio performance. On these scenarios, the original is replaced by the karaoke version, which is a related but different multimedia work for live performance in at least some of its parts (Davies 1997*b*).

the performance to the work's creation. In addition, a performance can be simultaneously and entirely of two works only if, despite differences in their contents and consequent identities, the one is such that its specification could record a performance of the other. Also, I proposed that live performances are individuated not solely in terms of the spatio-temporal unity of the playing event, but also with respect to the performing group involved. Studio performances, by contrast, are identified with the simulated or virtual performances encoded on a master, or its clones. Studio performances should be evaluated in terms of criteria reflecting the advantages and challenges afforded by the recording context, rather than by those applying to the live setting, but, in the case of classical music that is conceived for live performance, we do expect recorded performers to be capable of playing similar pieces live.

PART TWO

Performance, Culture, and Recording

Introduction to Part Two

Part Two draws on the contextualist ontology outlined in Part One to develop an account of authenticity in musical performance. Or rather, I should say 'accounts', because three very different aspects of authenticity are discussed. They are the authenticity with which a performance instances its topic work, the authenticity with which works and playing styles represent the performance tradition and musical ideals of the culture within which they are presented, and the authenticity with which recordings represent the live performances they simulate.

The first kind of authenticity is most often invoked and challenged in relation to the performance of classical music from earlier eras. The rise of the 'authentic performance movement' during the second half of the twentieth century occasioned considerable debate among musicologists and others.[1] The controversy has generated more heat than light.[2] It is not difficult to see why the topic excites passion. 'Authentic performance' challenges established traditions of playing and teaching. It calls into question the hegemony held previously by famous orchestras over large parts of the classical repertoire and it casts doubt on the integrity of their performances. It impugns the credentials informally bestowed by the performers' Guilds described in the previous chapter. Until recently, these Guilds endorsed for almost all performances the use of techniques and instruments that belonged to the late nineteenth century. It 'defamiliarizes' works of the Baroque and Classical periods (Dreyfus 1983). Many specialist groups have taken up the gauntlet on behalf of 'authentic performance'. The claims they sometimes make about their efforts—that only these have the imprimatur of the composer, that other approaches to the music are inadequate, even morally irresponsible,

---

[1] It is sometimes alleged that the performance practice of the past did not advocate authentic performance when older music was played (Morrow 1978; Taruskin 1984, 1988; Howard Mayer Brown 1988; Kivy 1988b). In fact, this is a gross simplification. For a history of the way 'old' music has been played since the early nineteenth century to the present, see Haskell (1988).

[2] To be frank, with a few exceptions, the level of argument among musicians and musicologists is appalling. No shot is too cheap, no inference is too shoddy. *Ad hominems* abound. I quote two for their culinary unity: 'Music played on the instruments composers would have known is very popular with the open-toed-sandal-and-brown-bread set, but the sound is coarse and rarely fluid' (Sir Neville Marriner in Walsh 1983: 67). 'A large number of the most radical seekers after authenticity as late as the 1950s were amateur musicians for whom Early Music was part of a style of life that included playing the recorder, eating brown rice and whole wheat bread, and making their own clothes. The movement has now developed into a genuinely professional and profitable one' (Rosen 1990: 49).

and that inauthenticity in musical performance is equivalent to defacing a painting[3]—add fuel to the flames.

In Chapter 5, I consider the key notions and issues that are presumed but not analysed by those whose musical ontology is merely a by-product of their musico-ideological prejudices. I discuss the nature of performance authenticity, its attainability, and its desirability. In particular, I examine the extent to which it might be legitimate to sacrifice authenticity for the sake of achieving other performance and reception values.

The second kind of authenticity is best examined in relation to the music of non-Western cultures subject to pressure from foreign sources. For comparison, consider a public performance at the Salzburg Festival of Mozart's Piano Sonata in D, K. 331. Questions might be raised about its authenticity, but it is unlikely that these would concern the following: the performance takes place in a public space, not in the home; the work's last movement clearly reveals that the composer was influenced by a foreign (Turkish) musical idiom; many of the audience's members are tourists, there to hear the music; the musician is paid for her work; she did not build the instrument on which she plays and ritual prayers and blessings were not involved in its making. When the authenticity of performances of non-Western music is debated, such considerations are likely to be raised. For instance, if the music played for paying tourists by the members of an African tribe has clearly been influenced by recent Western pop styles, its credentials as a faithful representation of the tribe's music and culture will probably be queried.

Where performances are inspected in these ways for their authenticity, at issue is the extent to which they are a genuine expression of the culture's music and, thereby, whether they reveal the values and qualities central to the home society's self-identity and continuity. In discussing such matters, it is necessary to consider whether cultural change can be meaningfully distinguished from colonization, and to reflect on the implications that accompany the commercialization and commodification of non-Western art.

Entirely different questions arise when one reflects on the present domination of the music scene by recordings. Most musical works are created for live performance, yet most people experience most performances via electronic mediation and, hence, at a remove from the playings that are done. They listen to the radio or to tapes or discs. In Chapters 1 and 4 I outlined some of the ways in which what occurs in the recording studio is unlike what happens on the concert stage. Despite these differences, we talk of the performances that are found on tapes, vinyl records, CDs, videos, and the like. Apparently we regard recorded performances as fair substitutes for live ones.

---

[3] These assertions are false or misleading, of course. To take the last, whereas oil paintings are singular, musical works are for multiple performance. One blatantly inauthentic musical performance does not prevent the possibility of other, authentic ones, whereas vandalizing an oil painting is liable to destroy the work.

It is important, then, to assess recordings for authenticity against the live performances they purport to represent, and to consider more broadly the implications for performance traditions and music making of the move towards technologically facilitated presentations of musical pieces.

Before getting down to the debates just promised, it is appropriate to clarify the general concept of authenticity.

What is authenticity?

Dictionaries register several meanings for 'authentic' and 'authenticity': of undisputed origin, genuine, reliable, or trustworthy. I recommend the following as a way of capturing the central notion: where 'X' names a type or kind or class of thing (and is not, say, a proper noun), an authentic X is an X. In other words, something is an authentic X if it is an instance or member of the class of Xs. An interest in authenticity reflects a concern with correct classification. In this view, a hamburger is an authentic McDonald's if it is made by McDonald's and displays the properties that distinguish their products.

Any individual might be seen as instancing different types—hamburger, nourishing food, instrument of US imperialism—and considered for its authenticity against these various categories. Judgements of authenticity are always class relative. If the type is not specified, usually this is because it is assumed we know which is in question. We might consider the authenticity of an item with respect to any classifications that interest us, so long as we make explicit which classifications those are.

Questions of authenticity come to the fore where things are difficult to categorize ('is this yellow metal gold?') and where matters of importance hang on how we classify them (gold is valuable and iron pyrites is not). The properties in terms of which a thing achieves authenticity are those by which it qualifies for class membership. Because classes can be generated in many ways, authenticity can be realized in many ways. Assessments of authenticity will refer sometimes to a thing's intrinsic, non-relational properties; at others, its relational or other properties will be crucial. Where the item in question is humanly produced, its authenticity often depends on its historical and causal provenance.

When membership in the class in question is a matter of precision, so that a thing has the decisive property or not, authenticity is an all-or-nothing affair. Many of our classifications are inherently comparative, however. Something qualifies as an instance if it meets a minimum standard, but it is better or clearer as an instance the more it exceeds that standard. All members of the class of tall people are above average human height, but some are taller than others. Where classes are of this kind, the authenticity of their members comes in degrees; all are (minimally) authentic, but some are more so than others. In general, classes that admit of a scale of well-formedness in their instances allow for comparative judgements about the authenticity of those instances.

There is another way some judgements of authenticity are relative. If it is the case that, on average, humans have grown taller over the years, the classification 'tall person' is time indexed. This does not rule out the possibility of cross-temporal comparisons—such as, Fred would have been tall had he lived in the Middle Ages. Judgements of authenticity are not rendered impossible or illegitimate by an extended history of change in the type in question, provided indices within the continuum identify the temporal locations of the elements being compared.[4]

The judgement that something is authentic does not, as yet, say something about its worth. In part, the value of an authentic item depends on the nature of its type, because, in qualifying as an instance, it faithfully exhibits the type's defining features. Some types will be essentially positive in value, others will be negative, and many will be neutral. Denis Dutton (1994) calls the kind of authenticity I have been describing, that which is concerned with the correct identification of an item, 'nominal'. He regards nominal authenticity as never concerned with evaluation. Though it is true that judgements of authenticity are neutral in value where the class to which they are relativized is the same, Dutton is wrong to make the universal claim. If value properties are essential to the type, then one must consider whether something has those properties in judging whether it is an authentic instance of the type. In assessing whether someone is an authentic moral paragon, one must examine whether she displays to a high degree the virtues of justice, kindness, and the like; so one must contemplate the moral value and significance of her actions.

Returning to the questions posed earlier we can ask, which classifications of music and its performance do they assume to be important? The first enquires whether a performance is representative of the work it purports to be of, and identifies that work as its author's. In other words, it assumes as primary an interest in performances as of works and in works as the products of their creators. The second attends to the work or performance as representing the styles and ideals of the performer's and composer's musical culture. Because of the social importance of art in contributing to the identity and self-image of the society in which it is made, these works and performances might also be seen as embodying and representing the given culture's wider cosmological, religious, ethical, and other values and attitudes. The third category focuses on recordings as representative of live perfor-

---

[4] To take one case, no inconsistency is displayed by Alan Lomax when, having recorded an unbroken line of development from African music to Mississippi delta blues, to modern urban blues, and to rhythm and blues, he goes on to compare urban, electronic blues unfavourably with older Mississippi blues (1993: 355, 360).

mances. This raises important issues because recording technology can alienate the listener from contextual features and human elements deemed significant to the proper appreciation and enjoyment of music as such. If recorded music is dislocated from its natal environment, the implications of this need to be recognized and explored.

Music and its performances can be classified with respect to as many features or functions as they can possess or be given. Their instances then can be judged for authenticity with respect to the categories in question. Most of these judgements will be silly, inappropriate, or trivial, because the classifications to which they are relativized are silly, inappropriate, or trivial. They pay no heed to what is distinctive to and important about music. A central task in the philosophy of music is to identify the interests that are crucial to our having music and to its having the (diverse) nature it displays. The categorizations crucial to our recognition of music as such mirror those interests. In Part Two, I discuss the significance of three ways of being interested in and classifying performances; as instances of works, as representative of the wider musical culture and of society in general, and as proxies for live renditions.

5

Authenticity in Western
Classical Music

Playing harpsichord music on the piano was simply not satisfying—
which eventually led me to take up the harpsichord. Something similar
seems often to be the case with violinists. There are certain things which
one finds in early violin methods which the modern violin and bow are
simply incapable of doing. During my first conservatory years I was
involved in a small baroque ensemble, using modern instruments. The
necessity of playing on early instruments became more and more clear
to us; it was not the public which demanded this, but rather our own
growing dissatisfaction. For us, the early instruments began where the
modern ones left off. This also became clear to me while working with
musicians in a modern orchestra; even the most outstanding results do
not come close to what one can achieve on baroque instruments.

(Koopman 1987: 4)

In this chapter I discuss performances judged for the authenticity with which
they represent the works they are of. In Chapter 1 I argued that musical
works are not of a single ontological type. It follows, then, that what is
required for authenticity in a work's instances will depend on what kind of
piece it is. For most of this chapter I restrict my attention to authenticity
in performances of pieces intended for live performance and specified by
scores written by their composers.[1] Such works are the most common and
familiar in Western classical music. It is pieces of this kind on which debates
concerning 'authentic performance' focus.

My discussion does not address the politics of performance. I approach
the topic under three headings. What is authenticity in respect of performances of works? Is authenticity attainable in practice? Is authenticity a
good thing?

---

[1] The position is developed from arguments outlined in Davies (1987, 1988b, 1990, 1991b).

Authenticity in works specified by composers' scores

In Chapter 3 I described scores as encoding instructions addressed by the composer to the player. These tell the musician what to do if she is to produce an instance of the work in question. In order to interpret them, the musician must know both the notational conventions and the performance practice assumed by the composer, because not everything that is required is recorded in the notation, and not everything written down is mandatory or should be read literally. A performance instances the work if the musician successfully executes the work-identifying instructions (or, at least, succeeds in satisfying a sufficient number of them that the performance is recognizably of the work). Combining these points with the account of authenticity offered earlier we get: a performance of a given work is authentic if it faithfully instances the work, which is done by following the composer's work-determinative instructions as these are publicly recorded in its score.[2]

Authenticity in performance comes in degrees. I allowed in Chapter 4 that a performance can be of a musical work, though it represents it imperfectly (owing to performance errors, for instance). Any performance that succeeds in instancing the piece is (at least minimally) faithful. A performance might fail to be ideally authentic, while being sufficiently authentic to qualify unequivocally as an instance of the given work. The more faithful a performance is, the more authentic it is.[3]

Because it is essentially implicated in a work's performance, authenticity is an *ontological requirement*, not an *interpretative option*. By this I mean that the pursuit of authenticity—enough, at least, to make the performance recognizably of its topic work—is not merely one interpretative possibility among many, equally legitimate, alternatives. If the work is designated by the composer's determinative instructions, one can perform the composer's work only by playing it authentically (that is, by respecting and executing those

---

[2] Haskell (1988: 175) writes: 'While it is generally agreed that authenticity of some sort is the ultimate goal of historical performance, no clear consensus exists as to what the word means.' Of course this is false. Koopman's view (1987: 2) is surely correct: 'In the context of early music, the meaning of the word "authenticity" is clear: the performance of music on period instruments, using rules of performance practice from that same period, according to the ideas developed at that time as skilfully and as accurately as possible.' I assume Haskell means that musicians disagree about how authenticity is to be achieved in particular cases. The term has become a 'buzzword', certainly, loaded with musico-political and ideological connotations (Morrow 1978; Leech-Wilkinson 1984; Kerman 1985).

[3] Since theorists analyse musical ontology differently, their views of what is required for authenticity in performance do not coincide (Davies 1991b; Edidin 1991). Someone who thinks musical works are pure sound structures would regard as irrelevant to the faithfulness of a performance that it uses instruments other than those specified by the composer, whereas someone who thinks musical works are performed sound structures will regard the use of appropriate instruments as essential for authenticity. For this, and for the reasons I am about to explain, issues of authenticity and of ontology cannot be separated.

instructions). If one is committed to playing the given piece then, equally, one must be committed to performing it authentically. To ignore a majority of the composer's determinative instructions is not to interpret her work in an unusual way; it is to fail to perform, and hence to interpret, *that* work at all. Where the goal is the performance of works specified by composers in the scores they write, achieving an appropriate degree of authenticity is a fundamental and unavoidable requirement; it is the default option; it is a prima facie obligation.

As it is an ontological requirement, I am disinclined to attempt to dodge the difficulties that attend talk of authenticity by resort to a new terminology. For instance, I think it is misguided to scrap mention of authenticity in favour of 'period performance' or 'historically informed performance'. The substitutions shun the controversy that surrounds the old terms, but in doing so fail to address the important questions provoked by that debate. Moreover, the new designations have unfortunate connotations of their own. 'Period performance' and 'historically informed performance' sound (to me) as if they characterize interpretative options that might be ranged alongside others, such as 'Romantic performance', or 'Gould-style performance'.

One feature of these alternative terminologies is worth noting: they imply that authenticity is an issue only with respect to the performance of works from past eras. In one sense, this is correct, in another not. Judgements of authenticity apply to performances of all music.[4] I agree with Kerman when he writes (1985: 210): 'The real issue is not a special repertory which has somehow acquired charm or prestige on account of its earliness, and which is to be played in a special, aberrant fashion, but a comprehensive theory of performance covering music from the earliest times we care about up to the present.' The pursuit of authenticity is not usually controversial, however, when the musicians are intimately familiar with the conventions and traditions that the composer presupposes, which is the case when trained musicians deal with scores of Western classical works from after 1920.[5] Aiming at authenticity is comparatively straightforward where the specified instruments are the familiar ones, the notation is transparently standard, and

[4] A different view, one that I believe is mistaken, regards authentic performance merely as a faddish twentieth-century style of playing older music (Leech-Wilkinson 1984; Temperley 1984; Howard Mayer Brown 1988; Haskell 1988; Taruskin 1988, 1992; Philip 1992).

[5] I do not deny that there is considerable debate over the legitimacy of many options taken in recorded performances from the early days of the twentieth century (see Philip 1992). For the most part, I believe these disagreements concern the success or otherwise of different interpretative strategies all of which are likely to be compatible with the authentic representation of the piece. For instance, Cook (1995) defends Fürtwangler's treatment of tempo in performances of Beethoven not only as interpretationally perceptive but as probably consistent with a performance tradition going back to Wagner and beyond. If he is right, Fürtwangler's approach may not be inauthentic, even if it is at odds with some current paradigms both for authentic performance and for tasteful interpretation.

the performance conventions are of the ordinary kind. Authenticity becomes a problem when we attempt to play works that require performance techniques about which we are uncertain, or that use 'strange' instruments or 'primitive' versions of modern ones, or that presuppose an intimate knowledge of performance conventions and notational systems that are no longer in use. In short, achieving authenticity becomes a live issue when there are difficulties in understanding the composer's instructions or in knowing how to execute them.

The mistaken suggestion that 'authentic' work performance is only one approach to interpretation that is rivalled by other, no less viable, ones often goes with these observations: many different-sounding performances are equally acceptable as accounts of the composer's work; at most, only one of these can be authentic; for the others, it must be something other than authenticity that accounts for their interest and acceptability. Hence the conclusion: authenticity is not the only target at which performers can aim legitimately, and its value does not trump or defeat other kinds of interpretationally rewarding readings of the score (Young 1988; Hermerén 1995).

This argument contains a false premiss: that the authenticist must hold that there is only one authentic performance. If the composer's determinative instructions settle everything that the performer must do in instancing her work, so that no two maximally authentic performances could sound different, one might suppose that only one performance type could be fully authentic.[6] Plainly this is not how the relevant works are, however. The composer's instructions underdetermine the sound of any particular, ideally authentic performance. Even if all the composer's determinative indications are followed to the letter, many matters that must be settled in generating a performance are not covered by them, being left to the performer (or conductor). It is for this reason that performing is creative, even where it aims at instancing a composer's work. A range of differing performances could all be ideally authentic (Ingarden 1986; Davies 1987; Thom 1993). Each shares with the others those elements produced in the faithful realization of the composer's instructions, but each differs from the others according to the performer's free choices.

The canard that there can be only one authentic performance of a work is put forward by opponents of the authentic performance movement. It is a straw person. Silly views are often attributed to the authenticist by her critics. One holds that an authentic performance must aim to recreate (the sound of) the work's *first* performance. Against this several points can

---

[6] This false supposition is invoked in the following argument offered by Morrow 1978; Taruskin 1982, 1988; Leech-Wilkinson 1984; Haskell 1988; Tomlinson 1988: because musical works are multiply interpretable and the performer is always free in some respects, there can be no such thing as an authentic performance.

be made. Conditions at the first performance were often far from optimal—the musicians were under-rehearsed and technically incompetent. In other cases, the performance contained elements we would (quite rightly) no longer regard as appropriate. For instance, at the first performance of Beethoven's Violin Concerto, Op. 61, between the movements the soloist played a novelty piece with the violin held upside down (Rosen 1971). Also, some works did not receive their first performances until long after they were written. These darts hit their target squarely enough, but there is no reason to think authenticity should be analysed in the fashion that is attacked here. Though my account of authenticity appeals to the musical practices of the composer's day, it does not assume that *actual* performances of the time set the standard for authenticity. The appeal is to optimized conditions—to the best that was possible at the time, whether or not it was available to the composer.

The optimizing clause does not suppose that composers work in the realm of 'pure sound', with scant regard for the resources and practical circumstances under which their works are performed. Though some virtuosic pieces have been deemed unplayable (in part) by their composers' contemporaries, they are the exception, not the rule. Composers almost always reveal a practical concern for the limitations of those for whom they write. In one case, a motet (usually attributed to Josquin) includes a monotonic part, marked 'vox regis', for the unmusical king (usually identified as Louis XII) (Reese 1954: 229). Edward Elgar composed wind pieces, *Promenades 1–6*, for himself and his friends, with differences in the difficulty of the various parts tailored precisely to the aptitudes of the players for whom he wrote. The optimizing clause assumes only that composers should be accorded, if possible, the best conditions and musicians for the performance of their works.

Here is another weakling argument. If the work is deemed to be what the composer heard in his head as he wrote the score, where this has the level of detail of sounded music, a performance is authentic only if it duplicates what he heard. Given that we do not know just what went on in the composer's mind's ear, we cannot perform his work authentically (except, perhaps, by chance and unwittingly).

This attack rests on a thoroughly implausible account of the nature of musical works. Though idealist ontologies have been proposed for works of art (by Benedetto Croce 1953, for instance), they have been deservedly criticized (see Wollheim 1968). Besides, the argument proves too much if it proves anything, for it seems to rule out the possibility of *any* performance, not just of authentic performance. At best, a performance could only gesture towards the work by playing an approximation that is roughly and inadequately captured by its score.

We are fortunate to have recordings of composers, such as Sergei Rachmaninov, Percy Grainger, and Igor Stravinsky, playing or conducting their own works. Where these were made under favourable conditions, they are bound to be of interest as indicating the interpretation preferred by the composer.[7] Nevertheless, we do not expect all other performers to follow these interpretations religiously. Composers' performances might bring to realization wishes they have regarding the interpretation of their works, but they do not thereby make those wishes work determinative. Music remains a *performance* art that, as such, conventionally allows that, in establishing the piece's properties, the composer permits interpretative freedom to the performer. As a performer of her work, a composer offers a performative interpretation that has a special status only to the extent that we expect it to be insightful, given her intimate knowledge of the piece. But, even where the performance succeeds in being revealing, alternative renditions may be no less interesting when they differ from the composer's account while remaining faithful to the work's score.

Another misconceived objection to the project of authentic performance takes this form: an authentic performance is one that matches the composer's intentions, but intentions are private mental events of which we can know little, especially when we are historically removed from the context in which they are entertained (Taruskin 1982, 1988). The caricature Cartesian view, according to which intentions are private mental events accessible only to the person who has them, has been rightly challenged by Ludwig Wittgenstein (1953) and others. But in any case, it simply is not true that we usually lack awareness of composers' work-identifying intentions. Those are expressed publicly in the scores they issue. Provided we are acquainted with the conventions on which their successful expression depends, we can often know quite clearly what was intended by the work's composer.

Mandates and recommendations

As is apparent from Chapter 3, I place considerable emphasis both on the conventions and ideals of the performance practice that provides the context for the composer's efforts and on the notational conventions the composer shares with those he addresses. These make possible the public expression of the composer's intentions, which concern what the performer is to do if she elects to produce an instance of the work in question. Though they make possible the communication of the composer's intentions, these conventions also set limits on what can be indicated as work determinative. Whether an intention issues in an instruction that must be obeyed, as against a recommendation that might be ignored by the performer, is not a matter of the strength with which the composer wills that intention. It is, rather, a

---

[7] Notice, though, that multiple recordings of a single work by its composer often display significant differences. For instance, compare Stravinsky's recordings of *The Rite of Spring* (see Chanan 1995: 123).

consequence of what the social practice allows the composer and performer to do. If the composer wants the string players to use instruments made only by Stradivarius, she could not thereby restrict the performers of her work, even if she expresses her desire by recording it in the score, because the social practice of music making does not recognize conventions permitting composers to issue that kind of instruction. In this case, the composer's note to the performer would be recommendatory, not mandatory. The conventions of musical practice have altered through time and have done so in a fashion that has given more control to the composer. The earlier the work, the more the score is silent, or contains advice only, about details that must be concretely realized in a performance. We must be aware of such changes, along with those in the instruments available and the techniques of playing them, if we are to interpret the composer's instructions correctly, which is to say in terms of the particular conventions that apply to his music and notation.

In acknowledging the role of musical and notational conventions, both as facilitating the expression of the composer's intentions and as restricting what he might command, I distinguish between the composer's definitive intentions or instructions and his recommendations, advice, or wishes (Davies 1987; see also Kendall L. Walton 1988; Predelli 1995; Edlund 1997). The pursuit of ideal authenticity requires of the performer only that he obeys the former. When it comes to wishes and advice, he can do what he chooses, provided he stays within the limits of choice allowed by the performance practice of the composer's day.

On this distinction, Peter Kivy (1995: 12) comments: 'it is a very nice question which of a composer's performance intentions are "determinate"[8] and which are "merely recommendatory"'. Yet he himself employs the distinction (see 1988*a*: 48), so it must be that the 'very nice question' concerns problems we sometimes face in judging between the two under conditions of epistemic opacity, rather than about the distinction's conceptual viability.

Take a deliberately outlandish example. Suppose a nineteenth-century composer wrote in the score of a purely instrumental work that, at a particular moment, each performer is to smile at the person on his left. Or take the case of Franz Joseph Haydn's Symphony No. 45, 'Farewell', in which the players are supposed to leave the stage in pairs before the last movement ends. Now, an orchestra's members might do what is suggested, but I doubt that the performance is less authentic as an instance of the musical work if they do not. Tradition has it that, in having the musicians exit, Haydn intended to remind his Prince that they should be granted holidays. I can see that it is

---

[8] I am misquoted. In 1987 and elsewhere, I use the word 'determinative', not 'determinate'. What is determinative is not always precise. 'Andante' can be no less determinative as an instruction than is 'crotchet = 70'.

desirable to explain this in the concert's programme notes, but it is not clear to me that the 'scena' Haydn envisaged is part of the symphony as such. (Kivy disagrees, though; see 1995: 104–5.) The conventions of instrumental musical genres do not provide composers with authority to make indications of those sorts determinative of their works.[9]

When it comes to recommendations the point of which is obviously musical, there is good reason to take them seriously. Where the soloist in a Mozart concerto has before her a version of the cadenza written out by Mozart, she would do well to follow it unless she is highly skilled in making up suitable ones of her own. But the performer who goes her own way, refusing to be guided in the matter by the composer's recommendation, does not compromise the authenticity of her performance so long as she remains within bounds set by the performance practice of the composer's time. It is only those instructions of the composer that are mandatory, those that specify what is constitutive of his work, that must be followed if authenticity is to result.

The conventions on which I place importance are ones governing the interpretation of the composer's work-determinative instructions. Many of the social norms that applied to performances in the past are irrelevant to the goal of authentic performance, I claim, because they have nothing to do with identifying instances of musical works as such. For instance, it is not required that the musicians wear wigs and light their music stands with candles, even if this was standard practice at the time of the work's first performance.[10]

Other conventions, ones that are 'musical', might also be ignored, if there is no artistic cost in doing so. Consider the repeats marked in many classical works (for example, at the end of the exposition of the first movement of a symphony). Often these are not played nowadays. If they served originally to help first-time audiences, many of whom would not be paying close attention anyway, to grasp the main thematic ideas, and if ignoring them does not unbalance the movement or its relation to other movements, their observance is unnecessary now because the audience is

---

[9] I allow that, within experimental music, such instructions can be mandatory. For instance, the score of Toshi Ichiyanagi's *Sapporo* (1962) specifies that the players watch each other (Nyman 1981: 95). In the context of avant-garde art and Ichiyanagi's œuvre, the action is part of the work, but this is because experimental music has moved in the direction of theatre and multi-media presentations, not because such gestures are normally integral to the identity of purely instrumental musical works.

[10] I would apply the same line to dramatic productions: in Shakespeare's day, boys played the roles of women on stage. I do not think this can be required now in the name of authenticity. This is not because performances with women are better, though this is likely to be true. It is because the original practice had a moral, rather than a strictly theatrical, basis. If the rule is merely a social convention applied to theatre, rather than one integral to the identity of dramatic works, there need be no loss of authenticity in ignoring it.

likely to be conversant with the work or to listen intently.[11] Notice, though, that the same argument does not apply to *da capo* structures, because ignoring the repeat would compromise the form, changing it from a ternary to a binary one. Because minuets have a ternary form, the trio must be followed by a return to the beginning, though the repeat is literal and the audience is already familiar with the material.

Prior to the early nineteenth century, the orchestra was directed by the soloist, the continuo player, or the leader of the violins. In performing these pieces now, is it inauthentic to employ a conductor? I do not think so. This departure from the practice of the day does not affect the identity of the work performed, so I see no reason to rule out the use of a conductor. In a similar vein, if the score calls for two percussionists, I do not think that the authenticity of the performance is compromised if the parts are redistributed to bring in a third player, so long as this does not alter musical properties relevant to the work's identity.[12]

Venues and social ritual

In general, I am inclined to regard its site or venue as relevant to the authenticity of a performance only in so far as this affects its sound. This is to say, what matters is the acoustic environment for which the music was conceived, not the social context. Physical aspects of the performance space contribute to the way music is experienced by affecting which pitch bands are reflected or absorbed and the period for which sounds remain audible. Composers write their music to suit the performance's setting. In the Renaissance, sacbuts and shawms were used only in music played outdoors; lutes and flutes were confined to interior locations. Much eighteenth-century court music was intended for the bright sound of wood-panelled rooms; liturgical music was for reverberant churches; nineteenth-century chamber music belonged in plush salons. Where the setting has unique acoustic properties, as is so for St Mark's in Venice, and the composer writes to exploit these (as in Stravinsky's *Canticum Sacrum* of 1955), the highest degree of authenticity might require that the works be performed at those places. Otherwise, it is sufficient that the site of performance has an appropriate

---

[11] I allow that the aesthetic cost in ignoring repeats is often unacceptable, though. Rosen (1990) suggests that, in eighteenth-century music, the repeats must be respected because the work's proportion and harmonic equilibrium depend on them. Later, in Schubert's music, the repeats are dispensable, he holds. Levinson (1997: 84) argues that the progression from the conclusion of the exposition to the outset of development may simply be more cogent or compelling with a repeated exposition than without it.

[12] If the piece is a percussion duet designed to showcase the virtuosity of the performers, the introduction of a third player would have dire consequences for the performance's authenticity. The different example I have in mind is one where the third musician takes over the tubular bells from the triangle player, where neither instrument is used very often.

soundscape.[13] So long as the acoustic features of the environment for which the piece was intended are duplicated in the concert-hall setting (by the use of adjustable baffles and the like), the authenticity of performances is not compromised by their removal to such locations.

The concert chamber, along with public performance, was an innovation that appeared at the end of the eighteenth century. Prior to this time, music was written for other venues and circumstances. For instance, J. S. Bach's *Cantatas* were conceived for inclusion in Lutheran church services. They can be performed authentically in the concert hall only if their identities survive intact when they are extracted from the ritual setting. Are musical works identifiable independently of the social context of presentation for which they were designed? If not, claims to authenticity on behalf of concert-hall renditions will be spurious, whatever care is taken over the use of period instruments and performance practices. The point is not, of course, that *we* are happy about abstracting what *we* regard as the musical work, which certainly is true enough. It is whether the composer and his contemporaries conceived of the work as distinct from the wider context for which it was intended. After all, if the work takes its identity from intentions and conventions operating at the time of its creation, then it is those intentions and conventions that set the standards to which judgements of authenticity should be relativized.

Kivy (1995: 98–9) thinks that works written before the end of the eighteenth century, which he calls the 'great divide', take part of their identity from their context (see also Morgan 1988 and Goehr 1992). They are inseparable from the multimedia events to which they belonged. When they are removed from these, what is played is a concert version or arrangement, much as one gets when an opera is performed in the concert hall. Though the result is inauthentic, this is counterbalanced by advantages afforded to the person interested in the music. She is not subject to the tedium of a vicar's sermon before she can listen to the piece.

I prefer a stronger line. If composers and musicians of the time regarded the work as a discrete musical entity, while fully recognizing that it was conjoined with other practices in a broader setting to which it contributed towards the overall goal, say, of promoting religious devotion and glorifying God, then they allowed in principle for the possibility that the work

---

[13] It may be that venues for public performance lack this. Rosen (1990) distinguishes between the music written by Bach for private, domestic use and that composed for public presentation. In a public setting, it might not be possible to play in an idiomatic fashion pieces of the former kind on the instruments, such as the clavichord, for which they were designed. He thinks Bach's *The Art of Fugue* and *Well-Tempered Klavier* are best presented in concert halls on the piano, because this is the instrument that can balance the parts while remaining audible. If Rosen is correct, what might follow is that recordings using the appropriate instruments are more authentic than public performances.

might stand as an object of interest in its own right. The claim is not that they would have preferred or intended the music to be divorced from its place in an extended ritual. It is, simply, that they viewed the work as identifiable independently of its social location. If they thought of the identity of musical works as not depending on the context with which they were integrated, then that conception would allow that performances of the work apart from their settings can be counted not as 'concert versions' but as genuine performances.

It is difficult, of course, to work out what conception these composers had. Much music was performed only once. Works that were repeated usually retained their ritual location. (A piece written for one coronation might later be used at another.) Lydia Goehr (1992) seems to interpret these facts as showing that composers did not conceive of their works as separable from the functional settings where they were used. It seems to me, however, that this account of the historical record does not do justice to other relevant considerations. There were many factors, ones falling beyond the composer's control, that determined what, when, where, and how his music would be played. Composers were employed as servants and wrote what was required by their church employers, their courtly masters, and so on. So, one should be wary of inferring from the incidence of performance how these composers thought of their activities. On the positive side, there are many indications that they regarded themselves as producing works taking their identity from musical features alone. It always was the case that playing and listening to music for its own sake was recognized as a worthwhile activity (Young 1996).

The use of period instruments

As I explained in Chapter 2, Jerrold Levinson (1980a, 1990a) holds that a work's instrumentation, its 'performance means', is partly constitutive of its identity (at least, in the case of pieces such as Beethoven's Quintet in E Flat, Op. 16). Accordingly, he maintains that an authentic performance of such a work requires the use of the instruments indicated (and that they be the versions with which Beethoven was familiar, not the modern equivalents). Authentic performance involves not simply making the 'right' sounds but eliciting them in the appropriate fashion from the relevant instruments (Levinson 1990c).[14]

---

[14] See also Kerman (1985), Harnoncourt (1988, 1989), Leppard (1988), Kendall L. Walton (1988), Donington (1989), and Thom (1990b, 1993). In the previous chapter I outlined Godlovitch's account of performance integrity. On the matter of authenticity, he is not a purist (see 1988, 1997). He is not devoted to the use of 'period' instruments, though he does think the performer must use an instrument of the *type* specified by the composer if the performance is to possess integrity.

As I have already made clear, I agree with Levinson on many of the relevant issues. We both think the use of appropriate period instruments *is* essential in achieving the highest degree of authenticity if their use is required by the composer. And I concur that some of the properties of musical works depend on the manner in which the sounds are elicited from the instruments in question. Where composers conceive their works for performance on specific kinds of instruments and issue determinative instructions that this be done, these are properties of the *work*, not solely of its *performances*. Though we share these conclusions and assumptions, Levinson and I differ in our arguments. He is inclined to suggest that there always is a gestural quality specific to playing the instruments in question, and that this affects the expressive properties of the resulting sound, though the perception of these properties is available only to the listener who is suitably informed about characteristics of the instruments in question. Also, he takes account of composers' expressed preferences. By contrast, I doubt that there always are relevant differences between the expressive character of performances using authentic and inauthentic instrumentations, and I am concerned with only those intentions of the composer that the musical practice of the day recognizes as work determinative. It was not always the case that composers' wishes as regards the instrumentation of their works were mandatory. Some of those earlier disagreements return in considering a question that is central to this chapter: is the use of period instruments, as against their modern equivalents, required for the fullest degree of authenticity in performance?

Levinson suggests there is a distinctive gestural quality involved in playing particular kinds of instruments, and that this affects aesthetic features that can contribute to a work's identity. Even if these claims were convincing, they could justify the use of *period* instruments, as against modern versions, only if playing them involves distinctive actions. Levinson accepts the challenge, but he does not spell out how the manner of playing differs in the case he considers.

The musical gestures in Mozart's Thirty-ninth Symphony, K. 543 . . . are presumably precisely those that are readily perceived in it against the matrix of the gestural repertoires and sonic capacities of just the instruments for which the piece was conceived—e.g., old-style clarinets . . . even if modern clarinets . . . could produce sounds *indistinguishable* from those that eighteenth-century clarinets would make in rendering the score of Mozart's Thirty-ninth Symphony, such a performance would not be expressively equivalent to *any* performance achievable on those older, and different, instruments. What expressiveness it would have is hard to say, bastardy being no simpler to deal with in the aesthetic realm than in the social one. But in any event, it would not quite be a proper representation of K. 543's own expressiveness, and hence not an authentic performance of it.   (Levinson 1990c: 407)

(Levinson allows, though, that the departure from ideal authenticity involved in using modern clarinets is a matter of degree and is not so serious as would be the substitution of an electronic synthesizer for the clarinet.)

Because I doubt that the playing of period instruments always requires different actions from those made in working with their contemporary equivalents, I am unconvinced by Levinson's argument. For instance, the gestures involved in sounding the modern pedal tympani cannot be very different from those in playing its non-pedal predecessors. Nevertheless, as before, I approve of the conclusion he draws: that the use of period instruments is required for the fullest degree of authenticity (given that their use is made work identifying by the composer).

If not by Levinson's argument, how is that conclusion supported? In the first place, one can appeal to the fact that period instruments usually sound different from their modern counterparts. Here is just one example:

[Beethoven's Symphony No. 1, Op. 21] calls for clarinets and horns in C. Neither of these instruments is common today, and the modern substitutes sound quite different, particularly the horns. The other instruments have also undergone changes to a greater or lesser extent . . . In addition, there is the problem of the relative weight of sound between the winds and the strings. Not only have the actual instruments and manner of playing them changed, but the proportion in the number of players between the families of instruments have changed. Playing the score in the modern orchestra, then, is only an approximation of the sound as Beethoven conceived it. (Silliman 1969: 106)

It is relevant to add a second observation to this first: period instruments, when played in the style of the day, sound different from modern ones, but, as well, they sound better. They make clearer or more salient features of the work that are aesthetically significant. The quotation at the beginning of this chapter from Ton Koopman illustrates the point.

To return to terms introduced in Chapter 2, even the timbral sonicist might be impressed by the difference made to the sound of the performance by the use of period instruments. If he believes that, in practice, authentic performances almost always sound different and better, he could support the use of period instruments and practices on aesthetic, if not ontological, grounds.

A different response is common, however. Though it is accepted that period performances sound different, it is often disputed that they sound better. Few would go so far as Webster (1974) when he claims there is nothing to choose between using a violin and a sousaphone in playing J. S. Bach's Violin Concerto in E, but many would see no problem with using a modern violin to play the work. Two considerations are brought forward in defence of this approach. (*a*) Modern instruments improve on their predecessors. For instance, valves have been added to brass, the Boehm system of keys is now used for winds, pianos have one-piece metal frames, strings are now made of metal rather than gut, and so on. (*b*) Composers looked forward to these improvements and would have welcomed the instruments that had them.[15]

As a first response, one can query the equation of change with improvement (Godlovitch 1988). Period instruments often had many distinctive and endearing qualities that were sacrificed in the name of progress and uniformity. The wooden Baroque flute has a warm intimacy of tone that is absent from its modern, metal counterpart. Harpsichords possessed stops and allowed for octave couplings, whereas pianofortes lack these. The fortepiano had a lighter, drier tone than the felt-hammered, modern grand. Some fortepianos had harp, bassoon, and Turkish stops (Kirkby 1966: 23). With its flatter bridge, the Baroque violin was more suited than the modern instrument to double stopping. Moreover, the wide variety among instances of cellos and oboes, for instance, allowed for a more subtle matching of instrument to work than is now possible.

The following also points to the danger of assuming that the 'improved' version is the better one to use: the Steinway grand, with its metal frame and sturdy construction, easily survives its use in a performance of Beethoven's 'Appassionata'. When one hears that work on a period fortepiano, the impression is very different. Then it becomes easy to appreciate the stories about the rate at which Beethoven broke pianos, for it is apparent that the instrument is deliberately pushed to its limits in the sonata. It sounds as if it might be shaken to bits by the fury of the music. One might compare this experience with watching two cars travelling down a road at the same speed. One is a Rolls Royce, cruising comfortably in something less than its highest gear, whereas the other is a Model T Ford, running at the limits of its engine's capacity and on the verge of blowing a gasket. Though both vehicles progress at the same rate, their motion appears very different to the person who is aware of their respective capabilities. That of the Model T is strained and dramatic, whereas the Rolls's is not. Returning now to the musical case, even if the sounds produced by the fortepiano and the Steinway were the same (which they are not, of course), they should sound different to the informed listener, and that difference would bring out an important feature of the music in the one instance that was lost to the other. (Kerman 1989 makes a similar observation in discussing performances of Mozart's piano concertos.)

[15] Morgan (1988: 68) quotes Phillip Spitta, Bach's nineteenth-century biographer, as saying that the piano 'floated in the mind of Bach' as an ideal instrument, and Howard Mayer Brown (1988) holds that it is more authentic to perform Bach on the piano than the harpsichord (as does Rosen 1990, but for different reasons). Though Adorno (1981: 143–5) is sceptical of such claims, he maintains that Bach's most mature instrumental works were 'waiting for the sound that would suit them' (see also Sessions 1950: 81). And Sir Neville Marriner is quoted as saying: 'If Bach had been offered modern plumbing, I'm certain he would have used it' (Walsh 1983: 67), which is not intended solely as a comment about toilets, I assume. Meanwhile, Brendel (1976) and Rosen (1990) hold that Beethoven would have preferred today's concert pianoforte for his works. Kerman (1985: 213) expresses the contrary view: 'We can feel sure that Beethoven would have been unhappy with his sonatas on the modern piano.'

These points obviously bear indirectly on the second claim: that composers would have opted for the improved instruments had they been available. In the first place, it is not obvious that the modifications would have been preferred, because they might not have been viewed as improvements. And, in the second, even if composers recognized limitations in the instruments for which they wrote, they adapted their music to these.[16] As indicated already in the discussion of the 'Appassionata', it might even be a virtue in the period instrument that the music seems to threaten its structural integrity.

Still, it might be said, it is not often that composers show toleration of the faults of instruments by treating these as quirky idiosyncrasies. One who does so is Benjamin Britten, when, in his *Serenade for Tenor, Horn, and Strings*, Op. 31 (1943), he elects to highlight the naturally flat seventh harmonic of the French horn. In this case, it is Britten's explicit rejection of the available alternative that makes clear his intention to exploit this quality.[17] But we should be wary of assuming the same where the composer had no choice in the matter. The fact that the seventh harmonic is usually avoided in brass and string music clearly implies that this partial's out-of-tuneness is normally regarded as a shortcoming. So, where a composer of 1800 uses it but could not easily avoid doing so, we should not assume that he enjoys its poor intonation. Horns with valves can avoid the seventh harmonic, so it is possible that he would have preferred such an instrument had it been available.[18]

[16] I do not suppose that any composer relished the poor intonation that was endemic to gut-stringed instruments, or the unreliability of harpsichord quills, but there was little they could do to avoid such problems by way of adapting their music. I agree with Donington (1989: 38) that little is lost to authenticity in employing plastic substitutes for quills in harpsichords if the instrument's sound is not affected deleteriously. And I would say the same of synthetic or metal substitutes for gut, except that, unfortunately, these do alter the instruments' sound. In the case of recordings, when sections with broken quills and poor intonation can be taped again, it would remain desirable that original materials be used.

[17] The same applies when a contemporary composer writes for an older instrument, as when Manuel da Falla and Francis Poulenc compose harpsichord concertos. We would never dream of substituting a piano for the harpsichord in professional renditions of these pieces (Godlovitch 1988). Indeed, doing so would make a nonsense of Elliott Carter's *Double Concerto for Harpsichord and Piano* (1961). In these cases, the composer excludes the piano by his choice of the harpsichord.

[18] The evidence for such preferences is explicit in some cases. As Rosen (1990) explains, the upper range of the piano was extended during Beethoven's lifetime. In his early works, passages of scales and arpeggios are transposed down an octave when the limits of the instrument's range is reached. Later, Beethoven revised these pieces for the higher compass. Should the original pitches be observed in an authentic performance? I think this depends on the facts of the case. The optimizing condition allows that, if instruments with a greater range were available, if not standard, at the time, they can be used. (Domenico Scarlatti may not have had a three-manual, 16-foot harpsichord, but the type was on sale in his home city when he wrote his late sonatas and, so, may be used for them.) Moreover, I allow that the same work can exist in more than one version, and can accept, therefore, that the later variant can be played so long as it is acknowledged for what it is. If only one version is authorized by the composer, its instrumentation is work identifying, and if the instrument the performer wishes to use was not extant at the time of composition, I think the performance will be less than ideally authentic.

EXAMPLE 5.1. Franz Schubert, Symphony No. 9, opening

The case of the natural French horn merits closer attention. The languorous majesty of its tone gave it a melodic potential that could hardly be ignored, but it could be employed in stepwise melodies in only two ways. Either a group of horns, each tuned to a different fundamental by the use of crooks (which became available in the late eighteenth-century), could combine their efforts, which was an approach not suited to flowing melodies. Or the upper harmonics of a single instrument could be employed, but some had to be stopped (by placing the fist in the bell), which inevitably compromised the evenness of the tone. The melody that begins the first movement of Franz Schubert's Symphony No. 9, D. 944, 'Great', of 1825-6 is a case in point (see Example 5.1). The As, B naturals, and Fs all require stopping, which is indicated by the symbol '+'. Though composers of a later era, such as Brahms, wrote horn parts that were playable on the natural horn (since the availability of valved horns could not be guaranteed), evidently they preferred the use of valved horns, which could perform such melodies without fist stopping. It is plausible, then, to suggest that Schubert would have chosen valved over natural horns for the performance of his symphony of 1825, had they been in use at the time.[19]

Does an *ideally* authentic performance of Schubert's symphony require the use of the natural horn, which is inferior to the alternative that Schubert would probably have chosen if he had the chance? And what of Beethoven's Symphony No. 3 of 1803-4, or Mozart's Horn Concerto No. 4, K. 495, of 1786? Though Schubert wrote his piece on the eve of the introduction of the valved horn, these earlier composers did not, though surely they were no less aware than he of the limitations of the natural instrument.

So far I have been considering the issue in terms of composers' preferences and the overall balance of aesthetic utilities, because that approach allows discussion of issues that can be acknowledged as relevant by timbral sonicists and other opponents of the instrumentalism I favour. Now it is time to appeal more squarely to the account of authenticity I developed earlier. An ideally authentic performance is one that meets all of the composer's work-determinative indications. In all but the rarest cases, the composer's directives are addressed in a very explicit and practical fashion to musicians who are interested in learning what they need to do now to perform the work

---

[19] The valve was invented in 1813 or 1815, but valved versions of the horn did not become standard until more than two decades later. The modern, F/B♭ horn was put on the market in 1899. (For discussion, see Apel 1966: 341; Baines 1966).

accurately, not in considering unrealized future possibilities. Inevitably then, if the composer determines anything as regards his work's instrumentation, what he requires must concern available instruments or ones for which he also supplies the design instructions. As I have already explained, the composer's non-determinative wishes and preferences may be ignored and, anyway, should guide the performer only where they are consistent with the execution of his work-defining indications. In the case of Schubert's Ninth Symphony, the instrumentation should be counted among the work's identifying features. Schubert's notation and the conventions of the time make the use of the natural horn mandated for this piece. Even if we know that Schubert would have preferred the valved to the natural horn for his theme, that does not mean a performance could be maximally authentic if it followed his desire.

I concede this much: where the valved instrument is used in the performance of Schubert's symphony, the infraction is innocuous (but less so where it is used for Beethoven's symphonies and less so again when it is pressed into service for Mozart's music). I accept that the trade-off between authenticity and other musical considerations might justify the approach. I have a similar attitude to the use of the tuba in Felix Mendelssohn's *Overture to a Midsummer Night's Dream* as a substitute for the (now obsolete) ophicleide he specifies. Achieving the fullest degree of authenticity is not worth the practical trouble in this case. Similarly, the current lack of castrati makes it appropriate that altos or countertenors are substituted for them, though this results in some loss of authenticity.

Where the change in instrumentation, and adaptations made to the music in the light of this, are significant, the result is a work transcription that is distinct from its model. One does not transcribe a work merely by crossing out the word 'harpsichord' on the score and replacing it with 'piano' (Davies 1988a), however. Neither does the substitution of the modern cello for its Baroque cousin result in a work transcription. If Domenico Scarlatti's sonatas are harpsichord specific, or if Bach's solo cello suites take part of their identity from their instrumentation, playing them on the piano or the modern cello will be less than ideally authentic. This is not to say that such renditions are heinous. There can be good reasons for the substitution. And the resultant lowering of authenticity might be relatively insignificant.

Rather than seeing the wishes (whether real or imagined) of composers invoked in the name of authenticity, I prefer to regard cases of the kind discussed previously as ones in which a small loss in authenticity is balanced against a practical or artistic gain. (Later in this chapter I reject the appropriateness of taking such trade-offs further than this.)

Kivy's counterfactualism

I have been considering the relevance of what the composer might have wanted for performances of her work. Peter Kivy (1995) develops this idea.

He asks what composers would have desired had they lived to the present. He claims that the issue of authenticity is better addressed by the counterfactual question 'what would the composer choose for the performance of his music now?' than by 'what did the composer determine for the performance of his works at the time of writing them?'

It seems to me that universal or overarching claims, along the lines of 'composers would always want their works played in the manner most familiar to performers who live hundreds of years after them', are likely to be false. If Kivy's approach is to amount to something more reliable than fanciful second guessing, the appropriate reasoning should be restricted to the particular composer's œuvre and alterations to the method of performance could be justified only if there were some clear evidence therein that he was not satisfied with the best that was available in his time. I suspect that evidence of that sort is usually rather difficult to come by. (Earlier I allowed that Beethoven's retraction of octave transpositions when the piano's range was increased is evidence of the relevant sort.) Composers are mostly very practical and, contentedly or not, accommodate themselves to the practices and resources that are their musical heritage. I doubt, therefore, that counterfactual speculation will endorse a radical approach to performance, such as Kivy seems to anticipate.

My main worry, though, concerns Kivy's claim that issues of authenticity are addressed by his method. It is reasonable to suppose that, had the composer lived and worked to the present, he would now be writing very different kinds of work. The pieces composed by Stravinsky at 80 contrast with those he penned in his twenties. If Mozart had lived to 1836, his late works would have been unlike those of 1776. But this observation proves nothing about how we should perform Mozart's *Divertimento in F*, K. 247, just as the contrast between Stravinsky's Symphony in E Flat (1906–7) and his *Requiem Canticles* (1966) implies nothing about how the symphony should be played.

Suppose we had asked Stravinsky in 1966 how he would like his Symphony in E Flat performed. The most likely answer, I guess, is 'just as it was written'. And I see no reason to assume that other composers would not usually say the same about their own works. But suppose that Stravinsky answers differently. In hindsight he thinks the symphony is too verbose, rhythmically predictable, and dull. It would benefit from defter orchestration, a clearer texture, and more astringent harmonies. He makes the changes and a performance takes place.

This example is fanciful, but some composers (such as Anton Bruckner and Stravinsky himself, in the case of *The Rite of Spring*) made new versions or revisions of their works after those works had received their first performances and publication. It also fits Kivy's model, except that we are dealing with a composer who happily outlived his earliest works by many years.

Kivy would have us conclude that the performance of the updated version of Stravinsky's Symphony in E Flat in the imaginary concert of 1966 is as or more authentic than one according to the score and the performance conventions of the time of its composition. My own intuition is quite different. I believe we would get a performance of a *re-composed* or *revised* version of the earlier work, not an *authentic* performance of the symphony of 1906–7. (For other criticisms of Kivy's position, see Edidin 1998 and Hall 1999.)

Whether adapting the original in the light of current performance practices and circumstances is consistent with authenticity depends on the outcome. (*a*) If the number of instrumentalists is augmented (and this seems to be one of the kinds of changes of which Kivy would approve), that might easily be consistent with authentic performance.[20] I noted earlier that authenticity does not require that the performers restrict themselves to the resources the composer had; authenticity is relativized to optimized conditions rather than to actual ones. Much early music needs 'bodying out' if it is to be given under conditions that would have been optimal in the composer's age. This might involve, as well as cadenzas, continuo, and ornamentation, new orchestrations and additional parts (see Donington 1989: 79–80). So long as these are consistent with the practice and style of the day, there should be no objection to their authenticity in my view. (*b*) If contemporary instruments are substituted for period ones, there is a departure from authenticity (though one that might be justified, perhaps, in practical or artistic terms). (*c*) If the performance style pays no heed to the conventions of the day, so that decoration is eschewed in favour of a heavy vibrato for instance, then the work is being revised. Alterations of that sort are not so different from note changes, since features constitutive of the work's identity are affected (even if those features belong to the performance practice, without being explicitly indicated in the score). (*d*) And when the arranger intentionally departs from features that the practice regards as fixed for the work, it is being decomposed, reconstituted as something else. I do not regard the revision or re-composition of old pieces as out of the question. What I baulk at is the suggestion that the result, when played, can be described as an *authentic* performance of the *original* work, which is how Kivy represents it. Kivy's counterfactual account is a thoroughly implausible analysis of authenticity in performance, I claim.

Another kind of authenticity

There is a familiar use of the term 'authentic' that differs from the one I have been considering. According to it, a person is authentic if she is 'true to

---

[20] Donington (1989: 75) observes: 'J. S. Bach . . . frequently used more restrictive forces than he would have chosen or than we have any need, merely from too literal a sense of historical correctitude, to impose on him today.' On 11 April 1781, Mozart wrote to his father: 'I forgot to tell you the other day that at the concert the symphony [K. 338] went magnifique and had a great success. There were forty violins, the wind instruments were all doubled, there were ten violas, ten double basses, eight violoncellos and six bassoons' (King and Carolan 1966: ii. 724).

herself'; that is, if her actions come from and express her personality and autonomy.[21] Applying this conception to the musical case, we can say that a person's playing is authentic if it flows from and reveals her character, intellect, emotions, and free choices.[22] An inauthentic performance, by contrast, would be one that slavishly copies another's interpretation or playing style.

I accept that we can and do sometimes talk of authenticity in such terms, though this is very different from considering how faithfully a performance presents the composer's work. The one view relativizes judgements about the authenticity of performances to persons and their characters, whereas the other measures performances against musical compositions. I allowed earlier that a given thing can be categorized differently and assessed for authenticity with respect to its various classifications, which is what happens here. Because it is possible to regard musical performance from the point of view of the player's agency, a concern with the sort of authenticity just mentioned can be appropriate. There are, however, two points to be made about this approach to the topic.

First, it does not reflect the focus of most musicologists and performers as revealed in their debates about authenticity in performance. Their interest (like mine) is in performances as of composer's pieces and in the conventions presupposed by those works. It adds or resolves nothing to observe that a different focus can lead to a concern with another kind of authenticity. Against this, it might be maintained that the two kinds of authenticity are connected and opposed, not distinct and complementary as I have implied. In developing this line, it could be held that the performer who is true to herself should not allow her decisions to be ruled by the composer in performing his work; that her enslavement to the score's instructions would entail a betrayal of her authenticity as a person and musician. Obviously, I regard this view as mistaken, and this leads to my second point.

Secondly, musical works of the kind I have been considering are written *for* performance. The composer's work-identifying instructions significantly underdetermine the detail that will be present in any actual realization of the work. As a result, the performer must make many decisions that go beyond the composer's instructions in playing his work. She is free, within limits set

---

[21] This notion has been developed by Sören Kierkegaard, Jean-Paul Sartre, and Martin Heidegger, among others. They regard authenticity as arising from the nature of human agency, of freedom, and of consciousness.

[22] Musical authenticity is analysed in this fashion by O'Dea (1993, 1994). Some musicologists (Taruskin 1982, 1984, 1988; Howard Mayer Brown 1988; Morgan 1988; Rink 1994) invoke this notion in insisting that a performance is authentic if the performer is sincere. Kivy (1995: chs. 5, 9) also identifies personal authenticity as one of several kinds that interest us in musical performance. He maintains that, if she is to express herself authentically in playing a Mozart concerto, the soloist should improvise the cadenza in a twenty-first-century idiom. In contrast, I regard such a cadenza as inappropriate, because it violates conventions resident to the musical conventions of the time of the work's composition.

by the score and the conventions of the relevant performance practice, to make those choices. And the exercise of her freedom is not something incidental or additional but is, rather, essential and integral to producing a performance that is faithful to the work she plays. She can satisfy the composer's instructions *only* by making such decisions. Her own creative contribution is not solely a bonus added after, and independently of, her complying with those instructions. We value the performer's technical and interpretative skill, because she contributes so much to the performance that brings the composer's work to life. There is no reason, then, to follow Goehr (1992: 273) in seeing an opposition between the performer's interpretative freedom and her pursuit of work faithfulness.

The performer can and should express her personality in performing the works of composers, so long as her personality complements the work's. But if she is to represent herself correctly as playing *their* works, she cannot treat their determinative instructions and the performance style of the time as irrelevant (Stubley 1995). In choosing to exercise her agency through the musical performance of others' works, she defines the *kind* of freedom she will pursue (Edidin 1997, 1998). The musician who takes no notice of the composer's instructions cannot achieve the personal authenticity that is her target if it is part of her goal to express herself through the manner of her playing *the composer's piece*.

It might be thought that the argument I have offered misses the point, which is that the performer of old music no longer has the freedom she had formerly. Her options, and therefore her autonomy as an artist, are reduced by the demands of authenticists. 'One interesting feature of the twentieth-century authenticity movement is that it decreases the role for artistry of the performer, for example, in interpretative degrees of freedom, making performers more the implementers of historical researches or other theoretical structures' (Dipert 1993: 200; see also Kivy 1995). Two observations are relevant to this claim. (*a*) What is at issue is not freedom but the difference between licence and legitimate liberty. If the pressure is on musicians to refrain from exercising licence with the works they offer to the public, what is wrong with that? (*b*) Even if interpreters of early music do not have the freedom they once thought they had, it remains the case that they retain more than the scores of Tchaikovsky and Mahler allow to them. If the music of the Romantics provides sufficient scope for artistry and skill, which no one seems to deny, where is the basis for the complaint that the performer of early music is straitjacketed?

Other kinds of musical works

In closing this discussion of the way the notion of authenticity applies to musical works, it is appropriate to renew the observations with which I began. Authenticity is a matter of ontology rather than interpretation. An ideally authentic instance of a musical work is one that faithfully reproduces the work's constitutive properties. Just what kinds of properties are determinative of musical works varies; musical works are not of a single ontological type. In consequence, what makes for authenticity also differs from case to case.

I have considered musical works for live performance, the instructions for which are encoded in musical notations, and I have concentrated on those from 1770 to 2000. These are complex, extended pieces specified in considerable detail. In them, instrumentation, phrasing, and dynamics are constitutive and the pursuit of authenticity must take this into account. In earlier periods (or in other cultures, or in non-Classical kinds of music), works for performance are not so thick with properties. In them, the conventions do not allow the composer to determine so many of the musical parameters. What in nineteenth-century pieces are constitutive details of the work are, in these other contexts, interpretative details of particular performances. Moreover, the performance practice in early music was extremely flexible and adaptable, permitting considerable variety in many aspects of the treatment of works. The choice of instrumentation, phrasing, tempo, and dynamics was left to the performer's discretion, as were many editing decisions, section orderings, and the like. Although the composer might have expressed preferences for one interpretation as against another, these are not determinative of what the performer must do in instancing his work accurately.

I have allowed that works might be specified via the presentation of model instances, rather than by scores. In that case, a performance will be authentic if there is a historical thread between it and the production of the original model, and if it recreates those features of the model that have a prescriptive significance, according to the conventions applying to this form of composition. Again, these conventions have varied through time or from musical type to musical type. In general, the composer's instructions are not likely to be as detailed in these cases as they are for works indicated by scores, if only because they rely for their communication and preservation on the reliability of performers' memories. As a result, such works are often thinner in identifying properties than those specified by written notations, which have more reliability and permanence than human memory. This generalization should be treated with caution, however, because systems of oral musical training, when coupled with attitudes of deep respect for the musical tradition, can lead to the rigorous preservation of complex musical works and repertoires. This is evident in Coptic chant, for instance. Where pieces are minimal, the emphasis falls primarily on performance skill, and faithfulness to the work is comparatively easy to attain. Performances are more likely to be assessed for authenticity in terms of the styles of playing they exemplify than for their accuracy as instances of works (Rudinow 1994). Where the tradition recognizes only music making *simpliciter*, the question of a performance's authenticity as an instance of a work does not arise. In this situation, again, it is the style of playing that is measured for its authenticity.

Where musical works are not for performance, as with purely electronic pieces, the notion of *performance* authenticity has no application. Authenticity here becomes a matter of the accuracy with which a playback device unscrambles the code representing the work, and on the accuracy with which this copy mirrors the master.

Is authenticity attainable in practice?

So far I have tried to analyse what authenticity amounts to in the performance of works specified by scores. Now I consider whether authentic performance according to this model is possible. It will be so only if certain conditions are met. An authorized version of the score must be accessible, as well as instruments suitable for its performance. The player must be familiar with the conventions governing the appropriate manner of reading the score and with the performance practice that is assumed by the composer. Moreover, she must have *practical* knowledge of such matters, so that she is able to *play* the music as written and in the appropriate style. A sufficient number of knowledgeable and skilled performers, along with an appropriate quantity and variety of instruments, all in the best working order, must be available.

There are many circumstances under which one or more of these conditions fails to obtain—especially in the case of medieval and renaissance vocal music—with the result that an ideally authentic performance of the work cannot be given (Morrow 1978; Howard Mayer Brown 1988). The score might exist in several discrepant versions without its being clear how many (if any) of these were authorized by the composer. (Note, though, that performances may be authentically of a given version, where more than one has the composer's blessing, as I indicated in Chapter 3.) Details of the performance practice can be known from period treatises on instrumental or vocal techniques, or from scores and part-books that have been annotated in unusual detail, but in many cases the information is scanty. Scholars debate the issues at length, as is evident in musicologists' exchanges about mensuration and rhythm in chant. Also, it is one thing to have the relevant information and quite another to put it into practice by using period instruments. This is apparent, for instance, in the recordings made in the 1960s of Claudio Monteverdi's music. Judging from these, the cornett—an instrument with a cup-shaped mouthpiece attached to a wooden tube with finger-holes, so that it combines features of the brass and winds—is an extremely difficult instrument to master, especially as regards intonation. These and other performances are poor as regards intonation, technique, and liveliness.[23]

Paradoxically perhaps, one of the most common complaints made by opponents of the authentic performance movement is that, in actuality, the performances are inauthentic.[24] This may often be true.[25] But, as Dreyfus (1983) points out, there can be no basis here for abandoning the pursuit of authenticity in favour of blatantly anachronistic styles of playing. The authentic performance movement should be judged in terms of its successes, not its failures. As it happens, considerable advances have been made in recent decades in our knowledge of appropriate instrumental techniques and performance practices (for instance, compare the relevant entries of older and newer editions of Grove or the *Harvard Dictionary of Music*), as well as in performers' executive skills and sensitivity (Donington 1989: 39–40). Nevertheless, so much in musical performance depends on nuances of timbre, attack, phrasing, stress, and articulation—that is, on matters that cannot easily be notated or described—that the person who aspires to produce idiomatic performances of works composed prior to 1900 faces an extremely difficult task.[26] On the evidence of many current recordings deserving the label 'authentic', these problems often are surmountable. Authentic performance of the kind I have characterized is frequently attainable.

As I have just indicated, many epistemological and practical difficulties stand in the way of authentic performances of the music of earlier eras. For the most part, it is these that occupy the literature on authenticity produced

[23] Adorno writes of 'mechanically squeaking *continuo* instruments and wretched school choirs' (1981: 145). According to Dreyfus, he went wrong in condemning authentic performance partly because he heard only 'the more barbaric gropings of the 1950s and a bit beyond' (1983: 303) before his death in 1969.

[24] See Neumann (1965), Rosen (1971), Brendel (1976), Morrow (1978), Adorno (1981), Leech-Wilkinson (1984), Temperley (1984), Taruskin (1984, 1988), and Howard Mayer Brown (1988).

[25] The charge needs careful evaluation, though. Sometimes it is made in a way that suggests that the objection is to an approach that disregards the variety of relevant practices in modelling itself on particular, prior performances. But, even if that strategy is narrower than it need be, it is not thereby inauthentic in my terms. At other times, what is objected to is the fact that the performer makes particular choices in the face of musicological uncertainty. But, if the music is performed, such ambiguities have to be resolved one way or another. And again, sometimes the objection is to the tastes and proclivities revealed by such choices, even where these are consistent with what is known of the relevant performance practice.

[26] What most upsets the musicologists, I think, is the advertising hype that presents such performances as definitive, along with the moralizing sanctimony with which some performers acclaim their own efforts. (Taruskin 1992 claims that all he has ever debunked is the hype.) The musicologists know better than most how much of the performer's personality is injected into the performance, and also that very different interpretations can be no less secure or justifiable on scholarly grounds. This is not to say, though, that one should deny the technical skill and musicianly intuitions of the professional performer. Donington (1989: 54–5) is exceptional in seeing both sides of the issue and in pleading for mutual respect.

by performers and musicologists.[27] Though I do not underestimate their importance, I put them aside. Instead, I examine arguments designed to show that authentic performance is impossible to achieve *in principle*. I argue against these.

The alleged impossibility of an Ur-text

A composer might always make a notational slip. In consequence, even the autograph score can contain notational errors. And, where the original score is lost, we must rely on copyists' versions or printed editions. Copyists and printers run the risk of adding new mistakes. We also know that composers' deliberate innovations sometimes look like infelicities. Early in the recapitulation of the first movement of his Symphony No. 3, Beethoven has the horn play the main tune in F major (not the tonic key of E♭). It is said that Beethoven boxed the ears of his pupil, Ferdinand Ries, who stopped the orchestra because he believed the horns had entered in the wrong key.[28]

Combining these observations, we are faced with this alarming prospect: the most innocuous and predictable notational progressions might, by a slip of the pen, disguise composers' intentions to introduce musically radical ideas, and the most outrageous continuations might be equivocal between innovations and unsuspected notational errors (Boorman 1999). If one marries all this to Postmodern doubts about the possibility of any textual determinacy in meaning, one might conclude that no musical score establishes an *Ur-text*. Where no definitive score is available, authentic performance, construed as the faithful rendition of composers' determinative intentions as expressed in such a text, must be impossible.

I think this argument turns a practical molehill into a mountain of principle. I do allow that questions might always be posed about the reliability of a musical score—that is, about whether the composer succeeded in representing notationally the instructions he intended. And I accept that, in some cases, limits to the evidence that can be adduced should incline us to an open verdict. I am receptive to case-by-case arguments that present particular reasons for regarding given musical scores as unreliable. I am intolerant, though, of this *general* argument for the uninterpretability of all texts.

Kivy (1990: 109–10) has rightly emphasized that there was a high level of professionalism among composers of the past. They very rarely broke the rules out of ignorance of those rules. Not all these composers were musical geniuses of the first rank. Nevertheless, they were all masters of their craft.

---

[27] For examples, see Dart (1967), Leppard (1988), Harnoncourt (1988, 1989), Donington (1989), Le Huray (1990), and Taruskin (1995).

[28] 'Even as progressive a musician as the young Wagner used to "correct" this passage in performance' (Harman and Mellers 1962: 641). In fact, Wagner, like many of his time, thought nothing of retouching Beethoven's works, including the Ninth Symphony (Cook 1993).

They did not always write great music, but they very rarely wrote music that was offensive in its crudity or incompetence. The same observation applies, I believe, to the use of musical notations by these composers. They were not illiterate as regards the notations they employed and they were not ignorant of the performance practices of their day or of the characteristics and limitations of the instruments for which they wrote. Given the detail and complexity of scores of extended works, the relative absence of notational clangers is surprising. There is ample evidence that composers took special pains to be accurate in what they wrote.[29] Notational mistakes are always possible, but they are very rare.

Musical innovations might sometimes look like notational errors, but there are direct and indirect tests of their genuineness. In the case of the 'Eroica', we know Beethoven meant what he wrote from his reaction to the attempted correction. Composers usually play their own music, or hear others do so, so they have opportunities to discover and remedy notational errors that might escape their notice initially. Moreover, we can judge one work against others, especially against the rest of the composer's œuvre. By considering her wider output, we can get a good idea of the likelihood that a given piece contains innovations. And by comparing it with other works, both earlier and later, in the same genre and style by her cultural cohorts, we can consider apparent anomalies in the light of developments and changes in the practice of the day. If something strange turns up in a composer's score, we can be sure that it is an intended innovation if it is repeated by her in later works, taken up and incorporated in the style by her successors, and so on.

The proposed argument, according to which no musical scores provide definitive texts, fails. It exaggerates a local, practical difficulty, one that we can frequently resolve with a bit of scholarship, into an objection of principle. There is no reason, I think, to regard musical notations as less trustworthy than other texts, nor any reason to consider all texts unreliable.

We cannot experience works as their original audiences did

I turn now to a second argument, one that is widely touted against the possibility of attaining authenticity in musical performance. It holds that authenticity is achieved only if the music is experienced by its present audience as it was by those who first heard it. It continues: since our experience of music cannot be the same as theirs, the attempt at authenticity is bound to fail.

Before considering this theory, I look to a point raised by Randall R. Dipert (1980*b*, 1988, 1993). He means to present a problem case for

---

[29] I mentioned one case of this in Chapter 3: though the distinction between G♭ and F♯ has no practical significance for the keyboard performer, composers are scrupulous in using enharmonic notations to indicate harmony and voice-leading, including for even-tempered instruments.

authenticists, not to provide a global argument against the possibility of authentic performance, but the example he considers helps set the stage for the more general issue I will discuss.

Dipert suggests that the composer's (joint) high- and low-level intentions can become unstuck. He offers the example of a composer who includes an unfamiliar instrument in the orchestra for the sake of its exotic tone. For instance, he writes for the clarinet at a time when it was newly invented. Later, the clarinet is standard and its timbral qualities no longer strike the audience as foreign. Now, even if our goal is to follow the composer's intentions in performing his music, which intentions should we respect?—the low-level intention (use the clarinet) or the high-level intention from which it was initially inseparable (use an instrument that is mysterious in its unfamiliarity)?[30] Dipert believes that composers' high-level intentions, which deal with artistic ends, are more significant than low-level intentions concerned with mere means. Scores mainly record low-level intentions. Where the two kinds of intention separate over time, the performer who seeks to perform authentically should be guided by high-level intentions (if these are known), which might mean ignoring some aspects of the score.

My response to this is the one I gave earlier to Kivy's position. I do not see how departing from the instructions that constitute the work as the one it is could result in an authentic performance of that work. My concern here, though, is with the way Dipert's legitimate point—that the composer's low- and high-level intentions can pull apart over time—might be developed into a principled objection against the goal of authentic performance.

At first sight it might appear that the issue Dipert raises is an isolated one. This is not so. Composers have often introduced into their music elements they intended to sound exotic, such as Janissary music in the late eighteenth century and Chinoiserie at the close of the nineteenth. In any case, the kind of phenomenon to which Dipert draws attention reaches much further than is indicated by his particular example. Composers have always intended to impart properties of tension and motion to their music. To do so, they rely on patterns of conflict and resolution generated by the treatment of harmony, tonality, rhythm, and the like. What counts as 'tense' is, however, no less contextual than what is exotic. In G. F. Handel's music, simultaneous major seconds function as discords; by 1840, such intervals were regarded as much more stable and more stringent harmonic clashes were needed to achieve the

---

[30] Here are some other examples: when Bach wrote for the harpsichord, he intended to write for an instrument that was familiar, unpretentious, and accessible, not quaint or scholarly. In playing his music, should we substitute the familiar piano for the now antique harpsichord? Also, he intended both that his cantatas be sung in the vernacular and that they be sung in eighteenth-century German, so which language should English speakers use? Equivalent issues arise in all the performing arts. If a playwright intends to set his piece in the present, which happens to be 1600, should a production use the dress of 1600 or of its own time?

same effect of tension. Later still, more extreme discords became the norm. Handel intended to write the interval of a major second (low level) and also intended that this be a strong discord (high level). Changes in the norms of musical 'syntax' have separated these layers of intention, with the result that, if Dipert is correct, the performer can no longer satisfy both intentions simply by playing what the composer wrote.[31]

Dipert's account supposes that authenticity involves following the composer's intentions. We can easily convert this view to one according to which authenticity depends on the listeners' experiences. Composers intend to impart to their music effects of expression, motion, tension, and the like. They expect the listener to apprehend the relevant qualities—for instance, to hear the sound of the clarinet as exotic. They also desire from the listener a level of engagement that goes beyond a purely intellectual, dispassionate awareness of musical properties. The listener should be moved, so that she comes to experience, not solely to observe, the music's features. In short, the composer wants the listener to feel the sound of the clarinet *as* exotic, not merely to register that it is (intended to be) exotic.

By this line of reasoning we are led to the conclusion that the nature of the listeners' experience of the music sets the standard for the authenticity of a performance—a performance is authentic if it is experienced as the composer intended. And if the listener who is historically removed from the composer's time experiences music in a fashion that is conditioned by her musico-historical situation, then she cannot apprehend an early work as its composer intended. In that case, the authentic performance of such music is impossible, whatever care is taken to make the performance sound (acoustically) as it would have done under ideal conditions in the composer's day (Dipert 1980*b*; Young 1988).

My first reaction to this position is to reiterate the view that authenticity is achieved in the manner of producing the sound of the music and in the sounds thereby made, not by inducing particular experiences in the listener (see also Sharpe 1991, 2000). As I see it, judgements of authenticity must refer to thoroughly public properties, because they concern matters of classification that operate at an interpersonal level. The experiences of individuals, because they are so variable and are affected by so many private factors, are not of a kind appropriate to furnishing standards for authenticity in musical performance.

Consider the account of authenticity I offered in the introduction to Part Two: a hamburger is an authentic McDonald's if it is made by McDonald's

---

[31] As I just noted, Dipert thinks we should follow the composer's high-level artistic intentions, rather than the low-level intentions recorded in the score. Should we add clusters of major seconds and sevenths to Handel's music? Dipert does not say, though consistency should force him to that conclusion. It strikes me as odd that anyone would think the addition of twentieth-century discords is required for the *authentic* performance of Handel's music.

and displays the properties that mark their products. Now, imagine that you are listening to the radio news as you are eating your hamburger. It is reported that the beef used in some hamburgers may be contaminated with Bovine Spongeiform Encephalitis ('mad cow' disease). I predict that your experience of eating your hamburger will be changed by this information. But if your hamburger was an authentic McDonald's when you bought it, surely it remains one. Its authenticity is independent of the fact that you can no longer experience it as you did formerly.

Is ideal authenticity desirable in practice?

Reference to the listener's experience plays no part in my analysis of authenticity in musical performance, but this does not mean that I see no connection between the two. I allow that there would be no point in valuing or pursuing a high degree of authenticity if achieving it could never afford to the listener a worthwhile experience of the music. This concession gives my opponent another recourse. He might accept my analysis of authenticity, but claim that maximal authenticity in performance never could be desirable or valuable because it does not produce the benefits that gave it significance in the original setting. He denies that it can lead the listener to an appropriate experience of the music.

Is it the case, as claimed previously, that we cannot appreciate period music because our ears are tuned to the different musical idiom of the present? Before tackling this question directly, consider how we experience the music of our own period, that with which we are most at home. Notice immediately that 'the music of the present' might better be termed 'the musics of the present'. There are many types and genres. Record stores display their wares under various categories: classical, world, rock, heavy metal, blues, rap, techno, jazz, musicals, easy listening, and so on. Each of these kinds displays its own musical syntax. Now, many people have catholic musical tastes and interest themselves in more than one variety of music. As they do so, they adjust their musical expectations. When a person listens to jazz, she does not expect to hear what she would if it were heavy metal that was playing; as she turns to heavy metal, she listens for different qualities and effects than when she goes to a musical by Stephen Sondheim. I am sure that we all know many listeners of the kind just described and would acknowledge them as people who appreciate and understand the types of music that interest them. If such a listener can experience different kinds of music all in an appropriate fashion, it must be the case that she adjusts the way she listens to accommodate the music that is her focus. Though she is equally at home with a spread of disparate musical idioms, she approaches any given piece in terms of the musical (and other) conventions that apply to it. Her awareness of other musical styles does not prevent her engaging at an intimate level with the particular kind of music to which she happens to be listening.

I believe the same applies when a listener interests herself in the music of other periods or cultures. Like anyone who hears music with understanding, she must learn the 'grammar' of the music, so that she can hear the aptness of an expected continuation, detect departures from the norm, sense the points of tension and repose, and so on. She must know something of the sonic ideals at which the composer aims and of the performance practice that is appropriate, but there is no barrier to her acquiring and assimilating this information through exposure to good performances, so that she comes to respond automatically to the music she hears. She may be familiar with types of music that employ different techniques and structural principles, but she can put her awareness of these off-line in order to listen with expectations appropriate to classical music of the eighteenth century, or whatever, just as the person who listens with understanding both to reggae and to rhythm and blues does the same.

It is false that the person who attends to music from eras earlier than the one she lives in is prevented by her awareness of later musical styles from hearing and responding to the music in an appropriate fashion. The position that denies this seriously underestimates our ability to control the way we listen to different kinds of music. Admittedly, the greater the discrepancy between the music of the past, or of another culture, and that with which we are most at home, the harder it will be for us to internalize its character and, hence, to make the adjustment in our expectations automatically. Nevertheless, the goal of hearing 'foreign' music with understanding and appreciation is not inherently unachievable.

A reply is available to the argument I have just sketched. Allowing what I have said, it remains the case that we cannot hear the music as its contemporaries did. They did not have to adopt *different* expectations from those appropriate to the familiar music of their time, because that is what they were listening to, whereas we must do so and cannot be unaware that we are listening to 'old' music even if we deliberately bracket our grasp of current musical practice as we listen. In other words, we listen *historically*, whereas the contemporary audience did not. Moreover, where the music is European from the period of Bach, Haydn, and Mozart, there is a further sense in which our listening is historically informed as the period audience's was not. At that time, there was little interest in, or knowledge of, the music of prior ages. Almost all the music played was newly composed and pieces were not often repeated. As a result, the period audience heard music as being in the current style and, also, they did not treat that style as part of a long heritage of musical development and change. The listeners of that day certainly knew that their music had its forebears, but they did not *experience* it in terms of that background. So, we do not hear the music as its contemporaries did.

(Several authors describe historically informed listening as 'inauthentic' (Rosen 1971; Keller 1984; Evans 1990: 111; McFee 1992; Kivy 1995: 71–2).)[32] The phenomenology of our experience must be different from theirs. The argument continues: if the modern listener cannot recapture the experience the music provided its period audience, the current vogue for authenticity in performance is exposed as without substance.

I allow that the awareness of the period listener differs phenomenologically from that of the audience of our own time. I doubt that this reveals anything about the desirability of authentic performance, though. The argument relies on the claim that the pursuit of authenticity has a point, and suggests that this can be satisfied only if the two kinds of listener experience the music in the same way. Surely, though, authentic performance aims to make the composer's work available to the audience and to produce a performance that is faithful to the work. The point of doing so is to facilitate the listener's apprehension of, and engagement with, the piece—that is, to allow the listener to understand and appreciate the composer's work. There is no reason to think that this is achieved only if all listeners have the same experience of the performance, where 'same experience' requires identity at the level of full phenomenological detail. The contrasts adduced between the experiences of the period listener and of one of the present day do not show that the latter is in no position to comprehend and enjoy the composer's work (Wolterstorff 1987). So the argument fails to demonstrate the pointlessness of an interest in the authenticity of performances given before an audience of listeners who are historically removed from the work.

Indeed, it is arguable that the differences between period and present audiences place the latter in a better position to appreciate the works they hear. Because our listening is historically informed and includes knowledge of music subsequent to the given work's composition, we are better positioned to recognize its historically relative artistic properties—to see it as the culmination of a musical style, or as a conservative attempt to prolong a style that was already exhausted; to hear it as an isolated masterpiece that was later unfairly ignored, or as pregnant with possibilities the full significance of which was exposed only when later composers exploited and developed them under the influence of the work in question. The advantages a historically removed listener has over the composer's contemporaries are not directly conferred by authenticity in performance, but they are relevant to the previous argument for indicating that we are not incapable of appreciating music from past eras. The undeniable differences between period and modern listeners,

---

[32] These writers exaggerate how ahistorical was the listening of the eighteenth-century audience, many of whom would have had a musical memory spanning thirty years or more and encompassing such radical changes as that from Baroque to Classical styles. I mean to endorse a less extreme claim than these authors: the earlier audience did not listen as historically as we do.

and in the phenomenological character of the experiences both groups have of the music, do not show that only the former can understand and enjoy the music. Authentic performance retains its relevance in the modern context by providing access to the work, since the present-day audience can engage with that work in appreciating it.

Unenjoyable authentic performances

In accepting that authenticity takes its point, and hence its value, from the experience of the music it affords the listener, I seem to have committed myself to the claim that maximally authentic performances provide a better or richer or deeper experience of the music than the alternatives. In general, I think this is true. I believe that musical works are almost always more interesting and worthwhile when represented as accurately as possible in performances. This is because they possess the relevant qualities by design, whereas aesthetic equivalents in nature or ones created adventitiously are only rarely of comparable value. Performances that are faithful to the work often produce clarity, balance, emphases, and nuances that are not apparent in other renditions. Typically, authentic performance allows one to hear more, and what one hears often reveals the work in a more favourable and intelligible light.

Not everyone agrees that authentic performances sound better and are more enjoyable. Some critics have found authentic renditions dreary, pedantic, sterile, and artificial, as well as technically poor (Crutchfield 1988; Taruskin 1988).

Two responses can be made to this charge. The first notes that optimal fidelity to the composer's intentions would include 'spontaneity, vigor, liveliness, musicality, aesthetic imagination . . .' (Kivy 1988*b*: 286). Earlier it was noted that authenticity is relativized to optimal performance conditions. So, this line implies that lifelessness in performance results in something less than the fullest level of authenticity. To the extent that they are poor, such performances are inauthentic. Rightly observing their inadequacy provides no argument against the desirability of authenticity, therefore.

The second response, which is the one I prefer, might be introduced with this observation: 'stilted performances are not the monopoly of some players of early music' (Godlovitch 1988: 262). The claim is not that we can justify or excuse poor authentic performance by pointing to similar faults in other performances. It is not like saying 'OK, I murdered, but lots of people do'. Rather, it points out that authenticity no more *guarantees* a fine performance than any other approach, but is not thereby shown to be without value or relevance. This line of argument does not assimilate the desired performance attributes to the notion of authenticity in work performance, as the first does. Instead, it allows that authenticity is only one of the aspects under which we assess performances. A performance is less good for being dull and mechanical, but need not be less authentic for displaying these qualities. Provided the fault is not a direct and inevitable consequence of the pursuit of authenticity, its presence reveals nothing about the desirability or otherwise of faithfulness to the composer's work.

It might be claimed there is, indeed, a connection between the pursuit of authenticity and the performance inadequacies that were mentioned. Where musicians are uncomfortable with the instruments they play and are unsure of the appropriate performance practices, simply delivering the notes claims their whole attention. They are so occupied with the business of getting from the beginning to the end of the work that they are unable to focus on interpretational niceties, and the performance suffers as a result.

No doubt this observation characterizes some attempts at authentic performance, but it is at this stage that one can reasonably refer to the optimizing clause mentioned previously. Ideal performance conditions require technically skilled musicians who are familiar with their instruments and the appropriate manner of playing the piece. Performances that are incompetent for the reasons just mentioned do count, therefore, as less than ideally authentic. An appropriate standard of musicianship, if not interpretational insight, is a prerequisite for attaining the highest degree of authenticity.

Both arguments I have discussed invoke the optimizing condition, but they do so at different points. The second insists that authentic performance presupposes the performer's competence, but allows that interpretative skill and ability go beyond this and, therefore, lie outside what is required for authenticity in work performance. Values other than, and distinct from, those associated with authenticity are involved in assessing the quality of performances. By contrast, the first argument attempts to implicate authenticity in all aspects of the evaluation of performances. It treats the optimizing condition as covering the full range of performance values, including ones normally associated with the performer's interpretation.

I observed that I prefer the second line of argument to the first. There are several reasons for this. According to my account, a performance authentically instances a work if it faithfully executes the composer's determinative instructions read in accordance with the appropriate performance practice. Those instructions leave many interpretative issues unresolved. Of course composers *want* good interpretations in the performance of their music, but they cannot *determine* these via their instructions. Usually, many options are consistent with authenticity and these need not be equally good. Indeed, some authentic performances could be seriously lacking in artistic sensitivity and taste. Where dreariness is an aspect of a technically skilled musician's interpretation, it is independent of, and can be consistent with, his following the composer's instructions. So, I see the assessment of interpretations as distinct from evaluations of performances for their authenticity as instances of the works they are of. In addition, we sometimes rate performances as good for their liveliness despite their manifest inauthenticity; for example, where they include many wrong notes. Wrong notes count against the authenticity of work performances on any theory. So, I do not think that all performance values fall under the umbrella of authenticity.

In discussing the listener's experience, I began with the claim that, for the most part, a high degree of authenticity in its performance makes the music more intelligible and enjoyable. This led to consideration of the charge that authentic performances are lacking. The connection was natural enough—poor performances are not likely to be enjoyed by listeners. I have rejected that critique; the performance can be weak because the interpretation fails, without this reflecting adversely on the desirability of authenticity. But this does not dispose of all the issues that must be faced. It remains possible that the listener does not enjoy a rendition that is exemplary in its authenticity and in its interpretation. The relevant case is one where the qualities that displease the listener result directly from the faithfulness with which the composer's instructions and the appropriate performance practice are followed. Suppose that the listener finds the tone of shawms unendurably rough and raucous, or the accents of vernacular French of the fourteenth century strike her ear as ugly, or the music seems excessively florid to her when it is decorated as it should be. She would prefer to hear oboes rather than shawms, modern French pronunciation, a less ornate style of performance. Suppose that the listener's preference is for an approach that is unequivocally inauthentic. How is the authenticist to respond?

If the listener's reaction comes from a failure to adjust her expectations to ones appropriate to the music, he might recommend that she educate her ear by exposing herself more often to authentic performances. Suppose she does what she can in this direction and that, from her point of view, no improvement results. She knows what to expect and what is required for the fullest degree of performance authenticity. Her problem is that she does not like what she hears, not that she listens wrongly. A less authentic performance would suit her better.

In that event, the authenticist could suggest that it is not so much the performance she dislikes as the music. No one expects all listeners to enjoy every kind of music. If she does not like this sort, she should concentrate on others. But she might truthfully reply that her objection is not to the music, less than ideally authentic performances of which she enjoys, but to the manner of its being played. And her response might not be idiosyncratic. Perhaps many people share her reaction. Should they all be denied access to performances they would like only because those performances are deemed unacceptable because not fully authentic?

The possibility just described strikes me as odd but plausible. Odd, because it is reasonable to anticipate that performances will generally be at their most revealing and enjoyable when the composer's instructions and appropriate performance styles are followed. Musical works are interesting and valuable because they are made to be so by their creators, who suit what they write to the performance practice of the day. Yet also plausible because tastes do change over time, along with styles of performance. During the last eighty years, voice production has moved to a cleaner, more 'forward' vocal timbre. Our affection for that quality might depend in part on its familiarity. But if we retain the preference through prolonged exposure to other (earlier) modes of singing, our tenacity in clinging to it cannot be explained simply as a function of naivety or ignorance. We favour it as a matter of taste, not of mindless conditioning. In view of this, should we allow for the possibility that the taste of our time recommends a degree of inauthenticity in perfor- mance, even where a higher level is attainable in practice? I would object if all performers sacrificed authenticity solely to cater for the inappropriate expectations of an unschooled audience. However, the case envisaged is one where the audience has made its best efforts to meet the challenge posed by fully authentic performances and, nevertheless, shares a widespread inclination to reject them.

I call the position of the listener just described a 'consequentialist' account of performance value. According to consequentialism, the value of authen- ticity resides solely in its consequences, and the relevant ones concern the audience's enjoyment, since it is this alone that motivates them to listen to music, so authenticity is a good thing sometimes and at others not. It is necessary to consider each case on its merits to see if authentic performances provide suitably informed and prepared audiences with a musical experience they find rewarding. Authenticity is only one among many features that might make a performance worthwhile. In assessing a given performance, we count its authenticity alongside, and in similar units to, its other virtues. If these other virtues can be attained only by sacrificing authenticity, the value of the performance is given by the net balance. A performance will be better for being less authentic if its being so allows it to realize other values that are greater in magnitude. Authenticity is only one source of value in performance, and it can be exchanged for others, provided the performance is improved (that is, is made more enjoyable to suitably informed audiences) as a result.[33]

The authenticist must oppose the consequentialist. This could be done by challenging the idea that the audience's enjoyment sets the standard for a per- formance's value. If the claim is to survive this interrogation, it surely will be necessary to characterize the pleasure that counts as deeply cognitive and complex. An alternative rejection of consequentialism queries the calculus of

---

[33] For an account of the various features that might be valued in performances, see Levinson (1987). Both Wolterstorff (1980) and Edidin (1991) defend consequentialism, arguing that, though authenticity sometimes promotes the value of a performance, at others inauthenticity is preferable because it does so more.

value that it assumes. It argues that authenticity is not negotiable in the way that other performance values may be. Both these lines of discussion are explored in the sections that follow.

Consequentialism and trade-offs

I suggested earlier that the pursuit of authenticity is not on the same footing as interpretative options in general (also see Thom 1993). This is because it is intimately connected with ontology. To interpret a work, one must instance it, and one cannot do that except by being faithful to the composer's work-identifying instructions. But I have also allowed that, for musical works, authenticity admits of degree. Any performance that is recognizably of the work is minimally authentic. Performances that are such could fall far short of ideal authenticity. For example, they might contain many wrong or out-of-tune notes.

The consequentialist can accept the first point: a performance must succeed in attaining a minimal level of authenticity, so that it counts as of the given work. The view rejected by consequentialism is this stronger one: a performance should seek to be ideally authentic. Some worthwhile interpretative options might be contrary to an obsessive interest in faithfulness. So long as a minimal degree of authenticity is achieved, the realization of these interpretative goals can and should take precedence over the pursuit of the ideal. There is a legitimate trade-off between ideal authenticity and other interpretative paths that might be taken by the performer. According to the consequentialist, the gap between ideal and minimally adequate authentic performances can and should be explored in the search for other performance virtues.

Kivy (1995) allows for consequentialist trade-offs of the kind I have outlined. Instead of describing these as implying a competition between authenticity and other performance values, he regards them as involving a contest between different kinds of authenticity.[34] It seems to me that this terminology is regrettable. It implies that a loss in one kind of authenticity is always compensated for by a gain in another, so appeals to the desirability of authenticity provide no guide to the performer's choices. At the outset, I indicated that authenticity is class relative, thereby conceding the legitimacy of terminologies such as Kivy's. What I find worrisome about his approach is Kivy's failure to consider which of the various kinds of authenticity is most relevant to the activity in question. If, as I claim, it is authenticity in instancing composers' works, then reference to other kinds of authenticity simply obscures the issue. I take seriously the possibility of a trade-off between faithfulness and other performance virtues—if it should be rejected, that

---

[34] His book of 1995 is titled 'authenticities' and he lists several types: sound, sensible, practice, and personal. See also Goehr (1992: 283).

must be shown. But I do not think the issues that need addressing should be fogged by introducing the word 'authenticity' left, right, and centre.[35]

A digression about Shakespeare and theatrical performance

When the issue of departures from ideal authenticity for the sake of other performance values is raised, without fail the contemporary attitude to the performance of William Shakespeare's theatrical works is mentioned (see e.g. Morrow 1978, Young 1988, and Donington 1989: 45). These plays are treated with great freedom. A wide variety of stagings, props, and costumes is used. (For example, *Romeo and Juliet* might be set among Sicilian Mafiosi or Los Angeles ethnic gangs.) The text is often cut and rearranged. Sometimes it is modified to include contemporary or local references for the sake of relevance or humour. Such productions are usually advertised not as adaptations or revisions, but as genuine instances of Shakespeare's plays. (To be more accurate, they are billed as '*X*'s version of Shakespeare's *Y*', where '*X*' is the name of the producer or lead actor.) All this is supposed to suggest that it is sufficient to aim only at low-level authenticity in performance—that is, it is supposed to demonstrate that consequentialism operates in an artform, theatre, that parallels the musical case.

It is not a straightforward matter to consider the relevance of these observations about theatrical practice to performances of instrumental musical works. I argue for two conclusions. Theatrical productions in general do not in fact settle for low-level authenticity. There is, though, more freedom allowed to the actor than to the musician in instancing the works they perform. The second point is about the particular case of Shakespeare's plays: although performances of these often sacrifice authenticity, this is appropriate only because special circumstances obtain—namely, the works in question are *extremely* well known. Where musical pieces are similar, they are also treated with more freedom. Even then, a standard much higher than the lowest possible level of authenticity is respected.

Though some playwrights (Bernard Shaw is one) provide detailed descriptions of sets and of other aspects of staging for their dramas, it is arguable that the relevant performance conventions do not regard these as determinative instructions. The interior of theatre buildings, their stages, their companies, and the resources available (including lighting, scenery, costumes, and props) vary considerably from place to place. In recognition of this, those of a playwright's specifications dealing with such matters are indicative or recommendatory, rather than mandatory, I think. (For a general account of

---

[35] The issues would be clearer if opponents of authenticism were prepared to say 'To hell with authenticity if we don't like the result. Who really cares about it anyway?' Instead, they often redefine authenticity in plainly unintuitive terms in order to pay lip-service to the idea that authenticity is always a performance virtue.

the conventions of the theatre, as well as of recent trends, see Hilton 1987.) As a result, differences between stagings of a given play do not necessarily indicate any falling-away from ideal authenticity. Some (though by no means all) of the liberties taken in the performance of Shakespeare's plays acknowledge a legitimate freedom granted by convention to the theatrical producer or actor, one that is consistent with ideal authenticity, since it concerns issues not determinatively controlled by playwrights, notwithstanding explicit indications in the script of their preferences.

In music of the past four centuries, more of the work's detail is determined by its creator than is so for plays. No doubt this became possible as a result of the standardization of the orchestra as regards the instruments, their relative numbers, and the level of performance skill that could be expected in their players. Simply, fewer of the details of performances are settled in the case of theatrical works than of instrumental musical pieces, so producers and actors have more interpretative freedom (without compromising authenticity) than do conductors and musicians.

Productions of plays differ considerably in their presentations and interpretations, but this does not indicate that they sacrifice authenticity for the sake of interpretative interest. If the requirements of authenticity are less stringent in the theatrical case than in the musical one, the variety of play productions provides no basis for the conclusion that it is acceptable for musical performers to aim only at low-level faithfulness. Actors and musicians both show a commitment to authenticity, to much more than the minimum if not to every aspect of the ideal, but they do so within the context of constraints that differ between the various artforms.

I turn now to the case of Shakespeare's plays. The treatment they receive is singular. The first production of a new play by Tom Stoppard or Harold Pinter would not be approached in a fashion that is similarly cavalier. If it were, this would be bound to attract censure and complaints. The same goes for the bulk of the dramatic repertoire. So why do Shakespeare's works come in for special attention? The answer, I think, is that they are so often done and are so familiar. This is relevant in two ways. The cynical view observes that producers and actors who want to make a name for themselves must adopt an outlandish approach if their efforts are to attract attention and make a memorable impression. The more charitable point stresses that these actors and producers can reasonably assume their audience's acquaintance with the pieces in question. New productions of well-known works, the war horses of the repertoire, are set against the background of a long performance tradition. This affects the performer's obligation to be authentic. That obligation might have been satisfied by prior performers, as it were, so that it no longer applies so stringently to the current artist, who can assume that his audience is conversant with staid, straightforward productions and looks to a more adventurous, spirited account of the work. Where the audience's familiarity with other productions cannot be taken for granted—for instance, where the play is new, or not often performed, or the audience is naive and unschooled—the demands of authenticity come back into force.[36] All this is to say: special circumstances apply to the performance of Shakespeare's works, so it would be an error to take the manner of their treatment as establishing the norm for the performing arts.

Are there equivalents to Shakespeare's plays within instrumental classical music? Bach's 'hits', Antonio Vivaldi's *Four Seasons*, Mozart's Symphony No. 40 and *Eine Kleine Nachtmusik*, Beethoven's Fifth and Ninth Symphonies, and Peter Tchaikovsky's Symphony No. 6 qualify, if any do. Do contemporary performers approach these works with more freedom than they would others that are less well known, such as Dmitri Shostakovitch's Symphony No. 2 (1927)? Apparently this is the case. Some (recorded) performances of these pieces are on instruments for which they were not intended. (I have in mind the recordings of groups such as Swingle Singers, Jacques Loussier Trio, the Kyoto Ensemble of Tokyo, and Cambridge Buskers.) Other versions, along the lines of 'switched on classics', and 'hooked on classics', abridge the music and add new parts, such as a drum 'beat'. The film *Saturday Night Fever* contains a disco version of Beethoven's Fifth Symphony.[37]

These various renditions do not fall within the mainstream, however, which is how the equivalent productions of Shakespeare's plays are represented and understood. Moreover, the result is often an arrangement or work transcription. There is a long and respectable musical tradition of making and performing work transcriptions, which have a standing in their own right. So, the parallel between these cases and the Shakespearian one is not very exact.

The musical performances that should be compared with the Shakespearian case are ones falling within the mainstream—that is, ones that are part of a continuing performance tradition dedicated to instancing the given work, if also to interpreting it in a distinctive fashion. When we examine these, we find that performers do take more liberties in playing the war horses than is usually done for other works, especially as regards tempo, balance, and expressiveness. This is probably for the reasons outlined; that is, conductors and soloists strive to create an impression, which leads to an interpretationally exaggerated treatment. Also, audiences are familiar with (perhaps jaded by overexposure to) these works and so might be expected to welcome unusual and provocative accounts of them. Nevertheless, the

[36] Suppose a hitherto unknown play by Shakespeare were discovered. I predict that, for the first performance, great care would be taken to be authentic. The text would be preserved intact, the locations would be those specified by Shakespeare, the historical period represented would be the one he indicated, and so on.

[37] Also, note that such pieces are the ones most often reincarnated in electronically synthesized renditions, though these are not performances and, therefore, are not directly analogous to the treatment of Shakespearian plays. Ontologically, these are for comparison with animated cartoon adaptations of novels and theatrical works.

musical pieces are not so radically transformed by their performers as are Shakespeare's plays. Generally speaking, the sound structure (which is equivalent to the text in Shakespeare) is kept intact, as is the instrumentation.[38] What is striking is the conventionality of the majority of performances of these works. It is a rare and brave conductor or performer—one such as Leopold Stokowski, perhaps—who actively exploits inauthenticity for the sake of interpretational excitement. Otto Klemperer, Arturo Toscanini, George Szell, Riccardo Mutti, and Claudio Abbado attempt to produce distinctively personal interpretations, but do so mainly in their treatment of fine detail or overall structure. They would be horrified, I suspect, if anyone were to suggest that their triumphs involve a systematic disrespect for features constitutive of the works of Bach, Mozart, Beethoven, and Tchaikovsky.

Mainstream performance practice is not consistent with consequentialism, I claim. The application of a Romantic manner to performances of works composed prior to 1825 is common, and involves a falling-away from ideal authenticity, though until recently this occurred more by habit than through a deliberate rejection of authentic practice. In other respects, most performances do not depart very far from the ideal in the search for interesting interpretations. They exceed by a considerable margin the threshold at which authenticity is at its lowest acceptable level.

These observations count against the truth of consequentialism, according to which authenticity can be traded for other performance virtues and an interesting interpretation provided that the minimum standard is attained. Is there an alternative to consequentialism that more accurately captures the commitments implicit in musical practice?

Opposing consequentialism with rights

In ethics, consequentialism (as in utilitarianism) is opposed by, among others, rights-based theories. These maintain that rights generating correlative duties on others trump other morally relevant considerations. Rights should be respected, even if doing so produces consequences that are, on balance, less desirable than available alternatives. If it applies to the musical case, this theory would explain why authenticity is not on a par with other performance values. If composers have rights concerning how their music should be played, ones imposing correlative duties on performers, the pursuit of authenticity would be a matter of moral obligation, not of choice. Do they have the rights claimed for them? People often have rights over things they own, rights specifying how and when those items can be used by others, for

---

[38] Among the most frequent departures from the composer's instructions are these: repeats are ignored, embellishments required by the appropriate performance style are absent, and modern, not period, instruments are used. Moreover, the style of playing is likely to be overly Romantic, for works dating before 1825.

instance. One way by which one might come to own a thing is as a result of creating or inventing it. So, it could be argued, composers have rights over the use of their compositions because those compositions are *theirs*, are created and owned by them. In this vein, some authors (Carrier 1983; Grossman 1987) suggest that performance has a moral dimension.[39]

Dipert (1980*b*) has dismissed a theory of this kind on the grounds that, in most cases where authentic performance is an issue, the work's composer is dead, and the dead do not have rights (see also Temperley 1984; Donington 1989: 45; Edidin 1991; Taruskin 1995: 24). Kivy (1988*c*) proposes, correctly in my view, that the dead can have rights. But, even if this is true in some cases, it remains to be seen whether dead composers have the rights claimed for them. I am inclined to think they do not. It is far from clear that musical works are owned by their composers.[40] And (contrary to Kivy 1988*c*: 233 and Sharpe 2000) it is not the case that performers are under an obligation to play any composer's works. The relevant rights might be regarded as conditional: if you perform my work, you are obliged to play it so-and-so (Urmson 1993). I doubt this, though, because I see no evidence that the practice of performance acknowledges moral obligations of this kind (see also Thom 1993). Generally speaking, the virtues and vices performers display in their manner of playing are aesthetic and musical, not *moral*, ones.[41]

Another suggestion holds that rights inhere in works of arts themselves. This view has been argued by Alan Tormey (1973), who suggests that works of art are bearers of special rights that are logically distinct from the rights of persons (artists and members of the art public). I find the claim implau-

---

[39] Grossman (1987), Young (1988), and Kivy (1988*c*) argue that we might also have a moral obligation to perform some music *inauthentically*. For instance, we should not use castrati in performing works that were written for them. It seems to me that this gets things back to front. We have a moral obligation not to castrate boys wrongly, and it would be wrong to do so solely for the sake of turning them into musical performers. But castration might occur by accident or could be medically justified under certain conditions. If a boy is castrated and later can sing the parts written for castrati, I see no moral objection to his being used in a performance. Indeed, he has a lucrative career before him.

[40] If the composer could forbid the performance of his work, even where the prospective players are prepared to pay the relevant fees, this would be an indication of ownership. Although there may be precedents of this kind—apparently Carl Orff's heirs rejected offers of payment and managed to get a performance of *Carmina Burana* (1937) banned—I doubt that they represent the norm. Certainly, recognition of 'intellectual property' raises many interesting legal and moral issues. Where it is the culture of one group that is adopted by another, special considerations may come into play; witness debates about whether white men can play the blues (Rudinow 1994, 1995; Young 1994; Taylor 1995) or jazz (Lee B. Brown 1999).

[41] O'Dea (1993) argues that both the discipline and the freedom of performance promote the moral development of the musician. For a wider perspective, see Richmond (1996). Dutton (1979) and Thom (1993) explain how the performer's attempt to disguise intentional departures from the composer's instructions could be represented as moral faults. My claim is that aesthetic and musical faults are not also moral ones if the performer sincerely attempts to comply with the composer's directives.

sible, since I think rights belong only to persons (or sentient beings). Admittedly, 'artificial persons', such as business corporations, can have rights, but it is far from obvious that works of art have the status of 'artificial persons'. It certainly is true that works of art should not be treated in just any fashion—and this might justify our protecting them from their legal owners—but it is not necessary to impute rights to them in explaining why this is so (Goldblatt 1976; Sparshott 1983).

If not composers and their works, do others have rights about what or how music is to be performed? If a public concert is advertised and money is collected from the audience that goes to see it, there is a quasi-contractual relationship between the musicians and the audience (Dipert 1980*b*; Urmson 1993). The audience has the right to receive what they paid for, and this imposes a duty on the orchestra to perform the works as advertised. I find this proposal convincing as far as it goes, but it does not go as far as the authenticist might prefer. The performer is obliged to play as she says she will, but she can make clear in the advertisement that her performance is not faithful to the composer's instructions. 'In tonight's performance, Donna Crystal will play Beethoven's Fifth Symphony while blindfolded, using two silver spoons and fifty glasses variously filled with water.' Moreover, it might not be necessary to be explicit in the advertisement if the context and mode of performance can be anticipated by the audience. It would be unreasonable to expect authenticity in this Christmas's performance of Handel's *Messiah*, given what happened in other years. Finally, the argument applies to a limited, if important, class of performances—namely, public presentations. Nothing is implied about the activity of the musician who plays in private and for her own amusement.

Talk of performers' moral duties to others strikes me as inappropriate in the context of arguments for authenticity. If the performer has a prima facie obligation to play a work authentically, this is not because another person (or thing) has the right that she do so. Rather, it is because a commitment to authenticity is fundamental to the enterprise of work performance. The obligation comes with the decision to play the work, for it is integral to the actions that would realize that decision.

Performances of works as of their composers

Music making has always been a very practical business. Typically, composers write for performance—indeed, for particular occasions of performance—and tailor their music to the instruments and musicians that will be used. They are often willing to adapt their music to changed performance circumstances (Leppard 1988). Moreover, the conventions for performance are also practical. It was not until orchestras became standardized and professionalized that instrumentations specified by the composer counted as mandatory.

Even when they are so, those instructions are sometimes ignored if it is impractical to meet them. If no one can be found to play the ophicleide in Mendelssohn's *Overture to A Midsummer Night's Dream*, a tuba is used instead. Where the choice is between no performance and a performance that is less than ideally authentic, the latter is preferable. This applies especially to amateur ensembles. If a suburban opera group puts on a Shostakovitch opera in English and substitutes a mixed chamber group for the full orchestra, it should be praised for its enterprise, not condemned for inauthenticity. If at home I amuse myself by playing Domenico Scarlatti's sonatas on a Yamaha upright—stumbling over the notes, ignoring those I cannot play, beginning again when I make mistakes—those who would complain must be musical pedants and puritans. This is all to say that it is a mistake to be overly prissy about the need to pursue ideal authenticity.

Notice, though, that the consequentialist is not asking us to excuse the accidental wrong notes of the amateur and is not drawing attention to the practical difficulties that can beset the professional pursuit of authenticity. Instead, he is advocating that the musician deliberately depart from what is instructed, even when she could meet the composer's requirements. This is an odd recommendation indeed. It is one thing to play wrong notes accidentally and quite another to play wrong notes deliberately for the sake of achieving an interesting interpretation. The consequentialist's recommendation is strange because it sets the player's intention at odds with the goal of work performance. Though the musician represents himself as playing the work— indeed, as offering an interesting interpretation of it—he intends to ignore some of the composer's work-determinative prescriptions. It is as if this performer does not understand what work performance is. He is like the chess player who knows all the moves but does not understand that the aim of the game is to capture his opponent's king. He misses the point of the enterprise and in that respect is not 'playing the game'.

A student of Zen might insist that it is a mistake to try too hard to hit the right notes. The musician should cultivate a studied indifference to correct playing. Perhaps this is right (though I doubt it). But notice that the advice is no objection to what I have written earlier. Zen masters might be casual in their approach to archery, but they are so just because that way they hit more bulls. What is recommended is a strategy for best achieving the end of the activity—for hitting more bulls or more right notes—not the consequentialist's rejection of that end.

Slippage from ideal authenticity can result from unintended mistakes or the unthinking acceptance of inappropriate performance practices. In other cases, the departure may be deliberately engineered for practical or artistic reasons, as when the ophicleide is replaced by a tuba. Nevertheless, there are limits to what can be excused by reference to the need to be practical. When it comes to performances by professionals or to recordings, one can reasonably expect a high technical standard of playing and a serious commitment to complying with the composer's instructions. It will not do to dispense with the second bass clarinet in *The Rite of Spring* solely on the ground that supplementary musicians come at expensive rates. If competent chitarrone and theorboe players are unavailable, one cannot mount a professionally satisfactory production of Monteverdi's *L'Incoronazione di Poppea*. In some cases, the appropriate response to practical barriers to performance is that they should be overcome.

Performances that are minimally authentic in being recognizably of the work can be very inaccurate. The minimum standard for authenticity is a low one. There is a considerable gap between the minimum and the ideal. In practice, only a small portion of this, one near the maximum, is explored for the sake of interpretative interest. The performer who intentionally goes further towards the minimum loses credibility in his claim to intend to play the composer's work. In other words, the approach to the ideal remains important, even when musicians are more concerned with being practical than with being ideally authentic.

I maintained at the outset that the value of authenticity depends on the value of its type. In the music under discussion, the type is the composer's work. If the particular work is good, an authentic instance will preserve and convey that goodness. If the work is poor, this also will be apparent in its authentic instances. This does not mean that authenticity is sometimes good and sometimes not, depending solely on the merits of the individual piece that is played. Authenticity is a virtue in performance, even if in some cases it exposes the performed work as poor (Carrier 1983). We can and do value the performance's authenticity for making this apparent. This suggests that authenticity is not a crudely consequentialist notion. The value of authenticity in the performance of a given work is not determined simply by aggregating the worth of the set of its authentic performances. When we consider the value of authenticity in performance, as against the merits of particular performances, the type to which the judgement is relativized is that of works as of their composers. If, in general, we are interested in musical works as of their composers, then authenticity will always be a virtue in performances, for its achievement is the means by which composers' works are transmitted.

William Lycan tells me that he does not like this view, regarding it as equivalent to the shift in utilitarian ethical theory from 'act' to 'rule' versions. The objection is the same in either case: why follow the rule when the balance of utilities that results is negative? If being faithful to a composer's score produces a worthwhile result, we should play authentically, but if it does not, we should go our own way regardless, not blindly adhere to a rule insisting on an authentic approach.

Lycan's objection would have bite if we were attracted to performances of composers' works merely because these tend to be the ones that result in pleasant playings. I reject this account of our interest in music making, however. We care for the works of composers and for performances at least in part for the works they reveal. We are not concerned with performances merely as pleasant playings that may be only incidentally related to the works they purport to be of. That is why we regard authenticity as important whether or not it always contributes to the maximization of the pleasure we take in hearing music played.

There is an intimate connection between the concern with music and with composers' pieces, for the music in question is just musical works regarded as of their composers. In the classical tradition, one does not get performance *tout court*. Performances are of works and works are identified in terms of their composers. The composer's name is not attached to the work merely as a convenient index that helps us to refer to it. It is not that we use composers' names only because other labels are less convenient. (Here I reject a view proposed in Jacobs 1990; see Davies 1991c.) Instead, we regard pieces as the *creations* of their composers. If we are interested in works that are identifiable from performance to performance, it must be works as of their composers that concern us, because, if we disregard the work's composer, we strip the piece of many of the contextual features on which its identity depends. Where such pieces are specified via sets of determinative instructions, one cannot set out to perform them without also intending to follow those instructions. In this way, a concern with authenticity is integral to the very business of work performance.

I do not mean that the work interests us mainly as a symptom of its composer's psychology, or as revealing the social ethos and structure of his society. Perhaps Mozart was exorcising the ghost of his father in *Don Giovanni* (as suggested by Peter Shaffer's play, *Amadeus*). (For Freudian accounts of Mozart's operas, see Brophy 1964.) Maybe Gustav Mahler integrated banal band music with music expressive of pathos because that was the kind of music heard at weekends when the unhappy family scenes of his childhood were enacted (as he revealed to Sigmund Freud). And possibly the structures of medieval music reflect the hierarchical nature of the society in which it was produced (Shepherd 1991). These observations are stimulating, but they are not what makes the music worthwhile. An interest in the work involves a concern with the musical achievements it displays, viewed for their own sake (and not solely as symptoms of something else). And the point about these achievements is that they are *done*. Music of this degree of complexity requires great skill in its creation; it is a sophisticated human product.[42]

---

[42] This does not mean Levinson (1980a) is right to hold that the composer's identity is among the features determinative of the work. It is sufficient that musical pieces are distinctive and complex enough that they are closely connected with their composers (see Currie 1988). Provided we can identify their period and context, we can also access the composer's work, even if we do not know who she is.

The point just made insists that we can appreciate the work that interests us only if it is accurately delivered, so a commitment to authenticity must be primary. An equivalent point can also be made about the composer. She is unlikely to take care over details (which, after all, are what separate the great from the ordinary works) if the performance practice treats her instructions in a cavalier fashion. Composers would not be motivated to do their best if it were common that their work specifications are deliberately flouted.

I have allowed that, in many kinds of music, we are interested in different matters—for instance, in the player's improvisational skills, or in the kinetic impulse that leads us to dance, or in the film to which the music is an accompaniment. In music of those kinds, authenticity in the delivery of a work might not be our prime concern.[43] But in a great deal of music, works are our focus and most of these are specified by composers. This applies to many non-Western and non-classical kinds of music, as well as to music in the European classical tradition. We are indifferent to authorship and context for only a few types of music.

Could it be otherwise? Yes and no. It is always possible that we could come to treat composers' works merely as jumping-off points for performers' fantasias. Then, authenticity of the kind I have been discussing would no longer be a performance virtue, because we would cease to be interested in those works as of their composers. Indeed, works would not concern us any more as such. If this is what people want, it will happen.[44] Nothing in the position I have presented *entails* that an interest in works as of their composers must remain primary. But, were this dereliction to occur, and now we get to the negative, it is arguable that the *concept* of music would be altered, for the interest in music that is an interest in composers' works goes to the heart of that. Music then would no longer be what it was.

Philosophers' analyses of musical ontology and musical authenticity are not what get people to engage with music. It is their pleasure that motivates them. Nevertheless, the philosophers' theses, even if they leave the world as it is, can be examined for what they imply. The analysis of the value of authenticity I have offered presupposes a certain attitude to, and interest in, music, one that gives a central place to works as the creations of their composers. The assumption is justified, I claim, by our musical traditions. Yet our

---

[43] It might be helpful to consider the debate about authenticity in music prior to the nineteenth century as involving a contest between those who think that compositions merely supply *occasions* for performance and those who believe that, despite their social embeddedness, musical works are thought of as creations with an identity and interest apart from the specific context of their presentation. Though I agree that compositions of this time were far less detailed and robust than their later, more easily decontextualized, counterparts, I see the difference between the two as one of degree rather than kind.

[44] Something like it might be happening now, with the late-twentieth-century trend to issue recorded compilations that abstract music from its historical, cultural, and work context. I discuss this issue in Chapter 7.

concerns, and the practices that reflect them, could alter, so that people take pleasure, not in musical works, but in other aspects of music's sound or of performances. (This would not spell the end of music. I have accepted that music satisfies many functions and comes in many kinds. It could be argued, for instance, that jazz caters to the sort of focus I have just described. Jazz undoubtedly counts as music.) But if we were to lose interest in the performance of complex musical works specified by composers' instructions, the result would be a sea change in our concept. There would be one fewer musical type and it would have been a historically crucial one that was gone.

Summary

For performances of Western classical musical pieces, the primary category in terms of which their authenticity is measured is that of 'works as of their composers'. Any performance recognizable as of a given work will be minimally authentic. An ideally faithful performance will satisfy all the work-identifying instructions conveyed by the score (taken in conjunction with the conventions and practices it presupposes). Whether a performance must comply with the composer's instrumentation, phrasing, tempo, and dynamics depends on whether these features are work determinative for the musical tradition within which the work was created.

Enormous difficulties can stand in the way of authentic performance—for example, where the score is equivocal, or we are not sure of the notational conventions and performance practices, or if we do not know how to make the appropriate instruments, or we cannot play them idiomatically. Many of these problems can be overcome. I dismissed some arguments designed to show that authenticity is impossible to achieve in principle. In particular, I claimed that a performance can be ideally authentic even if it cannot be experienced by today's listener as it would have been by the original audience. I did allow, though, that we would not value authenticity as we do unless, in general, it leads to a greater appreciation of the works that are played.

In analysing this last claim I argued against the view I called consequentialism, which holds that authenticity can be deliberately traded against other performance values in the search for interesting interpretations, provided minimal faithfulness is attained. This is not what usually happens. It is true that practical considerations, recently entrenched traditions, and the possibility that performers can take for granted the audience's prior familiarity with orthodox readings, all might count against the pursuit of ideal authenticity. Nevertheless, the territory explored for its interpretative possibilities by professional performers always lies much nearer the ideal than the minimum end of the spectrum along which authenticity is measured. It is not duties that are correlative to composers' or others' rights that restrict the performer. Instead, it is her recognition that a commitment to authenticity is integral to the enterprise that takes the delivery of the composer's work as its goal. If we are interested in performances for the works they are of, then authenticity must be valued for its own sake. So long as we remain concerned with composers' works, and in performances for the light they shed on these, we must regard a commitment to work faithfulness as fundamental to performing.

I see no point in moralizing about authentic performance, which is why I express my conclusions in a conditional fashion. People will do what pleases them. If they are concerned with the work only to the extent that it provokes and inspires the performer, or if the work is so minimal that it lacks intrinsic appeal, or if they are engrossed solely in musical playings, they will not attach to authenticity the importance that I have done. (Or they will be interested in different sorts of musical authenticity—for instance, in the extent to which a given performance event is faithful to the values and idioms of a particular style.) My account presupposes that many people are deeply concerned with the works that performances are of, as well as with what the performer brings to the interpretation of these. In many musical traditions, the creation of works of sufficient complexity and subtlety to sustain the involvement of the performer and listener is central. The survival of works of that type requires a commitment to authenticity of the kind I have been discussing. Authenticity will continue to be an essential aspect of performance provided that a sufficient number of people seek out such works, or undertake to play them.

6

Authenticity and Non-Western Music

They are tourists and we are civilized.[1]

In the previous chapter I discussed performances with respect to the authenticity with which they instance the works they are of. For the most part, this concern ignores the wider social setting for which the music was intended and assumes that works and performances can be contemplated for their own sake, rather than for the functional contributions they make to wider social practices. I confined my attention to the Western classical tradition, but some non-Western societies—those of the Middle East and of Japan, China, India, and Indonesia—have a 'classical' (court) practice that regards music in similar terms.

In general, though, a broader relativity is invoked in discussing authenticity in non-Western than in Western music. Ethnomusicologists are often interested in the characteristics of genres or styles, rather than in works taken as individuals. And, in the context of cultural studies, the social setting and function of musical presentations become the object of attention and are measured for their typicalness. In other words, questions about the authenticity of such music usually consider its relation to the wider culture, rather than focusing narrowly on works and performances regarded as autonomous individuals.

Earlier, I indicated that the New Musicology regards as 'mythological' talk of works and of the authenticity of their performances. Similar trends are apparent within anthropology and ethnomusicology as a new generation repudiates what it regards as the dogmas of its teachers. In consequence, the word 'authenticity' is now studiously avoided in these disciplines and the notion is debunked. In the following section, I sketch this attack on the old

---

[1] 'Mereka adalah wisatawan dan kita adalah orang yang berbudaya.' A Balinese opinion from a research report of the 1970s issued by Udayana University (cited in Picard 1990: 17).

orthodoxy and, as I have done before, I argue against the current stance by defending the continuing relevance of appropriate judgements of authenticity. Indeed, I maintain that such evaluations are inescapably required in achieving an understanding of other societies. Later in the chapter, I take Balinese tourist music as a case study and ask if it might authentically represent the culture's musical works, values, and practices.

The old mythology of authenticity

Following the lead of contemporary anthropologists, the philosopher Larry Shiner (1994) maintains that the view of 'ethnic' art taken by Westerners is conditioned by an outdated, Romantic ideology that reveals more about the image Westerners have of other cultures than about the reality of life within them. Shiner enumerates the elements of this mythology. Non-Western art is made in a long-established style, uncontaminated by external influences, to serve some ritual or other traditional purpose. The artist, by working within the indigenous heritage to serve its religion, taps into and gives expression to the spiritual ethos of the community. It is only under these conditions that his art is authentic. It becomes inauthentic or 'fake' if the artist is influenced by foreign (especially Western) art or ideas, or if he creates works for use apart from their original ritual context (especially if he takes money for his efforts and sells to tourists), or if he becomes mechanical in his approach to its production rather than working from a sense of spiritual vocation. 'What is conceptually interesting about this situation is that carvings *not intended* to be Art in our sense but made primarily as functional objects are considered "authentic" Primitive or Traditional Art, whereas carvings *intended* to be Art in our sense, i.e., made to be appreciated solely for their appearance, are called "fakes" and are reduced to the status of mere commercial craft' (Shiner 1994: 226–7).

Who was guilty of adopting this false ideology? Everyone, perhaps, given that a form of cultural Romanticism was the prevailing paradigm. More particularly, historians and artists have been. They cherished the aesthetic features they discovered in non-Western art, but were ignorant of, or indifferent to, the context in which it was created and used. They were more concerned to enfranchise it within the Western artistic canon and to relate it to works within that tradition. Whatever inspired Pablo Picasso at the Palais du Trocadéro in 1907 when he viewed 'Negro sculptures', or Claude Debussy when he heard Indonesian gamelan music at the Paris World Fair of 1905, was filtered through Western sensibilities, having no regard for the cultures in which such works come to life. Also culpable were earlier anthropologists, whose accounts of the arts and religions of other societies all too often reveal ethnocentric biases and unsuitable assumptions. They focused on practices that were judged 'authentic' because they seemed to be stable, homogenous, and insular. James Clifford (1988: 200) sums up the situation this way:

Since the early years of modernism and cultural anthropology non-Western objects have found a 'home' either within the discourses and institutions of art or within those of anthropology. The two domains have excluded and confirmed each other, inventively disputing the right to contextualize, to represent these objects . . . Both discourses assume a primitive world in need of preservation, redemption, and representation. The concrete, inventive existence of tribal cultures and artists is suppressed in the process of either constituting authentic, 'traditional' worlds or appreciating their products in the timeless category of 'art'.

Johannes Fabian (1983) writes that even those who claim to reject the myth of the 'primitive' employ a framework of objectification that allows the Other to speak only on their terms.

Ethnomusicology is a hybrid discipline, with practitioners coming both from anthropology and from Western musicology. As Clifford's view predicts, a tension is evident between the two approaches. On the one side, Danielou (1971) insists that, to be appreciated at its true value, non-Western music must be studied by musicologists, not 'scientists', while Becker (1986) addresses musicologists in arguing that non-Western music is not inferior to Western varieties (see also Howes 1962). Yet both types of ethnomusicologist previously perpetuated the ideology that is here in question. For instance, some of the early folklorists assumed that styles arising genuinely as expressions of culture are stable and homogenous. As Cecil Sharp put it in the introduction to his collection in 1916 of folk songs from the Appalachians: 'a national type is always to be found in its purest, as well as in its most stable and permanent form, in the folk-art of a nation' (1952: p. xxxv). The songs of cowhands are musically impoverished because the cowboy 'has been despoiled of his inheritance of traditional song' (1952: p. xxxvi). Bruno Nettl (1983: 316) comments: 'Sharp evidently did not wish to collect all of the music extant in the Appalachian communities but had specific ideas of what music properly belonged, and it was music believed to be old, to have uniformity of style, and to be unique in comparison to other musics that might be around. These criteria determined purity and authenticity.' A related view prevailed among ethnomusicologists. They focused on 'pure' material, uncontaminated by Western music. In Asia, the first studies concentrated on 'classical', court styles, whereas urban, mixed, and popular genres, which were Westernized and sounded familiar, were ignored. Music that seemed to be recent and to represent instability was dismissed in favour of often tiny remnants of traditions that were assumed to have long persisted. (The strong reaction of earlier ethnomusicologists against hybrid and recently influenced musics is catalogued in Kartomi 1981, Thomas 1981, Nettl 1983, and Richard Moyle 1993.) Nettl (1964: 181) diagnoses the aetiology of this attitude as follows:

The interest in the 'real' style of a people stems perhaps from the time, around 1900, when the idea of folk music was closely associated with nation and with nationalism, and when the students as well as the political directors of folklore were eager to cleanse their heritage of foreign elements. Another root of the interest in pure styles is the belief, formerly quite common among ethnomusicologists, that the music of a nonliterate culture does not change readily, and that the student, if he can only find a people's 'true' or 'pure' style, is assured of having material of great age.

Work in the later decades of the twentieth century on African, Pacific, and Native American history exposed the mythology as false by demonstrating that traditional societies were not self-contained and unchanging.

Sub-Saharan Africa, for example, was an area of enormous cultural diversity, where there was constant exchange of goods and stylistic borrowing among indigenous peoples, especially after Islamic penetration following the eighth century and the arrival of Portuguese traders in the sixteenth. Today's carvers who make reproductions which incorporate stylistic features from various African groups or even from European Art traditions are not violating the practices of some mythical self-contained 'traditional society' but are carrying on a process of continual cultural exchange.   (Shiner 1994: 228)

I agree. Cultures are not always static, conservative, and homogenous. Their art-making traditions are often dynamic and eclectic. Most cultures have traded their crafts and artefacts in the past, as they do now. No a priori principle can show that the commercialization of a practice alienates it from its cultural home. What follows from the dismissal of the old mythology, though, and what, if anything, should be put in its place?

The continuing relevance of authenticity

Many anthropologists see the deconstruction of previously held models as altogether undermining the usefulness of the categorial distinctions used formerly to describe other cultures. Gone, they say, are the differences formerly assumed to hold between high art/folk art, art/craft, artist/artisan, authentic/inauthentic, religious/secular, and so on. As a result, some (e.g. Maquet 1971: 16; Graburn 1976: 3–4) deny that non-Western cultures have art: the concept is a peculiarly Western one and its use imposes ethnocentric categories on cultures that have different, incompatible ones. Others, even if they do not go this far, agree with Shiner (1994) that the notion of authenticity is so compromised as to be meaningless and unusable (Fabian 1983; Clifford 1988; Sally Price 1989; Torgovnick 1990; Kasfir 1992). According to Errington (1994: 202), 'the received notions of "authenticity" have been thoroughly discredited.' The accepted view now is that any concern with authenticity, however qualified and ameliorated, introduces Western values that have no proper place in the study of other cultures.

It is true that many non-Western societies do not have Art, in the Western sense of High Art. Many of the value notions of Western Fine Art, with its emphasis on museums, non-utility, and contemplation distanced from functional and historical concerns, do not apply to their artefacts. It is not obvious, though, that they lack art, lower case 'a', or its concept. In many cultures, humanly created items are made to achieve aesthetic effects that are essential to their intended function, which suggests that those cultures have art (Blocker 1993; Dutton 1993, 1994, 2000; Davies 2000). If anthropologists seem blind sometimes to the art of the societies they study, this might reveal more about their methods and values than about their subjects.[2]

Fortunately, I do not think that it is necessary to pursue the question of whether there is a notion of art that applies across cultures. My interest is mainly in music. The term 'music' carries less baggage than 'art'. Though some people might deny that non-Western cultures have art, because they associate that term with institutions and values with no home outside the West, few would claim that non-Western cultures lack music. I assume, then, that I will be allowed to talk of non-Western music without being accused of cultural imperialism.

Am I also allowed to invoke the notion of authenticity in describing the music that interests me? It no longer appears respectable within anthropology and ethnomusicology to use the term. That attitude of condemnation is misplaced, though. It is mistaken to regard as authentic only music that is old and unchanging (if there is any such) and wrong automatically to dismiss as inauthentic music that bears the mark of foreign influence and innovation. That a notion sometimes is misused does not show that it is meaningless, though.

I maintain that a concern with authenticity is essential, not merely useful, in considering cultures and their musics. Sometimes we are surprised to learn that categories we took to be stable and clear are not so. Their contents have altered through time, or their applications are flexible in a way that is responsive to subtle differences in circumstances. Moreover, the boundaries between neighbouring concepts, instead of being sharp and fixed, sometimes turn out to be hazy, permeable, and revisable. None of this means that concepts change their identities moment by moment, or that distinctions between concepts cannot be drawn. Rather, it indicates that we must be careful when mapping conceptual space to note and respect the appropriate relativities. If

---

[2] The point is argued in Dutton (1977, 1995). For an example of the way anthropological methods filter out the artiness of the works of their topic cultures, consider Alfred Gell's requirement that the anthropologist adopt 'methodological philistinism'. 'Methodological philistinism consists of taking an attitude of resolute indifference towards the aesthetic value of works of art—the aesthetic value that they have, either indigenously, or from the standpoint of universal aestheticism . . . the anthropology of art has to begin with a denial of the claims which objects of art make on the people who live under their spell, and also on ourselves . . .' (1992: 42).

a vague boundary succeeds in keeping two things separate, then we can consider how they differ in their paradigm instances, even if we should also acknowledge that they share equivocal examples. Indeed, where concepts are not sharply articulated, it might be more, rather than less, useful to consider their differences. A great deal of importance can hang on our ability to make delicate discriminations between close shades of grey. An interest in fine distinctions is all too often mistaken for a style of logic chopping that tries to reduce everything to black and white.

In the Introduction to Part Two, I analysed what is basic to the notion of authenticity. Judgements of authenticity assess items for their membership in kinds. The making of such estimates need not be inhibited by a history of change in the type in question, so long as the relevant temporal indices are specified. Neither are such assessments prohibited by close relationships between kinds, so long as it is clear which are in question. Finally, to the extent that a given item can be variously categorized, a range of different, non-conflicting appraisals of authenticity can be applied to it, each relativized to one of the classifications under which it can be viewed.

If we wish to map 'conceptual space', whether our own or another culture's, we must be interested in the history of the relevant concepts and of the practices through which they are applied, and we must be interested in the relationships—the connections, the similarities, the differences—between those concepts and the classifications, hierarchies, and descriptions they generate. When anthropologists study other cultures, I take it that this kind of cartography is central to their task. They might see how the locals make the relevant judgements, or they might make them for themselves, but, either way, in studying how a society understands (and creates) its physical and cultural world, anthropologists must discover the conceptual schemata it uses. They can do so only by making or uncovering assessments of authenticity, by finding out for the group in question what does or does not count as a genuine classificatory category, and what does or does not count as a proper member of that category. Whatever anthropologists may say, they could not begin to comprehend foreign cultures without sorting the authentic from the inauthentic within them.

If a culture makes music, as all do, it will always be appropriate to ask of a piece if it is authentic. One can ask if it is representative of the group's musical types; if it possesses to an exemplary (or, at least, typical) degree the features they value; if, in their terms, it is one of *their* works and, as such, representative or expressive of their aesthetic goals and ideals. I believe, that is, that questions of authenticity arise meaningfully for any culture that has music. When these questions are posed by cultural outsiders, great care must be taken to avoid unapt and ethnocentric assumptions. But, to the extent that irrelevant norms and values wrongly imported from the domain of Western High Art can be put aside, issues pertaining to authenticity inevitably remain.

It might be objected that the kind of authenticity I have defended as relevant to the enterprise of understanding other cultures is weak and weedy by comparison with what was thought at issue by those who followed the old mythology. This need not be the case, though. I have observed previously that, even if something can be classified in countless ways (and can be assessed for authenticity in each of these), some modes of identifying an item are likely to be more compelling and salient than others. Correspondingly, some dimensions or types of authenticity will be more important or revealing than the alternatives. One crucial classification is that under which an object expresses or reveals a society's values and beliefs. Denis Dutton (1994) calls a concern with an item's status in this regard as dealing with 'deep' authenticity. Because of the care invested in them and the central role they play in other socially significant institutions and rites, artistic practices are usually central to a community and the ways it conceives its identity. Studying them is likely to be especially revealing of the culture's ethos and character, its ways of thinking, its religion and cosmology. So, where our goal is to understand a culture, we are bound to be interested in sorting its art from more mundane artefacts, and in discriminating among its works of art those that display 'deep' authenticity.

A concern merely with an item's causal provenance might reveal little about the values and ideas that are foundational within a culture. After all, one is unlikely to learn much about Western civilization in considering whether a particular hamburger is an authentic McDonalds. In Dutton's terms, 'nominal' and 'deep' authenticity need not be connected. Nevertheless, I think he is wrong to regard these two kinds of authenticity as always opposed. In the case of art and music, I think they are liable to correspond.

If art is important, then its production will call for care, attention, commitment, concentration, and deference, both for the material of the medium and for the heritage of works, genres, and styles. Artistic traditions survive only by being preserved and passed down, not by chance or in the face of indifference. (Change, innovation, and novelty might be highly valued within them, but these notions can apply only where continuities with which they can be contrasted also are recognized (see Layton 1981: ch. 5).) And, where art is regarded as important (though not necessarily also as autonomous and non-functional) by those who make and enjoy it, this must be at least because it is partly symptomatic or expressive of their more pervasive and foundational values and beliefs. Where the works of art of a culture are significant within it, their 'nominal' authenticity *as art*—taking into account their ritual and other uses, not narrowly viewing their aesthetic properties as if 'for their own sake'—will correspond with their 'deep' authenticity. No serious attempt to identify a culture's art and to discover what is distinctive and significant within it can avoid addressing questions of authenticity. And, for kinds of art or music that are so important that they shape the culture's sense of itself and its history, considerations of authenticity reveal a great deal more than neutral genealogies.

Ethnomusicology and the old mythology

As I have already allowed, we find among earlier ethnomusicology some of the approaches and attitudes rightly despised by the current generation. Yet we also find an engagement with legitimate and compelling questions of authenticity that are now passed over without comment. While many ethnomusicologists of the past accepted parts of the Romantic mythology rightly criticized in the last section, it is not obvious that they swallowed the whole package. They were by no means so naive about culture as their current critics imply.

Not all ethnomusicologists supposed their topic societies were culturally static and unaffected by cultural transmission prior to modern times. For instance, having emphasized the need for the folklorist to exercise discrimination in selecting the best folk music to record, weeding out music damaged by exposure under modern conditions to foreign influences, Karpeles (1951) accepts that modern ingredients that do not stand out as misfits but merge with the older elements have as much claim to authenticity as the music produced by the peasants of some isolated region who have had no contact with modern ways of life.

Admittedly, most ethnomusicologists were very selective about the music they studied, preferring to concentrate on traditional types as against ones developed in contemporary times. In some cases the preference was dictated by the goals of a particular study, such as the desire to record the treatment of British folk song in the Americas (Sharp 1952) or to provide evidence of past patterns of emigration (Saygun 1951). More often, it arose from the desire to catalogue musical traditions that were thought threatened by the rapidity of modern change. Mutual interaction between cultures can have an invigorating, fructifying effect when the local culture has time to adapt to its altered circumstances, but, where one culture quickly overwhelms another, the second may be crushed or extinguished, not strengthened. There is a difference between assimilation from within and conquest from without. Many ethnomusicologists in the first half of the twentieth century believed they were witnessing the latter, not the former, and that this justified their attention to older types of music.

In rare cases, dramatic, culturally destructive change is initiated from within the culture. In the 1930s in Bali, Colin McPhee observed that much new music was being composed as classical repertoires of unknown age and authorship were fast disappearing and traditional types of gamelan were being displaced by the new *gong kebyar* ensembles.[3] He writes: 'To try to pre-serve in some form of record this period in Balinese music, while older styles and methods survived, became my desire' (1966: p. xiv). More often, it was not internal development but the global spread of popular Western culture that was identified as the main source of danger. 'One can no longer go into the jungle, or on a fishing raft in the middle of a lake, or in the rice fields far away from all settlements, without hearing a heavy dose of "pop" music . . . The transistor has become the distraction of everyone' (Danielou 1971: 46; see also Hood 1959: 208–9; Kunst 1973: i. 4). Others experienced similar worries. During a three-year sailing expedition begun in 1934 to the South Pacific and South-East Asia, Bruce and Sheridan Fahnestock came to believe that the influx of Western culture and a burgeoning tourist trade would wipe out the indigenous musical traditions of the region. They returned in 1940–1 to record music they believed to be doomed: 'many collectors in the 1940s and 50s feared that the world's lesser-known musical cultures were rapidly disappearing . . . Sheridan Fahnestock, a preservationist at heart, was determined to document the musics of the Pacific islands before mass culture contacts and the influence of Western popular music (particularly swing and country) changed them forever' (McKee 1988: 5).

Even if the kind of music a society recognizes as traditional is not deemed to be in danger, the increased rate of contemporary change provides a reason for distinguishing recently from distantly influenced types of music. Nettl observes that the music of Amerindian and Polynesian cultures has not been static or homogenous. He adds this, however:

But the amount of change which these musical repertories have undergone in recent decades, under the stimulus of increased communication with each other, with Western civilization, and in certain cases with Oriental high cultures, must generally exceed the amount of change previously experienced. Thus the student of a contem-porary nonliterate culture may be confronted with a large amount of material which was acquired recently, and he may wish to separate this from the older material of the culture. (Nettl 1964: 182)

I conclude: although it is true that the past interest in non-Western and folk music has appealed to a notion of authenticity, this did not always involve Romantic ideas of the kind identified and rejected by recent critics of the notion. Ethnomusicologists did not automatically assume that musical traditions are conservative, static, and homogenous. Instead, it was the comparative rapidity and dramatic consequences of change earlier in the twentieth century that led them to concentrate on types of music identified

---

[3] Though these changes were activated by the Balinese themselves, the effects of Dutch coloniz-ation over the previous twenty years may have created the circumstances under which this occurred (Ornstein 1971: 18; Seebass 1996). I describe *gong kebyar* and the other musical types mentioned here later in this chapter.

within the culture as traditional, for they feared these might soon be lost or become thoroughly alienated from the settings and observances that gave them life and significance. They wished to put on record aspects both central and distinctive to life within the cultures they described, and many were concerned to appreciate how musical practices are rooted in, and give voice to, a cultural context encompassing the political and economic organization of the society, along with its aesthetic, moral, and religious beliefs. A person does not have to believe that everything modern is bad, or that all change is pernicious, to view with alarm the trend towards global homogenization that goes with the spread and adoption of Western technology, goods, arts, and values. Cultural diversity is of intrinsic interest, as are sophisticated and complex human practices that have been developed and maintained painstakingly over many years. No excuse need be made for the desire to describe these and their histories. As I see it, the attempt to debunk the notion of authenticity as applied to non-Western art fails to tarnish the reputations of these pioneers and does not devalue the importance of the contributions they made to understanding and conserving the music they studied.

Acculturated music

Since the 1980s, ethnomusicologists have become more interested in newly influenced or developed kinds of music. Nettl (1964: 183) foreshadowed the trend:

> We should, I believe, guard against an attitude which places greater value on the old, and which assumes the existence in the world of a group of pure musical styles whose change, in recent decades or centuries, is to be considered a contamination. Many collectors, especially those of Western folk music, have failed to describe some of the most interesting musical phenomena because they insisted on collecting only the old, 'pure' songs.

Steven Feld (1994) is another who rejects the equation frequently assumed by ethnomusicologists of popularity with both vulgarity and loss of authenticity.

The emergence of this more liberal attitude has led to the study of hybrid and acculturated musical types. In part, this followed the recognition that traditional musical styles might be plural, as is the case with music of Amerindian Shawnee (Nettl 1964), but it also reflected an awareness that recently introduced kinds of music often come to display features formerly associated with older types. Studies have shown that some non-Western cultures are more resilient than was predicted. The music that comes to them from foreign sources is frequently adapted, lending to it a character distinctive to the local region (Kartomi 1981; Thomas 1981; Richard Moyle 1993).

The growing interest in the acculturation of imported musical types could be interpreted as showing that ethnomusicologists have abandoned the earlier concern with authenticity. In fact, I do not think this is the case. Rather, it shows how the notion can be applied not only to the consideration of works, styles, and performances but also to the patterns or processes according to which there is change or evolution in works, styles, and performances. It is no longer assumed that, for a culture's music to qualify as authentic by the indigenous standards, it must be impervious to Western influence.

It is worth considering the conditions under which it is possible to see newly emerged musical genres as authentic to the local culture. *Gong kebyar* appeared in Bali in the second decade of the twentieth century. It was recognized by Balinese as one of their kinds of music because it built on established features of older forms. In being accepted as such, it changed what later counted as 'Balinese music in general'. *Gong kebyar* is no less authentic as Balinese music for the fact that it is not the most ancient variety, that it introduced new elements as well as incorporating much that was old, and that it is constantly changing and evolving. The same applies to the *barong* dance and the *kecak*, which were created a few decades later, though the former departed significantly from its sources and the latter was created specifically for tourists. They count as Balinese music through their historical, aesthetic, symbolic, stylistic, and other continuities with more traditional kinds, though they also contain their own innovations. In effect, they qualify as new kinds or types of Balinese music by being recognized as such by the Balinese on the strength of these continuities.[4]

Gong kebyar, the *barong* dance, and *kecak* are examples of a society drawing inspiration from indigenous sources in creating new types of music. But it need not be like this. Music from sources external to the society could furnish material for its own kinds. There always has been musical interchange between different cultures. What matters is not the origin of the musical material, but the extent to which it is assimilated. Music adopted from elsewhere and adapted to the local style might qualify as authentically representative of the culture's music, provided both that it is counted by the locals as one of their musical kinds and, once established, that it is resistant to modifications inconsistent with the culture's musical practices and idioms. One example is provided by Pan Pacific Pop. Though unashamedly derived from European sources, the songs are adjusted to bring them into line with local types and styles. For example, the melody is shifted to the second lowest voice part (Tonga), or the piece closes with a shouted call (New Zealand), or it employs locally distinctive cadence features (Fiji, Samoa, Cook Islands, and Hawaii) (Richard Moyle 1993).[5] In several parts of Polynesia, two musical

---

[4] Dutton (1995) rightly challenges the fashionable idea that *anything* is authentic just in case a member of the culture calls it so. As I have indicated, the identification counts only if relevant connections can be drawn between the present practice and precedents that are themselves widely accepted as representative of the culture.

[5] Thomas (1981) presents a detailed analysis of the way 'You are my Sunshine' is reworked to the local style by the Banaban Dancing Group of Rabi Island, Fiji.

traditions exist—the old, with fixed repertoires of works, and the new, which is constantly augmented by recently created and imported compositions—and both can claim to be authentic (Richard Moyle 1993).[6] Where the accommodation of musical influences according to recognizable principles is no less native to an area than is the tendency to preserve its core traditions and genres, the process of acculturation can transmit authenticity to the musical product that is its outcome.

What of music that is appropriated or imposed from one society onto a different one? Could music that is taken or inflicted just as it is, without being adapted to fit it to its new cultural context, be authentically representative of the music of its new setting? The obvious answer is 'no'. Usually, a foreign kind will not be absorbed into a society's music unless it is altered in ways that make it congenial to its new location.[7]

Nevertheless, in a few special cases appropriations might claim authentic status. American Samoans copied Tongan *lakalaka* they saw at the 1985 South Pacific Arts Festival, claiming it as their own (Richard Moyle 1993). Their doing so is plausible, since they now identify themselves with a wider geographical and cultural context than they did formerly. As Polynesians (if not as Samoans) they can take possession of the *lakalaka*.[8] A similar example is discussed by Jeffrey Summit (1993). Celebration of the Jewish religious holiday Simh at Torah traditionally involves the use of popular, secular tunes as settings for prayers. Instead of 'folk' melodies, Boston's Jewish community uses ones associated with the USA, such as 'Yankee Doodle Dandy'. It is because the group identifies itself biculturally, as Jewish Americans, that this extension of the practice might be viewed as consistent with the tradition.

Tourist music and authenticity

I have suggested that practitioners in the academic disciplines have rejected the old mythology, laying to rest its ethnocentric biases and its admirable qualities alike. But the Romanticization of non-Western culture persists in other arenas. Indeed, it is sustained by those who promote and consume ethno-tourism. According to Dean MacCannel's influential account (1976), members of pluralized modern cultures are alienated by their social circum-

---

[6] Tatar (1987: 5–7) recognizes six kinds of music in Hawaii, of which four are traditional. Three of those that she identifies as traditional arose in the twentieth century and were influenced by tourism.

[7] I do not deny that Western pop music is often avidly consumed by the people of other cultures. My point is this: the popularity of the Spice Girls' music in Bangladesh is not sufficient to make their songs authentically representative of the music of Bangladesh.

[8] Tatar (1987) records that Tahitian and Samoan music influenced Hawaiian forms through contact in the 1930s. She observes that this trend became more marked when the Hawaiians began to think of themselves as Polynesians in the 1970s.

stances and, as tourists, they engage in an existential quest for a mode of life that is authentic. They hope to find this in foreign contexts that are primitive, pre-urban, and organized along traditional lines. They regard non-Western cultures as sources of personal renewal by imagining that these preserve an older, more spiritual, real, and vital mode of existence, one that derives its soul-healing powers from the vigour with which it can repel change and outside influence. By partaking in these cultures as tourists, they aim to achieve a psychologically healthier sense of self.[9] Tour promoters appeal to these desires and fantasies by advertising tourist destinations as exotic societies untainted by Western commercialism. Bali, for instance, is represented as 'an isle of mystery and enchantment, an exotic South Seas island of dreams, where the people live untouched by civilization, close to nature, with a culture that is artistic, static, harmonious, and well integrated' (Bruner 1996: 157; see also Vickers 1989).

There are two ways of regarding the relation between tourists and native artists. According to the first, tourism merely continues a history of cross-cultural trade, for there is no credibility in the notion that the indigenous maker works strictly within an inherited local style and for consumption solely by the culture's members. Those who make pieces for tourists sometimes make identical ones for local ritual use (Jules-Rosette 1984; Dutton 1994), and, even where this is not so, the new trade is often fully consistent with traditional practices. The mistaken idea that the indigenous artisan must work for 'spiritual', not financial, reward presupposes the Western distinction between art and craft, which is a dichotomy with no basis in cultures requiring functionality in all their artefacts (Shiner 1994). Besides, tourist trade often contributes in an essential way to the survival of indigenous art styles. Christopher Anderson makes this observation concerning Australian Aboriginal acrylic paintings of the Western desert:

Because money can be made, young people are interested in painting. The only way they can do this is to go through the normal ceremonial training, and learn their culture in the traditional way. This reinforces their identity, and strengthens the authority of the older people at a time when other factors work to undermine them. The attention of the outside world through interest in the art is also a positive reinforcement towards cultural maintenance. (1993: 142)

The perpetuation of traditional forms of Asian art (and African carving) depends indirectly on trade with tourists, according to Jules-Rosette (1984: 233).

The second perspective is more negative and sceptical. The economic power of tourists leads to the commodification of the local arts, which are

---

[9] Some of MacCannel's critics (Spooner 1986; Cohen 1988) remain wedded to his account of the psycho-dynamics of ethno-tourism. Like Bruner (1996), however, I doubt that tourists typically are insecure about their own identities.

adapted to the tastes and predilections of foreign visitors, and are presented in hotels and airport foyers (Selwyn 1992: 356). Forced to dance to the tune of the tourist dollar, the hosts dish up (an often disappointing version of) what tourists have been led to expect by tour promoters, and thereby compromise the autonomy and quality of their culture's art (Greenwood 1978; for criticism, see Cohen 1988). Some are appalled by this situation, regarding it as a form of prostitution that is in no way integral to native cultures. For instance, Cornet (1975) and McLeod (1976) *define* authenticity in ethnic art so that it excludes any work made for a commercial, tourist market.

Dutton (1993) has argued for the degradation of indigenous art in a tourist market. He imagines two tribes, the Jungle People and the Tourist People. The carvings of the former are extremely important to them in their relation to their gods, whereas the latter have abandoned their faith but continue to make 'traditional' carvings for sale to tourists at the nearby Club Med. Dutton predicts that, in time, the works of the Jungle People will be, for those informed about the genre, discernibly superior to the pieces made by the Tourist People. Perhaps corn-grinding songs survive, notwithstanding the fact that the natives now buy ground maize at the local supermarket, because they have been incorporated into the 'ethnic' concerts performed for tourists. If so, Dutton's prediction is that the quality of the songs and their performances will erode over time. (For discussion and criticism, see Kelly 1994 and Saltzstein 1998.)

No doubt this scenario is realized all too often. The art and music offered to paying, foreign visitors in non-Western cultures is often an ersatz pap, a kind of ethno-kitsch, which, at best, cartoons the traditional genres. Among the common changes to indigenous practices and conventions are these: the performance is translocated to social venues, including hotels and clubs. Long pieces are shortened and a variety of different types are juxtaposed. Songs are presented in the tourists' language or, alternatively, the words sung become subsidiary to the visual display. Costumes become more opulent than would be typical otherwise. Performers are selected in part for their attractiveness (according to tourist ideals). In some cases, native scales are tempered to Western tunings (Malm 1967: 57, 100–1; Danielou 1971: 6). Traditional instruments are modified, or supplemented, or replaced by Western ones. For instance, Polynesian music has been adapted in such ways for tourist consumption (Richard Moyle 1993). In its indigenous setting, much of the song poetry of the region is semantically dense and stylistically refined. It uses esoteric language and presupposes knowledge shared only by members of the local community. In the tourist context, melisma is replaced by note-against-note melodies; the subject matter becomes more 'universal', dealing with themes such as romance; phrases of English or French are introduced; dance movements become more realistic; guitars and ukuleles accompany the ensemble; and, above all, movements, rather than words, become the focus of attention.[10]

Despite these observations, I think the first view could also be correct sometimes—that is, the relation between tourists and non-Western peoples does not guarantee the cheapening of indigenous art. The locals might take considerable care to preserve their hunting and corn-grinding songs, though they give them for tourists, just because they do not have the same opportunities to associate them with the ancestral activities. If a people's sense of themselves as a distinctive group is retained, they are likely to persist with the practices they value as expressing their character and values, even if the social function of these is altered or supplemented. Suppose the Jungle People also make pieces for tourists while retaining a fierce devotion to their standards, to the religious significance of their products, and to the universal appeal of their cultural artefacts. In that case, there may be no difference between what they make for their own use and those they sell to tourists. Indeed, I believe tourist music sometimes might be authentic in the sense of interest to ethnomusicologists. It could be just like the music that would be played in indigenous contexts; it might be faithful to the works, styles, genres, and practices recognized by the locals as distinguishing 'their' music. It could conform to and exemplify their sonic and cultural ideals.

The case of Bali

Bali is a tourist Mecca (Vickers 1989; Picard 1990). It is also famous for its rich and diverse culture.[11] If tourism inevitably erodes the integrity of indigenous arts, this should be readily apparent in this instance. Before considering that thesis, though, I need to describe the music and its performance for tourists.

Tourists encounter Balinese music in a variety of settings. In hotels and restaurants, a musical backdrop might be supplied by a pair of *gender*[12]

---

[10] The ukulele has been used in Hawaiian music from the early years of the twentieth century. For a discussion of alterations in Hawaiian music in response to tourist demand, see Tatar (1987: 25), and for an account of similarly induced changes in Pacific music in general, see van der Veen (1993).

[11] Some twenty types of gamelan ensemble are in use. Of these, the most common is *gong kebyar*, each of which requires about twenty-five players and usually involves a further fifteen dancers. There are about 1,500 *kebyar* groups. (New Zealand has the same population as Bali, but supports only about eight similarly sized orchestras competent to give public performances, as almost all Balinese groups are.) Some other types of ensemble, such as *beleganjur, anklung,* and *gender wayang,* are also common, but *gong gede, semar pegulingan, gambuh, gambang,* and *selonding* are represented by far fewer groups.

[12] For descriptions of these and other instruments mentioned in what follows, see McPhee (1966), Kunst (1973), and Tenzer (1991). The names of most dances and instruments are Balinese, not Indonesian. Where other terms are specific to Bali, I mark their first occurrences with '(B)'.

or by *tingklik* (bamboo xylophones), though, more often, cassettes representing a range of Indonesian and Western varieties of music are played. When they attend live concerts arranged for them, tourists most often encounter *gong kebyar* or *kecak*. These concerts last about ninety minutes. In the area of Ubud, the visitor has the choice of four or five tourist performances for every night of the week. Such events became frequent and were organized on a weekly schedule in the 1970s, but it is important to recall that musical performances were presented for tourists from the 1930s or earlier. Also, a group from Peliatan travelled in 1931 to the Paris Colonial Exhibition and to the Netherlands. Since then, numerous groups have made international tours.

In some respects, Balinese music is not modified for presentation to tourists. The costumes are sumptuous, certainly, but they were so previously. Some concerts are given for tourists (or Indonesian government officials) in hotels, but many take place in traditional locations—temple forecourts, palaces, and *bale banjar* (B) (village halls). Only indigenous instruments are used. Balinese gamelan temperaments have not become Westernized.[13] The musical works, instruments, and dances are Balinese in origin. But alterations have been introduced into tourist performances. Some pieces, such as *legong* dances, are reduced in length.[14] Tourist shows bring together suites of elements—a welcome dance, a *baris* dance, a *legong*, some instrumental numbers, and a *kebyar* dance—though this is also now common in temple festivals for the Balinese. Some programmes present dramatic works, based on the Ramayana or on the *calonarang*.[15] The *barong* dance is performed in daylight, not late at night. The trances of dancers in *barong*, *sanghyang jaran* ('fire dance'), and *sanghyang dedari* ('angel dance') are usually faked. Also, dancers sometimes play to the audience, posing for photographs.

It is expensive to form and maintain an active gamelan group. Indeed, past princes bankrupted themselves through their devotion to *legong*. Income from tourism has long been important in sustaining the orchestras and performance traditions. As Miguel Covarrubias observed in the

---

[13] The Balinese tonal/modal systems and the techniques of tuning gamelans are outlined in Ornstein (1971: 81–106) and Tenzer (1991: ch. 3).

[14] When President Ronald Reagan visited Bali in 1986, the welcoming dance was reduced from fifteen to seven minutes, but the White House people said that this was too long, so it was cut to two minutes. The embarrassment and consternation this caused the Balinese is evident in the fact that these events are still retold.

[15] An account of *baris*, *barong*, and *calonarang* as they were in the 1930s is given in Covarrubias (1972) and De Zoete and Spies (1979). The current state of these dances is described in Bandem and DeBoer (1981: 93–4, 131–42) and Fred Eiseman (1990). For discussion of the extent to which the *barong* has been altered for tourist concerts, see Bandem and DeBoer (1981: 147–8) and Bruner (1996). For a more general account of the 'artification' of Balinese dance for tourist presentation, see Picard (1996).

1930s: 'The cost of a fine set of instruments often amounts to quite a fortune. The estimated value of the gong Belaluan was put at about fifteen hundred guilders. The actual monetary expenses were paid in instalments, and even after four years of profitable playing for the hotel, there still remained four hundred guilders unpaid' (1972: 208). At that time, it cost 5–30 guilders to hire a gamelan for a night (1972: 163). Writing of a later time, when mass tourism was still in its infancy, Philip McKean comments:

Many hamlet cooperatives have worked strenuously to acquire the necessary capital to upgrade their orchestras, to obtain costumes, and rebuild the meeting halls used as performance centres—based on the risky expectation that they would be able to attract paying tourists on a regular basis. They have, in effect, invested in their cultural traditions, and planned for repayment, with accrued interest that could be both monetarily and culturally.   (1978: 96; see also Ornstein 1971: 15, 56)

Even now, the vast majority of musicians and dancers do not earn their living solely from music (Tenzer 1991: 117). Much of the revenue earned in playing for tourists is paid into the coffers of the gamelan club (*sekaha* (B)).

Also, money derived from tourism has been used to revive threatened forms of gamelan and to restore older instruments (Margaret Eiseman 1990: 340). The Walter Spies Foundation, which supports endangered kinds of Balinese music, is partly funded in this way. In Peliatan in 1996, it sponsored a *legong* festival.

An animist form of Hinduism is present throughout Balinese life. In understanding the Balinese attitude to music, it is necessary to appreciate its religious significance. David Harnish observes:

Nearly all traditional Balinese performing arts are ultimately rooted in religion and ascribed functions relating to religious practices. The major theater, dance, and musical performances, and even those seemingly nonreligious in character, are frequently presented at festivals to enhance the ritual's power. In addition, arts considered relatively 'secular,' such as *drama gong*, are held in spaces ritually purified, and both performers and performance space are positioned to acknowledge the mountain–sea axis that also informs the positioning of temples.   (1991: 9; see also Hood 1971: 15; Ornstein 1971: 65–6, 369–73)

The orchestra and its music are an icon of the spiritual universe no less sacred than the temple itself (Dibia 1989; DeVale and Dibia 1991). 'The "knowledge" of music, the aural organization of the cosmos, is magical and secretive. Anyone who misuses this knowledge will be punished by being sent to hell' (Harnish 1991: 13).

The religious connection runs to the heart of the orchestra and the music, so that it travels with the gamelan to tourist and other secular locations. The same instrumental groups that perform for the gods and Balinese in temple ceremonies also play for tourists.[16] I Wayan Rai comments: 'Most of the performances in [Ubud] are for tourists, but now the general attitude is that if you're not active in the temples then you're just a money-grabber and not a true musician' (Tenzer 1991: 119). Even in tourist settings, the ritual blessing by a priest of the musicians and instruments is observed prior to performance. Also, in many places, tourist concerts are given in the outer courtyards of temples, which are themselves representations of the cosmos (Budhardjo 1966; Covarrubias 1972: 264–70). Ruby Sue Ornstein (1971: 8–11) sums up as follows:

Balinese music in its traditional setting is essentially religious . . . Every performance is an offering to the gods or an attempt to placate evil spirits . . . Music for entertainment is also religious. Unlike ceremonial music, however, it is a spectator performance. Although the visible audience is composed of Balinese, its primary purpose is to entertain and propitiate an invisible audience: the gods . . . However, the same music that is played for the entertainment of the gods is also used on secular occasions when it is performed for tourists or official government guests.

In other words, the Balinese do not insulate their 'real music' from tourists by offering a different, inferior fare at tourist venues.[17]

Moreover, the Balinese make a conscious effort to maintain the highest standards in all performance contexts: their approach to music making is highly competitive, tertiary institutions for the performing and plastic arts train the emerging generation, and the people in general place a very high premium on perpetuating the quality of their arts, as I now consider.

In Balinese music, an atmosphere of rivalry ensures groups are constantly compared and thereby encouraged to perform at their best. Formal competitions are regularly organized for groups playing such music as *beleganjur*. The most intensely contested are those for *gong kebyar*. These have been arranged since about 1915, when this type of music first appeared. At first they were held every few years, but they became annual long ago. Representatives selected from the eight administrative regions compete in the Arts Festival held in Denpasar in June–July. At

---

[16] This is not to deny that there are differences between performances in the two settings. Some pieces are reserved solely for the temple. Whereas the *barong*s used in the temple are holy, those used in the tourist setting are not. Artforms, including *gong kebyar*, that have been classed as secular are performed in the temple's outer courtyard, whereas more sacred ones are reserved for the inner sanctum (Lansing 1983: 94–7; Harnish 1991; Picard 1996: 144–5).

[17] This strategy, which is described in Selwyn (1992), has been said to apply to Balinese painting and carving (Hood 1971: 15; McKean 1978: 103; see also Noronha 1979: 201–2; Jules-Rosette 1984: 196). As I have indicated, the same appears not to be true of music and dance performances (Picard 1996: 143–6).

the festival, the vast majority of the audience are Balinese (Picard 1990: 22), who take a discriminating interest in the music (Tenzer 1991: 110). Many groups aspire to play well enough to take part. Margaret Eiseman (1990: 339) writes: 'gamelans are extremely competitive, and most groups actively seek to improve their skills and maintain their equipment... A Balinese musician loves to tell you about the year he won first prize; a *gamelan* group might tell you that they are striving to be in first place next year.' The following remarks reveal the importance musicians place on the quality of their playing: 'In 1980, a gamelan competition to include groups from Ubud and the surrounding villages was proposed, but Ubud nearly walked out because tensions were so high and musicianship so low that coordinators were stumped by the difficulty of choosing a sekaha to represent the village' (Tenzer 1991: 118; for an account of the political differences that debilitated gamelan groups in Ubud in the 1960s, see Ornstein 1971: 34–6).

In addition, government-sponsored conservatoriums have been established: KOKAR, ASTI, and their more recent successor, the STSI academy in Denpasar, which provides tertiary level training in the performing and plastic arts (see Hough 1995). These institutions recognize a need to resist the negative effects exerted by tourism on the quality of performances. Dr Made Bandem (head of STSI) says: 'We have a responsibility at STSI to be involved in the upholding of artistic standards, particularly where tourist performances are concerned' (quoted in Tenzer 1991: 116–17). Also, the government arts council, LISTIBIYA, is officially charged with regulating groups that play for tourists by auditioning them and certifying to their quality and authenticity (Noronha 1979: 198; Tenzer 1991: 122). Some musicians question its present effectiveness, however.

The formation of music conservatoriums in Indonesia involved a conscious attempt to preserve traditional styles of music, as well as to foster their continuing development. Their role has always been controversial, though. The worry is clear: where the musical style is varied and fluid, the rigidity that goes with formal education and government policy could stifle the music that it so earnestly hopes to save. (Observe, though, that the opposite thought—that the conservatoriums are too innovative— has also been expressed.) From the outset, there was concern about departures from traditional methods of teaching and cultural transmission (for discussion of the Javanese case, see Becker 1980: 35). Ornstein sees the position in the 1960s in Bali this way: 'The conservatory attempts to teach traditional Balinese music in a non-traditional manner. Thus, music that until recently has been transmitted orally is now being taught by means of notation. Moreover, entire *gamelan* are played by women students' (1971: 41).[18] A more up-to-date assessment is supplied by Margaret Eiseman (1990: 333–42):

To some critics, the Indonesian government's creation of special music schools, where the *gamelan* is studied and innovations in its performance are introduced, seems to have brought about a stifling uniformity of style on [Bali] . . . Some people feel that KOKAR and STSI are having undue influence upon the development of music . . . But I think that there is great hope for Bali. Music and dance were never more popular than now. I don't mean in tourist shows, I mean in the villages themselves. Traditional music—whatever 'traditional' means—played by the Balinese for the Balinese.

So far I have argued that a competitive approach to the evaluation of musical performances, along with the formation of institutions that specialize in preparing students for a life in the performing arts, speak for the seriousness with which the Balinese view the maintenance of the quality of their musical performances. A third consideration appeals to the faith displayed by the Balinese in the intrinsic appeal of their traditional artistic practices. If their traditions and taste survive the impact of Western culture and technology, along with the influx of tourists, it is because of the pride they take in their own culture.[19] McKean (1978: 102) recognizes the point: 'An analysis of the production of art illustrates Balinese involution. The maintenance of self-respect through "presentation of culture" may be one of the primary factors in continued Balinese existence as a unique cultural entity.' The view is also presented by Dr Made Bandem: 'There is nothing Bali is more proud of than her arts, and music and dance are the most expressive of these. Through them, Westerners will know the Balinese mind, soul and personality' (Tenzer 1991: 117).

---

[18] On the appearance in Bali of women's *gong kebyar* groups, see Tenzer (1991: 109–10). A women's group, Mekar Sari, performs for tourists in Peliatan and women's troupes appeared in the annual Arts Festival between 1985 and 1997. Women's groups began in the 1990s to play *gamelan beleganjur*, a type that has been widely regarded as exclusively masculine (see Bakan 1997–8). Several studies have shown that tourism creates conditions for the emancipation of local women (Selwyn 1992; Fairbairn-Dunlop 1994), but Bakan (1997–8) is sceptical of such claims in the case of Bali, as are Hatley (1990) and Scott-Maxwell (1996) in their discussion of women's gamelan in Java.

[19] A similar point could be made with respect to central Javanese gamelan music, which has proved very resistant to Western influence. Despite changes consequent on the move to notations, rising nationalism, and the adoption of a national language, along with innovations in the treatment of melody, metre, and *patet* (mode), there has been no assimilation of contemporary Western popular music, according to Becker (1980: 67). (For a more detailed account of the interaction between Javanese and other musics over five centuries, see Sumarsan 1995.) Kartomi (1981) identifies the chauvinism of the central Javanese as the main reason for the resilience of their music. I would not describe the Balinese as cultural chauvinists—they are tolerant of belief and value systems different from their own—but they share this much with the Javanese: they are confident of the satisfactoriness of their way of life for themselves.

The ideology behind Balinese cultural tourism

So far I have suggested that the Balinese do not keep traditional types of music away from the tourist context and that they strive to maintain the established, high standards. According to Michel Picard (1990), the local government's position and that of the Balinese intelligentsia is that tourism has revived the interest of Balinese in their traditions, stimulated artistic creativity, and reinforced their sense of identity and pride. A debate in *Bali Post* between December 1988 and April 1989 closed by endorsing the view that Balinese culture is alive and well, thanks to tourism.

Picard is suspicious of this opinion, nevertheless, seeing it as glossing over the conflict of interest between tourism and culture. The optimistic views I have been presenting come as often from Balinese as from Westerners, but it is time to consider the possibility that the Balinese may be no less blinded by a Romantic mythology about their island and culture than are Western tourists.

In the 1960s, the Indonesian government attempted to direct the arts in Bali to promote its economic and social policies, as well as the national language. These efforts were viewed as inappropriate by the Balinese and were strenuously resisted (Ornstein 1971: 37–51). There was a change in the 1970s, when the Balinese government adapted national policy to the local scene by promoting Cultural Tourism with the slogan 'the tourists must be for Bali and not Bali for the tourists' (*bukan Bali untuk turis tetapi turis untuk Bali*). The doctrine of Cultural Tourism maintains the need to develop tourism and to preserve Balinese culture, while holding that these two objectives are compatible.[20] As Picard (1990) interprets it, there was an official move to blur the distinction between economic and cultural value by linking 'construction of culture' with 'development of tourism' to the point of entrusting the fate of Balinese culture to the interested care of the tourist industry. It was only after the investment of capital in tourism that the Balinese started regarding their culture as a heritage to be carefully preserved and nurtured. (Individual Balinese and particular villages have strived in the past to maintain ancient artforms, but this has never before been a policy fostered across the wider society.) As a result, the Balinese came to assess the value of their culture according to the worth of their island as a tourist destination.

Earlier I observed that anthropologists are now inclined to view culture not in terms of an ongoing history of practices, values, and traditions, but

---

[20] Elsewhere in Indonesia, though, government support for the arts has been conditional on the 'reconstruction' of local culture. Kartomi (1992) describes the 'appropriation' of traditional court dances on the Indonesian islands of Ternate and Tidore in the districts of North and Central Maluku by the Department of Education and Culture and the Department of Tourism. Drastic changes are introduced in packaging such music so that it is attractive to tourists.

as an identity constructed in the present in response to current circumstances. Picard (1990: 24) takes up the theme:

One might suspect that the supposedly indivisible and harmonious unity of agama [religion], adat [custom] and seni [art], in terms of which the Balinese readily define and circumscribe their culture, far from expressing the primordial essence of their identity, is the outcome of a process of semantic borrowing and conceptual adjustment which the Balinese had to make, as a result of the recent opening up of their social space to the outside world.

Other Balinists have arrived at a similar conclusion:

Tourism defines what Balinese culture is in a context where such definitions have hitherto not been needed . . . Tourism encourages Balinese to reflect on their own culture . . . This process of articulation has meant that the Balinese have had to be conscious of their own culture, producing both a sense of pride in their cultural identity as Balinese, and an ability to sum up what may be considered as the essential.   (Vickers 1989: 198)[21]

Edward M. Bruner (1996) draws out the implications for the arts of the observations just made. *Kecak* is presented to foreign dignitaries as emblematic of the culture, though it was created specifically for tourists only in about 1940. The frog dance, composed for tourists in Batuan in the 1970s, was chosen as an entertainment for Balinese at an indigenous wedding in Batuan in the 1980s. The tourist *barong* dance that an earlier generation of ethnographers helped to construct is described by a more recent ethnographer as the incarnation of 'the Balinese version of the comic spirit'. Bruner concludes that even the Balinese themselves are not entirely sure what is 'authentic' and what is touristic. Ethnography/tourism, centre/periphery, and authentic/ inauthentic are outdated, faded binaries that should be rejected.

I agree with these authors that the relation between tourism and culture is complex and subtle. Tourism is not something apart from Balinese culture, not something that impacts on it only from the outside. Rather, it is internal, because it connects with and grades into all aspects of social life and because it can be as responsive to them as they are to it, so that the causal interactions not only flow in both directions but are also reflexive. This perspective gives the lie to an older view that regarded 'ethnic' cultures as self-contained, conservative, and unchanging. On the other hand, though, I regard some of the claims as exaggerated and misleading. For instance, unlike Vickers, I think it is absurd to claim that people are generally unaware of practices they have grown up with unless they are confronted with an alien perspective or government bureaucrats. That a person need not explain what she is doing

---

[21] Vickers (1996) accepts that this process is not new. Balinese have been explaining themselves to foreigners for centuries; for instance, to the Javanese, Bugis pirates, and sixteenth-century Dutch sailors.

to those who share her cultural habits does not mean that she is ignorant of the relevant customs.[22] After all, such matters are taught to children and can be described if necessary. These practices may be 'unconscious' in the sense of being enacted unthinkingly under normal circumstances, but not in the sense of being beyond the agent's ken. Besides, the Balinese have always been self-conscious about their culture and the history of its genres. It is not as if it took the arrival of tourists to bring to their awareness the importance of their arts. So long as music retains its place in the life of the Balinese people—both as a central element in temple ritual and as an aesthetic delight to be appreciated as such—it is difficult to believe that 'travelling dollars' alone could determine what Balinese culture means and becomes to the Balinese. I also disagree that the interactive, volatile nature of culture renders point-less suitably contextualized and relativized questions about the authenticity of social practices, though I accept that such questions must be approached warily. That tourism is integrated with, and subsumed by, other dimensions of social existence within Bali does not demonstrate that we cannot consider issues that draw us into an examination of the intricacies and functional dynamics of these relationships.

The main relevance of the preceding discussion to my current project—con-sidering the quality of musical performances in Bali and the possibility that this has been eroded by the prevalence of tourist concerts—is as follows: I argued that the significance of music within the Balinese religion, the com-petitive attitude to musical performance, the institutionalization of proce-dures by which musical techniques and the heritage of works are transmitted, and the confidence of the Balinese in the artistic worth of their own musical practices should together lead to the maintenance of their performance stan-dards. But, to the extent that the influence of tourism extends beyond the narrow sphere of public concerts and the like, so that it pervades and trans-forms Balinese culture in general, my line of argument cannot be entirely convincing. It could be that the wider musical and cultural context that I have invoked is itself corrupted or altered, with the result that the values informing Balinese music making have been progressively undermined. Moreover, this process may be so gradual that it is almost imperceptible to the participants.

One who detects just such a falling-away in the standards of musicianship is the ethnomusicologist Jacques Brunet. In his view, this trend is caused both by responding to tourist demand and taste and by the formalization of musical training.

The recordings presented here are an echo of the spirit in which *kebyar* was played during the 60s . . . But tourism has wrought havoc. Young people go off to learn music

[22] Some folklorists (e.g. Karpeles 1951) associate cultural unself-consciousness with authen-ticity. Jolly (1992) argues that it was usually (and wrongly) assumed by anthropologists that Pacific societies were not culturally self-aware; see also Dutton (1977).

at the conservatory and come back playing a standardized, almost official, art that has little by little destroyed what made the very essence of Balinese music: respect for many diverse regional styles and freedom in playing technique and interpretation, which are now tending to disappear. One of the greatest dangers for contemporary Balinese music is the attraction of musicians for accelerating the *tempi*, which pays no regard to nuances. The modern world, the desire to put on 'spectacular shows' for tourists, and more and more 'technical' virtuosity taught at the conservatory have created the current situation which, with the exception of a few villages that have held on to their cultural autonomy, have made us spectators to the decline of the great *kebyar* tradition into insipidness . . . The Peliatan *gong* 'Gunung Sari' was the most prestigious in Bali for a long time . . . Unfortunately since the old master [Anak Agung Gede Mandera, who directed the ensemble for nearly fifty years] passed away in the 1980s, the musicians have given themselves over to giving almost daily performances for tourists and have perhaps lost their soul forever. (Record notes to [12], 22–5)[23]

Interviews with Balinese musicians

How can we test Brunet's claims? Balinese musicians are musically self-conscious and sophisticated. They are aware of the history of works and of the styles they play, they have a developed theory and technical terminology,[24] and they make aesthetic evaluations in a way that is familiar to Westerners. The critical comparison of different performances is thoroughly familiar to the Balinese.

Yet, can we trust their judgements to be more reliable than Brunet's if it is possible the Balinese mythologize their cultural history? We can do so, I believe, because we can confront indigenous musical experts directly with their musical past. Balinese music was first recorded by the companies of Odeon and Beka in 1927–8 (see McPhee 1979: 10, 71).[25] More recordings were made on 16-inch acetate discs by the Fahnestock expedition in 1941 (see McKee 1988). Since the early 1960s, many discs and tapes have been

[23] The Peliatan *gong* (as it was known formerly) travelled to Paris in 1931. McPhee (1979: 148–9, 182–3) describes the group as it was in the 1930s. The orchestra won the Bali-wide *gong kebyar* competition in 1937 (thereby earning for its members exemption from the compulsory labour of road building). The group as it was in the earlier 1950s and, again, in the late 1960s, is described in Coast (1953) and Ornstein (1971: 29–36). Gunung Sari has now visited all continents except Antarctica.

[24] Most cultures possess theories and technical vocabularies in terms of which they discuss their musical practices. For instance, Zemp (1978, 1979) has shown that the 'Are'are of the Solomon Islands, a group with a very small population, have a highly developed musicology. Note, though, that where a society has institutions for formal music education, these sometimes codify a 'music theory' that is at odds with that used by practising musicians (Weintraub 1993).

[25] According to Chanan, European companies (Gramophone, Columbia, Odeon, Pathé) went into Africa and other countries in the 1920s. 'These foreign-based companies recorded indiscriminately, mixing traditional songs and modern dance music, Christian mission hymns and Islamic chants, issuing the local music and the imported alongside each other' (1995: 90).

issued. Because they span so many years, these recordings allow for detailed comparison of performances, thereby revealing what has altered, what is variable, and what has been retained. In some cases it is possible to hear how a given work has been treated, or how a particular group has played, over several decades.

I interviewed acknowledged Balinese musical experts and respected young musicians, using tapes that juxtaposed past and present performances. My aim was to discover whether they acknowledge a deterioration in performance standards over the years. I also hoped to identify the factors seen by them as influencing performance and musicianship. Though I was mainly interested in *kebyar*, which is performed at tourist concerts as well as for Balinese in the temple, I also included *legong*, *kecak*, and *gender wayang* for the sake of comparison. *Legong* is a 'classical' dance genre often featured in tourist performances; *kecak* is presented exclusively for tourists; *gender wayang* is sacred and has a Balinese audience. Rather than asking directly about changes in performance standards, or about possibly deleterious influences on these, I invited the musicians to compare the taped excerpts. This they were most willing to do.

The interviews were conducted in August 1996. I Wayan Loceng of Sukawati[26] and I Nyoman Sudarna of Denpasar[27] conversed about *gender wayang*, as did I Wayan Wija of Sukawati.[28] *Kebyar* was covered by I Wayan Tembres of Blahbatuh[29] and by I Wayan Gandra of Petulu.[30] Dewa Putu Berata of Pengosekan[31] and I Wayan Sanglah of Lodtonduh[32] represented the views of the younger generation (that is, of those in their twenties or early thirties). The dancer Anak Agung Gede Oka Dalem

[26] He is the most famous player of Sukawati style *gender wayang* and a teacher at the STSI conservatory. He has made many recordings. In 1992 he won an international music competition in Japan. He has also toured in Canada and the USA.

[27] Son of the famous Bapak Konolan, he is an exponent and teacher of Kayu Mas *gender wayang* style, as well as a leader of *gong kebyar*, and has made many recordings. He is an instrument maker and has taught at the KOKAR conservatorium and at the Indonesian Museum in the Netherlands.

[28] He is a *dalang* (puppeteer for the shadow puppet play) and puppet maker, as well as a former teacher at the STSI conservatory. In 1981 he won the Ramayana competition for *dalang*s. He has toured the USA, Canada, Japan, Netherlands, Germany, and India and has made many recordings.

[29] He is the former leader of the renowned Pinda *gong kebyar*, a teacher of more than thirty-five gamelan groups, and a composer. He has made many recordings. The Balinese government has honoured him with an award (*Darma Kusume*) for his services to Balinese music.

[30] A son of the famous Made Lebah, he leads Gunung Sari and has taught many *kebyar* groups, in Australia and the USA, as well as in Bali. He was an instructor at the KOKAR conservatory and is a composer. He has made many recordings and overseas tours.

[31] A former member of Tirta Sari and Semara Ratih, he now leads the Pengosekan *gong kebyar*. He was the instructor of Sekar Jaya in San Francisco for six months in 1995–6.

[32] He now plays the rebab with Tirta Sari and has performed in Singapore, Taiwan, and the USA.

of Peliatan[33] discussed *legong*, as did Tembres. I Wayan Gandra of Peliatan[34] discussed *kecak*. I was assisted in the interviews by I Made Berata of Peliatan.[35] The interviews with Wija, Gandra of Petulu, and Oka Dalem were in English. The rest took place in both Indonesian and Balinese, with Made Berata asking the questions and consulting with me about the replies. All the interviews were taped. Translations were made by Made Berata, Ni Kuming Tirtawati, and myself.

The most valued quality in works, performances, or musicians is *taksu* (B), which means inner (spiritual) power or authority. Another general term of praise was *bagus* (good). When the interviewees were asked to be specific about the technical features responsible for conferring quality on a performance, they referred most often to the manner of playing *kotekan* (B), which is the interlocking combination of two parts and is characteristic of all Balinese music. It was the steadiness, clarity, and rhythmic accuracy of the *kotekan* to which their evaluations most often drew attention. Precise (*incep* (B)) drumming or key striking was praised, as was definiteness and clarity in the space (*jarak*) between drum or key strokes. In the case of the metallophones, exactitude and clarity also depend on key-damping technique (*tetekep* (B)), so this also was evaluated.[36] Because of their central role as leaders of the ensemble, the two drums are expected to provide an unwavering (*mantap*) beat (*tambur*). Any playing that was unclear (*ngaur*) thereby was bad. Poor playing was sometimes described as *mentah* (unripe, raw).

I begin by reporting discussion of the specific examples I presented to the interviewees, ending with a summary of their evaluations. Then I move to a range of topics, including wider social issues, that emerged as significant to the proper interpretation of the specific evaluations. While there is some evidence of a lowering of standards, and some indications that tourism plays a part in this, more significant are changes in the attitudes of the Balinese and changes to their traditional ways of life, I conclude.

Gong kebyar

Gong kebyar originated in north Bali in the second decade of the twentieth century and spread to other areas in the 1920s and 1930s. The orchestra

[33] Son of the legendary Anak Agung Gede Mandera, he is a dancer and teacher and has made many overseas tours. He is dance director of Tirta Sari and a director of Sangar Padma Naraswara (PANAS), a Balinese modern dance organization.

[34] He is musical leader of the Semara Madya kecak group of Peliatan, with which his family has been associated since its inception in the 1960s. The group has toured Japan and made many recordings.

[35] He is a *gender* player and member of Tirta Sari. His carvings and paintings have been exhibited in Japan and he has performed in the USA.

[36] In the north, the keys sit on the top of the resonators, like Javanese ones, whereas in the south they are suspended. The sound in the north is shorter and less precision in damping technique is required.

differed somewhat from standard gamelans of the time—in the number of keys and tuning of the instruments, and with the inclusion of a large *reyong*. *Gong kebyar* pieces drew on melodies from older forms, but also introduced passages in a new style. 'Kebyar', which means 'bursting open', refers to the aggressive, loud, metrically irregular passages that characterize this music. Above all, *gong kebyar* emphasizes technical virtuosity in the speed and accuracy with which various instrumental voices combine their parts to produce a melodic Gestalt, in dramatic contrasts in timbre and volume, and in brilliance of sound.

In the 1920s and 1930s, the composer and teacher Wayan Lotring of Kuta developed the style and composed new works, many of which were based on and referred to other types of gamelan, such as *gambang* and *anklung* (McPhee 1979: 159–68). (Lotring can be heard playing his compositions near the end of his life on [1].) I Mario (Ketut Maria) from Tabanan introduced dancing (*Kebyar Duduk* and *Kebyar Trompong*) to the form in 1925 and his performances created a sensation (Covarrubias 1972: 232–5). So popular did *gong kebyar* become that earlier forms and ensembles came under threat. By the mid-1930s, many *gamelan gong, semar pegulingan,* and *pelegongan* orchestras were being dismantled and melted down to make *gong kebyar* (Seebass 1996: 86–8). About 1950, a five-section form became standard. Though a number of works introduced in the 1950s are still widely played, new compositions are constantly made and former favourites are dropped when groups tire of them.[37] Overall, *gong kebyar* remains the most popular and dominant form of ensemble music in Bali.

Early recordings of kebyar   Two 1928 versions of *Kebyar Ding*, one from Badung and another from Pankung, were on [17]. The piece was composed in the north specifically for *gong kebyar*. Its structure is not of the modern five-part type. Though he judged the playing to be very good, Tembres thought the piece was monotonic and long-winded (*bertele-tele*) and the *kotekan* too simple for the current taste. A modern version would alter the form, shorten the piece, and repair the *kotekan*. Gandra of Petulu first heard these recordings in the 1960s, when he was an instructor at the University of California, Los Angeles. He brought the piece back to Bali and taught a modernized version of it at the KOKAR conservatory. He also taught it to Gunung Sari, but the spirit, the feeling for the music, was not good. Both

---

[37] For further comment on the history of *kebyar*, on the instruments and techniques of performance, and on the structure of works, see McPhee (1966), Bandem and DeBoer (1981), Margaret Eiseman (1990), Tenzer (1991), and Seebass (1996). For an account of the music and of the dances that go with it, see De Zoete and Spies (1979: 232–41). The most detailed discussion is provided in Ornstein (1971: history of *kebyar*, 15–19, 25–8; the style of kebyar and developments between the 1930s and 1960s, 20–5, 107–21, 351–67; the instruments, 68–80; the form, 122–99; and instrumental techniques, 200–350).

Dewa Berata and Sanglah were familiar with the contemporary interpretation of the piece (*Kebyar Ding Sempati*) currently taught at the STSI
conservatory. Sanglah, who had never heard the original, believed that
the younger generation would find it lovely, but Dewa Berata thought the
rendition of 1928 is not to the taste of modern audiences or musicians.

Two other kebyar performances, *Genderan* and *Gambang*, were recorded in
1941 [15]. These pieces derive from the music for shadow puppet plays and
have remained in the *gender* repertoire, as well as being incorporated in
subsequent *kebyar* works. The 1941 renditions were regarded as unsuitable
for modern performance. The *kotekan* was too simple and the notes were
simply transferred to *gong kebyar*, without being altered or developed to suit
its different instrumentation. Also, their structures were not of the modern
variety. New works based on these pieces would use and develop the borrowed material in only some sections, with newly composed music introduced
in the others. (*Manuk Nguci*, composed by Tembres in the early 1980s, was
based on *Gambang*.)

Kebyar *'classics'*   For the comparison of performances in the contemporary
style and form, I chose *kebyar* pieces that have the status of 'classics'.[38] All
of these have been played often since their composition and are currently
featured in tourist performances in the Ubud region, as well as in temple
ceremonies. The group discussed by Brunet in the quote given earlier, Gunung
Sari, appeared often in my chosen excerpts, which included the performances
from the 1960s that Brunet recorded and judged to be far superior to the
current fare.

The selected works were as follows: *Teruna Jaya* dates from before 1920
and was composed by Gede Manik, but it first appeared in south Bali
(Belaluan, Denpasar) in 1954 and was revised in 1960 (Ornstein 1971: 118).
It is 'a long and difficult dance of great subtlety and beauty that has become
a true Balinese classic. *Teruna Jaya* is a virtuosic effort for both musicians
and dancers and is considered to be the quintessential kebyar-style piece'
(Tenzer 1991: 78). Seven taped excerpts covered the period 1970–90.
Oleg Tambulilingan was created by Mario of Tabanan in 1951 (see Coast
1953: 107–14). Five recorded excerpts covered the period 1966–90. *Kebyar
Trompong* was created by Mario in the 1920s (see Covarrubias 1972: 232–5).
The recorded excerpts were from 1962 and 1970. *Sekar Jepun* dates from the
late 1960s and was composed by Wayan Gandra of Petulu. Unlike the other
pieces, which are dances, it is an instrumental piece. Four recorded excerpts
covered the period 1970–90.

---

[38] The interviewees contrasted these works with *kreasi baru* (new pieces). New compositions
are written constantly for use in competitions. The vast majority of these have a shelf life of just
a few months. Popular pieces may become established in the repertoire, however, as happened
with *Gambang Suling*.

Changes in the works   Alteration is expected and valued in most kinds of Balinese music, as regards the treatment of a given work from group to group, from region to region, and by particular ensembles over time. Classic *kebyar* pieces are no exception. The general trend since the mid-1960s has been towards more complex *kotekan*, a faster tempo, and a reduction in overall length. Different groups have introduced their own alterations, with the result that regional variants are common. What is at issue, then, is the type or quality of change, not change as such.

Tembres compared recordings of *Oleg Tambulilingan* from the 1960s [8], [12] and 1970s [16] with those of the 1990s [9], [22]. In the early days, the tempo was slower, because, at that time, the dance involved more constant action. The basic melody was varied a little, but only the five highest keys were used for *angsel* (B) (sharply accented syncopations introduced in response to dance movements). The later versions employ more variations and use more *angsel*, including ones on the five lower keys.

Gandra of Petulu noted that the long *kotekan* for *reyong* featured at the opening of *Sekar Jepun* was faster in the 1990s and more complex [9], [22] than it had been when the work first appeared [2], [3]. He also noted that, compared to the playing of the mid-1960s, the later style of *kebyar* in general was aggressive. He lamented this and commented on the difficulty of teaching musicians to adopt the older, comparatively more relaxed, method of playing.

Tembres believed that, though changes and variations should be incorporated in the classic works, these should not become excessive. In the case of *Teruna Jaya*, he thought that the recordings of Gunung Sari (1970 [2], 1990 [9]), Sebatu (1972) [20], Tirta Sari (1985) [6], and Sadha Budaya (about 1990) [4] all introduced too many alterations to the basic work. He preferred the performances from Sawan (1970) [12] and Tejakula (1993) [5], both from the north where the piece originated. *Teruna* had more significance and was more dearly loved in the north, he felt. Similarly, both Dewa Berata and Sanglah thought the northern *kebyar* style, with its dramatic contrasts, was better for *Teruna*. The STSI conservatorium treatment employs more gradual crescendos and diminuendos, which, though the result is aesthetic and refined, are inappropriate for this piece.

Performances compared for quality   The standard of performance was judged high for all the excerpts. In general, though, the performances of the 1990s were thought to be less good than the best of the older ones. For instance, Tembres thought the playing of *Kebyar Trompong* by all groups in the 1990s was always less precise than that of Gunung Sari in 1970 [3]. In the rendition of *Oleg Tambulilingan*, Tembres regarded Gunung Sari and Tirta Sari in about 1990 [9], [22] as neither so steady nor so clear as Gunung Sari in the 1960s and 1970s [8], [12], [16]. Gandra of Petulu thought that earlier versions of *Oleg* were better because the musicians then had 'more heart' for the music.

Not all the performances of the 1960s and 1970s were regarded as good, however. Tembres thought the playing of Gunung Sari in 1970 [2], [16] was poor in *Teruna Jaya* and merely adequate in the *reyong* part of *Oleg Tambulilingan*. The performance from Sanur in 1962 [21] of *Kebyar Trompong* was not satisfactory. Also, not all performances from the 1990s were equal, though all groups could be faulted in some respect.

Legong

Legong is a repertoire of dances that originated in the nineteenth century.[39] Since the 1980s, only *Legong Lasem* (also known as *Legong Keraton*) has been played widely. Tourist concerts often include it. Other *legong* are more diffi-cult, both for the dancers and the musicians. *Lasem* is of about fifty minutes' duration in its longest variant. For most tourist performances, the piece is cut to about fifteen minutes. The versions performed in temple ceremonies tend to be longer, but only by about ten minutes. Three taped excerpts of *Legong Lasem* covered the period 1969–90.

The type of gamelan traditionally associated with *legong* is the *semar pegulingan*, which employs a seven-note scale, whereas *gong kebyar* uses a five-note scale. The Balinese regard the sound of *semar pegulingan* as sweet (*manis*), by contrast with the weighty (*bobot*) and aggressive sound of *kebyar*. *Semar pegulingan* ensembles now are rare. *Gong kebyars* play *legong*, both in tourist concerts and the temple. All the interviewees mentioned that *gong kebyar* is not best suited to *legong* and that, in turn, the *semar pegulingan* group Tirta Sari, which appeared often on my tapes, was not best suited to *kebyar* works. Despite this, Tembres thought the playing of *Legong Lasem* by Gunung Sari (a *gong kebyar*) in 1969 [12] was superior to that of Tirta Sari in 1985 [6] and to Sadha Budaya, a *kebyar*, in 1990 [4].[40] For his taste, there were too many drum strokes in all these performances, but the playing was of a high standard.

The interviewees expressed concern about the future of *legong*. Tembres thought that works like *Legong Semarandhana* could be lost because young musicians are not learning them now. Gandra of Petulu suggested that young musicians do not enjoy playing such music. This was denied by Dewa Berata, though he was of the view that some in the Balinese audience no longer like or understand *legong*.

[39] For discussion, see Coast (1953), McPhee (1966), De Zoete and Spies (1973), Bandem and DeBoer (1981: 76–80), and Fred Eiseman (1990).

[40] Douglas Myers writes: 'In 1974, the producer recorded the traditional repertoire of the gamelan Semar Pegulingan. When the producer plays that recording today in the village where it was made, the people smile. They shake their heads. "We cannot play like that any more", they say' (record notes for [19]).

Attempts have been made to revive *legong* in the 1990s and 2000s. Tirta Sari, under the artistic direction of the dancer and teacher Anak Agung Gede Oka Dalem, includes seven *legong* in its current repertoire and aims to master more. It was Mandera of Peliatan, Oka Dalem's famous father, who first responded to the worry that *legong* might be lost by reintroducing them to the repertoire. On 20 February 1999 Ed Herbst made this comment on an Internet list:

When I was [in Peliatan] in [19]72, Anak Agung Gede Mandera and his son Anak Agung Bawa each told me at various times that [Bapak] Gerindem was the only repository of the variety of Peliatan tradition's *legong tabuh* and their relationship to the choreographies, such as *Kuntul* and *Jobog*, which had fallen out of the Peliatan repertoire. (They acknowledged Sang Ayu Muklin as a respected teacher of *Legong Lasem*). They lamented Peliatan's exclusive use of *Legong Lasem*, which they said was the result of routine tourist performances—performing for an uncritical audience.

Oka Dalem in the interviews also complained at the domination of *Legong Lasem* in tourist concerts and observed that *legong* is unsuited to the format of tourist concerts, because the pieces are shortened too much.

Kecak

If any music is debased and inferior by indigenous standards, it should be that created and performed *only* for tourists. *Kecak* (or 'monkey dance') is not given for Balinese. The drama was commissioned for tourists in the 1930s by Walter Spies and Katharane Mershon and the form was developed by the *baris* dancer Limbak. The first performances took place in the 1930s, either in Bona or in Bedulu. Despite its instigation by Westerners, this musical form is purely Balinese in its conception. *Kecak* draws on traditional sources. It derives in part from the *sanghyang dedari*,[41] a trance dance involving two girls. The use of the Ramayana story brings *kecak* into line with older Balinese forms of drama.[42]

　　Performances of *kecak* last 40–60 minutes. They involve an unaccompanied chorus of about 100 men, who sit in a close circle around a 'tree' of oil lamps as dancers enact the Ramayana epic. In this music, sections of the choir chant patterns of 3, 5, 6, or 7 syllables (called '*kecak 3*', '*kecak 5*', and so on) per unit time. These patterns are variously syncopated against an underlying, regular four-beat pulse. Seven recorded extracts covered the period 1941–90.

---

[41] *Sanghyang* is discussed by De Zoete and Spies (1973: 67–80). Chanting on the syllable 'cak' also appears in the social dance, *janger*, where it is present on recordings of 1928, apparently pre-dating the appearance of *kecak*. Like *kecak*, *janger* derived from *sanghyang* (De Zoete and Spies 1973: 83, 211–17).

[42] For further description, see De Zoete and Spies (1973: 80–5); Bandem and DeBoer (1981: 146–7); Fred Eiseman (1990: 288–9). For discussion of choreographic innovations introduced in the 1980s, see Tenzer (1991: 98–9).

In the 1941 recording from 'southern Bali' [15], the tempo was slow and only the simplest interlocking pattern (*kecak 3*) was used. As Gandra of Peliatan explained, it was not until the late 1960s that *kecak 5, 6, 7*, and *kecak pengadeng* (a variant on *kecak 6*) were used. The narrator's singing was striking for its 'classical' style. In the next two decades not many changes were introduced, but, in the 1990s, *cak* groups everywhere became obsessed with departing from the basic pattern, with each introducing its own variations. Gandra of Peliatan was negative about the rapidity of change.

The best of the recordings, Gandra of Peliatan thought, was that of the Peliatan group from 1966 [8]. It was only a few years before that the group had been taught *kecak* by Bapak Tanu, who came from Bona. The performances from Bona in 1962 [21] and Peliatan in about 1970 [16] were less good. One performance of the Peliatan group from about 1970 [13] was poor; in particular, the beat was not positive. Gandra of Peliatan regarded recent recordings from Bona [10], [11] as rhythmically unclear and believed that his Peliatan group was better. Nevertheless, he allowed that the quality of the Peliatan group was down in 1996, following the deaths of some of its most important and long-standing members.

Gender wayang

Gender wayang is played by a quartet of *gender* to accompany the Balinese shadow puppet plays (*wayang kulit*) deriving their stories from the Mahabharata epic. It is among the oldest and most sacred of Balinese musics, as well as one of the most demanding in instrumental technique. The four instruments form two pairs tuned at the octave, with those at the same pitch tuned slightly apart. Shadow puppet plays are not presented for tourists (an exception being a drastically abridged and altered version presented weekly in Ubud).[43] The taped excerpts used in the interviews covered the period 1928–90 and were all from the *Pemungkah* (the instrumental introduction to the shadow puppet play). The interviewees judged the 1969 performance from Teges [14] to be poor. The other renditions—[7], [15], [17], [18]—were all of the highest standard.

Sudarna could identify three of the players on the Kuta recording of 1928 [17]. The leader was I Wayan Lotring, one of the most famous Balinese musicians of the twentieth century, who taught Sudarna's father, Bapak Konolan. To his surprise, there was a slight difference in part three of *Pemungkah* between what was on the recording and his father's playing. (He surmised that Lotring did not teach the piece exactly, or did not teach all of it.) In other words, he expected the 1928 version to be exactly the

---

[43] For further discussion of Balinese *wayang kulit*, see McPhee (1981), Covarrubias (1972: 235–43), and Margaret Eiseman (1990: 322–32). I Wayan Loceng wrote a booklet (English and Indonesian) titled 'Gender Wayang Music' in April 1990.

same as that played in 1996 in Kayu Mas (a few kilometres distant) where his father lived.

The 1941 Ubud recording [15] displayed the influence of Sukawati style in its more complex *kotekan*, as compared with the Kayu Mas style of the 1928 recording [17]. As Loceng described, Bapak Granyam and others from Sukawati played at Ubud palace in the 1920s and 1930s.

Most of the discussion concentrated on distinctions between the dominant styles of Kayu Mas and Sukawati. Sudarna said that, in the Kayu Mas style, the old works (*gending*) are fixed (*tetap*). He would not dare alter them. (If a new piece is called for, which is rare, he would write it afresh.) The Sukawati style is faster in tempo and introduces many innovations to the old works, along with more conspicuous use of decoration and elaboration. Loceng made similar observations and stressed how the complex *kotekan* of Sukawati style is difficult to execute at speed. Both Sudarna and Loceng punctuated their comments with sung and played examples of the dominant styles and of local variants.

Overall evaluations

In interpreting these evaluations, care must be exercised. I should reiterate, the issue concerns the kind or quality of change over time, not change as such. Alteration is expected and valued in most kinds of Balinese music. Also, the negative evaluations of some of the recorded performances depended on discriminations that were fine even by the standards of Balinese musical experts. Finally, the interviewees often emphasized the personal aspect of the judgements they were making and were aware that others might differ. Though all agreed that 'classic' *kebyar* works should be subject to creative development, they did not coincide, and neither did they expect to, on the extent of change that is appropriate.

With these caveats in mind, I think the interviews indicate there were some poor performances in the 1970s and earlier, and there were some fine ones in the 1990s. In the case of *kecak* and *gong kebyar*, not every group that performed well in the 1960s or 1970s did so consistently. Nevertheless, the overall judgement seems to be that the best 1990s performances of *gong kebyar*, *legong*, and *kecak* were not quite so good as the best of those recorded in the 1960s and 1970s. The standard of *gender wayang* has remained high over many decades, and performances from the 1920s remain acceptable. In the case of *gong kebyar*, however, the styles and structures that pre-date the 1950s are regarded as too dated for later tastes, even if the playing is fine. Of the genres discussed, only *legong* was identified as under threat.

If there has been decline, how seriously should we view it? And what is responsible? Does the blame lie with tourist performances? Questions like these were addressed by the interviewees. In the remainder of this report, I turn to the considerations indicated as affecting the maintenance of traditional musical standards and practices.

Tourist performances

Dewa Berata thought that many changes (in dynamics, the interpolation of new material, and faster tempos) were a result of trying to please tourists, and Oka Dalem noted that *legong* dances must be drastically abridged for tourist performances, which is unfortunate. Apart from these observations, the subject of tourist performances was not raised by the interviewees. When the conversation was steered to the topic, the comments were interesting.

Tembres insisted that, when he was its leader, the Pinda group played in hotels in a positive and serious manner, just as they did in the temple. Their tourist performances were orderly (*tertib*), not casual. He also thought that it was good that skilled orchestras should play for tourists, who might thereby learn about the musical culture of Bali. On the negative side, he noted that tourist performances are sometimes given by groups with not yet competent student musicians and that the hotels sometimes want pieces cut too drastically. He commented that it was bad for Bali if the groups are not skilled, because the tourists can tell adequate from poor performances and serious from casual playing. He thought that, if the performances are weak, this is not good for Bali generally; the reputation of Bali as a whole is damaged.

It is perhaps surprising that Balinese believe tourists can recognize bad performances, but McKean (1978: 100) makes this point: 'tourists expect the perpetuation of ancient traditions, especially in the performing and plastic arts, and would not visit in such numbers if Bali were to become a thoroughly modern island. Both conservatism and economic necessity encourage the Balinese to maintain their skills as carvers, musicians, and dancers in order to have the funds for modernization.' My experience is that a majority of tourists in Bali have no clear idea of what the music and dance should be like, even if they expect to be delighted by what they find and are interested enough to seek it out.[44] It is true, however, that many foreign visitors attend temple and street festivals arranged primarily by Balinese for Balinese and find there the kind of music they encounter at tourist venues. And it is also likely that unserious, sloppy performances can be recognized as such, even by tourists. In any case, if a group were poor, word of this would quickly spread among Balinese.

---

[44] Also notice, as MacCannel (1976) astutely observes, that tourists' quest for authenticity is often met by admitting them not to the 'backstage' but to 'a staged back region', something created to give them the impression of penetrating beyond the surface of the culture. A detailed discussion of a relevant African case is provided by Bruner and Kirshenblatt-Gimblett (1994).

Paid performance

Although the prevalence of tourist concerts was rarely identified as having a detrimental effect on Balinese music, such performances were indirectly implicated in a common complaint: that musicians now play for money rather than from love of the music they perform. Both Tembres and Gandra of Petulu made the charge in discussing the younger generation of musicians.[45]

Taken literally, the claim is hard to believe. In one leading ensemble, all participants (about fifty in number) received the equivalent of about $US1 per tourist performance in August 1996, regardless of rank or experience. (Tourists in Ubud paid about $US3 for a concert and as many as 200 attended the weekly performances of the more famous groups, though audiences at other venues were as low as twenty.) In addition, the musicians received a bonus at *galungan* (the holiday that marks each Balinese year of 210 days). In August 1996, one could buy about twenty Indonesian cigarettes or a meal in a cheap, roadside *warung* with the equivalent of $US1. Many of the group's members rehearse many hours per week. It is not the level of remuneration, obviously, that accounts for their participation in the performance group. Indeed, several of its members are independently wealthy, even by Western standards.

So, what lies behind the complaint that musicians now play for money? I understand it as revealing a general worry about threats posed by commercialization to the traditional Balinese way of life, not a particular worry that can be laid solely at the door of paid tourist performances. In the past, musicians played for the sake of the activity and of the music, as well as to please the gods. Famous teachers received only food and accommodation in return for their services. All this was made possible by a cooperative social system that emphasized group goals and the pooling of common resources. Many aspects of Balinese life were organized communally. Under this system, money earned went towards the group. Though this social system remains largely intact, everyone, musicians included, needs money for their families and the temple. All dimensions of life in Bali, not solely those connected with musical performance, have become more materialistic and individualistic than they were formerly. This is an inevitable, if regrettable, consequence of modern economic development, with tourism but one element in this. It is a recognition of the dangers posed by this new regime to the traditional social fabric and, more specifically, to the place of the arts within it, that lies behind the reproach that musicians now are motivated to play for money. As Gandra

---

[45] Elsewhere Tembres says: 'We get a token fee for performing in the hotels now that we never used to get, but it's not enough for anyone to consider that a reason for doing those performances. We do them for the activity and the challenge, and for the strength of sekaha organization. In the temples, of course, it's our duty to play for free and it always will be. No one fails to meet those obligations, and that's why our tradition is so strong' (quoted in Tenzer 1991: 115).

of Petulu put it: 'Before the social system was stronger, but now everything is a little bit money.'

The role of conservatoriums

More frequently mentioned than tourist concerts for their impact on Balinese music was the role played by conservatoriums, such as STSI. Most of the leading musicians of the current generation, including Dewa Berata, Wayan Sanglah, and Made Berata, are products of STSI.

Gandra of Petulu (a former teacher at KOKAR and STSI) noted that, whereas the traditional approach to the study of music was entirely oral, notations supplement the teaching process in the conservatorium.[46] But the resulting performance standard is still the same, he concluded. Tembres, on the other hand, thought that the playing taught at STSI is sometimes of a lower or less even quality than was achieved previously by traditional methods.[47]

Both Dewa Berata and Sanglah observed that the STSI *kebyar* style, along with its versions of standard works, has become widespread as its graduates have become teachers.[48] They regretted the way local styles and work variants have disappeared as a consequence. Both believed, however, that STSI is very important for the development and continuity of Balinese music and dance. Students there received lessons in style, feeling, and technique. Also, rarer types of gamelan ensemble, and the repertoires associated with them, are taught.

Jacques Brunet, in the quotation offered previously, regards the influence of conservatoriums as no less negative than that of tourism. Obviously, Balinese musicians share some of the concerns he expresses, but regard these as balanced and mitigated by other considerations.

The younger generation of musicians

Though the interviewees were not inclined to identify performances for tourists as a source of concern, they were quick to locate a potential threat to Balinese musical traditions in the attitude adopted by the generation of emerging musicians. It was widely maintained that, as regards executive competence, younger players are no less technically skilled than their predeces-

[46] These notations are sparse, indicating only the melodic skeleton, and they are used in teaching only some kinds of music.

[47] Tembres has been more conciliatory: 'Some things are more difficult for musicians now than they used to be, and some are better. When I was young, school and outside pressures were not present to keep my friends and me from playing music all day every day. Now, obviously, it's harder for younger people to find that much time for gamelan, unless they enter a conservatory. But the ones that are serious play very well. Music is just as well-performed today as it ever was' (quoted in Tenzer 1991: 115).

[48] Hough (1995) notes that the STSI versions of certain religious dances—*Baris Gede* and *Rejang Dewa*—have become *de facto* state standards.

sors. What is in question, apparently, is their interest in, and commitment to mastering the intricacies of, difficult 'classic' works.

Tembres thought that the younger generation of musicians is not serious and prefers easy music. Gandra of Petulu held that young players do not enjoy *legong*. They look for dynamic contrast and constant change. They do not care if the work is good, only if playing it makes them happy. But he detected a growing interest in 'old' music, such as *legong* and *Kebyar Ding*. He predicted that, by about 2010, a respect for the musical precedents of the *Kebyar* style would be reawakened.

It is so common in all cultures for older musicians to allege that young players lack interpretative depth, despite being technically skilled, that one is likely to be wary of taking these comments at face value. And it was obvious that these generalizations did not apply to the younger musicians I interviewed; there could be no doubting the seriousness of Dewa Berata, Wayan Sanglah, and Made Berata. Yet they, too, expressed reservations about the attitude of their contemporaries. It was said that younger players are not always prepared to practise difficult passages and that the commitment to excellence is not what it was in the mid-1960s.

The attitude of the Balinese audience

The temperament of younger musicians appears to reflect that of a wider Balinese public, especially the younger generation as a whole. Dewa Berata noted that Balinese audiences are beginning to complain that the temple performances are too long and to say they do not like or understand *legong*. They prefer STSI style and new pieces, not the older works played in a traditional manner. What and how the musicians play, even in the temple, is dictated by what the people enjoy. This situation is very bad, he thought, and threatens the traditions of music and dance.[49]

Earlier I observed that the quality of the music for the shadow puppet plays shows no signs of decay. Notwithstanding this, the *dalang*, Wayan Wija, worries about the way *wayang kulit* is changing in response to pressure from the Balinese public. Few Balinese are expected to follow dialogue in the old Javanese language of Kawi, but, increasingly, audiences can no longer understand the parts of the drama that are spoken in High Balinese. It is the humorous interludes supplied by the clowns in Low Balinese or Bahasa Indonesia that attract their attention. As a result, performances are becoming briefer and more diverting. The musical interludes and accompaniments are also being reduced—repeats are cut, shortening pieces by a minute or more.

---

[49] The complaint is not new, of course. Walter Spies wrote in 1936: 'Bali's "modern" youth with their semi-European school-wisdom are no longer in touch with their own classic art. Danger is imminent that the art of Bali as a whole is destined to degenerate' (quoted in Picard 1996: 134).

Wija is no conservative. He is the sole performer of *wayang kulit* based on *Tantri* (Balinese fables involving animals) and has been involved (along with Larry Reid) in experimental forms of *wayang kulit*. Nevertheless, he bemoans the changes just observed and regards them as stemming from an alteration in the wider Balinese sensibility to tradition and the arts.

Of course, these remarks must be put in perspective. The music described here percolates more deeply into the fibre of the average Balinese than most Westerners can comprehend. For instance, it remains true that everyone in Bali knows the music of *Legong Lasem*, even it is no longer to the taste of all, which is not something that can be said of Westerners with regard to their own 'classical' music traditions. Still, that the Balinese public no longer identifies so completely with older works and styles of playing truly is alarming for indigenous musicians who prize them.

Conclusions

What is the overall picture? On the positive side, many musicians retain a deep devotion to the music of Bali and are equipped to communicate this on a practical level. The negative picture is more complex. For many kinds of music, there may have been a gradual decline in the last half of the twentieth century in the level of the very best performances. Brunet, who detects a more significant collapse of standards, blames this on tourist performances and the dominance of the conservatoriums. The interviewees do identify these factors as potentially relevant to the quality of performances, though their concerns were qualified. Uniformity of style has followed from the teaching at STSI, but some of the interviewees found that style to be congenial and all saw compensating advantages to Balinese arts in their promulgation through such institutions. Also, the shortening of works for tourist performances was regarded as regrettable. And such performances were implicated in the creation of an environment in which musicians play more for money than for love of music.

It was the attitude of the Balinese to their music, however, not the influence of tourism, that was more often identified as a source of concern. Many of the current generation of musicians do not deeply feel works and styles central to the traditional repertoire, though they are as technically competent as was ever the case in rendering such music. And this coincides with a loss of interest in and comprehension of such music by young people in general. The threat to Balinese dance and music, if there is one, comes primarily from within. This is apparent in pressure from the Balinese public for changes in the shadow puppet plays and in musical performances for the temple. Even in *kecak*, the current trend towards innovation arises from the musicians, rather than from tourists.

The most significant influence on Balinese music appears to be the shifting attitude of the Balinese to their own cultural heritage. This change in attitude is more readily explained by alterations within the wider society, ones affected by international trade and communications, than solely by the impact of tourism. It is important to recall that the last four decades have been ones of extremely rapid technological and economic development. Bali has gone from kerosene lamps to electricity, from *setrop* to Coca-Cola, from bicycles to four-wheel drive Toyota Kijangs. To take just one of the more obvious cases, television is present in many homes and eating-houses. The Balinese are inundated with information, products, and values that have origins outside their culture, not only from the West but also from Muslim Jakarta. At the same time, the assumptions of entrepreneurial capitalism that underlie the moneyed economy adopted in Indonesia (as elsewhere) are in tension with Bali's traditional social systems organized along cooperative lines. To my mind, these factors create much more powerful pressures for social change than does the immediate presence of tourists as such.

A similar conclusion is reached by Djelantik (1995) in his discussion of change in Balinese aesthetics. He focuses on architecture and the plastic arts and records that, though the Balinese are flexible in adopting new ideas, styles, and technologies, their evaluations are based on traditional notions of beauty. Changes in the artist's position in society depend mainly on wider alterations in society, and on tourism also, but to a lesser extent.

As for Western commentators on Balinese music, I believe Tenzer comes nearer than Brunet to identifying the factors that might threaten the traditions. Though he mentions tourism as both beneficial and dangerous, he places the emphasis on the wider social context when he writes:

The yearly Festival Gong and Bali Arts Festival, the constant stream of musical performances emanating from the conservatories, and the ever-increasing number of village sekaha with regular work performing for tourists, have created a broader range of contexts for gamelan in secular life than has heretofore been known in Bali. This has often had the effect of strengthening the sacred ties which are the root of the tradition, simply because there are more sekaha available and eager to play their part in rituals . . . At the same time, many young Balinese, bombarded by a hail of outside influences resulting from Indonesia's increasing international presence, and the influx of tourists, foreign goods and Western culture, are perhaps less aware than ever of the history and diversity of their own music.   (Tenzer 1991: 110–11)

Summary

When the authenticity of performances of non-Western music is debated, the considerations invoked differ from those that arise in evaluating the authenticity of performances of Western classical music. As well as considering its faithfulness with respect to the work it is of, and to the genre to which the music belongs, the non-Western performance is likely to be assessed for its cultural integrity as an expression of the society's historically important musical traditions, repertoires, and practices. Moreover, where the culture's music is closely tied to its religious and cosmological commitments, the performance might also be judged by the extent to which it mirrors or reveals the relevant non-musical values and beliefs.

Anthropologists and ethnomusicologists of the past sometimes based their judgements concerning the authenticity of the cultural products of their topic societies on mistaken assumptions about the nature of 'primitive' societies. These assumptions have rightly been challenged and rejected, and more interest was shown by the close of the twentieth century by ethnomusicologists in hybrid and acculturated musical types. Nevertheless, their tendency to abandon all talk of authenticity is deeply misguided, I have suggested. Indeed, it is not possible to map the flux of cultural change without judging what falls within the relevant categories and whether a given category has been replaced by another, or has absorbed the other, and so on—evaluations that presuppose prior assessments of identity and authenticity.

As I see it, three morals emerge from the critique of older models of ethnic authenticity. (*a*) If judgements of authenticity are to be meaningful, they must be carefully indexed to the times and contexts that are being compared. Because change that is responsive both to internal developments and to external influences can be consistent with preserving and expanding the repertoire of works and practices that authentically express a culture's musical ethos, considerable subtlety and sensitivity is required in those who would make the relevant judgements. (*b*) Where a society is culturally self-aware, as most surely are, appraisals of authenticity should come from within the culture or be informed by its views. This does not mean that the locals can say what they like, regardless of historical facts and musical practices. It is, rather, to acknowledge that their teachers and musicians are the ones with the relevant expertise—that is, with the appropriate knowledge of works, styles, techniques, and performance practices, and with the artistic and religious sensibilities that are required. They are best placed to judge if the music they perform and listen to belongs to them, accords with their view of what is musically proper, apt, and so on. (*c*) The extent to which we can expect their evaluations to coincide with those of Westerners depends on the ground that is common; on whether, whatever else is involved, both cultures value similar qualities in music and in its performance. Though it is fashionable to emphasize the differences that undoubtedly exist, I would not be surprised if there are many similarities, given our shared humanity. We could not expect to understand their views, though, unless we learn the conventions of their musical repertoires, styles, and genres, the characteristics of the instruments they employ, the technical and other demands imposed on the performer, and the functions that music fills in their lives.

With these morals in mind, I considered whether the quality of performances of Balinese music is compromised by the prevalence of tourist concerts. There are grounds for being concerned about the future of Balinese music, and tourism provides a scapegoat for those looking to assign blame, but, in fact, the social changes that impact on the vigorous perpetuation of the musical ethos and traditions of the Balinese people are of a very general, if complex, kind.

The discussion of topics as important as this last, which interrogates the status of art and culture within a global context, cannot proceed without taking seriously considerations of the authenticity with which performances represent indigenous musical styles and practices and thereby give expression to wider cultural values embodied within them.

7

Recordings

I thought John [Lennon] had liked all the production techniques we had pioneered on Pepper, but no sooner was it finished than he rebelled against them. He wanted to get back to what he called 'honesty', in recording—in other words, he wanted to make them as near to live performances as possible. I reckoned we were making little movies in sound, not stage plays. If a little artifice gave a better result, why not use it? After all, we were honest and up front about the tricks we used.

(George Martin 1994: 139)

Most musical works are created for live performance and most live performances are of works, yet most people experience music via electronic mediation and, hence, at a remove from the playings that are done. They listen to the radio or to tapes or discs. In Chapters 1 and 4 I outlined some of the ways in which what occurs in the recording studio is unlike what happens on the concert stage. Despite these differences, we talk of the performances that are found on tapes, vinyl records, CDs, videos, and DVDs. Apparently we regard recorded performances as fair substitutes for live ones.

Though I will consider the social impact of the prevalence of recording technology and electronic transmission later, I begin by discussing how recorded performances differ from live ones and the significance of this, both for the way music is played and for the experience of the listener. The topic is important because most philosophers of music assume the paradigm—that is, real time playing before an audience—when they discuss musical performance.[1] Yet, in practice, most of the music heard by most people comes to them via the TV, the radio, the record player, or other electronic playback devices. The paradigm is such, that is, because of its historical importance. It does not represent the kind of performance most often encountered now. The significance of this technologically facilitated shift in the means by which

---

[1] Among the few who are sensitive to the fact that recordings are very different from live performances are Higgins (1991), Lee B. Brown (1996), Gracyk (1996, 1997), Fisher (1998), and Edidin (1999).

we hear music will be missed if recordings are thought to be on a par with, or are heard as reproductions of, live performances.

Live performances and electronic media

Suppose that a person listens to a radio broadcast of a live concert of instrumental music—that is, to a performance that is broadcast (in FM stereo) just as and when it is played for an audience present in a concert hall. Also imagine that this person's radio (the complex of tuner/amplifier/speakers) is of the highest quality.[2] How is his experience different from that of a suitably placed member of the audience in the auditorium?

The radio listener, call him Ham, has more control over his situation than is normal for the person at the concert, call her Cecilia. He can sing along, dance, or wave his arms, where such behaviour would not be acceptable in many kinds of concerts (though they are encouraged in others). He can augment the bass or turn down the volume, and can switch off the radio when he wants, whether or not the broadcast is finished. He can use the music as a background or accompaniment to other matters. Let us assume, though, that Ham is just as interested in hearing the performance as is Cecilia. He attends to it closely, listens from the beginning to the end, and takes care to set his receiver so that it reproduces as faithfully as it can the sound of the performance. For both listeners, the conditions are as ideal as possible. Ham is not disturbed by background noises in his vicinity and Cecilia is seated near the middle and towards the front of the hall, which lacks pillars and balconies or other sources of acoustic 'dead spots'. What discrepancies between their experiences distinguish Ham from Cecilia?

One obvious difference is that Cecilia can see the music played and Ham cannot. If the broadcast work were an opera or a ballet, this would impair Ham's access to crucial aspects of the performance (Harris and Fender 1995). The same applies if the event is a rock concert, because these are offered as multimedia performances, with the staging, the prancing, the undressing, and the seduction of the microphone integral to the show. Suppose, though, that the concert is of the symphonic variety. How important is it to see that kind of music played?

There is an attractive visual aspect to such performances, both in the general panorama and in the delicate choreography of the players' movements. The bows of the string section proceed in unison, the lights are caught and softened to gold orbs as they are reflected by the brass instruments, the conductor hangs in a crucifixion pose, like a limp puppet, as the final notes die away. When asked if a concert is a theatrical activity, John Cage replies: 'Yes, even a conventional piece played by a conventional symphony orchestra: the horn player, for example, from time to time empties the spit

---

[2] On the technology of speakers and amplifiers, see Shorter and Borwick (1980).

out of his horn. And this—when I was as a child, taken to an orchestra concert—frequently engaged my attention more than the melodies, harmonies, etc.' (quoted in Kostelanetz 1988: 101). Peter Kivy (1995: 100–2) concludes that visible features of a performance may be an aesthetic part of the work, so long as they are relevant to its playing (see also Laszlo 1967). The beauty of the musicians' clothing is additional to and separable from the music, but the elegance or energy of the players' movements does contribute to the performance's aesthetic manifold, he thinks.

Though I do not deny the attractiveness of such factors in performance, there is a more important reason why performances should be seen. An awareness of the limitations and potential of the medium is necessary to an understanding of the composer's achievements and purposes, as well as to an appreciation of the performer's contribution to the result. In other words, one cannot fully apprehend music without knowing how it is elicited from the instruments for which it is written, and that knowledge must come either from playing the instruments or from watching them played (Levinson 1990c; Putman 1990). But someone who has previously acquired the appropriate knowledge need not see music played before he can follow the treatment of the medium or recognize the performer's contributions.

Another point deserves consideration: there is a distinction between silences that are part of the performance and those that are not (Judkins 1997a). A performance is framed by moments of stillness, with the musicians poised to play at the beginning or posed at the end in the attitude of playing. Moreover, some works exploit this boundary by starting almost imperceptibly or by fading gradually to nothing at their close. Unlike Cecilia, Ham is in no position to distinguish the framing silences from those that are contiguous with them, such as the hush that precedes the conductor's raising his baton at the start and the pause that anticipates the applause at the end. In this case, Ham's knowing what he would see if he were present is no substitute for witnessing it, because the actual timing of the particular events is crucial. But, again, I do not think that Ham's experience of the performance is crippled by his inability to locate the framing silences as precisely as Cecilia does.

In brief: Cecilia, in being present, may know that matching cummerbunds and jackets are being worn by the orchestra's members, while Ham knows nothing of such things, but his ignorance of these matters need not inhibit his understanding of the music if the ensemble is one of a kind with which he is familiar. If the concert is of Balinese *gong kebyar* and Ham has been to many of these, so that he can picture the orchestra and can discriminate in what he hears the contributions of the individual instruments, he is not disadvantaged by his inability to see the performance. (Indeed, if Cecilia is attending her first concert of music of this kind, she may recognize far less of what is going on than Ham does.) Ham's failure to see the music played need not produce a significant difference in his listening experience from Cecilia's, provided he can make the appropriate auditory discriminations and knows the kind of thing he would see, moment by moment, were he to be present. On the other hand, if the music and the ensemble are of types with which neither Ham nor Cecilia is acquainted, he is much worse placed than she to appreciate both the work and its performance.

A change to the case would allow Ham to see the orchestra in action. Imagine that he is viewing a radio–TV simulcast of the concert. Television, as a medium, displays features distinguishing it from ordinary perception. As a result, it is unlikely that Cecilia and Ham would see exactly the same things.[3] Cecilia observes the orchestra from her seat and is likely to remain there throughout. The heads of those in front of her might occupy as much of her field of vision as the orchestra does. By contrast, Ham is likely to be treated to different perspectives, including ones from behind and above the orchestra, along with close-ups, panning shots, and so on. He is shown the conductor's face and particular players at times when their parts are musically salient.[4] Ham will probably see something very different from Cecilia, even if the TV producer refrains from 'enhancing' the effect with superimposed images (for example, of swans during a performance of Camille Saint-Saëns's *Carnival of the Animals*). The style of television presentation can be distracting or irritating sometimes,[5] but, if it is not so, Ham may be better situated than Cecilia to note the musicians' use of their instruments. Such differences are not usually so great that they count against the claim that Ham and Cecilia share a relevantly similar experience of the music. Just as it is sufficient that Ham is aware of what he would perceive if he were present, so it is sufficient that Cecilia knows what the TV viewer is likely to be exposed to, whether or not she sees this for herself.

Another of the differences between Cecilia and Ham is inconsequential. Cecilia has a programme telling her what the works are, something about them, and identifying the performers. Ham does not have a programme, but

---

[3] They might see very similar things, of course, if the solitary TV camera were mounted on Cecilia's forehead, though this would make for rather poor viewing by the standards of the medium.

[4] Notice that, as against the conventions of some genres of television and film, the microphone does not follow the camera. There is no diminution in the orchestra's volume as the camera's viewpoint shifts from close to far. When we see the cor anglais player in close profile, we do not also hear what she plays brought into special relief.

[5] 'In a live concert the visual element is important . . . but the movement of the eye is controlled by the listener. The television viewer has no choice as to what he will look at and will tend to listen for whatever he is being shown. At best this characteristic can be effective as an elementary means of analytic highlighting; at worst it results in distracting images and the fragmentation of the music. The dangers of televising symphony orchestras in this way can be softened by such technical devices as superimposition and cross-fading of several images. The essential element is a sensitive producer with a thorough knowledge of the work being televised' (Goslich *et al.* 1980: 322).

I assume that the radio schedule identifies the works and the performers, and that he has books in which he can read about the works. Perhaps an announcer is at the concert and, in hushed tones, describes the scene prior to the commencement of the concert.

The most important distinction between Ham and Cecilia consists in the fact that the former's experience of the music is mediated by its electronic promulgation. If the medium of transmission is transparent, there may be no significant difference between their experiences, but, if it is not, there is likely to be. Is radio a transparent medium?

To answer this question, consider how the technology works. The sound of the orchestra is picked up by microphones, amplified, modulated by being imposed on a 'carrier' signal that has a much higher frequency, and transmitted from an aerial by electromagnetic waves travelling at the speed of light. A receiver tuned to accept the relevant bandwidth detects this signal via its aerial. It amplifies and demodulates the signal, passing it to speakers.

Older methods of transmission restricted the broadcast range of pitches to about 5,000 Herz, thereby losing the upper harmonics that contribute to the timbre of the sound. The amplitude of the signal was often narrower than the volume range of music heard live, so that a technician had to adjust the recording apparatus during the performance to accommodate changes in dynamics. As a result, the sound emitted from the receiver was noticeably louder in the quiet passages and softer in the loud passages than was the case in the concert hall. Also, in those days, only monaural transmission was available. Finally, speakers often did not reproduce sound with even sensitivity across the relevant pitch spectrum. Under these circumstances the medium was far from transparent and its effects might easily have been regarded as impoverishing the experience of the radio listener to a significant degree (Apel 1966: 623–7; Goslich *et al.* 1980; Shorter and Borwick 1980). Many of these deficiencies have been remedied. A wider spread of dynamics is conveyed.[6] Similarly, the pitch range covers a much greater compass and the transmission is in stereo. Speakers are improved or can be corrected by the use of graphic equalizers. Allow, if only for the sake of the argument, that the technology now generates at the receiver more or less exactly what impinges on the microphones. Then is it the case that the medium is transparent? There is reason to think not.

At a live concert there is a considerable amount of background noise. Much of this is made by the audience, however silent it tries to be. Some extraneous sound penetrates from outside the building. In a famous British radio broadcast during the Second World War, the 'crump' of exploding bombs could be heard as the musicians played on. Now, Cecilia's 'noise

---

[6] It remains the case that the technician must still set and alter the recording's levels (see Shorter and Borwick 1980: 573).

detectors', her ears, are 'mounted' in such a way as to allow her to focus on sounds coming from a particular source or direction to the exclusion of other, local noise. She is able to concentrate on the music, despite the ambient sound that surrounds her. Ham, though, is in a different position. If the microphones pick up background noise, this is conveyed to him, along with the music, from the speakers to which his listening is directed. It is much more difficult for the radio listener to exclude from attention such irrelevant noise as is transmitted along with the music he hears.

Broadcasters are aware of this problem, of course. To counter it, they place their microphones above the front of the orchestra, thereby reducing the volume of noise picked up from the auditorium. This produces some side effects, however. The radio audience is more likely than the concert hall listener to hear ambient noise produced on the stage, such as the musicians' grunting, humming, or singing as they play, or the 'clack' of the keys on wind instruments, or the creak of piano pedals, and so on. (The noises made by musicians and their instruments are rarely discussed, but see Judkins 1997*b* and James R. Hamilton 1999.)

I am inclined to think that the placement of the microphones, if not the technological limits of transmission, affect the sound of radio broadcasts in a way that prevents the medium from achieving complete transparency.[7] Moreover, differences in the phenomenology of the listening experience will remain, even if superior technologies improve on those of the early twenty-first century. (1) With multiphonic broadcasts transmitted to many speakers located around the auditor, and with each speaker taking its signal from microphones scattered through all parts of the hall, the radio listener might sort ambient from other noise as the concertgoer does. Nevertheless, the listener's experience can be expected to differ, given that the disposition of the playback speakers is unlikely to mirror the placing of the microphones at the performance venue. (2) Alternatively, imagine that the listener attends a 'holodeck' performance, with holograms creating a virtual performance space and generating sounds that come as if reflected by walls and the like within that setting. Assuming its technical perfection, such a medium would come close to auditory transparency. Despite this, the user's experience of the sound might differ from that of a person at a live performance if it is apparent to her that the virtual musicians do not respond to her reactions to their efforts. (3) Or, to up the 'ante', imagine technologies so sophisticated that they remove the listener's isolation from the virtual performers. Perhaps the listener can take the conductor's role, with her actions directing the virtual

---

[7] There is an interesting exception to this observation. If the instruments used in playing the work are themselves electronic, the broadcaster might intercept the signals before they reach the speakers used in the auditorium, bleeding them from the amplifiers and mixers which themselves are part of the work's medium. In that event, the radio listener could be spared all the ambient noise generated in the concert hall.

musicians, or perhaps the simulated musicians can be influenced by her visible responses as a member of the audience. Under these conditions, near-perfect transparency is achieved. Even so, the user's experience might differ from that of her equivalent at an actual musical performance. This is not because of what is (seemingly) done or heard, but because of the intrusive influence of general beliefs she has about her situation. Unlike the person who rightly believes that she is conducting or attending a real musical performance, the listener who is aware that she is involved in a simulation realizes that aspects of her experience that seem interactive and social are mechanically contrived.

I have suggested that radio is not a perfectly transparent medium at this time, even where it faithfully reproduces the sounds that reach the microphones. This does not show that the difference between Ham's and Cecilia's experiences are aesthetically or artistically significant. In fact, I do not think that they need be. Ham can claim acquaintance with the work, provided that it calls for instruments and techniques of playing with which he is familiar. Just as someone can truly say 'I saw the first game of the World Series yesterday', though he watched it on TV, so Ham can truly say 'I heard the first performance of Minimo's new quartet last night', though he listened to the radio and was not at the concert.[8] And Ham is not in a weaker position to assess the performance of a well-known work than is Cecilia.[9]

Recordings of live performances

So far so good. One might access a broadcast performance either by being at the performance site or by listening to one's radio. Recall, though, that my concern lies more with records than with radio. So assume that, instead of being broadcast, the concert attended by Cecilia is recorded onto a master tape and issued on disc as a recording.[10] Is this medium as near to transparency as is that of (live) radio?

In its history, the phonograph has been limited in the faithfulness with which it reproduces the sounds recorded. The moves from wax cylinders to

[8] This way of talking depends on our temporal nearness to the events in question. A person born in 1980 who watches film of John F. Kennedy's assassination is more likely to say 'Yesterday I saw a film of Kennedy's assassination' than to say 'I saw Kennedy killed yesterday'.

[9] I admit that we would be disconcerted to learn that the music critic for the *New York Times* does not attend the concerts he reviews, listening to them at home on the radio instead. In part, this is because of views we hold about the ethics of his profession—he *should* be there because convention has it that direct reporting takes the form of earwitness accounts. And, in part, it stems from concerns about the electronic medium—even if the radio might come close to transparency under ideal conditions, in actuality those conditions might be achieved only rarely, or only under conditions of uncertainty, since there is no easy way to check that the settings of the playback device do justice to any particular musical event.

[10] For a revealing account both of the special difficulties posed to the sound engineer by recording in the live situation, and of contrasting strategies for meeting those challenges, see Wilkinson (1997).

shellac to vinyl to CDs, from 78s to 45s to LPs, from wooden styluses to electronically sophisticated cartridges to laser beams, from valves to solid-state
chips and circuits, from diaphragms to modern speaker complexes, from
mono to stereo to quad to all-round sound—all these developments have
improved the reproductive potential of the recording medium.[11]

Even where the production conditions are ideal, the effect of the playback
equipment on the result is often striking. For instance, the best Sure cartridges
produce a svelte, even sound, whereas the best Garrard cartridges used on the
same record gives the sound an immediacy and physicality that seems to place
one on top of the performer's instrument.[12] I cannot discuss here all the technical changes that have been introduced to playback equipment, but one comparatively recent development deserves comment. Like others of its ilk, the
Sony Mini Hi-Fi Component System (MHC-E90X) offers settings allowing
for the digital modification of the output. Some of these ('car' and 'head-
phone') seem designed to adjust for the fact that the playback environment
can differ from that presupposed by the record manufacturer, which is the
living room of a home, I guess. Some ('night', 'hall', 'studio', and 'stadium')
modify the sound to give the impression of a different playback environment
from the listener's. Others ('rock', 'pops', 'background music', and 'classic')
are tailored to the characteristic features of particular kinds of music. For the
novelty of the experience, one might select the 'rock' setting ('lively rhythm
and powerful bass') in playing recordings of Mozart, but I assume that the
intention is that one adopts the mode matching the kind of music played. This
is odd, though, because it implies that the recordings are deficient and that the
playback device can compensate for this. (I wonder how the producers of Sony
recordings feel about this.) To listen without these audio effects, the user selects
the 'direct' mode. 'The direct circuit on this unit passes the music signals
directly to the outputs without sending them through the [Digital Sound
Processor]. This feature can be used when you want to listen to the music in
its pure, unprocessed state' (MHC-E90X Manual, ch. 5:21).

For fifty years, companies have insisted of each new product that it deliv-
ers 'pure, unprocessed' music. This time, it is said, one is in the presence of
the musicians. The rapidity of technical change inevitably leads to scepticism
regarding the hyperbole with which each 'advance' in recording or playback
equipment is advertised. Stravinsky says:

---

[11] On the history of developments in recording, see Read and Welch (1976) and Shorter and
Borwick (1980: 573–8). In the case of discs read by a stylus, some forms of inaccuracy are more
or less ineradicable: the groove waveform of the disc is originally inscribed by a plough-shaped
cutting stylus but picked up by a hemispherical playback stylus; there is a fall in linear recording speed across the disc, which results in a loss of high frequencies; because the playback stylus
is mounted on the record's side, whereas the cutting stylus is in the disc's centre, tracking errors
are introduced; inevitably, the stamper that creates the discs wears over time, thereby degrading
the faithfulness with which the master is reproduced.
[12] On cartridges and styluses, see Shorter and Borwick (1980: 579–82).

The short life-expectancy of a recording has become a deterrent to the composer-conductor . . . for he knows that the march of technical innovation will crush even the best musical performance. Last year's record is as *démodé* as last year's motor car. In fact, active interest in a new recording lasts for only six months, obsolescence sets in after that, and death occurs by the end of the year, in spite of geriatric treatment by sound engineers.   (Stravinsky and Craft 1959: 110–11)

Lee B. Brown (1996) suggests that improvements (or otherwise) in recording are better gauged against earlier records than against live music, because the medium is omnipresent and by no means transparent. Such cynicism is justified, I allow, but if we confine our attention to the acoustic profiles generated by live musical performances and by playings of recorded music, I think it is the case that a gradual improvement has been achieved and that digital recordings on CDs achieve the near transparency that I attributed earlier to radio.[13]

What differences, if not acoustic ones, distinguish the recording of the live performance from the radio broadcast of the same concert? Some are relatively minor. The recording is likely to omit the orchestra's tuning up, which is often included in the broadcast concert, and to cut the applause at the end, along with encores played at the concert.[14] Also, liner notes substitute for the concert's announcer. More significant, perhaps, is the fact that breaks between movements are likely to be replaced by shorter periods of 'dead' sound.[15] As a result, the framing and structuring function of these breaks is altered or destroyed.

---

[13] This is not to deny that the improvements have been purchased at a price. The person who played 78s was more or less obliged to *listen* to the music because, to keep it going, he had to turn the discs over every three or four minutes. Moreover, one should recall how fine is the sound quality on some recordings made in the 1930s and how inadequate sometimes are the pressings of commercial LPs later, with surface noise and distortion, echoing between tracks, and pitch oscillation caused by off-centre holes.

[14] Nigel Kennedy's recording (EMI Classics 7 54574 2, 1992) of Beethoven's Violin Concerto is presented as 'the new live recording'. The CD includes a tuning track, minutes of applause, and two encores.

[15] '[John] Atkinson [editor of *Stereophile*] recommends that you record a few minutes of silence in the hall before the audience arrives and insert this between the selections. "You don't want to fade to black between cuts; you want to fade into the natural sound of the hall . . ."' (Wilkinson 1997: 73). Though this approach is an improvement on the use of 'black' silence, it is not ideal, as is explained by Judkins. 'Live' breaks between movements both divide and unify the work. 'Between-movement silences are also structured by the conductor or performers who are challenged to retain musical involvement and the thread of the piece, while making necessary mechanical adjustments such as shifting [music] or emptying water keys. They prepare us for the movement to come and dissipate the one preceding—offering a neutralization of involvement . . . such silences rarely only resolve musical tension; in fact, they may often prolong it. It seems that these between-movement silences are most effective when just long enough to contain an afterglow from the previous movement, a neutral zone, and then a brief *crescendo* of expectation for the next movement' (1997*a*: 45–6) As she notes, all these effects are lost to recordings that separate movements with empty tracks.

One important difference derives from the permanence of the recording.[16] Ham can play his disc repeatedly, whereas the live performance takes place (and can be experienced as such) once only. Features that may be innocuous in a live performance are liable to take on a new significance when one has a recording of it. For instance, the audience's coughs become harder to ignore when they can be anticipated—and one knows from the first hearing that they will be present in all subsequent playings at the same moment, just before the flute solo, say. The same goes for mistakes or infelicities in the performance. A few wrong notes and fluffed entries need not mar the listener's enjoyment of a concert but they can be baneful on a recording. Meanwhile, an idiosyncratic, exotic interpretation may be exciting when one hears a familiar piece live, but soon can become irksome with repetition. Equally though, a performance that is rather too conservative for the occasion might become desirable on disc when one is looking to add a work to one's collection while expecting to possess only one interpretation of it. Also, a record might take on a special significance because it turns out to be of a famous musician's last public performance.

Typically, one listens to a recording with the expectation of hearing it again—with an awareness of the reproducibility of its content—and this inevitably affects how one experiences and evaluates it. Records are lived with (are taken to desert islands) in a way that live performances cannot be.[17] In this respect, the experiences of Cecilia at the concert and of Ham playing his record at home can be importantly different, despite the acoustic faithfulness with which the recording reproduces the sound heard at the time of live performance. This difference flows from the character of the medium through which the performance is transmitted.

There is another aspect of recordings of live performances that should be noted. As I have argued previously, performance necessarily involves a creative aspect (even if a composer's score is followed). In the live situation, this is added as and when the performance occurs, in the here and now. But when the real-time performance is recorded, this dimension is permanently fixed and thereby ossified.

Sometimes it is held that, because the listener experiences the disc as constantly reproducible, she cannot hear the performer's decisions as

---

[16] I use 'permanence' loosely: some early recordings became unusable after only a few dozen playings, and all recordings, whatever the medium, deteriorate with use or over time.

[17] Here I disagree with Edidin (1999), who argues that the ephemeral nature of live performances is purely contingent and not aesthetically significant. Though I accept that recordings present performances, I deny they are transparent and I claim that their repeatability can and should affect how they are heard and appreciated.

spontaneous, so they lose their immediacy and vibrancy. The composer Roger Sessions make the point more forcefully than most:

[A recording] ceases to have interest for us, however, the instant we become aware of the fact of literal repetition, of mechanical reproduction—when we know and can anticipate exactly how a given phrase is going to be modelled, exactly how long a given fermata is to be held, exactly what quality of accent or articulation, of acceleration or retard, will occur at a given moment. When the music ceases to be fresh for us in this sense, it ceases to be alive, and we can say in the most real sense that it ceases to be music. (1950: 70–1)

Ted Gracyk (1996: 55–6) replies to Sessions by pointing out that we do regard works of art, such as paintings and novels, as things to return to. As he is aware, that does not address Sessions's main concern, which is that the musician's inventive contribution becomes petrified when the performance is recorded. To try to explain why recordings are of continuing interest when they are reheard, Gracyk develops a second argument. Diana Raffman (1993*b*) claims that nuances of musical pitch, timbre, and rhythm are finer than the mental representations in terms of which we structure perception and, hence, that they cannot be stored in memory. Gracyk (1996: 57–61, 236) cites Raffman's analysis in suggesting that music on records retains its freshness because, quite literally, we cannot remember between playbacks exactly how a disc sounds. As a result, we encounter the performance anew each time we listen to the record. I am not convinced by this last argument. I accept that people are not capable of 'replaying' a recording, with all its perceptible detail, in memory. The issue, though, is whether they can anticipate what is coming next as they listen to a recording. My experience suggests to me that this is possible. If I know the disc very well, sometimes I have an eidetic aural 'picture' of what is about to happen a few milliseconds before it occurs.

Here is another response to Sessions's stance, at least as it applies to the classical music that he has in mind: a recording contains at least two things regarded as meriting repeated hearings, a work and an interpretation. This point blunts the force of Sessions's objection, but it does not remove it, as is apparent when we consider recordings of music that is primarily improvisatory. Lee B. Brown (1996: 366) writes of jazz: 'Once embedded in the grooves or bytes of recording media, improvized music is in danger of becoming seriously alienated from itself. It takes only one punch of the "repeat" button to bring home the fact that the effect of recording on what I have called "presence" is corrosive'.

Neither of the arguments considered so far succeeds in meeting Sessions's worry that recordings kill performances, but here is one that I regard as stronger. If one *knows* that a recording is of a genuinely live performance,[18] then one also recognizes that the performance options were taken in real time and under the usual circumstances. That knowledge informs the way one listens, even when replaying a disc (Edidin 1999). I allow that the mediation of the technology is likely to affect the listener's experience of the performer's creative input, but I do not accept that the appeal of the performance is killed stone dead as a result. That the kinds of experiences differ does not mean that the second preserves nothing that is valuable in the first. Moreover, it is an error to overlook the advantages of permanence in such discs. There are at least two. Whereas felicities introduced to the playing by the musician fly past the audience that is present, which can experience them only in the moment, the disc's auditor can savour them, recognize them more clearly, and analyse them if she is so disposed, as a result of being able to replay the recording. Moreover, though we find delight in novelty, we also take pleasure in the familiar. Too much repetition can pall, but an amount that suits the listener can be a source of enjoyment in its own right.

I began this discussion by comparing a live performance with a (not-to-be-repeated) radio broadcast. I did so because I think our first, crude intuition is that recordings are analogous to such broadcasts. If the medium of radio conveys the concert transparently, then a recording of the concert should do the same. Behind this view is the assumption that the transparency of the medium depends solely on the faithfulness with which it conveys the acoustic information it receives. There is room to doubt that radio is a perfect sonic reproducer, but I argued that the radio broadcast is adequate, so there is no reason to expect an important difference between the experience of the listener at the concert and a suitably informed listener by his radio. The former need not be in a significantly better position than the latter to apprehend and appreciate the work or its performance. The modern technology of recordings allows for a degree of acoustic faithfulness similar to that achieved by radio. But I also suggested that awareness of matters that are a consequence of the medium—in particular, knowledge of the relative permanence of recordings—affects the listener's experience of what he hears from his record player. As a result, his awareness need not follow that of the radio listener or of a member of the concert audience. Therefore,

---

[18] The proviso is not idle. Many recordings that are represented as 'live' have been modified in the studio before being issued. Nigel Kennedy writes: 'When you buy an album of a classical concert you are, nowadays, buying no such thing. Even though the album has been sold as "live", the performing artists have invariably gone back to the hall (after the concert(s) have been completed) and, in studio conditions (often for a few days), have patched over various offending passages of music' (Beethoven Violin Concerto, EMI Classics 7 54574 2 (1992), pp. 3–4). Obviously Kennedy believes that he occupies the high moral ground, but note that his 'real live' recording is compiled from two performances (on 11 and 12 June 1992), though it preserves 'complete unedited movements'. For discussion of the electronic doctoring of 'live' performances of rock music, see Gracyk (1996: ch. 3).

the assumption just mentioned is unfounded—that is, the transparency of the medium is not solely a function of the sonic fidelity it achieves. The listener's knowledge of the nature of the medium and of its adjuncts, such as discs and tapes, plays a crucial role in shaping his perceptions. As a result, the experience of the recording differs from that of the radio broadcast, even where both achieve the same, high measure of acoustic verisimilitude. First thoughts notwithstanding, recordings are not best thought of as broadcasts of live concerts, even where they are recordings of live performances.

Most philosophers who are aware of the differences between recordings and performances are quick to fault the former, especially if their interest lies mainly in jazz or classical music. Where there are deficiencies inherent to the medium, its proper assessment requires a balanced view. It is important to stress the many real benefits provided by recordings and to acknowledge that, when profits are weighed against losses, the result often appears on the credit side of the ledger. As long as the prevalence of recordings does not threaten the continuing tradition of live performances, we are not forced to choose between the two.[19] The two kinds of playing can and do coexist. The philosopher should concern herself with identifying their respective strengths and values, rather than dwelling on the weaknesses inherent in one or the other approach.

Studio recordings

Most recordings (with the possible exception of those of jazz and 'ethnic' music) are not of live performances—that is, are not of unedited real-time performances presented to an audience in a public venue. They are made in studios, or in deserted churches or concert halls in the dead of night. As already mentioned in Chapter 4, with the move to the studio and the technology it offers, many of Stan Godlovitch's (1993, 1998) conditions for (live) performance are abandoned. No audience is present, never mind one 'in a position to receive the entire performance in its detail'. The 'proper sequence' of the work need not be respected, since it is the editor or producer who splices together the takes that will be used, whatever the order of recording. The performance as given by the musicians is unlikely to be 'continuous'; many takes of passages or sections might be recorded.

Previously I identified ambient noise and mistakes in performance as more significant defects in a recording of a live performance than they are in the

---

[19] When Thom (1993: 172) and Gracyk (1997) consider the issue, they write as if one must choose between worlds one of which has only live performances and the other has only recordings. But neither of those worlds is like the real one, fortunately. Although fewer people now play musical instruments than once was the case—and, perhaps this is an indirect consequence of the domination of recordings—I think that real-time musical playing is bound to continue while there are people who retain an interest in traditional musicianship and in works designed to exhibit it.

performance itself. The approach to studio recording acknowledges this. Great care is taken to avoid extraneous, background noise. If possible, errors and crudities are eliminated when the composite is created by the producer, who brings together the best of a series of takes. In addition, it is easier to employ more microphones and more complex sound-mixing techniques in the studio than at live venues, thereby achieving greater clarity and definition where the texture is dense, as well as more subtle shadings of balance between the parts.

In earlier sections I discussed limitations on the acoustic faithfulness with which the technology in question reproduces the music played. Here I draw attention to the problem posed to studio recordings by the need to create a soundscape that approximates that of the setting where one would expect to hear the music live. The acoustic properties of the performance environment are not incidental to the character of the music if it is written for, or assumes, a given setting. So, the playback of a recording should reproduce the appropriate conditions. Achieving this is no straightforward matter, given that the recording most likely will be played in the carpeted living room of a suburban house; that is, in an environment with acoustic properties unlike those of the type of venue for which the work was intended, which may be a cavernous opera house filled with people, for instance (see Shorter and Borwick 1980: 589). Now, recording studios tend to have dry (flat, matt, dead) acoustics. The sound engineer must try to generate a sound with an appropriate resonance—one adapted to the 'standard' playback environment, not a 'straight' sound as such. She does this either by using directional microphones pointing away from the performers or by electronically controlling the balance of instruments and, with filters, the relative strengths of pitch bands, but neither technique is entirely satisfactory (see Shorter and Borwick 1980: 571–2).[20]

I will again disregard these technical shortcomings and suppose that, with the use of quadrophonic speakers or 'surround' systems, the listener can hear from the recording just what she would hear at an equivalent performance in an appropriate venue. Also, I will hold to the suggestion mentioned earlier by comparing the studio recording not with a live performance, but with a disc made at a live performance. How are experiences of these two recordings likely to differ?

[20] Earlier I mentioned the settings available on a Sony playback device: hall, stadium, studio, car, and the like. These impose changes on features that the recording sound engineer has already fashioned. It is possible that, when one plays back a studio performance of music recorded with the characteristics of music played in halls, while also selecting the 'hall' setting, one would hear an output that is like the playing of a record in a hall, rather than one that is like the playing of an orchestra in a hall. In this mode, the recording, which already captures the resonance typical of halls, would sound slushy and indistinct, because the reverberation caused by the hall during the recording playback would exaggerate that which is already on the recording.

In comparing a live performance, first with a broadcast, then with a recording of that same concert, I ignored the musicians. I assumed that, from their point of view, there would be no difference. This presumption is questionable. Knowing that a recording will be made of their performance, the players might cater their interpretation not to the audience that is present but to that projected for the disc.[21] Suppose they do not do this. What differences are likely to be found in their approaches to (recorded) live performances and to those given in the studio solely for the purpose of recording?

The pianist, Alfred Brendel (1990: 200–1), makes an astute response:

In a concert one plays just once, in the studio several times if necessary. In a concert you must convince the audience at once; in the studio it is the accumulated result that counts . . . In a concert the performer must get to the end of the piece without a chance to make corrections. In the studio he can make corrections, learn while he records and get rid of nerves. The player before the public must do four things at the same time: he must imagine the performance, play it, project it and listen to it. In the studio he has the opportunity to hear it again after playing, and to react accordingly. In a concert it is the broad sweep that counts. The studio demands control over a mosaic; while it offers the performer the possibility of gradually loosening up, there is also the danger of diminishing freshness. And there is the painful business of choosing between takes. When playing before the public, details must be projected to the furthest ends of the auditorium, just as the whispers of an actor must be heard throughout the theatre. In front of the microphone one tries, on the contrary, to get away from exaggerations and aims for an interpretation that will bear frequent hearing. In the concert hall the concentration of the audience brings about a mutual influence between the performer and his listeners. In the studio nobody has to be conquered—but there is nobody to disturb you. The player sits as though in a tomb. A fit of coughing or the chirping of the alarm on a watch may break the spell of the most delicate moment of the concert. The studio offers silence. Weaknesses in a concert performance tend to result from spontaneity, from a break in concentration or from nervous pressure. In the studio they may have their roots in excessive critical awareness. The ability to convince the public in the concert hall is quite independent of absolute perfection. The studio is ruled by the aesthetics of compulsive cleanliness.

There are several points to notice here. Though Brendel titles his piece 'A Case for Live Recordings', it seems to me that he is arguing as much for studio recordings as for recordings of live performances, because he clearly acknowledges that the former have some advantages over the latter. Studio recordings permit an intimacy that is not available in the concert hall, they allow for reflection and correction, they avoid some of the distractions that attend live performances, and they can aspire to a kind of perfection that is likely

---

[21] Brendel (1990) argues that, in the 1930s, classical musicians played in the studio as if they were at a live concert, whereas now they are liable to mimic the kind of playing that belongs in the studio when they play live. Others have observed that there is more variability and personality in the playing found on the earliest recordings (Taruskin 1988; Chanan 1995).

to elude the live performer. At best, Brendel establishes that *more* 'live' record-ings should be issued; he does not show that all studio recordings are worth-less. Secondly, he implies that each context creates the possibility of errors that are distinctive to it. The musician who records in the studio need not fear wrong notes or other technical solecisms because they can be avoided in subsequent takes, but new risks replace the old ones: the performance might lack spontaneity and freshness, and the possibility of repeated takes promotes a fastidious obsession with detail that may be at the expense of a wider interpretative vision. The third and most important point is that different interpretative approaches are called for. Live performances are at their most convincing when they convey the sweep of the music, which depends on their freshness, a degree of exaggeration, nervous pressure, and the rapport established with the audience. By contrast, studio performances are at their best when they present a perfect mosaic that lends itself to multiple hearings.

For Brendel, an important factor is that listeners are present when live recordings are made. There is an interaction between the performer and the public that generates an aura of physical presence and results in heightened intensity. The point is often emphasized:

Naturally 'live' or recorded relays of public concerts or operas convey the realistic atmosphere of the event, which includes a sense of tension and audience participa-tion that often manifests itself both in technical imperfections (usually edited out of commercial recordings) and in a more vital performance. Indeed many artists are at their best only in the presence of an audience, and the public concerts given by most broadcasting orchestras are arranged partly in view of the recognized value of having the players communicate directly with their audiences.   (Goslich *et al.* 1980: 320)

In addition, there are many gestures that the live performer may exag-gerate or make very plain, such as lifting the hands off the keyboard languidly, with the purpose of drawing the audience's attention to expressive and other qualities of the music.

When I compared a live performance with a radio broadcast of that performance, I did not mention the fact that, at home, Ham cannot partici-pate in the event as Cecilia does. That was because I assumed the ambience of the performance would be conveyed to him through the broadcast. This could be doubted. It might be argued, for instance, that an aspect of the enjoyment afforded by musical performance is the sense of community engendered among the participants, including the audience (Higgins 1991). There is also a certain frisson in being close to a famous, charismatic musician. These aspects of the experience are available to Cecilia, but not to Ham. Some of them involve a general pleasure in the sociality of musical concerts, but others are directed more specifically to the enjoyment of the work and its performance. These last cannot be dismissed as irrelevant to the musical experience (cf. Gracyk 1997), but it could be argued that they are less central to an appreciation of the work and its performance than is a concern with features of form, style, and expressiveness. In any event, it cannot be the pleasure of relating directly to fellow listeners that Brendel has in mind when he stresses the importance to the performance of the live context, because he believes that *recordings* of live performances can capture the relevant features.

Brendel's claim (1990: 204), that the presence of the audience increases the player's vision, courage, and absorption, receives this reply from Gracyk (1997: 148): 'At best, this is a hit or miss result. Besides, this is to argue that the mediation of recording makes the world of the performer, not the world of the listener, aesthetically poorer. [Not all] musicians may have trouble performing at their best under studio conditions.' It seems to me that, here, Gracyk misses Brendel's main point, which is neither that the audience inspires the performer nor that, together, they share a sense of community. Brendel argues that the live context invites an approach to musical interpretation unlike that appropriate to the studio. With an audience present, the performer should project the work on a public scale, whereas in the studio he should think of himself as soliloquizing, or as communicating on a more intimate level. It is not (or not solely) that the musician before an audience is likely to play the same way as in the studio, but better. Rather, it is that the two contexts call for different approaches to the music's interpretation. They offer contrasting opportunities and challenges to the performer, which, in turn, give rise to distinctive virtues (and vices) in the interpretations that are suitable.

Brendel prefers live recordings for their spontaneity, finding studio recordings sterile by comparison, despite the higher technical polish they usually achieve. A different view is favoured by Glenn Gould, who abandoned the concert platform for the studio (Goehr 1996). His goal was to avoid the circus element of live performances, what Eisenberg (1988) calls 'the lions-and-Christians atmosphere of the concert hall'. He aimed to remove that aspect of appreciation depending on the audience's admiration of the mastery needed if the musician is to avoid disaster gracefully and with dexterity. With risk eliminated through electronic purification, more room would be left for a proper admiration of the music itself and of its interpretation.

What are the roles of risk and spontaneity in live musical performance? The major danger, of course, is that of fluffing the notes or losing one's place in the ensemble. Musicians practise long and hard to reduce the likelihood of such things occurring. In striving for spontaneity, it is not usual that they set out to surprise each other. Rather, they work together to make possible a harmonious and mutual interaction that arises from the immediacy and urgency of the performance situation. Those who have attended or played in a series of orchestral rehearsals leading to a performance will be aware that there can be an unexpected electricity in the final outcome that lifts it onto a new level, even where the rehearsals were competent and efficient. Although musicians do what they can to sidestep the pitfalls and the insecurity that come with the unexpected, risk cannot be eliminated from live performance, and, though audiences do not relish seeing performances come to grief, they must be aware of the challenges faced by the player in appreciating both the work and its rendition. There is no inconsistency in recognizing that professional musicians eschew avoidable risks while appreciating their success in negotiating those that are integral to the conditions of live performance.

The more the performance calls for creative input from the performer— for instance, because the music is largely improvised—the more we rightly value the contributions made by risk and spontaneity to the qualities of the performance. Jazz musicians do not create music from thin air when they improvise. They draw their material from formulas and phrases that have been practised often, so that they lie easily under the hands. Some of these will be common stock within the style, others will be distinctive to the individual. According to Lee B. Brown (2000), jazz musicians are expected to confront risk, rather than minimize it, because they are expected to go beyond their own repertoire when the opportunity to do so presents itself. To improvise successfully is to bring all this together with the specified theme (or chord sequence, or whatever) in a manner that generates a satisfactory whole. Music making *simpliciter* achieves this synthesis at the time of performance. Where the music depends for its authentic delivery on the exigencies of live performance, the evaluation of risk and spontaneity must be relevant in assessing its performance.

The same applies when we move from improvisations to the performances of works. Much music is concerned with instrumental techniques, either because it aims to highlight them directly, as in the virtuoso concerto (Mark 1980), or because it pursues effects that depend on their use. In many cases, awareness of the demands placed on the performer is not readily separable from an appreciation of the performer's interpretation. 'Abolishing the risk taking in performances is to abolish an essential part of the traditional conception of performances' (Carrier 1983: 211).

Now, a performance recorded in a studio could *involve* the kinds of risk and spontaneity present in a successful live performance, but it cannot *display* these as a live performance can. Unless we are naive listeners, we will assume that editing is involved in the recording. This conditions our experience of what we hear. Something is lost, then, to the listener with an awareness of the technical possibilities offered by the recording technology, for she will not hear in the recorded performance the same risk taking and spontaneity that might enliven her experience of a live performance.[22] Moreover, even if the playing is the same, she will not readily hear identical interpretations in the two settings. A performance that would be studied, introverted, and precise in the live context might be more dynamic, outgoing, and relaxed on record, because the auditor would hear in it the rejection of possibilities provided by the technology that were not available to the live player.

This is not to say, though, that the studio recording is merely an impoverished version of a live concert, for the technology provides its own opportunities and difficulties, thereby replacing one kind of risk with another. As noted previously, Brendel observes that the studio recording, if it is to be convincing, must present a technically perfect interpretation that can survive repeated hearings and close scrutiny. Poor interpretations and technical imperfections, when recorded, live on to embarrass the musician (Gracyk 1997). They should have been remedied by further takes and better editing. The fact that a recording of a forty-minute piece takes a week to make does not show that the musician is 'cheating'. It does mean, though, that we listen for a level of technical polish and of interpretational unity and conviction that we would not require in the live context. We expect musical compensation for what is lost in the move from the concert platform to the studio, so further and different demands are made on the performer.

The purpose of the previous discussion is not to argue that studio recordings are not performances, and neither is it to claim that studio recordings present falsely works that were originally designed for live performance. My aim is to show that, as performances, they are different, and that the relevant distinctions depend as much on opportunities facilitated by the technology as on what is actually done. As fish, live and studio performances belong in different kettles. It is possible to appreciate properly neither their strengths nor their weaknesses unless they are considered in terms of their respective types. Each is legitimate in its own way. The person who listens exclusively to studio recordings, or solely to (recordings of) live performances, is limiting herself unnecessarily to only one kind of delight. Provided she is aware of the way the possibilities and demands of the studio differ from those of live performance, so that she does not mistake studio recordings for documentary traces of live performances, the auditor can find much that is enjoyable and different in studio recordings. Brendel is not wrong to maintain that the listener's record collection is the worse if it does

---

[22] If the use of the technology is minimal, it is common to draw attention to this in the liner notes. 'For the studio recordings, long takes were the norm (complete movements often performed without a break) and corrections made with the minimum of patching' (Peter Czornyj's notes on John Eliot Gardiner's edition of Beethoven's symphonies on period instruments, Archiv Produktion 439 900-2 (1994)). This information is relevant to how the recording may be experienced, but it does not remove the barrier between live and studio recordings. However long the takes are, we know that they always could have been redone.

not contain discs of live performances. But, as I read him, he means to redress an imbalance, not to suggest that recordings originating in the studio are without interest or value.

Deeper into the studio

The studio technology introduced so far is minimal. Studio recordings of classical music acknowledge the 'live' paradigm they approximate. I have assumed that musicians, occupying a contiguous space, play the vast majority of the notes that find their way onto the recording, even if the final result depends on an editor's decisions. They use the specified instruments; the notes are executed mostly in the order indicated by the composer; the orchestra advertised on the label is one comprised of musicians who do (or could) adequately perform the same pieces live, in real time. If Molto Fandango is presented by a record company as performing Beethoven's pianoforte sonatas, we can reasonably assume that Maestro Fandango executed most of the notes as we hear them, though he might make many takes over several days, not that he played the pieces at half the tempo and an octave lower than Beethoven indicated, with the sound engineer doubling the speed of the tape to make the record. Moreover, I have assumed that the producer is dedicated to achieving an overall sound that comes as close as it can to the ideal conditions of live performance.

In the early days of phonography, the deficiencies of the technology prompted departures from the usual performance norms. For instance, the number of instrumentalists on a part was increased if its line would otherwise sound weak on the recording. It was quickly realized that the balance of sound could be controlled by the technology, with the result that new and distinctive soundscapes, ones that could not be achieved in the live setting, might be created. For instance, Sergei Prokofiev used the microphone to achieve new effects in creating the music for the film *Alexander Nevsky* (1938). He says:

Since the sound of Teutonic trumpets and horns was no doubt unpleasant to the Russian ear, in order not to miss the dramatic effect, I have insisted that these fanfares be played directly into the microphone. Also, in our orchestras we have very powerful instruments, such as a trombone, and in comparison the more feeble sound of a bassoon. If we place the bassoon right near the microphone and the trombone some twenty metres away from it, then we will have a powerful bassoon and in the background a barely audible trombone. This practice can offer a completely 'upside-down' means of orchestration, which would have been impossible in compositions for symphonic orchestras.   (quoted in Eisenberg 1988: 94)[23]

---

[23] For a discussion of the special requirements and techniques of music written specifically for film, see Burt (1994).

Moreover, similar methods have sometimes been adopted in recording music from the standard repertoire. Gunter Schuller recalls Leopold Stokowski's treatment of Aram Khatchaturian's Symphony No. 2 (1943):

[Stokowski] sat down at the board with all those knobs and dials, and started doing the most *incredible* things in terms of balances. He was practically recomposing Khatchaturian's piece. Mind you, the orchestra had played it as written with all the correct dynamics . . . But when we got into the mixing studio—my Lord—flutes became twice as loud as brass sections; he was bringing out the viola's inner parts *over* the melody in the violins and other strange distortions . . . He made the music bigger than life-size.   (quoted in Eisenberg 1988: 125–6)

As these examples indicate, the use of the microphones can be significant. Crooning, as a style of singing, was made possible by the microphone, because it allowed vocalists performing publicly to sing softly (Frith 1986; but see Chanan 1995: 70). Also, the placement of the microphone can be crucial. For instance, close miking can 'enhance' (emphasize) stereo separation. It can be used to dissociate the soloist's part from the orchestra, promoting its individuality and its opposition to the ensemble, thereby reducing the impression of dialogue and cooperation between the two. Other effects are generated by the management of stereo spacing, especially if the orchestra's disposition is unusual or if the settings are altered for different passages of the music. The way the input from many microphones is mixed can dramatically affect the final sound.

Multi-tracking makes it possible to record parts of a work at different times and places. Igor Stravinsky's *Oedipus Rex* (1927) was taped in October 1951 in Cologne, but Jean Cocteau's narration was dubbed from a Paris performance of eight months later (Eisenberg 1988: 93). Also, overdubbing allows a single musician to take on different roles within a given piece. Wynton Marsalis plays all the solo parts in Vivaldi's *Concerto for Two Trumpets* and in Heinrich Biber's *Sonata in A for Eight Trumpets and Orchestra* (Sony No. 42478, 1988), and Peter Damm does the same in Robert Schumann's *Konzerstücke for Four Horns and Orchestra* (Berlin Classics No. 9324, 1998).

The latest digital technology permits yet more radical innovations. Gérard Corbiau's 1994 movie about the life of Carlo Broschi, *Farinelli: Il castrato*, uses a soundtrack that edits together the voices of countertenor Derek Lee Ragin and soprano Ewa Mallas Godlewska and digitally enhances the result to recreate (an impression of) the voice that enchanted eighteenth-century Europe. What can be done for a film soundtrack obviously can be also done for a recording. Soon, no doubt, it will be possible to purchase a recording of Geminiano Giacomelli's *Merope* (Venice, 1734) performed by a virtual castrato.

Earlier I recognized as one ontological type works that are intended for studio performance. Pieces of this kind rely on the paraphernalia of the

studio for their realization. When recordings of works created for live performance employ technology to achieve results that cannot be produced
under the conventional conditions of public presentation in real time, they
treat those works as if they are for studio performance. In the case of jazz,
where we expect to hear a spontaneous musical conversation between
the musicians, the intrusion of studio techniques—of multi-tracking and
patching, for instance—can seriously undermine the listener's experience.
As for classical pieces created for live performance, the result depends both
on the prominence of the electronic manipulation and on how this relates
to traditional performance values. Wynton Marsalis's multi-track renditions
of classical concertos display many of the virtues we associate with the
instrumental tradition. On the other hand, if the sound is synthesized or
drastically modified by filters, the work, as well as the performance, is transformed.[24] I do not deny that these can be of interest, but I think that we
are likely to regard them as work transcriptions rather than as performances
of the original.

In defending recordings, Gracyk (1997, 1999; see also Niblock 1999) argues
that they allow for a new kind of virtuosity, that of sculpting sound for effect,
not for fidelity to live performance. I have just indicated that, for works
intended for live performance and for recordings that are presented and
advertised as of those works, the relevant technical skills are best directed
towards fidelity, which is not to say that the goal is to trick the listener into
mistaking the recorded for a live performance. It is clear that Gracyk has a
different case in mind, however, since all his examples are of popular music.
These pieces are conceived for studio performance or as electronic compositions. As the Beatles' record producer, George Martin, so aptly puts it, he
and the group were creating 'little movies in sound, not stage plays' (1994:
139). Within the domain of popular music, the composers, producers, and
performers are free to use all the resources of the studio.

Electronic technology has led to the development of new instruments (such
as the Ondes Martenot and the Theremin) and to significant modifications
in older types (such as the guitar, organ, piano, and violin). Amplified instruments often call for different playing techniques and can generate distinctive
effects (for instance, of flutter and feedback). Meanwhile, the development
of electromagnetic tape, multichannel mixers, filters, and transistors allowed
sonic events to be stored, modified, and edited (Manning 1993). Ring
modulators, tone generators, computers, and the like permitted all manner
of sounds to be synthesized. Other developments (such as cylinders, tapes,
and discs, along with playback devices) allowed for (more or less) faithful
reproduction of masters, and hence for the wide dissemination of recordings.

[24] Consider, for example, Vanessa-Mae's version of Bach's *Toccata and Fugue in D Minor* on
the electric violin—(EMI 5 55089 2, 1995).

Naturally enough, musicians and composers have set themselves to control and explore the new world of sound all this made possible.[25] Many kinds of recorded music are conceived in terms of studio technology and could not exist without it. It goes without saying that the listener's appreciation of such music should be in terms of the situation for which it is created (Gracyk 1996; Fisher 1998), rather than by reference to live performance.

In a prior section, I argued that the experience of an informed listener is likely to differ in artistically significant respects as between a live performance and a recording of a live performance. The relative permanence of a recording, as a result of which it can be played several times, affects how we should judge the sounds it encodes. In the present section, I have indicated that a further difference, one of considerable magnitude, separates the recording of a live performance from one made under studio conditions. Studio recordings trade immediacy and spontaneity for accuracy, consistency, and finish. This is a proper response to the medium, since successful studio recordings display properties that distinguish them from successful live performance in virtue of their relative permanence and the intimate circumstances of their creation. Live and studio performances can be compared in many respects, but they should not be equated or regarded as intersubstitutable. They promote different values, ones depending on the contrasting contexts where they are made, and they should be approached with this in mind. In producing a studio recording of a piece conceived for live performance, the methods adopted usually acknowledge many aspects of the intended mode of presentation, but this does not eliminate the distinction between the recording's *modus vivendi* and that of the paradigm. Other pieces, ones made in and for the studio, should be heard and judged in terms of other recordings, not live performances.

Recordings, performances, and authenticity

In the Introduction to Part Two, I indicated that I would discuss the authenticity of recordings. Much of what I have written so far has been on that topic, albeit indirectly. Here are some more explicit reflections on the subject.

A recording of a purely electronic work is authentic either if it is a master or if it is cloned from a master encoding the given piece, with industry conventions and rulings determining when a master is authorized and the

---

[25] Also, composers writing works for live performance are not indifferent to the recording industry. Stravinsky's *Serenade in A* (1925) is in four movements, each long enough (about three minutes) to occupy one side of a (78) disc. 'In America I had arranged with a gramophone firm to make records of some of my music. This suggested the idea that I should compose something whose length should be determined by the capacity of the record. I should in that way avoid all the trouble of cutting and adapting. And that is how my *Sérénade en A pour Piano* came to be written' (Stravinsky 1962: 123–4). Bartók's *Contrasts* (1938) for piano, violin, and clarinet was commissioned by Benny Goodman to fit on two 78s.

level of accuracy needed in a clone. Such a work is authentically sounded when a master or clone is decoded and transmitted by an appropriate device. Again, it is industry conventions and rulings that determine when decoding and transmission are sufficiently accurate to generate an instance of the work, and, within instances, the scale from high to low in the quality of realizations.

A recording of a performance of a work for studio performance is authentic either if it is a master or if it is cloned from a master encoding the given (virtual) performance, with industry conventions and rulings determining when a master is authorized and the level of accuracy needed in a clone. Such a performance is authentically sounded when a master or clone is decoded and transmitted by an appropriate device. Industry conventions and rulings settle when decoding and transmission are sufficiently accurate to generate an instance of the performance, and, within instances, the scale from high to low in the quality of realizations.

A recording of a work for studio performance is a fully authentic work instance provided the virtual performance it presents follows and satisfies all the relevant work-determinative instructions. Works for studio performance can be ontologically quite thin, with the result that very different sounding recordings could all encode ideally faithful performances of the piece. But, however thin they are, it is a work-constitutive convention or practice that faithful performances of such works are generated at least in part by electronic manipulations. This is what is meant by the insistence that works for studio performance are instanced in performances that are virtual.

A recording of a performance of a piece for live performance is authentic either if it is a master or if it is cloned from a master encoding the given (actual or simulated) performance, with industry conventions and rulings determining when a master is authorized and the level of accuracy needed in a clone. Such a performance is authentically sounded when a master or clone is decoded and transmitted by an appropriate device. Industry conventions and rulings settle when decoding and transmission are sufficiently accurate to generate an instance of the performance, and, within instances, the scale from high to low in the quality of realizations.

Where the recording encodes an actual, live performance, the *performance* is a fully authentic work instance provided it follows and satisfies all the relevant work-determinative instructions. What is on the *recording* then is perhaps best regarded not as a work instance, but as a representation of a work instance—that is, a representation of the performance.

Most recordings of works intended for live performances encode what I have called simulated performances, not actual ones. Is the simulated performance a fully authentic instance of its topic work? In one way, it is not. There is no actual, real-time, continuous playing event corresponding to what is instructed as work determinative. In another way, it is. As it is presented phenomenally to the listener, the performance on the recording faithfully follows and satisfies all the relevant work-determinative instructions. As just indicated, the hint of paradox can be removed by regarding what is on the recording as a representation of a work instance—that is, it is the representation of a performance.

In other words, there is an ambiguity in asking about the authenticity of a recording. One question concerns the process by which information gets onto the record. In this sense, a recording is authentic if it is cloned in the appropriate fashion, and it produces an authentic sounding of what is on it provided that the process of decoding and transmission meets the required standard. On the other hand, the question can concern the faithfulness with which the performance represented on the recording instances the work it is of. And that question can be asked of the recorded performance not only when it had an independent existence as a live performance event but also when it is the simulation of such an event (or is a virtual replacement for such an event).

As I have noted previously, we do talk of recordings as encoding performances of works for live performance, even where they are made in the studio and do not pretend to be of continuous, real-time playing. That is very fortunate for both symphony orchestras and proponents of the authentic performance movement. Here I have suggested that such talk relies on our willingness to treat the representations of performances found on recordings as acceptable substitutes for live performances. This willingness could arise mistakenly and naively from the belief that the electronic medium is fully transparent and that what happens in the studio mimics what would otherwise occur on stage. More likely, though, it comes from our entering deliberately into a kind of collusion with the record maker, so that we entertain the actuality of the performance simulated on the recording. And this imaginative engagement is harmless and appropriate provided that the musicians on the recording are capable of playing the relevant pieces live, and that real-time playings of recognizable musical chunks take place in the studio, even if the final release is an edited composite of the best of these.

Unless our relation to recordings is understood, it can seem odd to claim for recordings that they are of authentic performances, when they are not of live performances at all. When we are careful to distinguish the objects of these judgements, and the categories under which they fall, the strangeness is resolved. We judge recordings sometimes for the integrity of their manufacturing process and at others for the accuracy with which what is on them stands to a given work specification, and we imaginatively consider 'what is on them' to be simulated (or virtual) performances, though we know events other than those whose existence is entertained were causally responsible for the detail of much that is heard.

Opera on film

Earlier I dismissed the necessity of Ham's seeing a live performance (or seeing a telecast of the concert) as he listens to an instrumental piece on the grounds that he could individuate the instruments and their contributions without the evidence of his eyes concerning such matters. Even if it is crucial to know what the instruments are and how they are played, the relevant knowledge is sufficient for his perceiving all that is constitutive of the work's performance, whether or not he witnesses that performance. That conclusion should not be generalized beyond instrumental music, however. Opera and ballet are art-forms in which the music is but one element and drama or movement are essential to their character. To experience a performance of such a work, one must see it enacted. What is seen is essential to the performance's identity, not solely a means to information that might be acquired independently of viewing the particular performance at issue.[26] For this reason, the equivalent of a radio broadcast of a live performance of instrumental music is, for opera or ballet, a television broadcast, and the equivalent of a recording of a live performance is a video or film of such a performance.[27]

This conclusion might seem unduly strong when it is recalled that operas are sometimes given concert renditions and that listeners are familiar with instrumental performances of many ballets that are hardly ever staged, such as Beethoven's *Creatures of Prometheus*, Op. 43, or Stravinsky's *Renard* (1915). Instrumental suites derived from longer ballets, such as Prokofiev's and Tchaikovsky's, are widely performed and recorded, as are ones from opera, such as Georges Bizet's from *Carmen* or Benjamin Britten's *Four Sea Interludes from Peter Grimes* (1945). I do not deny that these derive from the works in question, but I do maintain that they are deficient as representations of the operas or ballets as such. Suites are like work transcriptions in that they have an identity independent of their models. One can learn much about how the music of an opera or ballet sounds from a suite taken from it, but one does not thereby achieve the fullest acquaintance with the work

---

[26] If I were to hear on the radio a broadcast of a live performance of Marius Petipa's choreography of Tchaikovsky's *Swan Lake*, I would have a fair idea of what I would see as I listen to the dance of the cygnets in Act II, having attended the ballet in that choreography on other occasions. The four ballerinas in white tutus would be in line, facing the audience, with arms crossed and joined, their heads turning from side to side as they danced on points in unison. But in this case, knowing what I would see is not the same as seeing it. I have not experienced the work in its entirety if I listen to the radio while recalling how other productions appeared.

[27] Of course, many operas and ballets have been written specifically for TV, including Carlo Menotti's *Amahl and the Night Visitors* (1951) and Stravinsky's *The Flood* (1962). (For a list, see Goslich *et al.* 1980: 322.) In the discussion here, I concentrate on works created for live performance. Most of these are written for stage presentation, but others are for performance outdoors, as was the practice with the seventeenth-century masque. Verdi's *Aïda* is performed regularly in the Roman amphitheatre of Verona. For a video of a performance in Verona, see that produced by Giancarlo Sbragia.

in question, because it involves more than music. The same goes for concert performances of opera, which leave out the dramatic element that distinguishes this genre from oratorio. Such performances are worthwhile, especially where there is not ready access to staged versions, but it would involve error to regard them as complete.

Many people collect recordings of opera on disc. These are sometimes of live performances but are more often made in studios, though they might contain sound effects that simulate crucial bits of stage action. For opera, studio recordings have several advantages over recordings of live performances. Some of these are of the kind outlined earlier: ambient noise is reduced, multiple takes allow the editor to eliminate mistakes, and a better sound quality is likely to be achieved by the use of supplementary microphones and more sophisticated mixing techniques. Additional benefits are likely to result from the fact that the vocalists are better able to concentrate on their singing, being freed from the need to act, to move, to wear uncomfortable costumes, and the like. Moreover, factors that might debar a great singer from performing a particular role on stage—such as her age, race, physique, or her inadequacy as an actor—can here be disregarded. There is no denying the quality and value of such recordings. The collector makes no mistake in prizing them. At the same time, though, he is unlikely to be fooled into believing that he has all in which the works in question consist. He will recognize that a studio recording should not be compared strictly to a live performance (for reasons given earlier for instrumental music) and that the opera recording removes itself yet further from the ideal of live performance in shedding its connection to the staged enactment of the drama.

The medium that should be preferred for works for which stage action is integral is television, video, or film. Previously, in discussing telecasts of live performances of instrumental music, I noted some of the ways the visual medium follows its own agenda, thereby producing a result unlike the one witnessed by a member of the audience. The same applies in the case of television presentations of live performances of ballet and opera. The performance that is filmed constantly from a single viewpoint (using only different magnifications, much as a member of the audience might resort to opera glasses) is very much the exception. Typically, many cameras in different locations are used, though, usually, these remain outside the proscenium arch.

Opera films that appear to be of genuinely live, public performances are comparatively rare.[28] Inevitably, these include coughs, applause after numbers, performance errors, and awkward passages or actions. An intrusive camera may reveal trickles of sweat, flying spittle, and straining muscles that would not be seen by the house audience. Moreover, it is difficult to place the

---

[28] See Weber's *Der Freischütz* (Stuttgart) and Mussorgsky's *Boris Godunov* (Bolshoi).

microphones for the best result and only a limited number of camera positions can be employed. Not surprisingly, then, many films that present themselves as of stage performances are made in empty theatres. Multiple takes
permit the use of a wider range of camera techniques. In many cases, the illusion of live performance is maintained—applause is heard and shots of an
audience may be interpolated.[29] Usually, the vocal parts are mimed.[30] (More
accurately, as they are filmed the artists sing along with a recording they
have made previously, but it is only the recording that finds its way to the
soundtrack.) The separation of musical and dramatic elements has the advantage of allowing the recording to be done under studio conditions, permitting the singers to concentrate on their vocalizing and on the conductor,
but it does create difficulties of its own.[31] Other films abandon the pretence
of live performance, though they confine the action to the theatre stage[32] and
a few are made in the studio, though they follow the conventions of the
theatre setting.[33]

Where films capture productions made for the stage, there is, then, a continuum of approaches: from that in which a live, continuous performance is
filmed and recorded as it happens; through ones in which the performance is
interrupted for the sake of the camera on some occasions, though the singing
is recorded at the time of filming (and overdubbing may be applied to the
soundtrack later); through ones in which the recording of the soundtrack and
the filming are separate and each is discontinuous, but with the illusion of
stage performance (and sometimes also of public presentation) maintained
in the editing. Most commercial videos fall nearer the 'managed' than the
'live' end of the spectrum, though the professionalism of their production
often makes it seem otherwise.

As is perhaps apparent from the variety of strategies adopted by film-
makers, the marriage of stage conventions and cinematographic techniques
is not always a comfortable one. Because of the intimacy of the camera's
engagement with performers, the styles of acting and make-up appropriate

---

[29] See Wagner's *Tannhäuser* (Bayreuth) and Verdi's *Sicilian Vespers* (Bologna). Strauss's *Der
Rosenkavalier* (Salzburg) is characterized as 'an actual performance of the Salzburg festival',
though the singers mime their parts.

[30] See Monteverdi's *L'Incoronazione di Poppea* (Zurich), the Drottningholm (Copenhagen)
productions of Mozart's operas, Rossini's *La Cenerentola* (Milan), Bizet's *Carmen* (New York),
Strauss's *Der Rosenkavalier* (Munich), and Strauss's *Salome* (Vienna).

[31] 'This obviates the technical difficulties of microphone placing but can cause new problems
in relating the acoustic of the recording to the perspective in which the singer is seen on screen.
Furthermore, miming results in the loss of tension inherent in live singing, aggravating the sense
of artificiality resulting from the fact that in most studio opera productions the orchestra is
placed in a separate studio from that in which the action is taking place . . .' (Goslich *et al.* 1980:
323).

[32] For examples of Wagner's operas, see Boulez's films of *The Ring*, Stern's *Mastersingers*, and
Nelsson's *Lohengrin*, all from Bayreuth.

[33] See Mackeras's version of Handel's *Julius Caesar*.

for film are more restrained than those for the stage, where expansive gestures and exaggerated expressions are needed to project character to a distant audience. Stage lighting is also often more intense than is required for movies and this too affects the kind of make-up and costume colourations that are required.

A rather special difficulty for films that retain their allegiance to the stage setting is provided by the overture, because the curtain remains down and the orchestra is difficult to observe. Cinematographers deal with this in various ways. The more conservative approach gets all the credits done before the start of the overture, the playing of which, with views of the conductor and orchestra, is shown uninterrupted.[34] An alternative begins with the conductor and the orchestra before quickly moving on to the credits presented against the backdrop of the stage curtain,[35] or to stills of the cast,[36] or to shots of the theatre.[37] In other cases, the orchestra is ignored and the credits plus stills of the stars,[38] or credits plus graphics,[39] or graphics alone[40] are displayed during the overture. A more adventurous approach is that adopted in Sweden's Drottningholm Court Theatre production of Mozart's *Così Fan Tutte*, K. 588. As the overture plays, the stars are shown travelling to the venue, changing into costume, and making their way to the stage. At the end of the final sextet, the leading singers are again presented in civilian dress. These filmic segments frame the opera's stage performance and acknowledge a connection with its plot, which concerns the nature of love and fidelity: at the start, the sopranos approvingly view a loving couple and, at the close, the tenor and baritone look suspiciously at couples at a feast before walking away from the sopranos.

One interesting response to the challenges posed to the cinematographer by the theatrical nature of opera is that taken by Ingmar Bergman in his account of Mozart's *The Magic Flute*, K. 620. Rather than suppressing the

---

[34] See Bizet's *Carmen* (New York), Mozart's *Abduction from the Seraglio* (Drottningholm) and *The Marriage of Figaro* (Drottningholm), Mussorgsky's *Boris Godunov* (Moscow), Strauss's *Der Rosenkavalier* (Munich) and *Der Rosenkavalier* (Salzburg), Tchaikovsky's *Eugene Onegin* (Chicago) and *Queen of Spades* (Moscow), Verdi's *Nabucco* (Milan), and Wagner's *The Ring* (New York). In some cases—Berg's *Wozzeck* (Vienna), Britten's *Peter Grimes* (London), Monteverdi's *L'Incoronazione di Poppea* (Zurich), Strauss's *Salome* (Vienna), and Verdi's *Don Carlo* (London)—this approach is more or less required because of the overture's brevity.

[35] See the Bolshoi's versions of Tchaikovsky's *Swan Lake*, *Sleeping Beauty*, and *Nutcracker*.

[36] See the Drottningholm version of Mozart's *Don Giovanni*, Glyndebourne productions of Mozart's *Idomeneo* and *The Marriage of Figaro*, the Australian versions of Mozart's *Don Giovanni*, *Così Fan Tutte*, and Bizet's *Carmen*, and Peter Hall's of Beethoven's *Fidelio*.

[37] See Rossini's *La Cenerentola* (Milan), Verdi's *Sicilian Vespers* (Bologna), and Pierre Boulez's version of Wagner's *The Ring* (Bayreuth).

[38] See Britten's *Gloriana* (London).

[39] See Handel's *Julius Caesar* (London).

[40] See Wagner's *Rheingold* (New York) and the Bayreuth productions of Wagner's *Tannhäuser*, *The Mastersingers*, and *Lohengrin*.

tension between the conventions of film and theatre, he makes a play of their relation. Most of the props (such as the dragon at the opening, the wild animals charmed by the magic flute, the flying balloon that carries the three genii) are plainly of the theatrical type. (In a purely cinematic version, all of these could be handled much more 'realistically'.) Moreover, the effect of a performance is invoked by shots of the 'audience' during the overture. A child in the audience is later shown reacting to the stage action. Yet, on the other hand, distinctively cinematic effects are featured. The image of Pamina revealed in the locket given to Tamino is 'live'; she moves, smiles, looks towards him, and, later, the lurking figure of Monostatos is seen behind her. When the three ladies interrupt the initiation of Tamino and Papageno, they are shown moment by moment at different stage locations in what is plainly an edited sequence. Moreover, the camera sometimes follows the performers backstage. Papageno is seen rushing to make his first stage entrance, and, between the acts, the artists are shown relaxing. By peering behind the scenes and out at the audience, Bergman makes explicit the special privilege of the camera. He makes obvious that the film is not of a continuous performance in real time, but is, instead, a staged film of a performance. As a result, the conventions of the theatre are made part of the film's content; they are represented, not merely used. (For further discussion, see Tambling 1987.)

The more common alternative has the cinematographer abandoning any pretence of filming a stage in favour of turning the opera into an ordinary movie.[41] The full panoply of cinematic effects can be applied, and the action and setting are freed of the many restrictions resident to a stage location. Meanwhile, the soundtrack can be laid down under the best studio conditions. Inevitably, the work is recorded independently of the filming, the satisfactory combination of the two being virtually impossible in practice.[42] Appropriate locations can be employed,[43] along with impressive outdoor settings,[44] and sumptuous interior sets.[45] Characters can be seen on horseback, or riding in gondolas, carriages, and trains. Sets can achieve a realism

---

[41] Classical ballet does not lend itself to filmic treatment so readily as opera. This might be because many ballets are abstract, and those with stories are more concerned with spectacle than drama. In addition, dancers need a suitable substrate, so the shift from the stage to outdoor settings can be difficult to manage.

[42] This can allow for special effects. For instance, in Losey's film of *Don Giovanni*, the avenging Commendatore's statue sings with a sepulchral echo whereas the other characters do not.

[43] Puccini's *Tosca* can really be staged in Basilica Sant'Andrea della Valle, Palazzo Farnese, and Castel Sant'Angelo, as in the TV production directed by Giuseppe Patroni Griffi.

[44] As in Losey's film of *Don Giovanni* and Weigl's film of Britten's *The Turn of the Screw*.

[45] As in Zeffirelli's film of Verdi's *La Traviata*, and Weigl's film of *Eugene Onegin*. In Szinetár's production for television of Bartók's *Duke Bluebeard's Castle*, the full effects of studio design and lighting are brought into play as Judith reveals the different, fantastic worlds behind each of the locked doors in the castle.

impossible on the stage, and the camera can track the performers from room to room. Action shown during the overture can be integrated seamlessly into the work.[46] The natural disasters and sword fights with which operas are peppered can be presented in graphic detail.[47] The various disguises and misidentifications on which the plots of so many operas hinge can often be made more plausible. Or, if he prefers surrealism to realism, the director can exploit the medium's potential in that direction.[48]

Distinctive techniques are available to the cinematographer in the presentation of action. These include slow motion,[49] the camera's adoption of a particular character's visual point of view,[50] and the 'internalization' of the music, so that the character is heard expressing her thoughts to herself rather than vocalizing them.[51] Almost every film of opera makes use of flashbacks. When characters recall their former happiness, idyllic depictions of those times are shown.[52]

The next step in transforming opera for the stage into a filmic work is predictable but uncommon—the actual singers disappear from the screen, replaced by actors. Earlier I pointed out that studio recordings of opera allow the use of singers who, for reasons apart from their vocal abilities, might be unsuited for the stage. Because the soundtracks of films are recorded in studios, with the singing simulated when the part is acted for the cameras, the singing and acting roles can be separated. This general practice, as we know, is standard in films. Even if we are shown Holly Hunter playing the piano, we realize that someone else laid down the soundtrack (just as we know that stuntmen and body doubles replace the stars in action scenes). When the movie features an orchestra of beautiful young women, you can safely bet that some bald old men were playing in the studio. It is no surprise,

---

[46] Ponnelle's *The Marriage of Figaro* begins with Figaro packing to move to his new quarters. Losey's *Don Giovanni* has the characters arriving by gondola at a glass-blowing factory on Murano, the flaming cauldrons of which later form the background to the Don's descent to hell. Zeffirelli's *La Traviata* anticipates the work's end by presenting Violetta close to death. Weigl's *The Turn of the Screw* precedes the opera with scenes showing the characters both before and after the period covered by the opera. Harder to understand is a prolonged slow-motion sequence of Pinkerton running in Ponnelle's film of Puccini's *Madama Butterfly*.

[47] Zeffirelli's film of Verdi's *Otello* features the near-wrecking of Otello's ship during the brief overture and opening scene.

[48] Syberberg's studio setting for Wagner's *Parsifal* uses back-projected images of works by Bosch, Titian, and Caspar Friedrich, and sets the opera on a rock island modelled on Wagner's death mask. The area of a character's clothing is sometimes treated as a 'screen' for the projection of film. For further discussion, see Tambling (1987).

[49] This is used, for instance, in Ponnelle's *Madama Butterfly*, as Butterfly and Suzuki scatter flowers on floors and paths.

[50] In Ponnelle's *The Marriage of Figaro*, this device occurs in Rosina's 'Porgi amor'.

[51] Ponnelle's version of *The Marriage of Figaro* employs this approach often and unconvincingly.

[52] To choose just one example, see the treatment of Alfredo's 'De' mei bollenti spiriti' in Zeffirelli's *La Traviata*.

then, that, in Franco Zeffirelli's versions of Giuseppe Verdi's *La Traviata* and *Otello*, several 'voices' are listed in the credits; these are chorus members who do not appear in the film.

Mostly, international opera stars, who are well known to the potential audiences for such films, take their places before the camera. Their status is such that it is unlikely they would agree to record the soundtrack for a movie in which they would not appear. But the substitution is common in films of musical comedy and light opera. Marni Nixon recorded the music for, among others, Natalie Wood in the film of Leonard Bernstein's *West Side Story*, Deborah Kerr in the film of Richard Rogers and Oscar Hammerstein II's *The King and I*, and Audrey Hepburn in the film of Alan Jay Lerner and Frederik Loewe's *My Fair Lady*. The practice occurs also in a few films of opera. In Weigl's version of Britten's *The Turn of the Screw*, the players and singers are quite distinct.[53] In Jürgen Syberberg's film of Richard Wagner's *Parsifal*, only two of the vocalists appear in the film. The role of Parsifal is acted by *two* non-singers—an androgynous youth and a young woman—who are often shown together.

Films of operas intended for the stage can be compared to recordings of music created for live performance. Most films are equivalent to studio performances, though they are often represented as of live performances. Despite using the resources of the studio, they respect conventions for presentation that belong to the theatre. Other films, those that follow cinematic conventions, are like studio recordings that introduce effects that depend on the use of technology. When singers are replaced on the screen by actors, the world of the stage has been left far behind. Cartoon animations of operas—I have seen one of *Carmen*—could be compared to electronically synthesized versions of Bach. In all but the last case, I think that films of operas count as performances of their works, just as I think studio recordings of music intended for live performance do. Equally, though, they should not be confused with stage renditions given in real time. Something important would be lost if opera films entirely replaced live performances, though this is not to deny that a movie is often superior to most live productions. The two media complement each other. They have their own strengths and weaknesses and are to be understood and evaluated in the light of the use they make of the technology on which they rely.

The social significance of recordings

In considering the experience afforded to the listener by recordings and video, I have concentrated on the local picture. It is time to consider the wider social implications of the dominance that recordings have achieved.

[53] The result is not entirely satisfactory, I think. Actors are not always convincing mimes and, if one cannot sing a high C, it is not easy to look as if one is doing so.

A large record collection permits the owner many advantages. She has access to a wider range of works than she could hear by attending concerts where she lives—the repertoire covers all periods, genres, and styles, as well as the music of most countries and cultures. Stravinsky writes:

Recording? When I think that a disc or magnetic tape of a piece of new music can be several thousand times as powerful (influential) as a live performance, that disc or tape becomes an awesome object indeed. At the present moment, not more than 3,000 to 5,000 records of my later music (*Movements*; *A Sermon, A Narrative, And a Prayer*; *The Flood*) can be sold in the United States, this by way of contrast with a possible 30,000–50,000 sale of the *Firebird*. These figures may ... indicate that only the tiniest fraction of the musically inclined population is curious to acquaint itself with new things ... But if I compare this tiny audience to the small group of courtiers who patronized the music of Marco da Gagliano, for example, my situation seems to me less bad. Marco's thirty courtiers and my three thousand record buyers are the same *élite* in the same relation and proportion to the whole population, and though this *élite* may grow it will never catch up ... recording of new music seems worth while when one thinks of all those young musicians in Reno, Spokane, Talahassee, New York, and other provincial cities who may hear a thousand performances of [Dvořák's] *New World Symphony* but who would never otherwise than on record hear such landmarks of contemporary music as [Arnold Schoenberg's] *Die Jakobsleiter* or [Pierre Boulez's] *Pli Selon Pli* ... (Stravinsky and Craft 1959: 110–11)

The record owner can hear performers who now are dead—Thomas Beecham, Bruno Walter, Arturo Toscanini, Enrico Caruso, Nellie Melba, Tito Gobi, Dinu Lipatti, Arthur Schnabel, Ignacy Jan Paderewski, Pablo Cassals, Fritz Kreisler, Jascha Heifitz, Charlie Parker, Billie Holiday, and Jimi Hendrix. She can listen to Pietro Mascagni, Richard Strauss, Sergei Rachmaninov, Béla Bartók, Edward Elgar, and Igor Stravinsky, conducting or playing their own compositions. She can hear works written for instruments, such as the clavichord, which, because of the quiet intimacy of their sound, are unsuited for public settings. She can compare Fritz Busch's 1935 *Così Fan Tutte* for Glyndebourne with Willy Decker's 1984 production for Drottningholm. She can contrast the youthful performances of Yehudi Menuhin or Alfred Brendel with their later efforts. Though she might live in New Zealand, she can hear the orchestras of New York, London, and Berlin, and all the greatest performers of the present era. The listener is empowered by recording technology in further ways, too. She has more control over her situation than is normal for the person who hears music played live. She can hear what she chooses when she likes in the comfort of her home (or office, or while jogging). She can play the tracks in any order she fancies, and she can switch off the player when she wants, whether or not the record is finished. If she desires, she can cocoon herself in sound for much of her waking life.[54]

With works created for live performance, too much reliance on recordings also carries some obvious dangers. Most collectors of discs accumulate works rather than performances—that is, most purchase only a single recording of any given piece. The result is that the owner becomes familiar with a single performance and interpretation. In that circumstance, even the accomplished listener may have difficulty in distinguishing the work from its interpretation and, hence, in assessing and comprehending the contributions made by the composer and the performer respectively. And, if she can do so, it is a yet rarer ability that would allow her to grasp the interpretative possibilities that the work provides to different performers. Arriving at an interpretation often requires considerable reflection and experiment, as well as sensitivity and skill. The record owner who starts from a solitary instance of the work is not well situated to recognize the potential it contains for divergent performances. As a result, she is not in a strong position to appreciate either the work or the performance of it. The listener who confines her attention to a single disc of each piece—however good the performance is—is liable to blunt her sensitivity to aspects of the work, to its demands on the performer, and to the performer's response to those challenges.

This problem is already acute where the instrumentation is of the most familiar kind, but is further exacerbated if the ensemble is not standard. (For example, Stravinsky's *Les Noces* is scored for pianos and percussion as well as singers; just which instruments are given salience, and how they are balanced against each other, dramatically affects the overall sonorities of the performance.) Moreover, even if a work is written for a solo instrument, in some cases individual examples of that instrument differ considerably. (For instance, harpsichords and organs vary in the number of manuals, octave couplings, pitch ranges, and stops they provide.) Matters become yet more complicated when we consider works that are indeterminate in aspects of their sound structure and orchestration. Pieces that assign considerable freedom to the performer—for instance, as regards melodic decoration, the filling-in of a figured bass, and improvised cadenzas, or concerning the forces and instrumental combinations—obviously allow for very different performances. Recall also that, in playing early music, the performer often must make her choices in the face of musicological uncertainty so that, however faithful she aims to be, a great deal depends on her own musical judgement. (For this reason, it is not exaggerated to claim that a person

---

[54] Early reactions to the radio were not always positive (Schafer 1977: 91–2), because it was regarded as intrusive and impersonal. Soon enough, though, it became 'the first sound wall, enclosing the individual with the familiar and excluding the enemy' (Schafer 1977: 93). Nowadays, the introspective version of this is shown in the 'walkman'; the aggressive form is apparent in the stentorian car stereo.

can have only a sketchy idea of, say, Claudio Monteverdi's *Vespers* of 1620 if she is acquainted with only one recording of it.) This point also applies more generally, even if it is at its most obvious in recordings of early music. The performer of any work necessarily rejects a huge number of legitimate options in settling on a particular rendition, and the fullest appreciation both of the work and of her treatment of it depends as much on the listener's awareness of what is excluded as of what is included. That knowledge is difficult to cultivate if access is restricted to a solitary performance. If that single performance is a recorded one, there is the further risk that it becomes self-authenticating, by habituating the listener to its idiosyncratic features through repeated playings.

Earlier, I suggested that an appreciation of music requires an awareness of the way sounds are summoned from the musical instruments for which the work is written. Though I do not go so far as Jerrold Levinson (1990*c*), I allow that the player's actions sometimes relate to the expressive character of the sounds she produces. The person whose acquaintance with music comes exclusively from recordings is unlikely to attain knowledge of such matters. She (like many of my students) may be unable to distinguish cellos from violins, harpsichords from pianos, clarinets from bassoons, and trumpets from French horns. She may be unaware that successive passages employing harmonics, pizzicato, mute, double stopping, and *col legno* bowings are all played on a violin, or may be incapable of distinguishing a phrase sounded by one flute and answered by another from a passage given by a single instrument. Here, then, is another danger created by an exclusive interest in recordings.

An obvious response can be made to the points just made. It may be said that the problems identified lie more with the listener than the technology. She will be unlikely to valorize or be confused by a recorded performance if she buys more recordings of each work, or listens to live broadcasts, or attends concerts. And she can come to appreciate the use of the instrumental medium in a similar fashion—by attending concerts, or by watching TV broadcasts, or by reading musical scores, or by learning to play a musical instrument for herself. Admittedly, such things can be expensive and time-consuming, but that is hardly the fault of the recording technology.

As a child, my fascination with music was awakened by an initial exposure to recordings, not live performances. I suspect that the same is true of a great many others who, like me, went on to cultivate the interest that might not have been kindled otherwise. Recordings introduced them to the wider musical world and, in time, they became musicians or concertgoers.

That is one true story, but there is a flip side that is no less real. Because we occupy social space, one user's empowerment can handicap others. The problem is not just that one's neighbour might like playing loudly music that one does not enjoy. More generally, the soundscape is filled with recorded music, whether or not one wants to hear it.

Moozak, the sound wall of paradise, never weeps. It is the honeyed antidote to hell on earth. Moozak starts out with the high motive of orchestrating paradise (it is often present in writings about utopias) but it always ends up as the embalming fluid of earthly boredom . . . Throughout history music has existed as figure—a desirable collection of sounds to which the listener gives special attention. Moozak reduces music to ground. It is a deliberate concession to lo-fi-ism. It multiplies sounds. It reduces a sacred art to a slobber. Moozak is music that is not to be listened to. (Schafer 1977: 96–8)

The danger is that, by habit and desensitization, what first goes for 'moozak' later applies to music. Where it is ubiquitous, all music, not solely the kind that is designed to paper the sound wall, is liable to slip below the horizon of consciousness. Manufacturers of hi-fis connive in this process, producing multi-disc players that, once set in motion, can be forgotten about for hours. The constant background provided by broadcast recordings encourages us to treat music as not requiring our attention.

Dumbing down and abstracting

As just indicated, the adaptation of music to the mass technologies that promulgate it, as well as the commercial motives of those who control those technologies, have implications that cannot be ignored in a discussion of recorded music. The making of recordings is big business. Like any other industry, it is concerned with profits and treats music and its performers as commodities. Though it is ruled by the market laws of supply and demand, it is as much concerned with creating, as responding to, the demand to which it caters. As those who write about popular music are aware (Frith 1983; Chanan 1995; Gracyk 1996), there is a complex relation, one conditioning who and what gets recorded, between image and marketability, between music making and profit. The world of classical music is not immune from such considerations. Companies face pressure to create a product that will stand out in a market crowded with duplicates and look-alikes. This might be done by offering idiosyncratic performances of standard works. More often, though, the desired result is achieved by promoting the cult of the performer,[55] or by

---

[55] For instance, witness the terms used by EMI in advocating Nigel Kennedy and, more recently, Vanessa-Mae. For a different example, consider the response to the world tour of the Australian pianist David Helfgott, who played to rapturous audiences and critical damnation. Whereas professional music critics considered his performances in terms of the usual norms, the audience seemed to regard the concerts as part of an ongoing, multimedia biography. Apparently, they reacted as much to the man and his history (or, at least, to the portrayal of these in the movie *Shine*) as to the works or the manner of their performance. Many of these audience members were encountering the music played for the first time, of course. For discussion, see the symposium in *Philosophy and Literature* (1997).

packaging the music in a way that might make it accessible to, and hence desired by, a wider, or previously untargeted, public.[56] Aesthetic values are regarded as market corners and reduced to shopping opportunities.

Noël Carroll sets out to analyse the ontological character of mass art, which includes commercial movies and TV sitcoms. He concludes:

x is a mass art work if and only if 1) x is a multiple instance art work 2) produced and distributed by mass technology, 3) which art work is intentionally designed to gravitate in its structural choices (e.g., its narrative forms, symbolism, intended affect, and even its content) toward those choices that promise accessibility with minimum effort, virtually on first contact, for the largest number of relatively untutored audiences. (Carroll 1997: 190, 1998)

If he is right, it is no fault in mass art that it offers 'accessibility with minimum effort' so long as we value its purpose, which, presumably, is to provide undemanding entertainment. Carroll's account answers those who would condemn such art from an elitist standpoint. The formulaic approach and unexacting content of such works is not an unfortunate accident that should be corrected or criticized. Rather, these are essential in facilitating the function of such art, and there is nothing reprehensible about the fact that people often pursue the relaxation of diversion. Mass technologies seek a mass audience and, to attract one, must offer a product that appeals to denominators that are common because low.

Recordings and radio are mass technologies. What happens when they are applied to subjects, such as Beethoven's Fifth Symphony, that do not display the hallmark qualities of mass art? It could be that such works can establish a profitable niche in the market by being offered just as they are. (Or it could be that interest is generated in the personalities or lives of performers and composers, with works and performances treated as emblematic of these.) Alternatively, there can be a tendency to dumb down the product, to make it more like mass art, and thereby to increase its market potential. 'Disco' and 'techno' versions of classical pieces illustrate this trend.

Dumbing down might apply to the audience, not solely to the product offered to them. I have already observed that the prevalence of recorded music might desensitize the listener, inclining him to be a hearer instead. Moreover, the nature of the technology depersonalizes music, by removing it from the human context of generation.

Since the invention of electronic equipment for the transmission and storage of sound, any natural sound, no matter how tiny, can be blown up and shot around the world, or packaged on tape or record for the generations of the future. We have split the sound from the makers of the sound ... Modern life has been ventriloquized.

[56] A recent issue from RCA Victor Red Seal, 'Out Classics', introduces 'seductive classics by eight of the world's greatest composers who just happen to be *gay*'.

Through broadcasting and recording the binding relationship between a sound and the person making it have been dissolved. Sounds have been torn from their natural sockets and given an amplified and independent existence. Vocal sound, for instance, is no longer tied to a hole in the head but is free to issue from anywhere in the landscape. (Schafer 1969: 43–4)

These effects are reinforced by the way the technology is managed. To take a non-musical example, it is widely held that news programmes now offer shorter and less penetrating items than was formerly the case. Their exposure to mass media might make people less exacting as consumers than otherwise they would be.

These general processes are accentuated for broadcast music by programming strategies adopted by the industry in their attempt to hold and expand the audience that is attracted to radio. Richard Peterson (1990) identifies four trends: transvaluation (demoting Western classical music from a position of aesthetic privilege, with a higher value placed on rock), collaging (juxtaposing music from many different traditions), serial discourse (ordering pieces to regulate a mood, rather than to teach, to improve the mind, or even to entertain by telling a story), and the use of music as ambient sound (selecting music for its appropriateness as accompaniment to an activity other than listening).[57] To this list, John Fisher and Jason Potter (1997) add: extraction (removing movements or sections from the larger works to which they belong). Recordings resort to similar practices; for instance, compilations of Adagios.

To some extent, these approaches perpetuate an established practice. Some kinds of music have always been used as functional accompaniments to other activities, such as eating, dancing, war, and sport. (In Bali, the *semar pegulingan* ensemble is named after the god of love because it played outside the palace bedroom.) Suites and songs have been extracted frequently from longer works. Music designed to provide the main fare was often ignored by sectors of the court or church audience for whom it was rendered.[58] Despite these observations, the modern situation contrasts significantly with the past.

---

[57] Peterson is no critic of these trends. He advocates that public radio should abandon classical music programming in favour of 'world music'. 'While works of Western classical music will comprise an important part of the emerging mix, the Western classical art music aesthetic is not the standard nor the model by which all other music is judged . . . So what is world music? Contemporary practitioners include Philip Glass, John Cage, Steve Reich, Keith Jarrett, Brian Eno, Meredith Monk, Frank Zappa, Olivier Messiaen, George Winston, Laurie Anderson, Ravi Shankar, Chick Corea, David Byrne, Paul Winter, Pink Floyd, Jimi Hendrix, Jean-Michel Jarré, Will Ackerman, and Claire Hammill. Also included are a wide range of acoustic ethnic musics from around the world and experimental electronic works' (1990: 222).

[58] Paul Morphy played one of his most famous games of chess during a performance of Rossini's *The Barber of Seville* in Paris in September 1858. Morphy might have had time between moves to take in the opera, but it is doubtful that Count Isouard, his opponent, had that luxury.

Peterson (1990: 212) claims that baby-boomers do play a wider range of musical styles, have music turned on more of the time, and attend to it less closely than their parents. Music plays constantly now, so that people are inured to its presence, as was not formerly the case to a similar degree.[59]

The consequence of these processes, according to Fisher and Potter (1997), is the abstraction of music from its historical context. Music from many eras, cultures, and styles are juxtaposed, and their original functions and home situations are not explained or acknowledged. On radio, sandwiched between advertisements, one is liable to meet with a pot-pourri concocted from pieces spanning many centuries and styles and with only the names of performers and composers mentioned. Movements are removed from their home works, so one is offered the 'Elvira Madigan' Adagio, for example, rather than the entirety of Mozart Piano Concerto in C, K. 467. Films, TV shows, and advertisements ruthlessly pillage the works of the past for good tunes. What goes for music applies also to the other arts. Altar panels are removed from churches and presented in art museums; images of works of art are used on T-shirts and in TV advertisements; contemporary artists (whether commercial or 'serious') display an eclectic interest in media and styles that pays no special regard to the context in which they were first employed and the issues addressed through their use. Although these trends pre-dated the modern era and apply to all the arts, Fisher and Potter maintain that modern technology accelerates the process and that music, above all the arts, lends itself to decontextualization. Music can be abstracted so easily from the art-historical setting where it was created, because its very nature already dissociates it from that location. They continue: in artforms that are primarily narrational or representational, artists' intentions are 'coercive' of interpretations that can be accepted as legitimate. For these artforms, interpretation cannot respectably remain indifferent to the context of creation and original presentation. By contrast, most instrumental music does not invite or require an interpretative narrative, and this is why listeners might be unmoved by historical information concerning the music they hear. The appreciation of music is not constrained by historically conditioned factors, such as composers' intentions, because the significance that formal patterns have for us is independent of, or separable from, such considerations. (For accounts locating music's distinctiveness in the extent of its abstractness, see Budd 1995 and Kivy 1997.)

An outcome of the decontextualizing of music is, as I put it earlier, the dumbing-down of the listener. She is trained to treat all music as if it belongs

---

[59] It is not my intention to moralize about these trends or to rail against popular music of the day, as Adorno (1941) and Bloom (1987) have done. I mean to emphasize the way the music recedes from the hearer's attention under the circumstances described, and to consider the implications of this for our concepts of music and musical appreciation, not to judge the hearer's ethics or intellect.

in the category mass art. She has (or is assumed to have) a short attention span and a preference for the diverting, the unambiguous, and the unsubtle, as opposed to the intellectual, the difficult, and the challenging. She looks for immediate access and effortless gratification. This person finds things to enjoy in the music of Vivaldi, Mozart, and Beethoven, but she attends only to those features of their works that are shared with mass art. She is attracted by the veneer of charm, or vitality, or emotional bathos, and is conditioned to expect no more and to explore no further. If classical works display an appealing surface, as many do, a wide market is ensured for them, though this is one that depends on their being appreciated at something less than their full artistic potential.

At worst, one gets a listener who is attracted to the noise made by music but who is not interested in the music that is there. This person wants music that sets a pleasant ambience or apt mood but does not demand his attention. He wants music that need not be listened to, and he thereby reduces everything he plays to the level of 'moozak'. A more likely result, though, is a listener who enjoys music very much. Indeed, her taste is eclectic. She likes Gregorian Chant, isorhythmic motets of the fourteenth century, rock music, Tibetan bells, Japanese shakuhachi music, Celtic pop, Indian ragas, Zimbabwean jit-jive, xylophone music from Mozambique, jazz, and Solomon Island panpipes. She is content to trade off the joys of a deep understanding of a few kinds of music for the delight she obtains from a limited grasp of many types. She hears enough to discern works (if there are any) in their performances and she has a fair appreciation of the performance skills involved, because, though she knows little of the particular instruments and techniques of playing them, she is familiar with their generic types. She loses something by focusing almost exclusively on recordings, but that loss is outweighed in her estimation by other benefits. She accepts that her listening habits might result in an experience that is impoverished by comparison with what is possible—for instance, she is deaf to reference, quotation, and parody, where these occur, as well as to subtle nuances of style and technique—but she is satisfied with the pleasure she receives. Even if more might be available, the effort of pursuing it is not worth her trouble, she judges.

I allowed earlier that an introduction to music via recordings or radio might awaken in the listener an abiding love for music that leads her to make every effort to understand and appreciate it. I do not suppose that Fisher and Potter would deny this, but they focus on a no less likely scenario. Their point is that many listeners are content with an inferior, or at least different, experience of music issuing from periods other than their own. These listeners are ignorant of the relevant musical styles, genres, practices, and repertoire, and of the history of development and innovation that lies behind them, so their attention must be restricted to the most obvious surface elements presented by the work. If they are not well situated to recognize all the properties apparent to the person who appreciates the piece's musico-historical setting, still they enjoy what they hear (see also Gracyk 1997).

Ontology again

I am interested in the philosophical implications Fisher and Potter tease from their observations. They note that many philosophers, myself included, have argued that the ontology of works of art, and of musical works in particular, is historically relativized. Some properties that belong to the work (and that contribute to its identity as the work it is) depend on a relation between the composer's specifications and the musical conventions of the time. It follows from such a view, apparently, that the work can be identified as such only by someone with an appropriate knowledge of its context of creation. But, and this is where the prior discussion of the prevalence of abstracting processes comes in, a majority of listeners have no awareness of the historical features alleged to be crucial, or take no account of the knowledge they have of them, when they attend to music. There is, then, a serious tension between philosophical theory and ordinary practice.

In drawing attention to the discrepancy between ordinary listening and the theory of the historical contextualist, Fisher and Potter are not offering a *reductio* of the ontology advocated by the latter. They are sympathetic to a historically contextualized analysis of musical ontology. They are puzzled, though, by the indifference shown to standard listening practice by the theory's proponents, since that practice seems at odds with what the theory would lead one to expect. Their aim is to confront this apathy. Throughout this book I have expressed interest in the ways we classify, talk about, and appreciate musical works and performances. If my analysis has some appeal, this is because the word 'we' has an appropriately wide scope. If it means only 'me and the philosophers who share my view', then few would be impressed. So I acknowledge the problem that Fisher and Potter highlight.

In Chapters 4 and 5 I allowed that a poor performance is of a work so long as the piece can be recognized in it. In the case discussed, the imperfections that obscure the work lie in its performance, but we can imagine another in which they belong, not to the performance, but to the listener's way of hearing it. The performance is ideally faithful, but the listener perceives the work only dimly because she is not well equipped to recognize and understand what she hears. Nevertheless, she comprehends enough to appreciate the work's and the performance's gross features, if not their subtle detail. With this in mind, it is open to the contextualist to argue that the ordinary listener misperceives and misunderstands the music she hears, though she grasps enough to identify correctly the work that is her object.

This claim cannot be fully convincing, however. It will not do to dismiss ordinary listening practice in this fashion because, where it sets the norm, it effectively establishes the subject of discussion.[60] Given her purposes, there is nothing inadequate about the ordinary listener's approach to music. Accordingly, and this is the point behind the argument presented by Fisher and Potter, we should conclude instead that it is not the music described by the philosopher that is the auditor's concern.

There is a sense in which the ordinary listener's practice affects the nature of the music she attends to. This is not to claim that she can alter the ontological character of Mozart's Symphony No. 39. To appreciate Mozart's work as the one *he* wrote, it may be that the auditor must take some account of the historical context in which the piece was produced. It is to allow, though, that the nature of her interest in the music might reveal that its object is not *Mozart's* symphony.[61] Her focus is on something else, on another kind of music for which the contextualist's ontology is inappropriate. The music that concerns her is much less tied to the historical setting in which it was composed than is Mozart's Symphony No. 39 heard as such. It shares with Mozart's Symphony No. 39 many sound structures (viewed as abstract patterns), as well as a style (considered merely in terms of syntactic regularities and rules, without regard to historical influences and contextually conditioned functions). The piece she listens to differs from Mozart's Symphony No. 39, though. For instance, unlike his work, it is not innovative in including clarinets and it does not prefigure Beethoven's seriousness.

As I interpret them, the observations of Fisher and Potter draw attention to the fact that the standard practice reveals that the kind of music that engages the listener could not be the kind of music analysed by the philosopher. Also they doubt the convincingness of any quick argument to the conclusion that there is only one correct way (the philosopher's) of concerning oneself with music, given that what I have called 'standard practice' is the statistical norm if anything is. If each person is entitled to approach music according to her own taste, without coercion from others, where is the basis for disputing with her about what the norm *ought* to be?

In fact, there are at least three arguments that might be relevant. If the person thinks that nothing is lost by listening to all music ahistorically and acontextually, one can query the truth of her belief. Deciding how to listen to music is not like choosing between muffins, ice cream, and yoghurt in at least one important respect: the enjoyment derived from those activities

---

[60] Neither is it appropriate or persuasive to disregard the listener who prefers popular forms of music on the grounds that her taste must be defective, as does Adorno (1941, 1973).

[61] The listener is likely to designate the work as 'Mozart's Symphony No. 39', but that is only because the composer's name and the symphony's number provide a convenient route for reference. That one refers to someone as 'the third on the right' does not mean, of course, that it is their location that interests one.

is not affected by the way they are understood. Indeed, one might wonder what it is for a muffin, or the experience of eating it, to be understood as such. By contrast, music is a sophisticated human product that is offered for comprehension. The listener who declines the invitation issued by the composer and the performer denies herself the kind of enjoyment that goes with appreciating what they have done, and why. Because they are deliberately and carefully made to be what they are, musical works and performances are almost always more deeply enjoyable when they are considered in terms of the categories and descriptions they are created to exemplify or instance, and they can be approached in that fashion only by being regarded historically and contextually (Davies 1994*a*: ch. 6, 1994*b*). The empirical claim, that nothing is lost when the work's musico-historical embeddedness is ignored, is false.

A different response is needed, though, to the person who allows that he gets less from music than he might, but says he is satisfied with the pleasure he receives via his uninformed mode of listening and that he does not have the time, the energy, or the interest to acquaint himself with the work's historical setting. One possible line of reply would make clear just how much is at risk, and thereby would try to undermine the utility calculation this person makes. Musical works made to be listened to, and much else beside, occupy a central place within the cultural history and intellectual traditions that shape the world we live in. We cannot know ourselves in the present if we cannot recognize our former selves in the past, and we cannot know where we are if we cannot see where we have been. Even if the current time is Postmodern, it does not follow that we can engage meaningfully with the present if we neglect our history. There is an important sense, then, in which the objects of history are always important to where we are now as a culture, and, even if those objects are open to reinterpretation in the light of the present, they cannot be reinterpreted without first being located, and they cannot be located when they are treated ahistorically and acontextually.

A less general and grandiose line considers the relation between our concepts of music and of listening, and asks which mode of listening is primary for music. This is not to ask which mode of listening is the most common statistically; neither does it enquire about the first used, chronologically speaking; nor even does it seek to discover which is morally superior (if that task makes sense). Instead, the priority invoked by the question resides in the notion's conceptual and explanatory power. Is there a kind of listening such that, without it, music making could have no point or interest?

I maintain that a keystone in our concept of music is that of works composed for performance. We could not explain why music became what it is, and became valued, without giving a central place to composers' works and the talents performers bring to their realization, along with recognizing that the creation of pieces worth hearing is difficult and that they are often hard to play. It is an interest both in works as of their composers and in the skills of the performer that is central to the concept of music, I maintain, and the rightness of historical, contextualist ontologies is that they focus on music as identified via that regard. This interest is not the only one we could have, but it is the one that must be accorded primacy in an analysis of *music*'s nature. Once music is in place, as it were, all sorts of concerns other than an interest in works and their interpretation can come into play. (For instance, music can be valued for creating a pleasant ambience that does not require the listener's attention.) These other interests presuppose the existence of music. Appeal to them could not explain why the concept of music has the content it does. And it could not account for our making music, as opposed to pleasant noises that are good for dancing to, or for setting a mood, or for aiding digestion, or for putting babies to sleep.

Suppose this was once true. Still, this foundational interest may not have remained primary (or even survived). Music could continue to be created even if the audience were to become indifferent to the fact of its being composed. The kind of appreciation that once was central could be superseded, so that historical information about the music becomes less relevant to and less coercive of the manner in which it should be approached. Or, the originary interest could be proved inadequate by developments in music itself. Composers might no longer have anything to communicate, or it might be that their techniques become so arcane and esoteric that they alienate all but the most dedicated listeners. Different focuses could be primary at different periods, in which case it would be appropriate to think of the concept of music as changing through time. In this view, even if the concept of music would not have arisen had there not been a concern with historically contextualized musical works, new concerns should motivate the music making that follows later. For instance, developments in music could now be propelled by a different, more abstracted, strategy of appreciation. In this account, the future not just of music but of the very concept is open.

Of course the future is open. From here it is hard to tell how things will go. The interest identified as primary by the historical contextualist might retain that status. In that case, works regarded as the creations of their composers will remain of concern. Alternatively, if the primary interest disappears, thereby making irrelevant all that is implicated in the context of original creation, music will increasingly be labelled not by reference to its composer or performer, but simply as Classical, Rhythm and Blues, and so on. Within classical music, labels such as Baroque, Rococco, Classical, and Romantic will name styles that are construed only in terms of superficial features of the musical surface and syntax. They will not indicate historical periods, each of which involved a reaction to its predecessors and, in its turn, influenced its successors. They will not identify historic periods each of which aimed at its particular artistic goals and ideals, identified and grappled with its own problems, and so on. On this scenario, future generations may regard musical works much as we regard hand-illuminated Bibles—as peculiar but interesting curios, though magnificent in their way. If people so choose, the concept and practice of music will be transformed into something we would find difficult to recognize.

My bet remains with the historical contextualist, though. The wager is on what people will find interesting, will enjoy, will find understandable, will value. That kind of thing does not change very quickly. It varies in a local way from one person to another and from one kind of music to another, but, behind such differences, common themes persist. It is in terms of these that we can recognize of all periods and all cultures that they have music. (For further discussion of these issues, see Davies 1997*c*, 2000.) This universality suggests to me that music calls to something very deep and important within our shared humanity, which is why I bet that it will not easily be transformed into something with a radically different kind of appeal.

I think that some people will continue to want to *play* and to *listen* to music, even if there will also be a demand for music to dance to—any music so long as it is good for dancing—or to play in lifts and airport bars—any music so long as it is good for lifting or drinking—or to use in TV advertisements—any music so long as it makes the product seem desirable. For those people, the music that will be most rewarding will require talent from the producer, so that not just anybody (or any machine) will be able to provide it. As a result, they will regard works as the creations of their composers. They will want to know of the music what was original and what derivative; which conventions were presupposed, or violated, or introduced; which constraints were accepted and which supplied challenges that were overcome; what goals were pursued and why. They will be touched to the quick by such music, and marvel that this should be so. Also, they will wish to know the identity of performers, given that some individuals are better than others at playing music and interpreting works. They will be interested in the skills and techniques displayed by musicians. They will be moved and fascinated by the talented few who have the ability to make their instruments speak so eloquently.

Summary

I have argued that neither direct broadcasts nor recordings of live performances are the same as live performances, because the technology involved renders the medium non-transparent even if acoustic verisimilitude is achieved in the transmission. Recordings of what I have called studio performances and videos of operas are even more unlike live performances. Studio performances are of the works in question, but they are performances of a special kind. To the suitably informed listener, they display different strengths and weaknesses from sound-alike live performances, and the two should be assessed and appreciated differently. At the chapter's close I mentioned the social significance of the present ubiquity of recordings. There are plusses, but it is not clear that these counterbalance the minuses that are a consequence of the extent to which the medium decontextualizes and abstracts the music it purveys. The work is alienated from the context of its creation and the performance is divorced from the human element that traditionally is essential in the generation of the appropriate sounds. Yet, if music chimes with human needs and experiences that are no less deeply important for humankind now than they were in the past, it may be changed but it should survive.

References

Ackerman, James S. (1981). 'Worldmaking and Practical Criticism'. *Journal of Aesthetics and Art Criticism*, 39: 249–54.

Adorno, Theodor W. (1941). 'On Popular Music'. *Studies in Philosophy and Social Science*, 9: 17–48.

——(1973). *Philosophy of Modern Music*, trans. Anne G. Mitchell and Wesley V. Blomster. London: Sheed & Ward.

——(1981). 'Bach Defended against his Devotees', in Adorno, *Prisms*, trans. Samuel and Sherry Weber. Cambridge, MA: MIT Press, 133–46. First published in 1967.

Alperson, Philip (1984). 'On Musical Improvisation'. *Journal of Aesthetics and Art Criticism*, 43: 17–30.

——(1991). 'When Composers have to be Performers'. *Journal of Aesthetics and Art Criticism*, 49: 369–73.

Anderson, Christopher (1993). 'The Art of the Sacred and the Art of Art: Contemporary Aboriginal Painting in Central Australia', in Philip J. C. Dark and Roger G. Rose (eds.), *Artistic Heritage in a Changing Pacific*. Honolulu, HA: University Press of Hawaii, 142–8.

Anderson, James C. (1982). 'Musical Identity'. *Journal of Aesthetics and Art Criticism*, 40: 285–91.

——(1985). 'Musical Kinds'. *British Journal of Aesthetics*, 25: 43–9.

Apel, Willi (1953). *The Notation of Polyphonic Music 900–1600*. Cambridge, MA: The Mediaeval Academy of America.

——(1966) (ed.). *Harvard Dictionary of Music*. Cambridge, MA: Harvard University Press.

Arnold, Denis, and Fortune, Nigel (1971) (eds.). *The Companion to Beethoven*. London: Faber & Faber.

Bachrach, Jay (1971). 'Type and Token and the Identification of the Work of Art'. *Philosophy and Phenomenological Research*, 31: 415–20.

Baines, Anthony (1966) (ed.). *Musical Instruments through the Ages*. London: Penguin Books. Revised version of 1961 printing.

Bakan, Michael (1997–8). 'From Oxymoron to Reality: Agendas of Gender and the Rise of Balinese Women's *Gamelan Beleganjur* in Bali, Indonesia'. *Asian Music*, 29/1: 37–85.

Bandem, I Made, and DeBoer, Fredrik Eugene (1981). *Kaja and Kelod: Balinese Dance in Transition*. Kuala Lumpur: Oxford University Press.

Bartók, Béla (1967). *Rumanian Folk Music*, ii. *Vocal Melodies*, ed. Benjamin Suchoff. The Hague: Martinus Nijhoff.

Baugh, Bruce (1993). 'Prolegomena to Any Aesthetics of Rock Music'. *Journal of Aesthetics and Art Criticism*, 51: 23–9.

——(1995). 'Music for the Young at Heart'. *Journal of Aesthetics and Art Criticism*, 53: 81–3.

Beardsley, Monroe C. (1958). *Aesthetics: Problems in the Philosophy of Criticism*. New York: Harcourt, Brace and World.

Becker, Judith (1980). *Traditional Music in Modern Java: Gamelan in a Changing Society*. Honolulu, HA: University Press of Hawaii.

——(1986). 'Is Western Art Music Superior?' *Musical Quarterly*, 72: 341–59.

Behrman, David (1976). 'What Indeterminate Notation Determines', in Benjamin Boretz and Edward T. Cone (eds.), *Perspectives on Notation and Performance*. New York: W. W. Norton, 74–89.

Bender, John W. (1993). 'Music and Metaphysics: Types and Patterns, Performances and Works', in John W. Bender and H. Gene Blocker (eds.), *Contemporary Philosophy of Art: Readings in Analytic Aesthetics*. Englewood Cliffs, NJ: Prentice-Hall, 354–65.

Bird, John (1976). *Percy Grainger*. London: Paul Elek.

Blacking, John (1973). *How Musical Is Man?* Seattle: University of Washington Press.

Blocker, Gene H. (1993). *The Aesthetics of Primitive Art*. Lanham, MD: University Press of America.

Bloom, Allan (1987). *Closing of the American Mind: How Higher Education has Failed Democracy and Impoverished the Souls of Today's Students*. New York: Simon & Schuster.

Bohlman, Philip V. (1999). 'Ontologies of Music', in Nicholas Cook and Mark Everist (eds.), *Rethinking Music*. Oxford: Oxford University Press, 17–34.

Boorman, Stanley (1999). 'The Musical Text', in Nicholas Cook and Mark Everist (eds.), *Rethinking Music*. Oxford: Oxford University Press, 403–23.

Boretz, Benjamin (1970). 'Nelson Goodman's Languages of Art from a Musical Point of View'. *Journal of Philosophy*, 67: 540–52.

Bowen, José A. (1993). 'The History of Remembered Innovation: Tradition and Its Role in the Relationship between Musical Works and their Performances'. *Journal of Musicology*, 11: 139–73.

——(1996). 'Performance Practice versus Performance Analysis: Why should Performers Study Performance?' *Performance Practice Review*, 9: 16–35.

——(1999). 'Finding the Music in Musicology: Performance History and Musical Works', in Nicholas Cook and Mark Everist (eds.), *Rethinking Music*. Oxford: Oxford University Press, 424–51.

Brendel, Alfred (1976). *Musical Thoughts and Afterthoughts*. Princeton: Princeton University Press.

——(1990). *Music Sounded Out: Essays, Lectures, Interviews, Afterthoughts*. New York: Farrar Straus Giroux.

Brett, Philip (1988). 'Text, Context and the Early Music Editor', in Nicholas Kenyon (ed.), *Authenticity and Early Music*. Oxford: Oxford University Press, 83–114.

Brophy, Brigid (1964). *Mozart the Dramatist*. London: Faber & Faber.

Brown, Howard Mayer (1988). 'Pedantry or Liberation? A Sketch of the Historical Performance Movement', in Nicholas Kenyon (ed.), *Authenticity and Early Music*. Oxford: Oxford University Press, 27–56.

Brown, Lee B. (1996). 'Musical Works, Improvisation, and the Principle of Continuity'. *Journal of Aesthetics and Art Criticism*, 54: 353–69.

——(1999). 'Postmodernist Jazz Theory: Afrocentrism, Old and New'. *Journal of Aesthetics and Art Criticism*, 57: 235–46.

——(2000). '"Feeling My Way": Jazz Improvisation and its Vicissitudes—A Plea for Imperfection'. *Journal of Aesthetics and Art Criticism*, 58: 112–23.

Bruner, Edward M. (1996). 'Tourism in the Balinese Borderzone', in Smadar Lavie and Ted Swedenburg (eds.), *Displacement, Diaspora, and Geographies of Identity*. Durham, NC: Duke University Press, 157–79.

——and Kirshenblatt-Gimblett, Barbara (1994). 'Maasai on the Lawn: Tourist Realism in East Africa'. *Cultural Anthropology*, 9: 435–70.

Budd, Malcolm (1995). *The Values of Art: Pictures, Poetry, and Music*. London: Allen Lane & The Penguin Press.

Budhardjo, Eko (1966). *Architectural Conservation in Bali*. Yogyakarta: Gadjah Mada University Press.

Bujic, Bojan (1993). 'Notation and Realization: Musical Performance in Historical Perspective', in Michael Krausz (ed.), *The Interpretation of Music: Philosophical Essays*. Oxford: Clarendon Press, 129–40.

Burt, George (1994). *The Art of Film Music*. Boston: Northeastern University Press.

Cage, John (1969). *Notations*. New York: Something Else Press.

——(1996). *Musicage: Cage Muses on Words Art Music*. In conversation with Joan Retallak. Hanover, CT: Wesleyan University Press.

Caldwell, John (1985). *Editing Early Music*. Oxford: Oxford University Press.

Callen, Donald (1982). 'Making Music Live'. *Theoria*, 48: 139–68.

Carpenter, Patricia (1967). 'The Musical Object', *Current Musicology*, 5: 56–87.

Carrier, David (1982). 'Art without its Artists?' *British Journal of Aesthetics*, 22: 233–44.

——(1983). 'Interpreting Musical Performances'. *Monist*, 66: 202–12.

Carroll, Noël (1988). 'Art, Practice, and Narrative'. *Monist*, 71: 140–56.

——(1995). 'Towards an Ontology of the Moving Image', in Cynthia Freeland and Tom Wartenberg (eds.), *Philosophy and Film*. New York: Routledge, 68–85.

——(1997). 'The Ontology of Mass Art'. *Journal of Aesthetics and Art Criticism*, 55: 187–99.

——(1998). *A Philosophy of Mass Art*. New York: Oxford University Press.

Chanan, Michael (1995). *Repeated Takes: A Short History of Recording and its Effects on Music*. London: Verso.

Chew, Geoffrey (1980). 'Non-Mensural and Specialist Notations', in Stanley Sadie (ed.), *The New Grove Dictionary of Music and Musicians*. London: Macmillan, xiii. 415–17.

Clark, Ann (1982). 'Is Music a Language?' *Journal of Aesthetics and Art Criticism*, 41: 195–204.

Clifford, James (1988). *The Predicament of Culture: Twentieth Century Ethnography, Literature, and Art*. Cambridge, MA: Harvard University Press.

Coast, John (1953). *Dancers of Bali*. New York: G. P. Putnam's Sons.

Cochrane, Richard (2000). 'Playing by the Rules: A Pragmatic Characterization of Musical Performance'. *Journal of Aesthetics and Art Criticism*, 58: 135–42.

Cohen, Erik (1988). 'Authenticity and Commoditization in Tourism'. *Annals of Tourism Research*, 15: 371–86.

Coker, Wilson (1983). 'Music as Art', in H. Curtler (ed.), *What is Art?* New York: Haven, 155–73.

Cone, Edward T. (1967). 'What is a Composition?' *Current Musicology*, 5: 101–7.

——(1995). 'The Pianist as Critic', in John Rink (ed.), *The Practice of Performance: Studies in Musical Interpretation*. Cambridge: Cambridge University Press, 241–53.

Cook, Nicholas (1990). *Music, Imagination, and Culture*. Oxford: Clarendon Press.

——(1993). *Beethoven: Symphony No. 9*. Cambridge: Cambridge University Press.

——(1995). 'The Conductor and the Theorist: Furtwängler and the First Movement of Beethoven's Ninth Symphony', in John Rink (ed.), *The Practice of Performance: Studies in Musical Interpretation*. Cambridge: Cambridge University Press, 105–25.

——(1996). 'Music Minus One: Rock, Theory and Performance'. *New Formations*, 27: 23–41.

——(1999). 'At the Borders of Musical Identity: Schenker, Corelli and the Graces'. *Music Analysis*, 18: 179–233.

Cooper, Grosvenor, and Meyer, Leonard B. (1960). *The Rhythmic Structure of Music*. Chicago: Chicago University Press.

Cornet, J. (1975). 'African Art and Authenticity'. *African Art*, 9/1: 52–5.

Covarrubias, Miguel (1972). *Bali*. P. T. Pustaka Ilmu, Jakarta: Oxford University Press. First published in 1937.

Cox, Renée (1985). 'Are Musical Works Discovered?' *Journal of Aesthetics and Art Criticism*, 43: 367–74.

——(1986). 'A Defence of Musical Idealism'. *British Journal of Aesthetics*, 26: 133–42.

Croce, Benedetto (1953). *Aesthetic: As Science of Expression and General Linguistic*, trans. D. Ainslie. London: Peter Owen. First published in Italian in 1902.

Crutchfield, Will (1988). 'Fashion, Conviction, and Performance Style in an Age of Revivals', in Nicholas Kenyon (ed.), *Authenticity and Early Music*. Oxford: Oxford University Press, 19–26.

Currie, Gregory (1988). *An Ontology of Art*. London: Macmillan.

Danielou, Alain (1971). *The Situation of Music and Musicians in Countries of the Orient*, trans. John Evarts. Florence: Leo S. Olschki.

Danto, Arthur C. (1981). *The Transfiguration of the Commonplace*. Cambridge, MA: Harvard University Press.

Dart, Thurston (1967). *The Interpretation of Music*. London: Hutchinson University Library.

Davies, Stephen (1987). 'Authenticity in Musical Performance'. *British Journal of Aesthetics*, 27: 39–50.

——(1988a). 'Transcription, Authenticity and Performance'. *British Journal of Aesthetics*, 28: 216–27.

——(1988b). 'A Reply to James O. Young'. *British Journal of Aesthetics*, 28: 388–91.

——(1990). 'Violins or Viols?—a Reason to Fret'. *Journal of Aesthetics and Art Criticism*, 48: 147–51.

——(1991a). *Definitions of Art*. Ithaca, NY: Cornell University Press.

——(1991b). 'The Ontology of Musical Works and the Authenticity of their Performances'. *Noûs*, 25: 21–41.

——(1991c). ' "I have finished today another new concerto . . ." '. *Journal of Aesthetic Education*, 25/4: 139–41.

——(1992). 'Mozart's *Requiem*? A Reply to Levinson'. *British Journal of Aesthetics*, 32: 254–57.

——(1994a). *Musical Meaning and Expression*. Ithaca, NY: Cornell University Press.

——(1994b). 'Musical Understanding and Musical Kinds'. *Journal of Aesthetics and Art Criticism*, 52: 69–81.

——(1996). 'Interpreting Contextualities'. *Philosophy and Literature*, 20: 20–38.

——(1997*a*). 'John Cage's *4′33″*. Is it Music?' *Australasian Journal of Philosophy*, 75: 448–62.

——(1997*b*). 'So, You Want to Sing with the Beatles? Too Late!' *Journal of Aesthetics and Art Criticism*, 55: 129–37.

——(1997*c*). 'First Art and Art's Definition'. *Southern Journal of Philosophy*, 35: 19–34.

——(1999). 'Rock versus Classical Music'. *Journal of Aesthetics and Art Criticism*, 57: 193–204.

——(2000). 'Non-Western Art and Art's Definition', in Noël Carroll (ed.), *Theories of Art Today*. Madison: University of Wisconsin Press, 199–216.

Deutsch, Otto Erich (1966). *Mozart: A Documentary Biography*. London: Adam & Charles Black.

DeVale, Sue Carole, and Dibia, I. Wayan (1991). 'Sekar Anyar: An Exploration of Meaning in Balinese Gamelan'. *The World of Music*, 33: 5–51.

De Zoete, Beryl, and Spies, Walter (1973). *Dance and Drama in Bali*. Kuala Lumpur: Oxford University Press. First published by Faber & Faber in 1938.

Dibia, I. Wayan (1989). 'The Symbols of Gender in Balinese Dance'. *UCLA Journal of Dance Ethnology*, 13: 10–13.

Dipert, Randall R. (1980*a*). 'Types and Tokens: A Reply to Sharpe'. *Mind*, 89: 587–8.

——(1980*b*). 'The Composer's Intentions: An Examination of their Relevance for Performance'. *Musical Quarterly*, 66: 205–18.

——(1988). 'Toward a Genuine Philosophy of the Performing Arts'. *Reason Papers*, 13: 182–200.

——(1993). *Artifacts, Art Works, and Agency*. Philadelphia, PA: Temple University Press.

Djelantik, A. A. M. (1995). 'Is There a Shift Taking Place in Balinese Aesthetics?' Paper presented to the Third International Bali Studies Workshop, University of Sydney, 3–7 July.

Donington, Robert (1989). *The Interpretation of Early Music: New Revised Edition*. London: W. W. Norton.

Dorian, Frederick (1942). *The History of Music in Performance: Interpretation from the Renaissance to our Day*. New York: Norton.

Dreyfus, Laurence (1983). 'Early Music Defended against its Devotees: A Musical Theory of Historical Performance in the Twentieth Century'. *Musical Quarterly*, 69: 297–322.

Dutton, Denis (1977). 'Art, Behavior, and the Anthropologists'. *Current Anthropology*, 18: 387–94.

——(1979). 'Artistic Crimes: The Problem of Forgery in the Arts'. *British Journal of Aesthetics*, 19: 302–14.

——(1993). 'Tribal Art and Artifact'. *Journal of Aesthetics and Art Criticism*, 51: 13–21.

——(1994). 'Authenticity in the Art of Traditional Societies'. *Pacific Arts*, 9–10: 1–9.

——(1995). 'Mythologies of Tribal Art'. *African Arts* (Summer), 32–43, 90–1.

——(2000). '"But they don't have our Concept of Art"', in Noël Carroll (ed.), *Theories of Art Today*. Madison: University of Wisconsin Press, 217–38.

Edidin, Aron (1991). 'Look what they've Done to my Song: "Historical Authenticity" and the Aesthetics of Musical Performance'. *Midwest Studies in Philosophy*, 16: 394–420.

——(1997). 'Performing Compositions'. *British Journal of Aesthetics*, 37: 323–35.

——(1998). 'Playing Bach his Way: Historical Authenticity, Personal Authenticity, and the Performance of Classical Music'. *Journal of Aesthetic Education*, 32/4: 79–91.

——(1999). 'Three Kinds of Recording and the Metaphysics of Music'. *British Journal of Aesthetics*, 39: 24–39.

Edlund, Bengt (1996). 'On Scores and Works of Music: Interpretation and Identity'. *British Journal of Aesthetics*, 36: 367–80.

——(1997). '*Sonate, que te fais-je?* Toward a Theory of Interpretation'. *Journal of Aesthetic Education*, 31/1: 23–40.

Eiseman, Margaret (1990). 'Gamelan Gong: Traditional Balinese Orchestra', in Fred B. Eiseman Jr. (ed.), *Bali: Sekala & Niskala*. Singapore: Periplus Editions, i. 333–42.

Eiseman, Fred B., Jr. (1990) (ed.). *Bali: Sekala & Niskala*, Vol. i. Singapore: Periplus Editions.

Eisenberg, Evan (1988). *The Recording Angel: Music, Records and Culture from Aristotle to Zappa*. London: Picador.

Epstein, David (1995). 'A Curious Moment in Schumann's Fourth Symphony: Structure as the Fusion of Affect and Intuition', in John Rink (ed.), *The Practice of Performance: Studies in Musical Interpretation*. Cambridge: Cambridge University Press, 126–49.

Erauw, Willem (1998). 'Canon Formation: Some More Reflections on Lydia Goehr's Imaginary Museum of Musical Works'. *Acta Musicologica*, 70: 109–15.

Errington, Shelly (1994). 'What Became Authentic Primitive Art?' *Cultural Anthropology*, 9: 201–26.

Evans, Martyn (1990). *Listening to Music*. London: Macmillan.

Fabian, Johannes (1983). *Time and the Other: How Anthropology Makes its Object*. New York: Columbia University Press.

Fairbairn-Dunlop, Peggy (1994). 'Gender, Culture and Tourism Development in Western Samoa', in Vivian Kinnaird and Derek Hall (eds.), *Tourism: A Gender Analysis*. Chichester: John Wiley & Sons, 121–41.

Feld, Steven (1988). 'Aesthetics as Iconicity of Style or "Lift-Up-Over-Sounding": Getting into the Kaluli Groove'. *Yearbook for Traditional Music*, 20: 74–113.

——(1994). 'From Schizophonia to Schismogenesis', in Charles Keil and Steven Feld, *Music Grooves*. Chicago: Chicago University Press, 257–89.

Ferguson, Linda (1983). 'Tape Composition: An Art Form in Search of its Metaphysics'. *Journal of Aesthetics and Art Criticism*, 42: 17–27.

Fisher, John Andrew (1991). 'Discovery, Creation, and Musical Works'. *Journal of Aesthetics and Art Criticism*, 49: 129–36.

——(1995). 'Is There a Problem of Indiscernible Counterparts?' *Journal of Philosophy*, 92: 467–84.

——(1998). 'Rock 'n' Recording: The Ontological Complexity of Rock Music', in Philip Alperson (ed.), *Musical Worlds: New Directions in the Philosophy of Music*. University Park, PA: Pennsylvania State University Press, 109–23.

——and Potter, Jason (1997). 'Technology, Appreciation, and the Historical View of Art'. *Journal of Aesthetics and Art Criticism*, 55: 169–85.

Frith, Simon (1983). *Sound Effects: Youth, Leisure, and the Politics of Rock 'n' Roll.* 2nd ed. London: Constable.

——(1986). 'Art vs. Technology: The Strange Case of Popular Music'. *Media, Culture and Society*, 8: 263–79.

——(1987). 'Copyright and the Music Business'. *Popular Music*, 7: 57–75.

Gell, Alfred (1992). 'The Technology of Enchantment and the Enchantment of Technology', in Jeremy Coote and Anthony Shelton (eds.), *Anthropology, Art, and Aesthetics*. Oxford: Clarendon Press, 40–63.

Godlovitch, Stan (1988). 'Authentic Performance'. *Monist*, 71: 258–77.

——(1990a). 'Music Performance and the Tools of the Trade'. *IYYUN, Jerusalem Philosophical Quarterly*, 39: 321–38.

——(1990b). 'Artists, Programs, and Performance'. *Australasian Journal of Philosophy*, 68: 301–12.

——(1992). 'Music—What to do about It'. *Journal of Aesthetic Education*, 26/2: 1–15.

——(1993). 'The Integrity of Musical Performance'. *Journal of Aesthetics and Art Criticism*, 51: 573–87.

——(1997). 'Innovation and Conservatism in Performance Practice'. *Journal of Aesthetics and Art Criticism*, 55: 151–68.

——(1998). *Musical Performance: A Philosophical Study*. London: Routledge.

Goehr, Lydia (1992). *The Imaginary Museum of Musical Works: An Essay in the Philosophy of Music*. Oxford: Clarendon Press.

——(1996). 'The Perfect Performance of Music and the Perfect Musical Performance'. *New Formations*, 27: 1–22.

Goldblatt, David A. (1976). 'Do Works of Art have Rights?' *Journal of Aesthetics and Art Criticism*, 35: 69–77.

Goodman, Nelson (1968). *Languages of Art*. Indianapolis: Bobbs-Merrill.

——(1970). 'Some Notes on *Languages of Art*'. *Journal of Philosophy*, 67: 563–73.

——(1972). *Problems and Projects* (Indianapolis: Bobbs-Merrill).

——(1984). *Of Mind and Other Matters*. Cambridge, MA: Harvard University Press.

Goslich, Siegfried, Mead, Rita H., and Roberts, Timothy (1980). 'Broadcasting', in Stanley Sadie (ed.), *The New Grove Dictionary of Music and Musicians*. London: Macmillan, iii. 313–24.

Gould, Carol S., and Keaton, Kenneth (2000). 'The Essential Role of Improvisation in Musical Performance'. *Journal of Aesthetics and Art Criticism*, 58: 143–8.

Graburn, Nelson H. H. (1976) (ed.). *Ethnic and Tourist Arts: Cultural Expressions from the Fourth World*. Berkeley and Los Angeles: University of California Press.

Gracyk, Theodore A. (1996). *Rhythm and Noise: An Aesthetics of Rock Music*. Durham, NC: Duke University Press.

——(1997). 'Listening to Music: Performances and Recordings'. *Journal of Aesthetics and Art Criticism*, 55: 139–50.

——(1999). 'Play it again Sam: Response to Niblock'. *Journal of Aesthetics and Art Criticism*, 57: 368–70.

Greenwood, Davydd J. (1978). 'Culture by the Pound: An Anthropological Perspective on Tourism as Cultural Commoditization', in Valene S. Smith (ed.), *Hosts and Guests: The Anthropology of Tourism*. Oxford: Blackwell, 129–38.

Grier, James (1996). *The Critical Editing of Music: History, Method, and Practice*. Cambridge: Cambridge University Press.

Griffiths, Paul (1979). *A Guide to Electronic Music*. London: Thames & Hudson.

Grossman, Morris (1987). 'Performance and Obligation', in Philip Alperson (ed.), *What Is Music? An Introduction to the Philosophy of Music*. New York: Haven, 257–81.

Hall, Timothy S. (1999). 'The Score as Contract: Private Law and the Historically Informed Performance Movement'. *Cardozo Law Review*, 20 (May–July), 1589–1614.

Hamilton, Andy (2000). 'The Art of Improvisation and the Aesthetics of Imperfection'. *British Journal of Aesthetics*, 40: 168–85.

Hamilton, James R. (1999). 'Musical Noise'. *British Journal of Aesthetics*, 39: 350–63.

Harman, Alec, and Mellers, Wilfred (1962). *Man and his Music: The Story of Musical Experience in the West*. London: Barrie & Rockliff.

Harnish, David (1991). 'Balinese Performance as Festival Offerings'. *Asian Art*, 4: 9–27.

Harnoncourt, Nikolaus (1988). *Baroque Music Today: Music as Speech: Ways to a New Understanding of Music*, trans. Mary O'Neill. Portland, OR: Amadeus Press.

——(1989). *The Musical Dialogue: Thoughts on Monteverdi, Bach, and Mozart*, trans. Mary O'Neill. London: Helm.

Harris, Kenton, and Fender, David E. W. (1995). 'Video-Preservation of Dance'. *Journal of Aesthetic Education*, 29/1: 69–78.

Harrison, Nigel (1975). 'Types, Tokens and the Identity of the Musical Work'. *British Journal of Aesthetics*, 15: 336–46.

——(1978). 'Creativity in Musical Performance'. *British Journal of Aesthetics*, 18: 300–6.

Haskell, Harry (1988). *The Early Music Revival: A History*. New York: Thames & Hudson.

Hatley, Barbara (1990). 'Theatrical Imagery and Gender Ideology in Java', in Jane Monnig Atkinson and Shelly Erington (eds.), *Power and Difference: Gender in Island Southeast Asia*. Stanford, CA: Stanford University Press, 177–207.

Hermerén, Göran (1993). 'The Full Voic'd Quire: Types of Interpretations of Music', in Michael Krausz (ed.), *The Interpretation of Music: Philosophical Essays*. Oxford: Clarendon Press, 9–31.

——(1995). 'Art and Life: Models for Understanding Music'. *Australasian Journal of Philosophy*, 73: 280–92.

Hernadi, Paul (1991). 'Reconceiving Notation and Performance'. *Journal of Aesthetic Education*, 25/1: 47–56.

Higgins, Kathleen Marie (1991). *The Music of our Lives*. Philadelphia: Temple University Press.

——(1997). 'Musical Idiosyncrasy and Perspectival Listening', in Jenefer Robinson (ed.), *Music and Meaning*. Ithaca, NY: Cornell University Press, 83–102.

Hilton, Julian (1987). *New Directions in Theatre Performance*. London: Macmillan.

Hoffman, Robert (1962). 'Conjectures and Refutations on the Ontological Status of the Work of Art'. *Mind*, 71: 512–20.

Hood, Mantle (1959). 'The Reliability of Oral Tradition'. *Journal of the American Musicological Society*, 12: 201–9.

——(1971). *The Ethnomusicologist*. New York: McGraw-Hill.

Hough, Brett (1995). 'Sekolah Tinggi Seni Indonesia, Denpasar and the *Tri Dharma Perguran Tinggi*'. Paper presented to the Third International Bali Studies Workshop, University of Sydney, 3–7 July.

Howat, Roy (1995). 'What Do We Perform?' in John Rink (ed.), *The Practice of Performance: Studies in Musical Interpretation*. Cambridge: Cambridge University Press, 3–20.

Howes, Frank (1962). 'A Critique of Folk, Popular and "Art" Music'. *British Journal of Aesthetics*, 2: 239–48.

Ingarden, Roman (1986). *The Work of Music and the Problem of its Identity*, trans. Adam Czerniawski. Berkeley, CA: University of California Press. First published in Polish in 1966.

Jackson, Frank (1997). 'Reference and Description Revisited'. *Philosophical Perspectives*, 12: 201–18.

——(1998). *From Metaphysics to Ethics: A Defence of Conceptual Analysis*. Oxford: Clarendon Press.

Jacobs, Jo Ellen (1990). 'Identifying Musical Works of Art'. *Journal of Aesthetic Education*, 24/4: 75–85.

Janaway, Christopher (1999). 'What a Musical Forgery Isn't'. *British Journal of Aesthetics*, 39: 62–71.

Jolly, Margaret (1992). 'Specters of Inauthenticity'. *Contemporary Pacific*, 4: 49–72.

Judkins, Jennifer (1997a). 'The Aesthetics of Silence in Live Musical Performance'. *Journal of Aesthetic Education*, 31/3: 39–53.

——(1997b). 'Signs of Struggle: Aesthetic Aspects of Musical Noise'. Unpublished.

Jules-Rosette, Bennetta (1984). *Messages of Tourist Art: An African Semiotic System in Comparative Perspective*. New York: Plenum Press.

Kallberg, Jeffrey (1996). *Chopin at the Boundaries: Sex, History, and Musical Genre*. Cambridge, MA: Harvard University Press.

Karkoschka, Erhard (1972). *Notation in New Music*, trans. Ruth Koenig. Austria: Universal Edition.

Karpeles, Maud (1951). 'Some Reflections on Authenticity in Folk Music'. *Journal of the International Folk Music Council*, 3: 10–14.

Kartomi, Margaret J. (1981). 'The Processes and Results of Musical Culture Contact: A Discussion of Terminology and Concepts'. *Ethnomusicology*, 25: 227–49.

——(1992). 'Appropriation of Music and Dance in Contemporary Ternate and Tidore'. *Studies in Music*, 26: 85–95.

Kasfir, Sidney (1992). 'African Art and Authenticity: A Text Without a Shadow'. *African Art*, 25: 41–53.

Kaufmann, Walter (1967). *Musical Notations of the Orient*. Bloomington, IN: Indiana University Press.

Keil, Charles (1994). 'Music Mediated and Live in Japan', in Charles Keil and Steven Feld, *Music Grooves*. Chicago: Chicago University Press, 247–56.

Keller, Hans (1956–7). 'A Slip of Mozart's: Its Analytical Significance'. *Tempo*, 42 (Winter), 12–15.

——(1984). 'Whose Authenticity?' *Early Music*, 12: 517–19.

Kelly, Michael (1994). 'Danto, Dutton, and our Preunderstanding of Tribal Art and Artifacts', in Carol C. Gould and Robert S. Cohen (eds.), *Artifacts, Representations and Social Practices*. Dordrecht: Kluwer Academic Publishers, 39–52.

Kerman, Joseph (1985). *Musicology*. London: Fontana Press/Collins.

——(1989). 'Mozart a la Mode'. *New York Review*, 18 May, 50–1.

Khatchadourian, Haig (1973). 'The Identity of a Work of Music'. *Music and Man*, 1: 33–57.

——(1978). 'The Identity of a Work of Music—II'. *Music and Man*, 2: 223–33.

Kieran, Matthew (1996). 'Incoherence and Musical Appreciation'. *Journal of Aesthetic Education*, 30/1: 39–49.

Kinderman, William (1995). *Beethoven*. Oxford: Oxford University Press.

King, A. Hyatt, and Carolan, Monica (1966). *The Letters of Mozart and his Family*, trans. Emily Anderson. 2nd edn. London: Macmillan.

Kirkby, F. E. (1966). *A Short History of Keyboard Music*. New York: Free Press.

Kivy, Peter (1983). 'Platonism in Music: A Kind of Defence'. *Grazer Philosophische Studien*, 19: 109–29.

——(1984). *Sound and Semblance: Reflections on Musical Representation*. Princeton: Princeton University Press.

——(1987). 'Platonism in Music: Another Kind of Defence'. *American Philosophical Quarterly*, 24: 245–52.

——(1988a). 'Orchestrating Platonism', in T. Anderberg, T. T. Nilstun, and I. Persson (eds.), *Aesthetic Distinction*. Sweden: Lund University Press, 42–55.

——(1988b). 'On the Concept of the "Historically Authentic" Performance'. *Monist*, 71: 278–90.

——(1988c). "Live Performances and Dead Composers: On the Ethics of Musical Interpretation', in J. Dancy, J. M. E. Moravcsik, and C. C. W. Taylor (eds.), *Human Agency: Language, Duty and Value*. Stanford, CA: Stanford University Press, 219–36.

——(1990). *Music Alone: Philosophical Reflection on the Purely Musical Experience*. Ithaca, NY: Cornell University Press.

——(1995). *Authenticities: Philosophical Reflections on Musical Performance*. Ithaca, NY: Cornell University Press.

——(1997). *Philosophies of Arts: An Essay in Differences*. New York: Cambridge University Press.

Koopman, Ton (1987). 'Some Thoughts on Authenticity'. *Musick*, 8/3: 2–6.

Kostelanetz, Richard (1988). *Conversing with Cage*. New York: Limelight Editions.

Kramer, Lawrence (1993). 'Music Criticism and the Postmodernist Turn: In Contrary Motion with Gary Tomlinson'. *Current Musicology*, 53: 25–35.

Krausz, Michael (1993a). 'Rightness and Reasons in Musical Interpretation', in Michael Krausz (ed.), *The Interpretation of Music: Philosophical Essays*. Oxford: Clarendon Press, 75–87.

——(1993b). *Rightness and Reasons: Interpretation in Cultural Practices*. Ithaca, NY: Cornell University Press.

Kroon, Fred (1987). 'Causal Descriptivism'. *Australasian Journal of Philosophy*, 65: 1–17.

Kunst, Jaap (1959). *Ethnomusicology*. 3rd edn. The Hague: Martinus Nijhoff.

——(1973). *Music in Java: Its History. Its Theory and Its Technique*. 3rd edn. 2 vols. The Hague: Martinus Nijhoff.

Langer, Susanne (1953). *Feeling and Form*. London: Routledge and Kegan Paul.

Lansing, J. Stephen (1983). *The Three Worlds of Bali*. New York: Praeger.

Laszlo, Ervin (1967). 'The Aesthetics of Live Musical Performance'. *British Journal of Aesthetics*, 7: 261–73.

Lawrence, John S. (1987). 'The Diatonic Scale: More than Meets the Ear'. *Journal of Aesthetics and Art Criticism*, 46: 281–91.

Layton, Robert (1981). *The Anthropology of Art*. New York: Columbia University Press.

Leech-Wilkinson, Daniel (1984). 'The Limits of Authenticity: A Discussion'. *Early Music*, 12: 13–16.

Le Huray, Peter (1990). *Authenticity in Performance: Eighteenth-Century Case Studies*. Cambridge: Cambridge University Press.

Leppard, Raymond (1988). *Authenticity in Music*. London: Faber Music.

Lester, Joel (1992). *Compositional Theory in the Eighteenth Century*. Cambridge, MA: Harvard University Press.

Levinson, Jerrold (1980*a*). 'What a Musical Work Is'. *Journal of Philosophy*, 77: 5–28.

——(1980*b*). 'Autographic and Allographic Art Revisited'. *Philosophical Studies*, 38: 367–83.

——(1987). 'Evaluating Musical Performance'. *Journal of Aesthetic Education*, 21/1: 75–88.

——(1988). 'Artworks and the Future', in T. Anderberg, T. Nilstun, and I. Persson (eds.), *Aesthetic Distinction*. Sweden: Lund University Press, 56–84.

——(1990*a*). 'What a Musical Work Is, Again', in Levinson, *Music, Art, and Metaphysics*, Ithaca, NY: Cornell University Press, 215–63.

Levinson (1990*b*), 'Music and Negative Emotions', in Levinson, *Music, Art, and Metaphysics*. Ithaca, NY: Cornell University Press, 306–35.

——(1990*c*). 'Authentic Performance and Performance Means', in Levinson, *Music, Art, and Metaphysics*. Ithaca, NY: Cornell University Press, 393–408.

——(1990*d*). 'Musical Literacy'. *Journal of Aesthetic Education*, 24/1: 17–30.

——(1992). 'Critical Notice of Currie's *An Ontology of Art*'. *Philosophy and Phenomenological Research*, 52: 215–22.

——(1993). 'Performative vs. Critical Interpretation in Music', in Michael Krausz (ed.), *The Interpretation of Music: Philosophical Essays*. Oxford: Clarendon Press, 33–60.

——(1994). 'Being Realistic About Aesthetic Properties'. *Journal of Aesthetics and Art Criticism*, 52: 351–4.

——(1996). 'Work and Œuvre', in Levinson, *The Pleasures of Aesthetics*. Ithaca, NY: Cornell University Press, 242–73.

——(1997). *Music in the Moment*. Ithaca, NY: Cornell University Press.

Lindley, Mark (1980). 'Temperaments', in Stanley Sadie (ed.), *The New Grove Dictionary of Music and Musicians*. London: Macmillan, xviii. 660–74.

Lippman, Edward A. (1977). *A Humanistic Philosophy of Music*. New York: New York University Press.

Lomax, Alan (1993). *The Land where the Blues Began*. New York: Pantheon Books.

MacCannel, Dean (1976). *The Tourist: A New Theory of the Leisure Class*. New York: Schocken Books.

McFee, Graham (1992). 'The Historical Character of Art: A Re-Appraisal'. *British Journal of Aesthetics*, 32: 307–19.

McKean, Philip Frick (1978). 'Towards a Theoretical Analysis of Tourism: Economic Dualism and Cultural Involution in Bali', in Valene S. Smith (ed.), *Hosts and Guests: The Anthropology of Tourism*. Oxford: Blackwell, 93–107.

McKee, James (1988). 'South Sea Collection Comes to Folk Archive'. *Folklife Center News* (American Folklife Center, The Library of Congress), 10: 4–6.

McLeod, M. D. (1976). 'Limitations of the Genuine'. *African Art*, 9/3: 31, 48–51.

McPhee, Colin (1966). *The Music of Bali: A Study in Form and Instrumental Organization in Balinese Orchestral Music*. New Haven, MA: Yale University Press.

——(1979). *A House in Bali*. Kuala Lumpur: Oxford University Press. First published by Victor Gollancz Ltd, London, in 1947.

——(1981). *The Balinese Wajang Koelit and its Music*. New York: AMS Press. Reprint of the 1936 edition: Printed from *Djåwå*, 16/1 (1936).

Malm, William P. (1967). *Music Cultures of the Pacific, the Near East, and Asia*. Englewood Cliffs, NJ: Prentice-Hall.

Manning, Peter (1993). *Electronic and Computer Music*. 2nd edn. Oxford: Clarendon Press.

Maquet, Jacques (1971). *Introduction to Aesthetic Anthropology*. Reading, MA: Addison Wesley.

Margolis, Joseph (1965). *The Language of Art and Art Criticism*. Detroit: Wayne State University Press.

——(1980). *Art and Philosophy*. Atlantic Highlands, NJ: Humanities Press.

——(1993). 'Music as Ordered Sound: Some Complications Affecting Description and Interpretation', in Michael Krausz (ed.), *The Interpretation of Music: Philosophical Essays*. Oxford: Clarendon Press, 141–53.

——(1999). *What, After All, Is a Work of Art?* University Park, PA: Pennsylvania State University Press.

Mark, Thomas Carson (1980). 'On Works of Virtuosity'. *Journal of Philosophy*, 77: 28–45.

——(1981). 'Philosophy of Piano Playing: Reflections on the Concept of Performance'. *Philosophy and Phenomenological Research*, 41: 299–324.

Martin, George (1994). *Summer of Love: The Making of Sgt. Pepper*. London: Macmillan.

Martin, Robert L. (1993). 'Musical Works in the Worlds of Performers and Listeners', in Michael Krausz (ed.), *The Interpretation of Music: Philosophical Essays*. Oxford: Clarendon Press, 119–27.

Morgan, Robert P. (1988). 'Tradition, Anxiety, and the Current Musical Scene', in Nicholas Kenyon (ed.), *Authenticity and Early Music*. Oxford: Oxford University Press, 57–82.

Morrow, Michael (1978). 'Musical Performance and Authenticity'. *Early Music*, 6: 233–46.

Moyle, Alice (1967). *Songs from the Northern Territory Companion Booklet*. Canberra: Australian Institute of Aboriginal Studies.

Moyle, Richard (1993). 'Save the Last Dance—for Me?' *Musicology Australia*, 16: 78–87.

Nettl, Bruno (1964). *Theory and Method in Ethnomusicology*. London: Free Press of Glencoe.

——(1983). *The Study of Ethnomusicology: Twenty-Nine Issues and Concepts*. Urbana, IL: University of Illinois Press.

Neumann, Frederick (1965). 'La Note pointée et la soi-disant "manière française"'. *Revue de musicologie*, 51: 66–92. Reprinted in English in *Early Music*, 5 (1977), 310–24.

——(1993). *Performance Practices of the Seventeenth and Eighteenth Centuries*. New York: Schirmer Books.

Niblock, Howard (1999). 'Musical Recordings and Performances: A Response to Theodore Gracyk'. *Journal of Aesthetics and Art Criticism*, 57: 366–8.

Noronha, Raymond (1979). 'Paradise Reviewed: Tourism In Bali', in E. de Kadt (ed.), *Tourism: Passport to Development? Perspectives on the Social and Cultural Effects of Tourism in Developing Countries*. New York: Oxford University Press, 177–204.

Nyman, Michael (1981). *Experimental Music: Cage and Beyond*. New York: Schirmer.

O'Dea, Jane W. (1993). 'Virtue in Musical Performance'. *Journal of Aesthetic Education*, 27/1: 51–62.

——(1994). 'Authenticity in Musical Performance: Personal or Historical?' *British Journal of Aesthetics*, 34: 363–75.

Ornstein, Ruby Sue (1971). 'Gamelan Gong Kebyar: The Development of a Balinese Musical Tradition'. Ph.D. dissertation. Los Angeles: University of California.

Paléographie Musicale (1970). Series 2, Vol. 1. Berne: Editions Herbert Lang and Cie.

Pearce, David (1988*a*). 'Intensionality and the Nature of a Musical Work'. *British Journal of Aesthetics*, 28: 105–18.

——(1988*b*). 'Musical Expression: Some Remarks on Goodman's Theory', in Veikko Rantala, Lewis Rowell, and Eero Tarasti (eds.), 'Essays on the Philosophy of Music'. *Acta Philosophica Fennica*, 43: 228–43.

Peterson, Richard (1990). 'Audience and Industry Origins of the Crisis in Classical Music Programming: Toward World Music', in David B. Pankratz and Valerie B. Morris (eds.), *The Future of the Arts: Public Policy and Arts Research*. New York: Praeger, 207–27.

Philip, Robert (1992). *Early Recordings and Musical Style*. Cambridge: Cambridge University Press.

Philosophy and Literature (1997), '"Please Shoot the Piano Player!" The David Helfgott Debate', 21/2, 332–91.

Picard, Michel (1990). 'Kebalian Orang Bali: Tourism and the Uses of "Balinese Culture" in New Order Indonesia'. *Review of Indonesian and Malaysian Affairs*, 24 (Summer), 1–38.

——(1996). 'Dance and Drama in Bali: The Making of an Indonesian Artform', in Adrian Vickers (ed.), *Being Modern in Bali: Image and Change*. New Haven: Monograph 43/Yale Southeast Asia Studies, 115–57.

Porcello, Thomas (1998). '"Tails Out": Social Phenomenology and the Ethnographic Representation of Technology in Music-Making'. *Ethnomusicology*, 42: 485–510.

Porter, Roosevelt (1996). 'Performances and Individuating Musical Works'. *Southern Journal of Philosophy*, 34: 201–23.

Predelli, Stefano (1995). 'Against Musical Platonism'. *British Journal of Aesthetics*, 35: 338–50.

——(1999). 'Goodman and the Wrong Note Paradox'. *British Journal of Aesthetics*, 39: 364–75.

Price, Kingsley (1982). 'What is a Piece of Music?' *British Journal of Aesthetics*, 22: 322–37.

Price, Sally (1989). *Primitive Art in Civilized Places*. Chicago: Chicago University Press.

Putman, Daniel A. (1990). 'The Aesthetic Relation of Musical Performer and Audience'. *British Journal of Aesthetics*, 30: 361–6.

Raffman, Diana (1993*a*). 'Goodman, Density, and the Limits of Sense Perception', in Michael Krausz (ed.), *The Interpretation of Music: Philosophical Essays*. Oxford: Clarendon Press, 215–27.

——(1993*b*). *Language, Music, and Mind*. Cambridge, MA: MIT Press.

Read, Oliver, and Welch, Walter T. (1976). *From Tin Foil to Stereo: Evolution of the Phonograph*. New York: Howard W. Sams.

Reck, David (1977). *Music of the Whole Earth*. New York: Scribners.

Reese, Gustave (1954). *Music in the Renaissance*. London: J. M. Dent and Sons Ltd.

Richmond, John W. (1996). 'Ethics and the Philosophy of Music Education'. *Journal of Aesthetic Education*, 30/3: 3–22.

Rink, John (1994). 'Authentic Chopin: History, Analysis and Intuition in Performance', in John Rink and Jim Samson (eds.), *Chopin Studies 2*. Cambridge: Cambridge University Press, 214–44.

Robbins Landon, H. C. (1989). *1791: Mozart's Last Year*. 2nd edn. London: Thames and Hudson.

Rosen, Charles (1971). 'Should Early Music be Played "Wrong"?' *High Fidelity*, 21: 54–8.

——(1990). 'The Shock of the Old'. *New York Review of Books*, 37, 19 July, 46–52.

Ross, James (1993). 'Musical Standards as Function of Musical Accomplishment', in Michael Krausz (ed.), *The Interpretation of Music: Philosophical Essays*. Oxford: Clarendon Press, 89–102.

Ross, Stephanie A., and Judkins, Jennifer (1996). 'Conducting and Musical Interpretation'. *British Journal of Aesthetics*, 36: 16–29.

Rudinow, Joel (1994). 'Race, Ethnicity, Expressive Authenticity: Can White People Sing the Blues?' *Journal of Aesthetics and Art Criticism*, 52: 127–37.

——(1995). 'Reply to Taylor'. *Journal of Aesthetics and Art Criticism*, 53: 316–18.

Rudner, Richard (1950). 'The Ontological Status of the Esthetic Object'. *Philosophy and Phenomenological Research*, 10: 380–8.

Sachs, Curt (1940). *The History of Musical Instruments*. New York: W. W. Norton.

Saltz, David Z. (1997). 'The Art of Interaction: Interactivity, Performativity, and Computers'. *Journal of Aesthetics and Art Criticism*, 55: 117–27.

Saltzstein, Peter A. (1998). 'Misperceiving African and Eskimo Art'. *Journal of Aesthetic Education*, 32/2: 99–107.

Samson, Jim (1994). 'Chopin Reception: Theory, History, Analysis', in John Rink and Jim Samson (eds.), *Chopin Studies 2*. Cambridge: Cambridge University Press, 1–17.

Savile, Anthony (1971). 'Nelson Goodman's "Languages of Art": A Study'. *British Journal of Aesthetics*, 11: 3–27.

Saygun, Ahmed Adnan (1951). 'Authenticity in Folk Music'. *Journal of the International Folk Music Council*, 3: 7–10.

Schafer, R. Murray (1969). *The New Soundscape*. Scarborough, Ont.: Berandol Music Ltd.

——(1970), *When Words Sing*. Scarborough, Ont.: Berandol Music Ltd.

——(1977). *The Tuning of the World*. New York: Alfred A. Knopf.

Scott-Maxwell, Aline (1996). 'Women's Gamelan Groups in Central Java: Some Issues of Gender, Status and Change', in Brenton Broadstock *et al.* (eds.), *Aflame with Music: 100 Years of Music at the University of Melbourne*. Centre for Studies in Australian Music, University of Melbourne, 223–30.

Scruton, Roger (1974). *Art and Imagination*. London: Methuen.

——(1994). 'Recent Books in the Philosophy of Music'. *Philosophical Quarterly*, 44: 503–18.

——(1997). *The Aesthetics of Music*. Oxford: Clarendon Press.

Seebass, Tilman (1996). 'Change in Balinese Musical Life: "Kebiar" in the 1920s and 1930s', in Adrian Vickers (ed.), *Being Modern in Bali: Image and Change*. New Haven: Monograph 43/Yale Southeast Asia Studies, 71–91.

Seeger, Charles (1958). 'Prescriptive and Descriptive Music Writing'. *Musical Quarterly*, 44: 184–95.

Selwyn, Tom (1992). 'Tourism, Society, and Development'. *Community Development Journal*, 27: 353–60.

Sessions, Roger (1950). *The Musical Experience of Composer, Performer, Listener*. Princeton: Princeton University Press.

Shaffer, Peter (1980). *Amadeus: A Play*. London: Deutsch.

Sharp, Cecil J. (1952). *English Folk Songs from the Southern Appalachians*, ed. M. Karpeles. London: Oxford University Press. First published in 1932.

Sharpe, Richard A. (1979). 'Type, Token, Interpretation and Performance'. *Mind*, 88: 437–40.

——(1991). 'Authenticity Again'. *British Journal of Aesthetics*, 31: 163–6.

——(1993). 'Review of Goehr's *The Imaginary Museum of Musical Works*'. *British Journal of Aesthetics*, 33: 292–5.

——(1995). 'Music, Platonism and Performance: Some Ontological Strains'. *British Journal of Aesthetics*, 35: 38–48.

——(2000). *Music and Humanism: An Essay in the Aesthetics of Music*. Oxford: Oxford University Press.

Shepherd, John (1991). *Music as Social Text*. Cambridge: Polity Press.

Shiner, Larry (1994). '"Primitive Fakes", "Tourist Art", and the Ideology of Authenticity'. *Journal of Aesthetics and Art Criticism*, 52: 225–34.

Shorter, D. E. L., and Borwick, John (1980). 'Sound Recording, Transmission and Reproduction', in Stanley Sadie (ed.), *The New Grove Dictionary of Music and Musicians*. London: Macmillan, xvii. 567–90.

Shusterman, Richard (1992). *Pragmatist Aesthetics: Living Beauty, Rethinking Art*. Oxford: Blackwell.

Silliman, A. Cutler (1969). 'The Score as Musical Object'. *Journal of Aesthetic Education*, 3/4: 97–108.

Snoeyenbos, Milton H. (1979). 'Art Types and Reductionism'. *Philosophy and Phenomenological Research*, 39: 378–85.

Spade, Paul Vincent (1991). 'Do Composers have to be Performers Too?' *Journal of Aesthetics and Art Criticism*, 49: 365–9.

Sparshott, Francis (1983). 'Why Artworks have no Right to have Rights'. *Journal of Aesthetics and Art Criticism*, 42: 5–15.

——(1987). 'Aesthetics of Music—Limits and Grounds', in Philip Alperson (ed.), *What Is Music? An Introduction to the Philosophy of Music*. New York: Haven, 35–98.

Spooner, Brian (1986). 'Weavers and Dealers: Authenticity and Oriental Carpets', in Arjun Appadurai (ed.), *The Social Life of Things: Commodities in Cultural Perspective*. Cambridge: Cambridge University Press, 195–235.

Stravinsky, Igor (1962). *An Autobiography*. New York: W. W. Norton. First published in 1936.

——and Craft, Robert (1959). *Expositions and Developments*. London: Faber & Faber.

————(1968). *Dialogues and a Diary*. London: Faber & Faber.

Stubley, Eleanor V. (1995). 'The Performer, the Score, the Work: Musical Performance and Transactional Reading'. *Journal of Aesthetic Education*, 29/3: 55–69.

——(1998). 'Being in the Body, Being in the Sound: A Tale of Modulating Identities and Lost Potential'. *Journal of Aesthetic Education*, 32/4: 93–105.

Sumarsam (1995). *Gamelan: Cultural Interaction and Musical Development in Central Java*. Chicago: University of Chicago Press.

Summit, Jeffrey A. (1993). ' "I'm A Yankee Doodle Dandy?": Identity and Melody at an American *Simh At Torah* Celebration'. *Ethnomusicology*, 37: 41–62.

Tambling, Jeremy (1987). *Opera, Ideology and Film*. Manchester: Manchester University Press.

Taruskin, Richard (1982). 'On Letting the Music Speak for Itself: Some Reflections on Musicology and Performance'. *Journal of Musicology*, 1: 338–49.

——(1984). 'The Limits of Authenticity: A Discussion'. *Early Music*, 12: 3–12.

——(1985–6). 'Review of Caldwell's *Editing Early Music*'. *Notes*, 42: 775–9.

——(1988). 'The Pastness of the Present and the Presence of the Past', in Nicholas Kenyon (ed.), *Authenticity and Early Music*. New York: Oxford University Press, 137–207.

——(1992). 'Tradition and Authority'. *Early Music*, 20: 11–25.

——(1995). *Text and Act: Essays on Music and Performance*. New York: Oxford University Press.

Tatar, Elizabeth (1987). *Strains of Change: The Impact of Tourism on Hawaiian Music*. Honolulu, HA: Bishop Museum Press.

Taylor, Paul (1995). '. . . So Black and Blue: Response to Rudinow'. *Journal of Aesthetics and Art Criticism*, 53: 313–16.

Temperley, Nicholas (1984). 'The Limits of Authenticity: A Discussion'. *Early Music*, 12: 16–20.

Tenzer, Michael (1991). *Balinese Music*. Berkeley, CA: Periplus Editions.

Thom, Paul (1990a). 'Works for Performance'. *Grazer Philosophische Studien*, 38: 139–56.

——(1990*b*). 'Young's Critique of Authenticity in Music'. *British Journal of Aesthetics*, 30: 273–6.

——(1993). *For an Audience: A Philosophy of the Performing Arts*. Philadelphia: Temple University Press.

Thomas, Allan (1981). 'The Study of Acculturated Music in Oceania: "Cheap and Tawdry Borrowed Tunes"?' *Journal of the Polynesian Society*, 90: 183–91.

Tomlinson, Gary (1988). 'The Historian, the Performer, and Authentic Meaning in Music', in Nicholas Kenyon (ed.), *Authenticity and Early Music*. Oxford: Oxford University Press, 115–36.

——(1993*a*). 'Musical Pasts and Postmodern Musicologies: A Response to Lawrence Kramer'. *Current Musicology*, 53: 18–24.

——(1993*b*). 'Gary Tomlinson Responds'. *Current Musicology*, 53: 36–40.

Torgovnick, Marianna (1990). *Gone Primitive: Savage Intellects, Modern Lives*. Chicago: University of Chicago Press.

Tormey, Alan (1973). 'Aesthetic Rights'. *Journal of Aesthetics and Art Criticism*, 32: 163–70.

——(1974). 'Indeterminacy and Identity in Art'. *Monist*, 58: 203–15.

Treitler, Leo (1992). 'The "Unwritten" and "Written Transmission" of Medieval Chant and Start-up of Musical Notation'. *Journal of Musicology*, 10: 131–91.

——(1993). 'History and the Ontology of the Musical Work'. *Journal of Aesthetics and Art Criticism*, 51: 483–97.

——(1999). 'The Historiography of Music: Issues of Past and Present', in Nicholas Cook and Mark Everist (eds.), *Rethinking Music*. Oxford: Oxford University Press, 356–77.

Urmson, J. O. (1976). 'The Performing Arts', in G. E. M. Anscombe (ed.), *Contemporary British Philosophy: Fourth Series*. London: Muirhead Library of Philosophy, 239–52.

——(1993). 'The Ethics of Musical Performance', in Michael Krausz (ed.), *The Interpretation of Music: Philosophical Essays*. Oxford: Clarendon Press, 157–64.

Valone, James J. (1985). 'Musical Improvisation as Interpretative Activity'. *Journal of Aesthetics and Art Criticism*, 44: 193–4.

van der Veen, Tjitske (1993). 'Historical Change in Pacific Art'. *Oceania Newsletter*, 11/12 (July), 30–8.

Vickers, Adrian (1989). *Bali: A Paradise Created*. Ringwood, Victoria: Penguin.

——(1996). 'Modernity and being "*Moderen*": An Introduction', in Adrian Vickers (ed.), *Being Modern in Bali: Image and Change*. New Haven: Monograph 43/Yale Southeast Asia Studies, 1–36.

Wacker, Jeanne (1960). 'Particular Works of Art'. *Mind*, 64: 223–33.

Walhout, Donald (1986). 'Discovery and Creation in Music'. *Journal of Aesthetics and Art Criticism*, 45: 193–5.

Walsh, Michael (1983). 'Letting Mozart be Mozart'. *Time*, 122, 5 September, 66–7.

Walton, Kendall L. (1973). 'Not a Leg to Stand On'. *Journal of Philosophy*, 70: 725–6.

——(1979). 'Style and the Products and Processes of Art', in Berel Lang (ed.), *The Concept of Style*. Philadelphia: University of Pennsylvania Press, 46–66.

——(1988). 'The Presentation and Portrayal of Sound Patterns', in J. Dancy, J. M. E. Moravcsik, and C. C. W. Taylor (eds.), *Human Agency: Language, Duty and Value*. Stanford, CA: Stanford University Press, 237–57.

Walton, Susan Pratt (1987). *Mode in Javanese Music*. Monographs in International Studies, Southeast Asia Series No. 79. Athens, OH: Ohio University Center for International Studies.

Weber, William (1999). 'The History of Musical Canon', in Nicholas Cook and Mark Everist (eds.), *Rethinking Music*. Oxford: Oxford University Press, 336–55.

Webster, William E. (1971). 'Music is not a "Notational System"'. *Journal of Aesthetics and Art Criticism*, 29: 489–97.

——(1974). 'A Theory of the Compositional Work of Music'. *Journal of Aesthetics and Art Criticism*, 33: 59–66.

Weintraub, Andrew N. (1993). 'Theory in Institutional Pedagogy and "Theory in Practice" for Sundanese Gamelan Music'. *Ethnomusicology*, 37: 29–39.

White, Harry (1997). '"If it's Baroque don't Fix it": Reflections on Lydia Goehr's "Work-Concept" and the Historical Integrity of Musical Composition'. *Acta Musicologica*, 69: 94–104.

Wilkinson, Scott (1997). 'Capturing the Classics'. *Electronic Musician*, 13/5: 56–73.

Wilsmore, S. J. (1987). 'The Role of Titles in Identifying Literary Works'. *Journal of Aesthetics and Art Criticism*, 45: 403–8.

Wittgenstein, Ludwig (1953). *Philosophical Investigations*, trans. G. E. M. Anscombe. Oxford: Blackwell.

Wollheim, Richard (1968). *Art and its Objects*. London: Pelican.

Wolterstorff, Nicholas (1975). 'Towards an Ontology of Artworks'. *Noûs*, 9: 115–42.

——(1980). *Works and Worlds of Art*. Oxford: Clarendon Press.

——(1987). 'The Work of Making a Work of Music', in Philip Alperson (ed.), *What Is Music? An Introduction to the Philosophy of Music*. New York: Haven, 101–29.

——(1991). 'Review of Currie's *An Ontology of Art*'. *Journal of Aesthetics and Art Criticism*, 49: 79–81.

Young, James O. (1988). 'The Concept of Authentic Performance'. *British Journal of Aesthetics*, 28: 228–38.

——(1994). 'Should White Men Play the Blues?' *Journal of Value Inquiry*, 28: 415–24.

——(1996). 'Review of Kivy's *Authenticities: Philosophical Reflections on Musical Performance*'. *Journal of Aesthetics and Art Criticism*, 54: 198–200.

——and Matheson, Carl (2000). 'The Metaphysics of Jazz'. *Journal of Aesthetics and Art Criticism*, 58: 125–33.

Zemach, Eddy M. (1992). *Types*. Leiden: E. J. Brill.

Zemp, Hugo (1978). ''Are'are Classification of Musical Types and Instruments'. *Ethnomusicology*, 22: 37–67.

——(1979). 'Aspects of 'Are'are Music Theory'. *Ethnomusicology*, 23: 6–48.

Ziff, Paul (1971). 'Goodman's *Languages of Art*'. *Philosophical Review*, 80: 509–15.

——(1973). 'The Cow on the Roof'. *Journal of Philosophy*, 70: 713–23.

Zuckerkandl, Victor (1956). *Sound and Symbol: Music and the External World*, trans. Willard R. Trask. London: Routledge and Kegan Paul.

Discography

A list of recordings of Balinese music mentioned in the text.

[1] *Bali: Hommage à Wayan Lotring.* cp 1989. Ocora, Radio France C 559076/77. Two compact discs [ADD]. Recording, photographs, and notes by Jacques Brunet; translation by Dinnie Lambert. [Recorded 2–11 October 1972—Jacques Brunet, pers. comm.]

[2] *Bali South: Compositions of Wayan Gandera: Teacher, Composer, Gamelan Master: Peliatan, Bali.* cp 1973. IE Records stereo ier-7503. (Institute of Ethnomusicology, University of California, Los Angeles.) One LP. Recordings and notes by Gertrude River Robinson. Recorded in 1970 in Peliatan, Gianyar.

[3] *Court Music and Banjar Music.* cp 1971. Philips 6586 008. One LP. Recording by Jacques Brunet and Ngac Him. Photographs and notes by Jacques Brunet. [Recorded September, 1970 in Peliatan, Gianyar—Jacques Brunet, pers. comm.] Reissued cp 1994. Unesco collection D 8059. (International Music Council.) One compact disc.

[4] *Dancers of Bali: Sekehe Gong: Sadha Budaya—Kelurahan, Ubud.* Maharani RCD-01. One compact disc. [Other details unspecified. Recorded about 1990 in Ubud, Gianyar.]

[5] *Gamelan Gong Kebyar [III]: The Ensemble of Tejakula Village.* cp 1994. Produced by Soh Fujimoto. JVC VICG-5352-2. (JVC World Sounds.) One compact disc. Recording, notes, and photographs by Tsutomu Oohashi. Recorded January 1993 in Tejakula Village, Buleleng.

[6] *Gamelan Semar Pegulingan [I]: 'Tirta Sari' Ensemble of Peliatan Village.* cp 1990. Produced by Soh Fujimoto. JVC VICG-5024-2. (JVC World Sounds.) One compact disc. Recording, notes, and photographs by Tsutomu Oohashi. Recorded January 1985 in Peliatan, Gianyar.

[7] *Gender Wayang of Sukawati Village.* cp 1992. Produced by Hoshikawa Kyoji. King Record Co. KICC 5156. (World Music Library.) One compact disc. Engineered by Takanami Hatsuro. Notes by Minagawa Koichi; translated by Gerald Groemer. Recorded 3 December 1990 in Sayan, Gianyar.

[8] *Golden Rain: Balinese Gamelan Music: Ketjak: The Ramayana Monkey Chant.* cp 1969. Nonesuch H-72028. (Nonesuch Explorer Series.) One LP. Recording, notes, and photographs by David Lewiston. Recorded in 1966 in Peliatan, Gianyar. Several tracks from this LP, including the kecak, have been re-released on *Music from the Morning of the World.* cp 1988. Elektra/Nonesuch 9 79196-2. (Nonesuch Explorer Series.) One compact disc.

[9] *Golden Rain: Gong Kebyar of Gunung Sari, Bali.* cp 1995. Produced by Hoshikawa Kyoji. King Record Co. KICC 5195. (World Music Library.) One compact disc. Engineered by Takanami Hatsuro. Notes by Minagawa Koichi; translated by Oshima Yutaka and Matthew Zuckerman. Recorded 6 December 1990 in Peliatan, Gianyar.

[10] *Kecak and Sanghyang of Bali.* cp 1991. Produced by Kyoji Hoshikawa. King Record Co. KICC 5128. (World Music Library.) One compact disc. Engineered by Hatsuro Takanami. Notes by Koichi Minagawa; translator unacknowledged. Recorded November and December 1990 in Bali; performed by 'Ganda Sari', Bona, Gianyar.

[11] *Kecak of Bali: Monkey Dance: Bona Sari.* Maharani MR-001. One compact disc. [Other details unspecified. Recorded about 1990 in Bona, Gianyar.]

[12] *Les Grands Gong kebyar des années soixante.* cp 1994. Ocora, Radio France C 560057/58. Two compact discs [ADD]. Recording, photographs, and notes by Jacques Brunet; translation by Peter Lee. [The Peliatan group was recorded in June 1969 in Peliatan, Gianyar, and the Sawan group was recorded in July 1970 in Sawan, Beluleng—Jacques Brunet, pers. comm.]

[13] *Music Atlas: Bali.* cp 1972. EMI/Odeon 3/C064–17858. One LP. Recording by Jacques Brunet and Ngac Him. Photographs and notes by Jacques Brunet. [Recorded in May 1970 with the kecak group of Peliatan, Gianyar—Jacques Brunet, pers. comm.]

[14] *Music for the Balinese Shadow Play: Gendèr Wayang from Teges Kanyinan, Pliaton, Bali.* Nonesuch H-72037. (Nonesuch Explorer Series.) One LP. Recordings, notes, and photographs by Robert E. Brown. Recorded 25 July 1969. [Other details unspecified.]

[15] *Music for the Gods: The Fahnestock South Sea Expedition: Indonesia.* cp 1994. Produced by Mickey Hart and Alan Jabbour. Rykodisc RCD 10315. (Library of Congress Endangered Music Project.) One compact disc. Notes by Sue Carole DeVale and Jim McKee. Recorded in 1941.

[16] *Music from Bali: Played by the Gamelan Orchestra from Pliaton, Indonesia.* cp 1971. Decca ARLP 2308. One LP. Recording and notes by John Coast. [Recording about 1970.]

[17] *Music from the Morning of the World, Bali.* 2 vols., 1920s. Recorded in 1927–8 by C. M. von Hornbostel for Beka and Odeon. Source: taped copies from 78s, Archive of Maori and Pacific Music, Department of Anthropology, The University of Auckland. Several tracks have been released as *The Roots of Gamelan: The First Recordings, Bali 1928, New York 1941.* cp 1999. World Arbiter 2001. One compact disc. [ADD] Notes by Edward Herbst.

[18] *Music of the Wayang Kulit [II]: A Shadow Play from the Dewa Ruci.* cp 1993. Produced by Soh Fujimoto. JVC VICG-5266-2. (JVC World Sounds.) One compact disc. Notes by Koichi Minagawa; translation by Robin Thompson. Photographs by Yuki Minegishi. Recorded 29 July 1983 in Tokyo, Japan.

[19] *Old Gold: Semar Pegulingan.* cp 1995. Produced by Douglas Myers. Aman 003. One compact disc [DDD]. Recording and notes by Douglas Myers. Recorded 1995 in Teges Kanginan, Gianyar.

[20] *The Earth Greets the Sun: Gamelan Music from Bali.* cp 1972. Produced by Dr Andreas Holschneider. Deutsche Grammophon 447 499-2. One compact disc [ADD]. Recording by Jacques Brunet. Notes by Neil Sorrell. Recorded February 1972 in Sebatu, Gianyar.

[21] *The Music from Bali.* cp 1962. Philips 631 210 LP. One LP. Recording and notes by Joachim E. Berendt. Recorded March and April 1962. [Group from Sanur, Bandung.]

[22] *The Very Best of Legong: Most Beautiful Music of Bali: Part 1: 'Tirta Sari' Semar Pegulingan of Peliatan Village—Ubud, Bali.* Maharani RCD-08. One compact disc. [Other details unspecified. Recorded about 1990 in Peliatan, Gianyar.]

Index

Abbado, Claudio 245
Ackerman, James S. 157, 158
Ackerman, Will 332 n.57
Adorno, Theodor 219 n., 229 n.23–4, 333 n.,
    336 n.60
African music 49, 61 n., 202, 204 n., 334
Alperson, Philip 13–14, 18, 177 n.
Amerindian music 88, 262, 263
Anderson, Christopher 266
Anderson, James C. 37, 42 n.34, 71, 73 n.16,
    75, 176 n.
Anderson, Laurie 332 n.57
Apel, Willi 49, 62, 117, 221 n., 299
Arnold, Denis 69 n.
Atkinson, John 303 n.15
audiences 157, 160–1, 186–8, 235–7, 247
    dumbing down of 330–6
    modern versus period 83–4, 231–7,
        239–40
    and recordings 301–7, 310–14, 317
    rights of 247, 252
'Auld Lang Syne' 164
Austin Lounge Lizards 8
Australian aboriginal music 49, 88, 131–2
authenticity 152, 203–4, 259, 293
    deep 260–1
    nominal 204, 260–1
    in non-Western musical traditions 201–5,
        254–94
        acculturated and hybrid music 263–5
        critique of old mythology of 255–8,
            267, 275, 293
        defence of old mythology of 259–63
        necessity of judgements about 255,
            258–61, 293–4
    in performances of musical works 20, 91,
        164–5, 201–24, 227, 318–19
        attainability of 107, 228–34
        consistent with differences in
            performances 20, 110, 117, 130, 152,
            154, 209, 238
        degrees in 153, 207, 241, 249
        departures from the ideal 166, 218,
            221–2, 241, 248–9
        as experienced by modern audience
            231–7, 239–40
        impracticality of 222, 247–9
        and instrumentation 66–71, 73, 98, 166,
            193 n.30, 216–22, 224, 252
        integral to the point of performance 17,
            112, 161, 207–9, 225–6, 241, 247–52
        may sound better 206, 218–19, 237–41

not to be traded for interpretative
    interest 202, 240–5, 248–50, 252
    value of 234–41, 248–52
in recordings 201–5, 319
    of performances of works for live
        performance 318–19
    of performances of works for studio
        performance 318
    of works for studio performance 318
    of works not for performance 228,
        317–18
see also performances of works;
    recordings; works
Avery, Oswald 79 n.

Babbitt, Milton:
    Compositions for Synthesizer 9–11
    Philomel 196
Bach, Carl Philipp Emmanuel 13, 15
Bach, Johann Christian (1735–82), son of
    J. S. 83
Bach, Johann Christian (1642–1703), cousin
    of J. S. 78, 82
Bach, Johann Sebastian 8, 19, 45, 50, 59,
    69 n., 70, 76, 78, 82–3, 86, 120, 181,
    215, 219 n., 222, 224 n., 232 n., 235,
    244–5, 326
    The Art of Fugue 55, 119–20, 215 n.
    Brandenburg Concertos 7, 10, 74–5
    The Musical Offering 13–16
    Partita for Solo Violin in D minor 168,
        169 n., 179–80
    'Sheep May Safely Graze' 144 n.31
    Suites for Unaccompanied Cello 70, 120,
        222
    Toccata and Fugue in D minor 316 n.
    Two Part Inventions 145–7, 163, 166, 175
    Violin Concerto in E major 43, 60, 68 n.,
        218
    The Well-Tempered Klavier 61, 173, 179,
        215 n.
Bach, Michael 23 n.13
Bachrach, Jay 37, 39–40, 42 n.33
Baines, Anthony 221 n.
Baird, John Logie 78–9
Bakan, Michael 273 n.18
Bali:
    tourism in 268–70, 274–5
    see also Balinese music
Balinese music 50, 52 n.6, 88, 188, 261–2,
    264, 268–94, 332
    conservatoriums 272–3, 289, 291